Praise for *The Digital Economy* 20th Anniversary Edition

"1994 was a good year. We released Netscape Navigator and the web took off. It was also the year that Don Tapscott wrote *The Digital Economy*, prophetically explaining how the Web would change business. With this anniversary edition, Tapscott provides lucid insights for the next stage of these amazing times."

Mark Andreessen, Cofounder and General Partner, Andreessen Horowitz

"We're now into three decades of terrific insights and analysis from Don Tapscott about the digital revolution! Read this book!"

Ajay Banga, President and Chief Executive Officer, Mastercard

"Twenty years ago this book gave us an invaluable and clear roadmap for an emerging revolution. In this timely update, Don Tapscott reminds us how far we have come, but, more importantly, the extent of the transformation that still lies ahead."

Dominic Barton, Chief Executive Officer, McKinsey

"Don Tapscott has produced powerful new insights that make the Anniversary Edition of *The Digital Economy* worthwhile reading for anyone seeking to understand both the promise and challenges of the digital age."

George Cope, CEO, Bell Canada

"Twenty years of hindsight prove how deeply Tapscott understood the impact the Internet would have on the way we live, work, play, and learn. The 'Age of Networked Intelligence' he accurately predicted two decades ago is what we call the Internet of Everything, in which all the new and better connections between us are making amazing things happen for people, businesses, communities, and countries. This important book, now updated, is just as relevant today as it was then."

John Chambers, Chairman and CEO, Cisco

"The digital forces of social media, mobility, cloud computing, robotics, and big data will fundamentally change all aspects of our lives. There is no better starting point to understand this shift than Don Tapscott's prescient *The Digital Economy*. I am happy to see the release of the Anniversary Edition of *The Digital Economy*. It will benefit many who are trying to fathom the extent of the impact of digital technologies."

N. Chandrasekaran, Chief Executive Officer and Managing Director, Tata Consultancy Services

"Don was one of the first and most important theorists on the importance and impact of networks. *The Digital Economy* contains important lessons for how we work in a networked age. And, as networks accelerate transformation, his new updates are critical advice for how best to navigate the new world of work."

Reid Hoffman, Executive Chairman and Cofounder, LinkedIn

"Don Tapscott defined the digital economy, through which connected individuals and organizations could transport dominant structures to networks. His concept of collective intelligence that changes how we innovate, produce, buy, communicate, and learn was profound. In this new edition, he shows how new generations can shape a sustainable social, technological, and economic future. Read this book."

Juan Hurtado, Chairman, Entel Chile

"No one has better explained the vast power of networks to tackle humanity's problems than Don Tapscott. *The Digital Economy* was a pioneering work—a watershed. The 20th Anniversary Edition has unsettling reflections on the past and profound insights for our collective future."

Georg Kell, Executive Director, UN Global Compact

"*The Digital Economy* was *the* book that defined the future 20 years ago. Tapscott charted the course in the early days of business on the Internet, and this new look forward is equally insightful."

Dave Kepler, EVP and CIO, Dow Chemical Company

"It's hard to believe 20 years have flown by since the publication of *The Digital Economy*. The prescience of Don Tapscott's views of how the Internet would change our professional and personal lives was unparalleled. Don and I spent considerable time discussing how the world would transform itself and how I could use this perspective to help transform Oracle. Looking back, I'm thankful to have such a visionary as part of my life."

Raymond Lane, Former President, Oracle Corporation; Partner Emeritus, Kleiner Perkins Caufield and Byers; Chairman, Carnegie Mellon University

"Over the last 20 years, *The Digital Economy* has had a significant impact on my leadership of, and strategic planning for, Seagate. The new chapters in this 20th Anniversary Edition once again provide unique insights as to the next evolution of our digital world and will serve as excellent guideposts for anyone leading a company or who is responsible for strategy."

Stephen Luczo, CEO, Seagate

"Information is the currency of the 21st century, and nobody understands and explains the transformational implications, both wonderful and wicked, better than Don Tapscott."

Tiff Macklem, President, University of Toronto

"As Canada's Industry Minister through much of the 90s, Don Tapscott's *The Digital Economy* and earlier *Paradigm Shift* energized me and my officials to try to turn the Canadian economy on its head! They were mandatory reading for senior staff and caused us to redirect the strategy and resources of our department in fundamental ways. It was the early days of the digital revolution, and we were fortunate that Don provided us with such an accurate roadmap to navigate the changing global environment."

John Manley, President and Chief Executive Officer, Canadian Council of Chief Executives

"Twenty years ago Don Tapsott showed again that he had his finger on the pulse of the digital world. His new perspective, insights, and analysis should be required reading for everyone from students to CEOs."

Bill McDermott, Chief Executive Officer, SAP

"It's amazing how a single person can influence the course of history. Europe is now committed to evolving a digital economy strategy that can have a material impact on prosperity and our future. This concept originated with and dates back to Don Tapscott's seminal work of 20 years ago."

Ann Mettler, Executive Director and Cofounder of The Lisbon Council

"Every business is a digital business, and leaders must take action now to ensure their organizations remain relevant. Don Tapscott offers practical new insights to help us understand and unleash the power of digital."

Pierre Nanterme, Chairman and CEO, Accenture

"Don Tapscott was the first to describe how our shared human experience is being reinvented by the emergence of the digital economy and the networked society in which we live today. Twenty years later Don is as insightful and profound as ever."

Joe Natale, President and CEO, TELUS

"The most important enabler of social, economic and human development today is a connected world; connecting people to each other, to better sources of information and to new business opportunities. Governments can learn from *The Digital Economy* how to democratize access to prosperity, minimize social and economic divides, and transform government and democracy."

Enrique Peña Nieto, President of Mexico

"I still remember reading *The Digital Economy* two decades ago. It opened my mind to the world of possibilities and threats made possible by a digital world. Today every business must become, as Don Tapscott says, a 'digital business.' The Anniversary Edition is teeming with fresh insights relevant to business leaders in every industry."

Indra K. Nooyi, Chairman and CEO, PepsiCo

"More than 20 years after writing *The Digital Economy*, Don's thinking on business strategy, organizational transformation, and the role of technology in business and society is more relevant than ever. Don gave us a glimpse into our future that has amazingly stood the test of time, and now he's at it again, pointing the way forward."

Filippo Passerini, Group President–GBS and CIO, Procter & Gamble

"As Don rightly predicted 20 years ago, the Internet has transformed many things that people do. But beyond that, it has disrupted many long-standing industries as basic as books and telephones, and has become the defining invention of our time. Given his foresight over the last 20 years, businesses that do not carefully monitor the trends he outlines about the next few years will do so at their own peril."

Paul Polman, Chief Executive Officer, Unilever

"Twenty years later, Don's insights into the age of networked intelligence and its impact on industry are like a journey "back to the future." Today more than ever, technology continues to disrupt the way we manufacture goods, power our communities, treat diseases, and, most importantly, interact with each other."

Eric Spiegel, CEO, Siemens Corporation

"In this fascinating reflection of predictions and trends from the past 20 years, Don Tapscott continues to provide valuable insights into the opportunities and challenges for business, government, and wider society in our increasingly digital and connected world. It is indeed sobering to see how the "age of networked intelligence" is in many ways just beginning to truly transform our world."

David Thodey, CEO, Telstra

"Twenty years ago HP's CEO Lew Platt endorsed *The Digital Economy* saying 'Read this book. It will scare you and excite you and teach you how to succeed.' His words were wise then and remain appropriate for today. The Anniversary Edition shines with important insights."

Meg Whitman, CEO, HP

"The networked society has arrived, and there has been no better chronicler and scrutinizer than Don Tapscott. Read this book and heed his advice!"

Hans Vestberg, CEO, Ericsson

THE
DIGITAL
ECONOMY

— 20TH ANNIVERSARY EDITION —

THE
DIGITAL
ECONOMY

— **20TH** ANNIVERSARY EDITION —

Rethinking Promise And Peril
In The Age Of Networked Intelligence

DON TAPSCOTT

New York Chicago San Francisco Lisbon London Madrid
Mexico City Milan New Delhi San Juan Seoul
Singapore Sydney Toronto

Portions of this book were previously published by McGraw-Hill in 1995.

1 2 3 4 5 6 7 8 9 0   DOC/DOC   1 2 0 9 8 7 6 5 4

ISBN: 978-0-07-183555-8
MHID: 0-07-183555-5

e-ISBN: 978-0-07-183556-5
e-MHID: 0-07-183556-3

Library of Congress Cataloging-in-Publication Data

Tapscott, Don, 1947-
    The digital economy ANNIVERSARY EDITION : rethinking promise and peril in the age of networked intelligence / Don Tapscott. – 2nd Edition.
        pages cm
    ISBN 978-0-07-183555-8 (hardback : alk. paper) 1. Information technology. 2. Electronic commerce. I. Title.
    HC79.I55T368 2015
    384.3–dc23   2014036453

Dedication to the First Edition
To Alex, Niki, and Ana,
who give me reason to keep searching.

Dedication to the 20th Anniversary Edition
To my most loyal supporter, Mary Tapscott,
who as a *nonagenarian* is still one of the clearest thinkers I know.

Contents

Foreword to *The Digital Economy:*
20th Anniversary Edition
by Eric Schmidt, Executive Chairman, Google

I'm pleased Don asked me to say a few words about the update to his landmark book, *The Digital Economy*, if for no other reason than to place it in context. Twenty years ago, I was at Sun Microsystems, a company that in its time was pushing the boundaries of hardware, software, and network architecture in a similar way to what Google is doing today.

But even with the advances Sun and other tech companies were developing, the Information Age was still in its infancy. It was a time of dial-up modems and bulletin board systems, CDs and VHS, books sold in bookstores, and phones hardwired to your home or, if you were lucky, your car. The world wide web was just slowly beginning to emerge.

Who could have foreseen the next two decades? Who could have seen the way open platforms like the Web would transform nearly every part of our society and economy? That the power of networking would redefine collaboration and leadership, expanding both humanity's productivity and its potential? That technology would suddenly begin to uproot major industries and challenge the power of incumbents? Who could have possibly known all that?

Well, to a large degree, Don did.

Don remains one of the most perceptive thinkers about the way technology is transforming business and society. Several of his predictions—from networked intelligence to the demands on leaders to embrace technology—have taken permanent hold, giving rise to what Jared Cohen and I describe in our own book as a "New Digital Age."

The age we live in now is one filled with opportunity and promise. The digital revolution was a once-in-a-generation event that continues to transform every corner of the global economy, allowing businesses to run more efficiently, increase productivity and develop entirely new and enriching business models. It's blown entrepreneurship wide open, lowering the cost for someone to deliver on the next great idea. It is transforming science and education, slowly but surely spreading knowledge and strengthening education worldwide. And it's even changing the way governments—those hidebound bureaucracies—interact and deliver services to their citizens.

But just as Don described the benefits of our new digital age, he was also clear-sighted about the perils. Like any revolution, the digital revolution depends on steady leadership and informed and empowered citizenry to guide it.

Already we've seen repressive governments use technology to spread propaganda and limit the flow of information amongst the public. We've seen countries as free and open as our own succumb to the temptation of widespread surveillance and indiscriminate data collection, with chilling implications for our personal freedoms. The idea of living as a private citizen these days seems quaint.

And then there's the way technology has accelerated what I believe will be the next great generational challenge: job scarcity and its implications for social inequality. We pay a price for our efficiency and our productivity gains and that is the uprooting of jobs and previously secure ways of life. For those content to write this off as a consequence only faced by blue collar workers or manual laborers, you need only look to the increased outsourcing and automation of fields like law, medicine, accounting and finance—domains long thought safe.

Still, we must remember that technology remains a tool of humanity—that it is up to us to use it to create new economic opportunities, expand freedoms and expression, strengthen governance and global education. It's not man vs. machine. It's man, tapping into the immense potential of machines to give everyone globally a better way of life.

That will take strong leadership and it will take people who fully understand the implications of the digital age: that growth and profit must be tempered with the needs of society; that privacy must not be a casualty of a networked citizenry; that we use the great potential that we are unlocking to beat back the threats of a new digital age.

As we enter the new age, the future won't just happen. It will be created.

If those words sound both prescient and familiar, it's no surprise. They're Don's.

Eric Schmidt, September 2014

Preface to *The Digital Economy*: 20th Anniversary Edition

Not everything I've written holds up well. I'd love to retract the Enron case study from one of my books, or at least add in the sentence: "Note to Enron leadership—don't commit fraud."

But in rereading *The Digital Economy* for this 20th Anniversary Edition I'm struck by how the book has withstood the test of time. I'm also struck by how far we've come since then.

The book was published in 1995. Flash back to the fall of 1994 when I was writing the book. Netscape, the first commercial Web browser, was released in October of that year and the first Web sites had started to appear. Web sites only published content and none did transactions. People accessed the Internet and the Web through dial-up connections, and they were fortunate to have a 9,600 bit per second (bps) connection. Today a typical home connects at 10 million bits per second.

Mobile phones were clunky and performed a single function—telephony. The first Research in Motion (RIM) pager did not appear until 1999, and it was well into the next decade that the mobile Web was available broadly. In fact it wasn't until 2007, 13 years after the book was written, that the first iPhone appeared on the market.

In 1994, primitive search engines made it very difficult, if not impossible, to search the Web and it was half a decade later that Google became available. There were no online auctions, let alone the vast marketplaces of today. In 1996, my company researched a little company called AuctionWeb and reported that they had huge potential to change retail, price discovery, and create a vast community of people who make a living through selling stuff. The company later changed its name to eBay (no I did not invest in it, but our report was very good.) Books were still sold in bookstores and nobody had heard of Amazon, as it was founded in July of that year. The concept of social media had not been invented and 1994 was a decade before the first glimmer of MySpace and YouTube, and 15 years before Twitter came on the scene.

It's tempting to wish you could be transported back then with today's knowledge. If you had carefully invested $100,000 then, you would be the wealthiest person in history. But I digress.

THE DIGITAL ECONOMY—THE BIG IDEAS

The book introduced a number of big ideas, some of which have become part of the vernacular, and others that companies and governments are still struggling to implement.

1. *Introducing Ronald Coase.* The book introduced the writings of Nobel Prize–winning economist Ronald Coase as key to understanding the meaning of the Internet. Coase died in 2013 at the age of 102. He was awarded the 1991 Nobel Prize in Economics, largely for his inspiring 1937 paper "The Nature of the Firm," which argued that transaction costs in open markets caused companies to bring business functions within the boundaries of the firm. After reading Coase, I was thunderstruck how his insights from 50 years ago could explain the impact of the Internet on the architecture of businesses. (See *Chapter 2.*)

2. *Themes of the Digital Economy.* Prior to the widespread use of the Web there was no language or taxonomy to discuss this revolution. The first attempt to elucidate a set of Themes holds up well today with prosumption, immediacy, molecularization, discordance, and disintermediation along with its flipside "re-intermediation" standing out. (See *Chapter 2*)

3. *The concept of Networked Intelligence.* This concept is still central to my current writing. It's great to read today:

> The Age of Networked Intelligence is an age of promise. It is not simply about the networking of technology but about the networking of humans through technology. It is not an age of smart machines but of humans who through networks can combine their intelligence, knowledge, and creativity for breakthroughs in the creation of wealth and social development. It is not just an age of linking computers but of internetworking human ingenuity.

The book mused about Nathaniel Hawthorne, who inspired the development of the telegraph, wrote in 1851 that through electricity, the world of matter had become a great brain, instinct with intelligence. I concluded by arguing:

> For over a century humanity has been taking steps to realize Hawthorne's vision of a world where human intelligence could be networked. That age has arrived. Organizations can become conscious on a global scale. Perhaps societies and even humanity can as well.

I still hold today that this is not primarily an information age. It's an age of networked intelligence.

4. *Taxonomy and Language.* In the early days of the Internet there was no taxonomy or language to discuss this emerging revolution. There is a "cascading hierarchy" to describe the potential of the Net for enterprises that is still helpful. It begins at the lowest level with enabling effective individuals, cascading to high-performance teams, then integrated organizations, then extended enterprises, and finally to the internetworked business—essentially a business ecosystem. (See *Chapter* 3.)

I remember at that time my company had a neologism committee. We employed so many smart and creative people that the proliferation of newly invented words was not helpful. I chaired the committee so I probably had undue influence and some of those early terms, including "The Digital Economy" itself, were adopted. I note that today several countries, and the European Union (EU) as a whole, are working on creating a "Digital Economy Strategy."

You'll read other terms that never took hold too. But today it's striking to think of the vast language that has emerged to describe this new age, with its thousands of conceptual models and neologisms.

5. *Industry Impact.* The discussion of the technology itself is interesting but mainly for historical purposes as all these trends, seemingly revolutionary at the time, played out with a vengeance: the rise of digital, microprocessor-based systems, network computing, high-bandwidth communications, smart information appliances, multi-media, open systems, intelligent networks, and high-level object-oriented programming languages. The last shift made me chuckle reading it today: The Shift from GUIs to MUIs, MOLEs, MUDs, MOOs, AVATARS, AND VR. (See *Chapter* 4.)

There are also interesting discussions of the impending transformations of many industries, including health care, government, manufacturing, retail, and the travel industry, along with some key business functions—logistics, design, sales, marketing, and human resources (HR). The discussion of the transformation of the media industries, in particular broadcasting, unbelievably provides a pretty good framework for today. Broadcasters are still struggling to embrace most of these themes. (See *Chapters 5 to 8.*)

6. *The Challenge of Leadership.* This is a dominant theme throughout the book. Some good advice for today's leaders: Leadership Can Come from Anywhere in an Organization; Leadership in the New Economy Is Leadership for Learning; Collective Leadership Is Becoming Possible; Internetworked Leadership Can Be (enhanced) Digital; Internetworked Leadership Is Incomplete Without the CEO.

7. *Privacy.* I honestly don't remember why I chose to write an entire chapter on Privacy, many years before social networking and big data. But it was clear at the time there was "a coming firestorm" on this issue. However my conclusions on how to safeguard our privacy in a networked world has been obviated by recent developments. (See Chapter 11 for the update.)

8. *The Dark Side.* The book was pretty breathless about the opportunities, but equally it warned of the huge dangers ahead. It's worth reflecting whether the digital revolution has fulfilled its vast potential or if our disruptions and problems are deepening:

> The Age of Networked Intelligence is also an age of peril. For individuals, organizations, and societies that fall behind, punishment is swift. It is not just old business rules but also governments, social institutions, and relationships among people that are being transformed. The new media is changing the ways we do business, work, learn, play, and even think. Far more than the old western frontier, the digital frontier is a place of recklessness, confusion, uncertainty, calamity, and danger.
>
> Some signs point to a new economy in which wealth is even further concentrated, basic rights like privacy are vanishing, and a spiral of violence and repression undermine basic security and freedoms. Pervasive evidence exists that indicates the basic social fabric is beginning to disintegrate. Old laws, structures, norms, and approaches are proving to be completely inadequate for life in the new economy. While they are crumbling or being smashed, it is not completely clear what should replace them. Everywhere people are beginning to ask, "Will this smaller world our children inherit be a better one?

9. *The Call to Action.* The book appeals to business leaders to step up. This challenge is as relevant today as it was then.

> The digital economy requires a new kind of businessperson: one who has the curiosity and confidence to let go of old mental models and old paradigms; one who tempers the needs for business growth and profit with the requirements of employees, customers, and society for privacy, fairness, and a share in the wealth he or she creates; one who has the vision to think socially, the courage to act, and the strength to lead in the face of coolness or even ridicule. The digital economy requires yesterday's managers to become tomorrow's leaders. As we enter the new age, the future won't just happen. It will be created. And if we all get involved, our values, aspirations, and growing expectations will shape and drive the transformation of our businesses and our world.

REVIEWING THE DARK SIDE

If there has been one criticism of my work over the years it is that I have been too positive about the digital revolution, emphasizing only the upside. It's true that I have been hopeful, even optimistic. This is particularly true when it comes to my polemics with the pundits who attack the first generation to grow up digital as being somehow inferior to past generations. My research shows that we can be very hopeful about the "Net Generation" (as I dubbed them in 1997 in *Growing Up Digital*) as the smartest generation ever, having the mental processes that equip them well for the digital age.

However as the subtitle of *The Digital Economy* indicates "Promise and Peril in the Age of Networked Intelligence," I don't accept the criticism that I have been a digital Pollyanna. As this chapter states:

> There is a vast new promise but also new perils. A looming dark side holds the potential for severe social stratification, unprecedented invasion of privacy and other rights, structural unemployment, and massive social dislocation and conflict. The future will depend on what we as businesses and as a society do—on our decisions and our actions.

In hindsight, the book pretty much nailed the tough issues, and looking forward today these problems are now unfolding with a pace and force that is shocking and sometimes bewildering. My somewhat discouraging conclusion is that the "promise" of a new, more fair, equal, just and sustainable world is in balance unfulfilled. The topics the book summarized in this chapter are pretty much the issues each of us must address today.

1. "Dislocations in labor markets, with old industries and jobs disappearing."

> The fact that we're entering a new economy is of little consolation to that displaced worker and his or her family. How will we manage the transition to new types of work and a new knowledge base for the economy?

Today: For the first time in history, economic growth is not generating a meaningful number of new jobs. Young workers are taking the biggest hit. Google's Executive Chairman Eric Schmidt says that job scarcity will be the biggest public policy issue for the next two or three decades. We are still suffering the hangover of the obscene American subprime mortgage crisis, and Nobel prize–winning economist Paul Krugman argues persuasively that major government stimulus will be needed for years to come.

However the biggest culprit is digital technologies. We've already seen knowledge work such as accounting and legal services being shipped offshore to cheaper employees. Soon the work will stay here, but be done by computers. A recent McKinsey report noted that IBM's Watson computer diagnoses cancers with much higher levels of speed and accuracy than skilled physicians do. The same software combined with robotics, 3D printing, and myriad other innovations will eliminate jobs throughout the workforce.

Technology is also the foundation of new species of businesses that are capable of wiping out entire industries. Digital Conglomerates such as Google are achieving leadership roles in a dozen industries, where they do a better job with a fraction of the employees. The New Aggregators like Uber, Lyft, and Airbnb hold the power to wipe out jobs in industries ranging from taxis to hotels. Data Frackers like Facebook are acquiring vast treasure troves of data that position them to dominate multiple industries.

Factor in the hangover from the financial collapse of 2008 and we're witnessing youth unemployment levels across the Western world from 15 to 60 percent. This situation is not only immoral it is creating a massive powder keg.

2. "The destruction of privacy in an unprecedented and irrevocable manner."

I believed this topic to be so important 20 years ago that I devoted an entire chapter about it (*Chapter 11*):

Most of us believe we have the right to decide what personal information we divulge, to whom, and for what purpose. Left unchecked, the Internet could render such thinking irrelevant. As human communications, business transactions, working, learning, and playing increasingly come onto the Net, unimaginable quantities and types of information become digitized and networked. How can we safeguard privacy in an economy that is digital?

Today: This is a major topic on the minds of most thoughtful people. But since the book was written there has been profound changes in how we need to safeguard privacy. So-called "data minimization" (limiting what information we give away) is no longer feasible. New approaches are required. (*I outline my new thinking on this topic in the introductory essay in Chapter 11.*)

3. The danger of "a severe bipolarization of wealth."

An ill-conceived transition to the digital economy could foster a two-tiered society… Is there an emerging 'revolt of the elites' who will use the new infrastructure to further cocoon themselves—children in private schools, paying for their own social services, surrounded by high-perimeter fences, identifying closer with friends and business associates in cyberspace, losing any sense of responsibility to others in their physical communities or country?

Today: Income inequality is one of the hottest topics on the planet. It was listed as the number one global risk by the World Economic Forum's 2014 meeting in Davos, Switzerland. It is the topic of the *New York Times* number 1 bestseller *Capital in the Twenty-First Century* by the French economist Thomas Piketty. While many disagree with his socialist conclusions, Piketty's scholarship has been pretty much unassailable, showing that growing social inequality is endemic to capitalism, even in the digital age. And reasonable people today are questioning whether the digital revolution might actually accelerate inequality.

4. "What impact will the digital economy have on quality of life?"

Will telework create new, flexible, enjoyable working environments, or will it enslave people to piecework done in isolation? Will we, as some pundits argue, drown in data or amuse ourselves to death? As technology invades our offices, homes, cars, hotel rooms, airplane seats, kitchens, and washrooms, is there a danger of the separation of work and leisure vanishing?

Today: This is a hotly debated topic and the jury is still out. As for technology making us stupid, many measures of smartness (improving IQ, standardized test scores, university graduates, etc.) suggest otherwise. However the quote from the brilliant Alan Kay in *The Digital Economy* seems prophetic: "Another way to think of roadkill on the information highway will be the billions who will forget that there are off-ramps to destinations other than Hollywood, Las Vegas, the local bingo parlor, or shiny beads from a shopping network!"

5. "What will be the impact of the new media on the family?"

"The new media hold the promise of strengthening the family by moving many family activities dispersed by industrial society back into the home… But are there other dangers? Despite its unhealthy impact on people, television at least brought families together around an electronic hearth. But in my family today, it's not unusual for the four of us to be clicking away on our keyboards in separate rooms."

Today: Many people are conflicted about such matters. On the one hand, they agree with some technology critics. On the other hand, they assert that the new media have brought them bounty, new connections, knowledge, and even joy. But as you sit in a restaurant and observe families silently staring into their devices, or get to the end of a day searching the Internet and answering e-mails, texts, and social media posts, you would reasonably question the digital balance sheet of the human condition. Alarmist voices are growing in number and volume. They represent more than a neo-Luddite backlash against change or a choir of "nattering nabobs of negativism" (as Spiro Agnew might say). Instead, it is clear that the digital revolution is outpacing our capacity as humans to effectively exploit and integrate it into our economies, social structures, and relationships, work and play, and our families.

6. "Many governments seem slow to comprehend the shift."

"Bureaucracies by definition resist change, thinking that heads-down is the route to survival. Can government become electronic, transforming the way government services are delivered? The so-called reinvention of government is not possible without reinventing the delivery system for government, and in doing so, dramatically reducing costs and improving the services government provides to its customers."

Today: Most governments spent a decade making existing models of government digital—"paving the cowpaths"—by putting existing services online through Web sites. However the economic crisis of 2008 has created a burning platform, causing governments to think seriously about using open data and social media to alter the deep structures of government and how we orchestrate capability to create public value.

8. "How can (we) change the democracy?"

"Will the electronic town hall become an electronic mob? Will cyber-democracy become hyper-democracy? Or can we craft a new age in which networked intelligence can be applied for the good of the people?"

Today: The problem is hardly too much citizen engagement through digital media, as I worried. The opposite is occurring. Industrial-Age governments have clung to the "you vote I rule" model. This is leading to a crisis of legitimacy for democratic institutions around the Western world as voting among young people declines. As I discuss later, during the past 20 years, voter turnout has dropped in most Western democracies, in some cases quite dramatically. In the 1992 U.S. presidential election, 89.9% of voters went to the polls. In the 2012 contest, the turnout plunged to 66.6%. Voter turnout has also fallen in countries such as the United Kingdom, France, Germany, Italy, Sweden, and Canada. In particular, young people are looking for ways other than voting to bring about social change and a new youth radicalization is fully underway.

Being elected to the U.S. House of Representatives is frequently a step into the revolving door to a K Street lucrative lobbying career. With two-year terms, these members of Congress spend their time in constant pre-election mode, and devote most of their time in office raising funds to fight the next election. Egregious gerrymandering is now common so that politicians can hold on to their seats regardless of the electorate's mood.

Politicians are increasingly beholden to wealthy contributors and interest groups. The health-care insurance industry thwarted the United States from joining the rest of the developed world with a single payer health-care system. Fully 92 % of Americans want background checks of people buying guns, but the "will of the people" cannot be realized because the National Rifle Association's (NRA's) clout prevents that from happening.

The American political sociologist Seymour Martin Lipset wrote that legitimacy is "the capacity of a political system to engender and maintain the belief that existing political institutions are the most appropriate and proper ones for the society." The ongoing abuse of trust by officeholders is not simply a series of isolated incidents, but manifestations of a deep and widespread rot. The result is a full-blown crisis in legitimacy.

To restore legitimacy and trust we need to do what *The Digital Economy* advised two decades ago—build a second era of democracy based on integrity and accountability, and with stronger, more open institutions, active citizen citizenship, and a culture of public discourse and participation.

9. "Can the formal education system transform itself?"

Can we create a virtual college or university system for all the other faculties that eliminates the lineups of tens of thousands of prospective students across the country? Will teachers and administrators be able to reinvent education? Talk to the students; they're willing. As Geoffrey Bannister, president of Butler University, says: "Just wait till the generation of teenage Internet users hit the universities where the average age of a tenured professor is 50. Sparks are going to fly!"

Today: Ironically, no institution has been more resistant to change than the schools and universities. They have used technology primarily to improve administration rather than changing the model of pedagogy.

In higher education this is all changing rapidly today, not because faculty and administrators have awoken to the new opportunities, but because the entire model of higher education is being bludgeoned by Massive Open Online Courses (MOOCs). Major universities are putting recorded lectures and course content online for free. Some analysts say that half of the universities in the United States will be gone within a couple of decades. Some universities want to develop a way to give students credit for the MOOCs they complete.

In a similar vein, a new kind of online training program, designed by businesses, will prepare thousands of workers and job seekers for high-demand jobs in the tech industry. AT&T and Udacity have launched the first "nanodegree" program using the MOOC format.

The first courses focus on entry-level software skills. Udacity will manage the program with personalized coaching and career services. AT&T will provide direction on course content and offer 100 paid internships for nanodegree graduates. Students will be certified for the skills they learn, and the nanodegree will be fully recognized for entry-level software jobs at AT&T.

Developments such as these underscore why educators must acknowledge that the current model of pedagogy is obsolete. The traditional Industrial-Age model has the teacher as the broadcaster. This may have worked for the past four centuries, but it fails woefully to meet the needs for today's students who are entering the global knowledge economy.

With technology, it is now possible to offload rote learning to multimedia computers or tablets that are used outside of class time. The computer customizes the material to each student's pace and abilities. Rather than devoting class time to a lecture, it can be used to discuss material that the students have learned. So it is now possible to embrace new collaboration models that emulate the nature of the small seminar and capture its benefits. The technology gives educators opportunities to develop a deeper and richer relationship with their students.

For sure, the model of collaborative learning existed before the Internet. For many years, some learning institutions offered small seminars where students learned by discussing topics in the subject being studied. The educator was less the fountain of knowledge and more the moderator. Such seminars were effective, but they were rare and only offered to advanced students.

READING THIS BOOK

The original manuscript for *The Digital Economy* is published below in its entirety. I have made one change. It's amazing to think that 20 years ago there was no certainty regarding what we would name this new network. The leading candidates were the Internet, the Web, and the Information Highway (which I not so cleverly attempted to dub as the "internet.") The term "Internet" didn't exactly take hold, and it's such a jarring term appearing in several chapters that I felt it would distract you as the reader. So I've done a global "search and replace" to substitute it with a more modern term.

As for things I got wrong or didn't anticipate, the biggest was mobility. The mobile revolution has intersected with the Web to revolutionize many aspects of business and personal lives. My only defense is that the mobile Web really kicked in a decade later, and the book was not intended to be a forecast but rather a guide for practitioners at the time. If you read these pages, you'll also see the notions of internetworking and collaboration throughout. The first time I heard the words "social network," was in the early 2000s from the brilliant Silicon Valley diva Kim Polese. I asked her what was next and when she said those magic words "social network" I just shrugged, wondering what the fuss was all about. After all, I thought, isn't that what we've been doing all along? In hindsight, I missed a hell of an opportunity there too.

You'll find much of this material relevant to today, but much has also become part of the vernacular and reads to be old-school or even naïve. You decide. However this Anniversary edition is not intended to be a history text.

For each of the 12 chapters I have written a preamble—a new introductory essay that reflects on how the world has changed, raises new issues and insights for today, and projects foreword to the next 20 years. I hope you find the new material helpful in figuring out how the ever-accelerating digital revolution can be harnessed for you, your organization, and for your planning for the future.

Don Tapscott, September 2014

Original Preface to the 1995 Edition

Today we are witnessing the early, turbulent days of a revolution as significant as any other in human history. A new medium of human communications is emerging, one that may prove to surpass all previous revolutions – the printing press, the telephone, the television – in its impact on our economic and social life. The computer is expanding from a tool for information management to a tool for communications. The Internet (Net) and World Wide Web (Web) are enabling a new economy based on the networking of human intelligence. In this digital economy, individuals and enterprises create wealth by applying knowledge, networked human intelligence, and effort to manufacturing, agriculture, and services. In the digital frontier of this economy, the players, dynamics, rules and requirements for survival and success are all changing.

Such a shift in economic and social relationships has occurred only a handful of times before on this planet. It is causing every company to think far beyond the likes of "reengineering" to transform itself. A new enterprise is emerging – the internetworked business-which is as different from the corporation of the twentieth century as the latter was from the feudal craft shop.

The Digital Economy attempts to answer the question: What does it all mean for *my* business? Whereas businesspeople are inundated with information, ideas, and theories on new technologies and new organizational forms as well as changing business conditions and strategies, there has been little success in developing a coherent view that synthesizes these factors. *The Digital Economy* explains the new economy, the new enterprise, and the new technology, and how they link to one another—how they enable one another. If you and your organization understand these relationships—the role of the new technology in creating the new enterprise for a new economy—you can be successful.

The Age of Networked Intelligence is an age of promise. It is not simply about the networking of technology, but about the networking of humans through technology. It is not an age of smart machines but of humans who work through networks to combine their intelligence, knowledge, and creativity for breakthroughs in the creation of wealth and social development. It is not just an age of linking computers but of internetworking human ingenuity. It is an age of vast new promise and unimaginable opportunity.

Think about scientific research. In the past, scientists would work with a powerful supercomputer to, say, simulate mechanisms of a biological cell membrane as a way of understanding the structure of biological molecules. But as networking permeates the plant, computers everywhere can be marshaled concurrently to attack the problem. Rather than a single expensive computer supporting a single group of scientists, a global network of computers can be internetworked to support distributed teams of scientists. The network becomes the computer —infinitely more powerful than any single machine. And networked human intelligence is applied to research, thus creating a higher order of thinking, knowledge—and maybe even internetworked consciousness—among people.

The same networking can be applied to business and almost every other aspect of human endeavor—learning, health care, work, entertainment.

Networking can change the intelligence of a business by bringing collective know-how to bear on problem solving and innovation. By dramatically opening the channels of human communication, consciousness can be extended from individuals to organizations. Unconscious organizations, like people, cannot learn. Through becoming conscious, organizations can become able to learn—and that's a precondition for survival. Networked intelligence is the missing link in organizational learning, and the conscious organization may be the foundation for the elusive learning organization. And perhaps networked intelligence can be extended beyond organizations to create a broader awakening—social consciousness—in communities, nations, and beyond.

But the Age of the Networked Intelligence is also an age of potential peril. For individuals, organization, and societies that fall behind, punishment is swift. It is not only old business rules but governments, social institutions, and relationships among people that are being transformed. The new media is changing the ways we do business, work, learn, play, and even think. Far more than the old western frontier the digital frontier is a place of recklessness, confusion, uncertainty, calamity, and danger. Some signs point to a new economy in which wealth is even further concentrated, basic rights like privacy are vanishing, and a spiral of violence and repression undermine basic security and freedoms.

Pervasive evidence exists that indicate the basic social fabric is beginning to disintegrate. Old laws, structures, norms, and approaches are proving to be completely inadequate for life in the new economy. While they are crumbling or being smashed, it is not completely clear what should replace them. Everywhere people are beginning to ask, "Will this smaller world our children inherit be a better one?"

Unfortunately, when people look at the new age, they tend to focus on one side or the other – the promise or the peril. Two camps have emerged: those exhilarated by the promise and those terrified by what the new technology and economy are bringing.

I have attempted to present both sides and some new directions, perhaps to break down walls between these two extremes. My goal is to equip you – today's emerging business leader – with the insights you need to transform your business for success in the new economy.

If you accept the mantle of leadership, you can participate in achieving, for yourself and all of us, a world of unrequited peril and promise fulfilled. If we all do it right, and do the right thing, the Age of Networked Intelligence can be an age of unprecedented wealth, fairness, true democracy, and social justice. Read on.

Don Tapscott, 1995

Acknowledgments for the 1995 Edition

To a considerable degree, this book is the product of collaboration with many persons associated with the Alliance for Converging Technologies. The Alliance is conducting a multimillion-dollar investigation into the impact of the new media on business. This program, initiated in 1994, is called "Interactive Multimedia in the High Performance Organization: Wealth Creation in the Digital Economy." The results of this research are proprietary to the companies and governments that are funding the effort. However, members, staff, and contributors to the Alliance have shared their views freely on nonproprietary matters.

My special thanks to Alliance president David Ticoll; OECD economist and Alliance contributor Dr. Riel Miller; and Chuck Martin, publisher of *Interactive Age* and a strong supporter and contributor to the Alliance's work. Also, special thanks to economic development consultant Phil Courneyeur, for the views of the social implications of the new technologies were developed considerably through a spirited discussion involving Phil, Riel, and me, that was conducted on the Net over several months from three continents.

Also my sincerest thanks to Alliance contributors Art Caston (who was my coauthor for *Paradigm Shift*), Alex Lowy, Carl Thompson, Paul Woolner, Wendy Cukier, Burnes Hollyman, Del Langdon, Max Hopper, Cynthia Rudge, Araldo Menegon, and Michael Miloff. Key insights on the transformation of broadcasting came from new media producer Michael Vaughan and from consultant Duncan McEwan. Thanks also to New Paradigm Learning collaborators Julia Gluck and Ruth Burgess for their insights and background information. Important research was conducted for the effort by Alexandra Samuel, a tireless Harvard Ph.D. student. Tim Fiala of Burson-Marsteller helped to develop the insights on networked intelligence, and consultant Bill Gillies has a way with words to clarify complex issues. Special thanks also to privacy authority Ann Cavoukian, who, with me, co-authored *Who Knows: Safeguarding Your Privacy in a Networked World*. Ann's insights on the privacy issue and review of that chapter are very much appreciated. And my usual thanks to Betsy Brown at McGraw-Hill, who has a knack for finding and developing books that are of considerable importance to business.

Many ideas were developed through my activities chairing Canada's first advisory committee on the information highway. Canada and I are indebted to Deputy Minister Elaine Todres and telecommunications strategist Joan McCalla—both of the Ontario government—and also former Premier Bob Rae and former cabinet secretary David Agnew, both of whom provided the drive behind this effort and critical personal support for me.

I am indebted to more than 100 business leaders and technology visionaries who spent time sharing their insights with me. Their names are listed throughout the book—reading like a *Who's Who* of the new economy.

Much of the work of researching, interviewing, and drafting case study materials was diligently performed by Toronto author and journalist Rod McQueen. Rod also acted as sounding board throughout the project—from conception to final product. This included a careful edit and review of the entire manuscript.

My wife and partner, Ana Lopes, was a source of insight and encouragement throughout. The book would not have been written without her. And because children often see complex issues clearly, I was fortunate to have two bright ones on the team—12-year-old Niki Tapscott and 9-year-old Alex Tapscott.

Two others deserve special credit, for they spent as much time on this project as I did—Antoinette Schatz and Jody Stevens, both of New Paradigm Learning Corporation. Antoinette coordinated the discussions with business leaders and researched key topics on the Net. Jody not only produced and edited the work but also handled the technology infrastructure, tricky negotiations, and finances.

My heartfelt thanks to all of you.

Don Tapscott, 1995

Acknowledgments for the 20th Anniversary Edition

It's not possible to thank my many collaborators over the last twenty years, but a few deserve special mention with regards to this new edition of *The Digital Economy*. David Ticoll has contributed significantly to my thinking about the current status of the digital revolution. Anthony D. Williams continues to be a great collaborator about all things digital, in particular leading the content development for our program on Global Solution Networks. And special thanks to long-time partner Joan Bigham for providing stellar business leadership for that initiative.

Bill Gillies, the chief editor for The Tapscott Group, contributed ably to my writings for the Anniversary Edition. Thanks to Jody Stevens for keeping the trains going: Carley Williamson for leading the book promotion; Alisa Acosta for research and presentation production; and to Amie Colquhoun, who designed and manages all of our spectacular Web properties. Over 20 years I've been grateful for my agent The Leigh Bureau, headed by Bill Leigh and Wes Neff, for keeping my ideas in front of audiences internationally. And thanks to the team at McGraw-Hill for bringing this book to market faster than any of my previous tomes.

I'm deeply grateful to the business leaders who have reviewed the new manuscript and provided me their endorsements. I don't remember seeing such a stellar list for any business book, and I'm humbled that they took the time. Special thanks to Eric Schmidt, Google's Executive Chairman for his deeply thoughtful Foreword and his support over the years. Also many thanks to Richard Florida, Roger Martin, and Jamison Steeve—my coconspirators at the Martin Prosperity Institute at the Rotman School of Management, University of Toronto—for their support and collaboration.

Increasingly my work is a family affair. My brothers Bob and Bill Tapscott both made important contributions to the ideas herein. My children Alex Tapscott and Niki Tapscott both provided specific insights for the anniversary edition, and Ana Lopes continues to be the source of my deepest intellectual stimulation.

Don Tapscott, September 2014

I T WAS APPROPRIATE that the first chapter of *The Digital Economy* began with a story about the band R.E.M. and how they used the Internet to promote themselves, and then speculate about how the entire music industry would be turned on its head. For if there is one industry that seemed to take forever to understand the disruptive force of the digital revolution it has been the music labels. With their heads in the sand for almost two decades, they viewed the Internet as a threat rather than the biggest opportunity to come along in their history. The record companies continue to cling belligerently to their old business model, where music is a physical product, and the industry has become the poster child of failed digital opportunities.

The music labels' problems predated the Internet. Recorded music was a bloated industry with huge distribution costs. It also had many intermediaries, such as distributors and promoters, looking for a cut of the action. Taking a band from obscurity to popularity was expensive, but that's what companies had to do to be given coveted shelf space at the record store. Less than 10% of CDs (compact discs) made a profit, so the best sellers covered the losses from their poorer-selling cousins.

The Internet should have been a godsend for music labels. By sidestepping the Industrial Age infrastructure, many more musicians could be profitable. Record companies—reinvented as digital networks of artists, fans, and entrepreneurs—could nurture many small artists, rather than focus all their energies on potential superstars. As a society and culture, we would be much better served by such an approach.

The solution to restoring the music industry to economic health is not to sell songs at a dollar a pop. Instead, it should embrace a revamped business model. Honestly, it took me a decade after the publication of *The Digital Economy* to figure out a point of view. In 2003, in a *New York Times* article,

"Some Advise 'Everywhere Internet Audio,'"[1] I advocated that music should stop being a product that one buys and instead be a service that one subscribes to for a small monthly fee. Recordings would be streamed to music lovers via the Internet to any appliance of their choosing—such as their laptop, mobile device, car, or home stereo. Musicians, songwriters, and their labels would be compensated through systems that track their popularity.

I called it "Everywhere Internet Audio." In 2003, the idea sounded revolutionary, but such services now exist and are growing fast. Companies such as Spotify, Rhapsody, and Pandora are being joined by cloud heavyweights like Amazon and Google to stream music. Netflix has extended the streaming model to movies and television shows. As music services grow more sophisticated, every customer will have his or her own channel and will slice and dice the massive musical database anyway he or she likes—by artist, genre, year, songwriter, popularity, and so on. Soon you will be able to ask the service to retrieve upbeat tunes from your high school years that feature great guitar riffs.

Going forward, get ready for Everywhere Internet Everything.

Reflecting: Is the Digital Economy Still a Capitalist Economy?

There is one substantive issue I want to address in this Introduction. For all the discussion about the so-called "new economy" that occurred in the 1990s, all advocates, including me, skirted a big issue. Our economy is called "capitalism." We all discussed various aspects of how the digital revolution was changing business, government, and society, but never actually addressed the fundamentals of the economy itself.

Today, the continuing global economic mess is causing many to question "the system," but there are few serious proposals to get rid of it. Still, from student protests in Europe to the Occupy movement globally, many are asking, What are the fundamental problems with capitalism and how do we fix them? And should the new economy be capitalist at all?

As one Occupy Wall Street sign read, reflecting on the so-called crisis of capitalism: "Capitalism *is* the Crisis."

Recently, the capitalists themselves are energizing the discussion. The *Financial Times* presented a multipart series on the topic. *The Economist*, a sophisticated defender and reformer of capitalism, has discussed capitalism's strengths and weaknesses at length. Business schools around the world are also debating the topic. And dozens of books written by business leaders— from *The Crisis of Capitalist Democracy* by Richard A. Posner to *The Road from*

Ruin by Matthew Bishop and Michael Green—discuss everything from how to save capitalism to whether it is even saveable.

In 2014, *Capital in the Twenty-First Century*, a book by the French Marxist economist Thomas Piketty, reached the #1 rank on the *New York Times* nonfiction book list. The most discussed nonfiction book of 2014, Piketty analyzes a massive data set from 20 countries to show that growing inequality is built into the capitalist system. He argues that capital (wealth) and inequality are likely to grow in the next few decades and that rather than seeing the broad and mutual prosperity we have come to assumes the natural state of advanced economies, the influence of wealth will make our economy look a lot more like the nineteenth century, dominated by massive fortunes. "The main driver of inequality—the tendency of returns on capital to exceed the rate of economic growth—today threatens to generate extreme inequalities that stir discontent and undermine democratic values."[2]

In a June 2014 tech-focused conference in Nashville, none other than Al Gore waded into the discussion saying that: "We have rising levels of inequality and chronic underinvestment" in public programs. He reminded the crowd that when "95% of all the additional national Income in the United States, since the recovery began in 2009, goes to the top 1%, that's not an Occupy Wall Street slogan, that's a fact."[3] His conclusion? "Democracy has been hacked" by mon-eyed interests.

But perhaps the problem is not capitalism per se that is ailing, but rather its first iteration: "industrial capitalism." All around us we see industries in crisis and governments that can't get things done. Media companies are failing and the financial services sector is increasingly reckless. Our energy grid and transportation systems need urgent renewal. Institutions for global cooperation and problem solving seem incapable of progress.

But at the same time, it's clear that we're in the early stages of a massive transformation. Society has at its disposal the most powerful platform ever for bringing together the people, skills, and knowledge we need to ensure growth, social development, and a just and sustainable world. The Internet slashes collaboration costs and enables deep changes to the way we orchestrate society's capability to innovate, to make goods and services, and to create wealth and public value.

Companies and communities are working together in new ways on shared concerns, endeavors, and challenges. People around the world are collaborating like never before. From education and science, and new approaches to citizen engagement and democracy, sparkling new initiatives are underway, embracing a new set of principles for the twenty-first century—collaboration, openness, sharing, interdependence, and integrity.

While the contours of new institutions and industries are becoming clear, it's less clear what this means for the fundamental nature of the economy itself. And what should we call the new economic system that appears to be rising from the ashes of the latter-day silk-hatted tycoons?

Clearly, it is a social economy. In a year or so, there will be a billion people on this planet using social media daily. More than 80% of the world's population has access to cell phones.[4] The social world is transforming the way we create wealth, work, learn, play, raise our children, and probably, the way we think. We're all collaborating like never before. In business the hottest concepts are social: collective intelligence, mass collaboration, crowd sourcing, and collaborative innovation.

"Social" is penetrating every aspect of the economy and society. Social media, social networking, social business, social government, social entertainment, and social everything. One might suppose that the logical term to describe the synthesis of all things social would be "socialism." Unfortunately, I'm told that term has already been taken, as it were, so let's opt instead for the term "Capitalism 2.0."

During the first era of capitalism, machinery was the means of production and the most important assets were physical and financial. Work was organized in hierarchies and capitalists had a single objective: maximizing their personal wealth. The Internet is becoming a new mode of production that changes the way we orchestrate capability in society to innovate, create goods and services, and even create public value. The most important assets are contained in the crania of knowledge workers. The most effective work systems are social and collaborative, and increasingly thoughtful people everywhere understand that an economy based on greed is not only unworkable, it threatens the planet.

If Capitalism 2.0 were the most natural umbrella term to describe the impact of social media on our economy and society, what would be its guiding principles? If you look at social technology, business models, and thinking today, you'd be in for some surprises.

To begin, rather than social (state) ownership of everything, it would be a society where innovation is driven by companies and market forces. Under capitalism there is private ownership of wealth and most goods and services are produced by firms, most of which are corporations. These firms provide limited liability for shareholders, management, staff, and markets. These are solid concepts and there is a broad agreement that markets have historically provided the best incentives for innovation and wealth creation. But sophisticated companies understand that traditional Industrial Age approaches can be radically improved by social business.

Today as Linux dominates large computers and mobile devices around the world, smart companies like IBM have embraced the open-source operating system, saving themselves hundreds of millions of dollars a year and generating billions of dollars in hardware and services revenue. Biotechnology (biotech) companies cooperated to place their intellectual property (IP)—the human genome—in a commons. Nike gave away 400 patents to the GreenXchange on the principle that "a rising tide lifts all boats." In industries ranging from pharmaceuticals to auto manufacturing, competitors are beginning to share some of their intellectual property as a step toward improving their industries and their own chances of survival.

Companies are learning that all intellectual property is not the same. Some intellectual property should be protected, while it's wiser to place other intellectual property in a commons. Like IBM, they save money, enhance their capability by sharing, and then compete on a higher level, all to the benefit of shareholders. I estimate that if IBM had fought Linux rather than embracing it, the company's revenues and likely market value today would be a third less than it is.

Customers love the new collaboration. They purchase goods and services collectively on Groupon. They find the best hotels by sharing knowledge on TripAdvisor and find the best restaurants through Restaurant.com. They lend money to each other through peer-to-peer banks like CommunityLend. And they collaborate with companies, helping coinnovate everything from Threadless T-shirts to Doritos Superbowl ads.

Under Capitalism 2.0, governments are still important. The notion that the best government is no government is foolhardy. However government bureaucracies could be smaller in many areas. The concept of "reinventing government" for better, cheaper government, has been around for two decades. Today, due to the social revolution, it's an idea whose time has come. The sovereign debt crisis in Europe and the spiraling debt in America and other Western countries call for more than tinkering. Social media not only changes the way we innovate and create goods and services, it can change the way societies create public value.

Governments can become a stronger part of the social ecosystem that binds individuals, communities, and businesses—not by absorbing new responsibilities or building additional layers of bureaucracy, but through a willingness to open up formerly closed processes and data to broader input and innovation. In other words, government becomes a platform for the creation of services and for social innovation. Government provides resources, sets rules, and mediates disputes, but allows citizens, nonprofits, and the private sector to share in the heavy lifting. This is leading to a change in the division of labor in society about how public value is created, and holds the promise of solving the debt crisis.

But while private wealth and market forces are necessary, they are proving to be woefully insufficient to move the economy and society forward. The Occupy movement is correct in saying that completely unfettered market forces would result in disaster. Loosely regulated bankers, driven by greed, almost brought down the global economy. The class divisions in society are growing, and governments have cozy relationships with corporations that often seem to prevent them from acting in the public interest.

The 2008 economic meltdown underscored how interconnected our world has become. We need to encourage and enforce mutual cooperation through a new division of labor among the four key pillars of society: business, government, the civic sector, and the new pillar enabled by the Internet—the individual citizen. There is no longer room for unilateralism. Part of the "social" philosophy is that business can't succeed in a world that's failing.

Warren Buffett was called a socialist when he suggested closing tax loopholes for corporations and the rich. Bill Gates is marshaling his vast personal wealth and influence to make a better world. Smart business leaders understand that the purpose of corporations goes beyond making money for shareholders.

Some political leaders are starting to shift from the Industrial Age model of democracy too. The "You vote, I rule" approach is stalled and citizens are increasingly cynical. But experiments with digital age democracy are growing. From electronic town hall meetings, challenges, digital brainstorms, and open data initiatives, governments at all levels are reaching out to engage citizens in developing new ideas and solving problems.

Capitalism 2.0 would have a different approach to regulation. To begin, business leaders would embrace good regulation, understanding that markets work best with strong foundations and good regulations. For example, Canadian banks avoided the entire subprime mortgage crisis and its aftermath because the regulatory environment kept the banks from getting into trouble. The upshot is that today 4 of the largest banks in North America are now Canadian, and of the largest 20 banks, the top 6 low-risk banks are Canadian. And if Thomas Piketty is right—most thoughtful analysts and economists think he is—about growing social inequality, then clearly mechanisms will be needed to help society better share the wealth. We can't accept a new century bifurcated by wealth, a society run by dynasties, and the elimination of a middle class. Among other things, that's a formula for social upheaval or worse.

With Capitalism 2.0, much greater transparency for every institution could change the regulatory paradigm, adding "citizen regulators" as a key element of the new economy. Governments could make everything transparent on the Web and let citizens and other parties contribute their data and observations. They could also let citizens help enforce regulations, perhaps by changing their buying behavior or by organizing public campaigns that name and shame offenders. This is not to say that transparency is a substitute for better regulation by national governments and international institutions. Rather, more disclosure and increased civic participation would add significant muscle to traditional regulatory systems.

Under Capitalism 2.0, there could actually be "a chicken in every pot," as the Marxists of the last century sloganeered. The principles of collaboration, sharing, openness, and self-organization outside the boundaries of traditional corporations, governments, and other institutions are already starting to drive unprecedented economic, political, and societal activity.

But we need to move further. We need to reinvent every institution in society around the social model for innovation, interdependence, sustainability, and integrity. In manufacturing, companies need to join initiatives like the GreenXchange, sharing know-how about creating sustainable companies. In pharmaceuticals, companies need to start collaborating on precompetitive research and compete on a higher level. University professors need to join Massachusetts Institute of Technology's (MIT's) open courseware movement and collaborate on the creation of learning for higher education. Car companies should be joining forces to advance fuel cell science. Banks aren't lending money to small businesses because they are saddled with a trillion dollars of toxic assets left over from the subprime mortgage mess. The details of these assets should be placed into a commons so that they can be valued by independent modelers, helping banks clear their balance sheets and kick-start job creation.

Capitalism 2.0 needs a global system with mechanisms for problem solving and governance that transcend nation-states. Today's institutions were created in a much different time, to govern a new world of nations after World War II. Institutions such as the United Nations, the World Bank, the International Monetary Fund (IMF), the G20 (Group of Twenty), and the G8 (Group of Eight), while necessary, are no longer sufficient. More often than not, national self-interests take priority when today's challenges demand solutions that transcend the traditional boundaries of nation-states. They make little room for the inclusion of authentic citizens' voices, such as the self-organized civic networks we have seen coalescing around important issues at city and regional levels.

There is a growing urgency to rethink our aging global institutions of the Industrial Age. Today, there are myriad new collaborative models that are self-organizing to address twenty-first century realities. These models have names such as global action networks, multistakeholder networks, global alliances, and stakeholder webs. In fact, the entire concept of social innovation—new thinking and action for the public good—is being extended beyond communities and nations to the global stage. The new collaborations and networks include some combination of the four "pillars" of society: the state, the private sector, the civil society, and now empowered individuals.

There is at least one big problem with this vision though. Such a model of capitalism can only be achieved in a smooth and managed way if today's capitalists get on board. Unfortunately, leaders of the old paradigms are the last to embrace the new. The transition from agrarian feudal economies and societies to industrial capitalism was punctuated by revolutions—such as the French, the American, and the National Independence revolutions across Latin America.

Many of the leaders of the old model of capitalism are tenaciously clinging to the past and hoping that things will get back to normal. The upshot is that the forces of change—especially today's young people—may have to find more extreme methods to achieve a new future. When extreme conflict, discord, rebellion, and even revolution occur it's anybody's guess what the outcome could be.

The Challenge of Leadership

In the original *The Digital Economy*, I discussed the challenge of leadership, arguing that every institution would have to find within itself the leadership for transformation to a new age. Many CEOs and government leaders agreed with me, and gave kind and thoughtful jacket endorsements.

Sadly however, it is instructive today to note that most of these executives had great challenges achieving the change for their own organizations. It is striking, and even shocking, to see how many of the original endorsers of the book had their organizations turned upside down or swept away by the tidal wave of change. On the jacket were enthusiastic quotes from the CEOs of Nortel Networks, MCI, Nynex, Ameritech, GE Information Services, and *BusinessWeek*—all of which were swallowed by competitors or went bankrupt. At least I didn't include the CEOs from Kodak, Borders, Blockbuster Entertainment, or Circuit City.

The companies of other jacket endorsers went through or are still going through their own massive transformations. Lewis "Lew" Platt, then CEO of

Hewlett-Packard (HP) provided great leadership for the company, only to have his successors drop the ball (although by most accounts Meg Whitman has picked it up again and is driving big changes). Frederick "Fred" Smith, the then-CEO of FedEx, proved that a company can constantly reinvent itself for success. To my knowledge *The Digital Economy* was the only book ever endorsed by former Vice President Al Gore, who after an unsuccessful run for president reinvented himself and brought the challenge of climate change to the world.

In fact, with two decades of "water under the bridge" the challenge of leadership continues unabated. As the pace of change accelerates, this is a time of uncertainty, confusion, and calamity, and the digital revolution seems to be outpacing our capacity as individuals and institutions to comprehend it. As with all new shifts, leaders of the old paradigm are having the greatest difficulty embracing the new.

Many household names didn't exist a decade ago let alone two decades back: Facebook, Twitter, Uber, Airbnb, OpenTable, TripAdvisor, StubHub, 1stDibs, iTunes, Spotify. There have been convulsive disruptions to leadership in many industries, ranging from the collapse of Wall Street giants to the upending of the auto industry, not just by European and Asians Juggernauts but also by the new auto innovators such as Tesla and Google.

Many industries are rethinking their entire industry model—such as pharmaceuticals. Under pressure from the patent cliff, big pharma companies are beginning to actually share clinical trial data; this is a step toward them competing on a different basis. The health-care industry is on the verge of a major disruption, but one led by the likes of Amazon, Apple, and Google rather than government or traditional providers.

Overall, I'm convinced we have a burning platform for change. It's a good analogy: the costs of staying where we are becoming greater than the costs of going to something very new. The crisis of 2008 is still shaking the windows and rattling the doors of the global business community. Today, because of transparency and the growing power to scrutinize, naked corporations are coming under pressure to behave with integrity and have sustainable business models. Increasingly, smart business executives are beginning to understand that business can't succeed in a world that's failing. Still, vested interests from Wall Street to Washington, D.C., are causing leaders to dig in their heels to fight change.

The good news is that new leaders are showing the way forward. For the new archetype look to visionaries like Elan Musk, the founder of (among other things) Tesla. A serial disrupter, his focus has not been on building the latest cool, social-software gadget, as many in Silicon Valley do, but rather to create great innovations for a world in search of meaningful sustainable solutions.

The Tesla Model S, a fully electric car was rated by *Consumer Reports* as not only the best electric car they have reviewed but the best car of any kind they have reviewed in their history. The company has a market value of $30 billion, making it worth more than Chrysler.

In 2014, Musk further disrupted the auto industry by releasing all of the Tesla patents. In doing so, he helped the electric car ecosystem as a whole compete against the traditional internal combustion engines. He contributed not only to his competitive advantage, but also to creating a sustainable planet.

Musk is an example of the new leader who sees improving shareholder value as complementary to improving the state of the world. He understands that businesses must operate with a new set of principles for the networked age.

Similarly, we need leaders in government who are focused on real digitally enabled change rather than personal power. These leaders must also see citizens as active participants in the democracy rather than passive spectators.

Sadly however, it is becoming clear that many leaders of today's old, stalling institutions are not equipped for this challenge and that leadership will come from new sources. Get ready for an age of discordance, dissonance, disruption, and upheaval or worse.

Notes

1. "Some Advise 'Everywhere Internet Audio,'" *New York Times*, September 15, 2003 (http://www.nytimes.com/2003/09/15/technology/15neco.html).
2. Thomas Piketty, *Capital in the Twenty-first Century*, Belknap Press, 2014.
3. http://www.salon.com/2014/06/12/democracy_has_been_hacked_al_gore_channels_his_inner_thomas_piketty_partner/
4. http://newsfeed.time.com/2013/03/25/more-people-have-cell-phones-than-toilets-u-n-study-shows/

THE AGE OF NETWORKED INTELLIGENCE

Are you looking to drive my dreams
You here to run my screens?

    R.E.M.

A TIME OF TRANSFORMATION

When the Atlanta-based rock band R.E.M. went on tour in 1995, the first time the supergroup had played so extensively in five years, much of the promotional effort was focused on the Internet. The dates for the North American portion of the band's tour were posted on the World Wide Web (WWW) in January, just days before the first concert in Perth, Australia. Fans could look in the R.E.M. folder created by MTV News not only for the schedule but also for audio and video interviews with band members, as well as concert footage. Want more? Well, just tap into the WWW for the entire list of R.E.M. bootleg records, band photographs, all the song lyrics, and even the sounds from some of their famous guitar riffs.

And coming soon? Click on your favorite hit from any singer, sit back, and enjoy the video. The marketplace for R.E.M. is an electronic one—the Net! Can it be long before R.E.M.'s distribution system is the Net as well? What will happen to their current publisher, Warner Brothers Records? What is the role of a record store in this new world? Or what will happen to the radio station when R.E.M.'s music can be accessed from the Net with the push of a button from the digital radio in your car? What will happen to MTV itself when you can say to your television, "Play me the first cut from R.E.M.'s new album?"

In music, and in everything, the times they are a-changing. A new age is upon us and no one can halt its progress. Unlike revolutions of the past, however, the opportunity to share more fully in the largesse of this revolution is huge. Aspects of this new age already exist; the rest is being born daily. Amid the apparent chaos of change, there are rhythms at work, and patterns are beginning to appear.

We are at the dawn of an Age of Networked Intelligence—an age that is giving birth to a new economy, a new politics, and a new society. Businesses will be transformed, governments will be renewed, and individuals will be able to reinvent themselves—all with the help of the new information technology.

There is a vast new promise but also new perils. A looming dark side holds the potential for severe social stratification, unprecedented invasion of privacy and other rights, structural unemployment, and massive social dislocation and conflict. The future will depend on what we as businesses and as a society do—on our decisions and our actions.

Look at what happened in April 1995 immediately following the blast at the federal government building in Oklahoma City. The Net became a focal point for all sides of the debate. Some messages went so far as to allege that the FBI was to blame. Others, posted by extremist gun cults, exhorted fellow members to more rebellious acts. But the Net was also the focal point for helpful information. The FBI, using its Home Page, quickly posted descriptions of the suspects. And the Net was used to spread pleas for heavy equipment that could be used in the rescue operation. The promise and the peril.

Even Newt Gingrich, the Georgia Republican who became Speaker of the House of Representatives in 1995, made the disruptions of the new age a major theme upon taking office. "The most accurate analogy to what is happening to us now is to look at the period between 1770 and 1800, when America was changing from a rural to a manufacturing society," said Gingrich in a speech. "What is happening to us now—the transition from the industrial era ... is forcing us to ask very similar and profound questions about ourselves."

But how can companies transform themselves for the new economy? In the 1980s, the main management tool for change was quality. The total quality and continuous improvement movement helped many companies respond to the newly emerging global situation.

In the 1990s the attention shifted to business process reengineering (BPR), a management technique that swept through corporations and governments around the world. It is true that the old business processes, management practices, organizational structures, and ways of working have become inappropriate for the new volatile, global, competitive business environment. Clearly, many large companies needed to reengineer to reduce their cost bases.

However, by all accounts, BPR is in trouble. A survey by *Systems Reengineering Economics*, a newsletter published by Computer Economics Inc., of Carlsbad, California, found that companies will spend $52 billion on business reengineering by 1997. Of that, $40 billion will go to information technology (IT). Will corporations be satisfied? According to *InformationWeek*, two-thirds of such projects fail. According to management consulting firm Arthur D. Little Inc., only 16% of companies are "satisfied." Of the rest, 45% are partially satisfied and 39% are dissatisfied. Other companies have simply wasted money; Citibank has frankly admitted that the $50 million it spent on reengineering produced no results.

The idea behind BPR seems to be a good one. So, what's the problem? The number one culprit on everyone's list is resistance to change. A study by Deloitte & Touche listed 60% of respondents as indicating resistance to change as the main factor behind the failure of BPR. Among the top five reasons, three were variants on resistance—lack of executive consensus; lack of a senior management champion; and unrealistic expectations.

Old business processes die hard. They have built-in resistance to their own transformation. But scratch the surface and you'll find that much of this so-called resistance is rational—at least from the perspective of the human subjects who are reengineered. Notwithstanding the lofty statements of BPR theorists about improving customer service, the real goal of most reengineering projects is to streamline processes and reduce costs—specifically head count. People, having heads, reflect that theirs might be one of those to be counted, and decide to resist. They openly resist. They passively resist. Or they superficially comply rather than buy in. But resist they do. And such resistance is basically rational.

Don't get me wrong. All companies need to control or reduce costs. Old processes, from the old economy and old enterprise, are an obstacle to competitiveness. They need to be reengineered for efficiency and high performance. This becomes especially clear when your customer calls on Friday and says that you must reduce prices by 10% by Monday or they will no longer do business with you. The 10% isn't going to come from reducing margins, which are already razor thin.

But increasingly BPR will not be adequate for success. Although downsizing may be laudable in some situations, it is not a strategy for the future. A vision for transformation beyond "neutron bombing" your enterprise is required. Success in the new economy will require inventing new business processes, new businesses, new industries, and new customers—not rearranging old ones.

For the 1990s and the next millennium, corporations need to get beyond reengineering to the transformation of the corporation enabled by IT. The goal should not just be cost control but the dramatic and profound transformation of customer service, responsiveness, and innovation.

Business process reengineering does not a strategy for the new economy make. Like quality, reengineering is a *necessary* but *insufficient* condition for competitiveness. The reason is that the world, the economy, and all the rules of business are changing.

The New World (Dis)Order

The superlatives to describe the changes underway are never-ending—tectonic shifts, revolutionary changes, a new paradigm, a tsunami of transformation (all adding up to a tsunami of superlatives). Such extreme characterizations don't arise because the world has acquired a new taste for hyperbole. Rather, the language flows from the attempts of baffled business leaders, boggled academics, and amazed journalists to somehow characterize the world we are entering and how the changes underway are unlike anything before.

Retired General Colin Powell tells the story of how the first 30 years of his 35-year military career were quite straightforward. For those years, the entire strategy of the United States in the world was summed up in one word: containment. The goal was to contain the military, political, and ideological advance of communism. The United States had a unifying systems theory of the world that everyone could understand. There was a single enemy—according to Powell, a "good enemy"—complete with villains like Stalin, who ordered horrible atrocities, and Khrushchev, who pounded his shoe on his desk at the United Nations. The United States built 30,000 nuclear weapons matched by the Soviets' 30,000 nuclear weapons. Both sides lined up their troops across Europe. And then suddenly it all changed.

General Powell describes a historic meeting with Gorbachev, who was getting frustrated trying to explain how the old model of the world was unworkable. Gorbachev finally leaned across the table to Secretary of State Schultz and said, "You need to understand, Secretary Schultz; today I am ending the cold war." And then Gorbachev said to Powell, "General, you will have to find yourself another enemy."

Powell thought to himself at the time, "I don't want to find another enemy. I've got a few years to retirement. You are a good enemy. You can't just sit there and kick out all of the assumptions, rules, trading systems, political structures that have held the world together for the last 40 years." And then, in December 1991, the Soviet Union ceased to exist as a country. The Soviets lost their economic system, their values, their system of beliefs. That ended the bipolar world, the policy of containment, and the unifying systems theory of how the world works.

The result today is the new world disorder, unfolding at warp velocity. Previously unimagined changes taking place in the world and their implications for our professional and personal lives are relentless. There is an openness and a volatility that seem rich with opportunity and fraught with danger for your country, for your organization, for you, and for humanity.

With the collapse of the bipolar world, East and West Germany were reunited, but there was more change globally. Nelson Mandela, once unacceptable as an alleged Soviet-supported "communist," was freed after 27 years in jail, and a multiracial state was created in South Africa headed by him. There was a war in the Mideast involving 20 countries in a coalition including the USSR and the United States—on the same side. Horrible civil wars broke out in Yugoslavia, Georgia, Bosnia, Chechnya, Croatia, and elsewhere. Hundreds of thousands of people in Somalia and half a million people in Rwanda fell victims to the unconstrained new world disorder. Two of the most bitter enemies in modern times, Israel and the PLO, signed a peace agreement; their respective leaders shook hands at the White House. The United States invaded Haiti. The United States invaded Somalia. The United States invaded. …Peace and war broke out all over the planet.

THE NEW ECONOMY

This new global situation is turning the world economy upside down. The CEO of Alcoa wakes up one morning to find that Russia is now dumping aluminum on world markets at half the current price. The first major survey of Chinese people shows that the top priority for two-thirds of the country is to get rich through hard work, whereas only 4% want to continue the revolution. Economist Lester Thurow asked his audience in a recent speech to U.S. business leaders, "Who do you think has more high school graduates—the United States or China?" He replied: "If you guessed China, you're right—by a couple of hundred million. Now why would I hire a graduate in the United States for $30,000 per year when I can get an equivalently educated person in China for $100 per month?" Many U.S. businesses have already answered that question with a resounding, "We don't." Millions of so-called virtual aliens are clicking away on keyboards in Shanghai, New Delhi, and Hong Kong—fully networked and employed as members of the U.S. economy. Except that they don't pay U.S. taxes or live in the United States.

The bipolar world has become a multipolar economy. In the 1960s, East Asia accounted for only 4% of the world's economic output. Today, that region accounts for 25%. At the same time, the GNP in the United States has been growing at a not-bad 3% annual rate, but the Pacific Rim has seen rates that have been more than twice that high. Taiwan and South Korea, not so long ago low-cost countries themselves, now find that they have to ship some work to lower-cost places like China.

The economy for the Age of Networked Intelligence is a *digital economy*. In the old economy, information flow was physical: cash, checks, invoices, bills of lading, reports, face-to-face meetings, analog telephone calls or radio and television transmissions, blueprints, maps, photographs, musical scores, and direct mail advertisements.

In the new economy, information in all its forms becomes digital—reduced to bits stored in computers and racing at the speed of light across networks. Using this binary code of computers, information and communications become digital ones and zeros. The new world of possibilities thereby created is as significant as the invention of language itself, the old paradigm on which all the physically based interactions occurred.

The technological whirlwind sweeping us into the digital economy is relent-less. Patrick Stewart, the great Shakespearean actor who played Captain Jean Luc Picard in the *Star Trek: The Next Generation* TV series, points out that the original *Star Trek* communicator—the device used to transmit the famous phrase, "Beam me up, Scotty"—now has a parallel in the cellular flip-phone. In the follow-on series, *The Next Generation*, the character Wesley Crusher, teen-age son of the ship's doctor, received his education via individualized online sessions through the ship's computer—not so much different from how engi-neers learn today through the networks of the National Technological Univer-sity (NTU). John Seely Brown, head of the Xerox Palo Alto Research Center (PARC), talks about the shift from tools that support the mind to tools that support relationships. All these future shocks have come in less than a genera-tion. David Ticoll, Alliance for Converging Technologies (Alliance) president says: "The pace of innovation and onslaught of new technologies is accelerat-ing so fast we have to have regular discussions in our research teams to define and maintain consistency of neologisms." As Nicholas Negroponte says in his lucid book *being digital:* "Early in the next millennium your right and left cuf-flinks or earrings may communicate with each other by low-orbiting satellites and have more computer power than your present PC. Your telephone won't ring indiscriminately; it will receive, sort, and perhaps respond to your incoming calls like a well-trained English butler. Schools will change to become more like museums and playgrounds for children to assemble ideas and socialize with children all over the world. The digital planet will look and feel like the head of a pin."[1]

The new economy is also a *knowledge economy* based on the application of human know-how to everything we produce and how we produce it. In the new economy, more and more of the economy's added value will be created by brain rather than brawn. Many agricultural and industrial jobs are becoming knowledge work. Already almost 60% of all American workers are knowledge workers and eight of ten new jobs are in information-intensive sectors of the economy. The factory of today is as different from the industrial factory of the old economy as the old factory from the craft production that preceded it. Farms are operated with agricultural equipment brimming with chips. Cargo is shipped in containers loaded by giant computer-controlled cranes or in jumbo jets loaded with software. Products themselves have knowledge content. There are smart clothes with chips in the collar; smart vehicles brimming with microprocessors that do a hundred new things every year; smart maps that tell a trucker's location and automatically change tire pressure according to the weather and road conditions; smart radios that store the traffic report for you when you want it; smart houses that manage energy, protect you from intrusion, and run a bath for you before you arrive; smart elevators that phone in when they're getting sick; and smart greeting cards that sing to you. These are only a few examples.

More than that, the knowledge content of dumb products is increasing in new ways. In the new economy, adding ideas to products and turning new ideas into new products is what the future is all about. Whether people act as consumers or producers, adding ideas will be central to wealth creation in the new economy. Take something as low-tech as bread. There are now boutique bakeries where you can specify the ingredients for your own custom bread, order it over a computer network, and have it delivered that afternoon. Your ideas, culture, knowledge, and tastes about bread become part of the loaf. The bread increases in knowledge content and is mass-customized rather than mass-produced to meet your individual needs. And the gap between you as consumer and as producer narrows.

The existence of "virtual aliens" points to the role of networks in this new age. In the agricultural age, what mattered was the plow and the mule. In the industrial age, steel, engines, fuel, and roads were king. In the Age of Networked Intelligence, silicon, microprocessors, and roads of glass fiber as thin as a human hair are enabling humans across the hall and across the planet to apply their know-how to every aspect of production and economic life. This is an age of networking not only of technology but of humans, organizations, and societies.

Nathaniel Hawthorne, who inspired the development of the telegraph, wrote in 1851: "By means of electricity, the world of matter has become a great nerve, vibrating thousands of miles in a breathless point of time. …The round globe is a vast … brain, instinct with intelligence." For over a century humanity has been taking steps to realize Hawthorne's vision of a world where human intelligence could be networked. That age has arrived. Organizations can become conscious on a global scale. Perhaps societies and even humanity can as well. As Vice President Al Gore puts it: "These highways, or more accurately networks, of distributed intelligence … will allow us to share information, to connect and to communicate as a global community. From these connections we will derive robust and sustainable economic progress, strong democracies, better solutions to global and local environmental challenges, improved health care, and—ultimately—a greater sense of shared stewardship of our small planet."[2]

The overall structure of the economy was changing as well. A new industrial sector was emerging from the convergence among computing (computers, software, services), communications (telephony, cable, satellite, wireless), and content (entertainment, publishing, information providers). This structure is depicted in Figure 1.1. This interactive multimedia industry was narrowly defined as 10% of the U.S. GDP. By the end of 1996, this industry will be an almost $1 trillion industry—44% computing, 28% communications, and 28% content. By 2005, the industry will have grow to $1.47 trillion. (See Appendix 1.)

Just as the automobile changed the landscape of the world, both physically and socially, interactive multimedia will revolutionize the world again. Already, Americans make more computers than cars, make more semiconductors than construction machinery, and work in data processing than in petroleum refining.[3]

The impact of the new sector can be seen when examining data on job growth (Appendixes 2, 3, and 4). Although output in this sector is growing faster than are jobs, there is significant employment growth. It is noteworthy that whereas output growth is fastest in the computing sector, jobs are growing fastest in the content sector.

A NEW ENTERPRISE REQUIRED

The new economy is creating a tyranny of conflicting drivers causing every company to rethink its mission. Virtual aliens and a hundred other factors

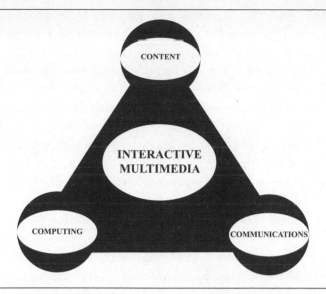

FIGURE 1.1 Converging Technologies. SOURCE: © New Paradigm Learning Corporation, 1996.

are pressuring the cost structure of large companies. Time to reach market is critical when products have a competitive life span of one year, one month, one week, or one afternoon, as in the case of some products in financial services. Innovation, rather than access to resources, plant, and capital, is what counts most. (Remember when eyeglasses took two weeks?) Customers have changed, expecting that companies must provide best quality, green products, fast, at lowest price, with best service, and ensuring social responsibility—to name a few.

Five years ago, competitors to Xerox were Kodak, Canon, and Ricoh. Today, the rivals are Hewlett-Packard, Microsoft, and IBM. Five years from now, it may be Sega-Genesis, Andersen Consulting, AT&T, and the banks. The most famous last words that could possibly be uttered inside any firm these days are: "We don't have any real competition." No one is secure, not even the Fortune 500 companies. Of the companies on that prestigious list in 1955, 70% are now out of business. Of the companies on the 1979 list, fully 40% no longer exist as corporate entities. By 1993, the combined market value of Intel and Microsoft was larger than that of IBM; the suppliers had become more valuable than the customer.[4]

The Queen of England's bank—Barings—was put under by a 28-year-old employee. American banks have faced different pressures. Fifteen years ago all the top money-center banks were based in the United States. Now, none are. In fact, of the world's 25 biggest banks, measured by assets, 15 are Japanese—and now many of them are in trouble.

In the digital economy, competition doesn't come from competitors only—it comes from everywhere. When information becomes digital and networked, walls fall and no business is safe. There is nowhere to hide. Take the case of Microsoft's ill-fated attempt to acquire the personal financial software company Intuit. The proposed deal was dropped by Microsoft in light of potential Justice Department opposition, which was in turn stimulated by the banks. The financial industry was worried that Microsoft would become a bank! Consumers would pay bills electronically using Microsoft software, generating almost instant annual revenues of hundreds of millions of dollars. Microsoft could then demand a share of the clearing house revenue of the banks. Over time, brand identities of the banks would fade as consumers would appear to use Microsoft products for banking. Microsoft could also enable investors to surf the stock market and execute trades themselves, "disintermediating" the investment banks. As *Fortune's* Terence P. Paré put it: "Microsoft would become, in effect, a nationwide consumer bank."[5] Banks would become commodity suppliers competing only on price. And although Microsoft backed off from the Intuit deal, it is clearly not backing off from being a player in the world of electronic banking.

In the 1980s, American business believed the answers would come from MBA graduates. Management also grabbed any passing guru with a catchy phrase covering customer satisfaction, high-octane productivity, and competitive culture. "Adopting 'new' ideas became a way for companies to signal to the world that they were progressive, that they had come to grips with their misguided pasts, and that they were committed to change. After all, the worst thing one could do was stick with the status quo,"[6] say Nitin Nohria and James D. Berkeley of Harvard Business School. In the 1990s, there was no status quo. The velocity of change in information technology were seen to that. Products are becoming digital. Markets are becoming electronic. Industries were in upheaval. Organizations were having to go far beyond reengineering to fundamentally rethink everything about themselves and their futures. As Tony Comper, president of the Bank of Montreal, says: "It's kind of like the early days of the universe after the Big Bang, when gases are congealing and galaxies are forming. No one is really sure how it will all sort out and it's not yet clear where Earth is."

Even the tried-and-true familiar clichés of business are no longer accurate. Take the old adage that executives used in the past to halt fresh thinking, "If it ain't broke, don't fix it." At Philadelphia-based Bell Atlantic, they've not only updated that phrase, they've stood it on its head, saying: "If it ain't broke, keep looking." Home Depot, with more than 300 stores—the largest home-improvement center in the United States—put the same case differently: "Unless you keep fixing it, someday it will be broke." For many companies with products having short life cycles, the message should be, "If it ain't broke, break it before your competitors do." What that means for the future of business is this: Only those organizations that understand the pace of change and can develop successful strategies—and are willing to ride that wild surf—can succeed. As Bette Davis said in *All About Eve*, "Fasten your seatbelts. It's going to be a bumpy night."

What's a business person to do?

For starters, create a company. Many of the brightest and most energetic people of the new economy would rather create a new small business than change an old big one. "Big" was what made companies successful in the old economy. Today, being big is often a liability, whereas innovation, agility, and organizational learning are the key variables for success. Besides, by growing your own, you get to share in the value you create.

Or maybe you've chosen to "reinvent" your current company. Just about everyone agrees that a shift from the traditional bureaucratic hierarchy is needed. The new organization has many names. Peter Drucker calls it the "networked organization."[7] Peter Senge has coined the "learning organization."[8] Davidow and Malone call it the "virtual corporation."[9] For Peter Keen, it's the "relational organization."[10] For Tom Peters, it's the "crazy organization."[11] For D. Quinn Mills, it's the "cluster organization."[12] Charles Savage calls it "human networking."[13] Russell Ackoff describes the "democratic corporation."[14] For James Brian Quinn, it's the "intelligent enterprise."[15] For Michael Hammer and James Champy, it is the "reengineered corporation."[16] For Gary Hamel and C.K. Prahalad, the challenge is not just a new organizational paradigm but a new strategy paradigm.[17] Call it what you like, fundamental change is necessary.

The new enterprise is a network of distributed teams that act as clients and servers for each other. Teams received a big push back in the 1980s when John Welch, GE's CEO, launched the workout program, which was centered on the creation of cross-functional teams. Now teams reach out to customers, suppliers, and others, thereby changing the relationships between organizations.

Easy? No, but it surely can't be as hard as Charles de Gaulle found running France to be. "How can you govern a country," the soldier-statesman once lamented, "with 246 varieties of cheese?"

Moreover, the answer lies not in new organizational structures. As Petronius Arbiter, an officer in the Roman Imperial Army, said in 60 AD, "I was to learn later in life that we tend to meet any new situation by reorganizing, and a wonderful method it can be for creating the illusion of progress, while producing confusion, inefficiency, and demoralization."

Companies need fundamentally new strategies for the new economy. Networking is enabling new structures and new strategies. But even more, it is enabling strong personal trusting relationships among people—relationships that are very different from those of the old hierarchy. Having trouble building a learning organization? Individual learning requires intelligence and consciousness. Such learning has been going on for millennia. But both can now be networked to create conscious organizations. Organizational consciousness is a prerequisite for organizational learning. The new networks are opening the bandwidth of human communication. But how?

THE INTERNET: HYPE, REALITY, AND PROMISE

At the heart of all this change is the much-hyped, much-maligned, but absolutely critical information highway (internet). Networks are the foundation of the digital economy and the Age of Networked Intelligence.

Now is a good time to hit the slo-mo button and sift through some of the internet's claims and criticisms. Even though the term *information highway* has been in common use for only a few years, some people are tired of hearing about it. Others object to the term on aesthetic grounds. But as Bob Allen, chairman of AT&T, points out: "There's good reason why the highway metaphor has become so widely used. It's a form of shorthand for the collective expectations people all over the world have for what information technology can deliver."[18]

There is also a justified sense of enthusiasm about the emerging opportunities for business and society, not to mention a widespread concern about how those benefits may or may not be achieved. If anything, the hyperbole is low key compared to not only the potential but what has already occurred.

Based on the model of the Internet—the vast, expanding network of networks—the internet is becoming a high-bandwidth web of communication systems that will pump huge quantities of text, sound, images, and video into and out of homes, businesses, factories, hospitals, schools, and government offices. Although there are other important technologies such as satellites and terrestrial wireless technologies, the Internet is emerging as the exemplar of the internet. Broadly defined, the publicly available network (referred to in this book as "the Net") is the means by which all computers in the world will be able to communicate.

And what will be the "killer application"—the software tool or use that will catapult the new technology into mass use? This debate is basically silly, making about as much sense as a hypothetical discussion of the killer application for the telephone from decades earlier. The telephone was and is used for financial applications (placing orders for stocks), management applications (supervising a remote employee), health care (collaboration between hospitals), personal applications (courting), and thousands more applications. But the telephone pales in comparison to the richness and capacity of interactive multimedia. The internet will be used for every kind of communication, information, business, learning, entertainment, and social development application we can imagine—and millions more.

The "Killer Application"?

Some internet applications will change the world. Others won't. For example, staff at the University of Cambridge Physics Department were wasting time walking down the hall to see if the coffee was ready. The solution? They put the coffee pot on the Net with a video camera. Their collaborators at Butler University in Indianapolis occasionally take a break to check on the status of Cambridge's coffee.

And will we be couch potatoes watching more TV? Chances are we'll be doing less watching and more interacting. The TV is converging with the home computer and telephone to create the information appliance that is intelligent, interactive, and multimedia. This appliance will look a lot more like a computer than a TV. The number of houses with PCs is growing phenomenally every year. In 1993, 21 million households had PCs; in 1994 the number reached 30 million, a 43% increase; by the end of 1995 the number reached 45 million. Networking has grown even faster. In 1994 the number of home PCs with a modem was about 5%. By the end of 1995 this had doubled to 10%. We can expect that the number will continue to double until 1998 when most will be connected.

Rather than enabling more MTV cartoon characters like Beavis and Butthead, there is a growing consensus in business, government, community, and social interest groups that the internet can be the key to economic and social success. Evidence is mounting that it will provide a new basis for everything from wealth creation, national competitiveness, the reinvention of the corporation, the renewal of the business of government, and the sustaining of social development, all the way to the saving of lives, protection of the environment, improvement of democratic processes, and nation building. This may sound like hyperbole. It is not. It is a conclusion based on the extension of the current experience with the new technology in changing the way we do business, work, learn, and live.

To begin, it is a misnomer to call the new economy a service economy. Industrial production and agriculture will continue to be central as long as humans need to eat, be housed, be clothed, and be mobile. However, just as agriculture was transformed by the Industrial Age (by tractors, milking machines, etc.), so both agriculture and industry are being transformed in the Age of Networked Intelligence. Industrial production now has robotics, computer-aided manufacturing, and mass customization. Farmers have PCs on their tractors. When the cow is sick, you log on to a network, do an interactive diagnosis ... and while you're there you might check prices on the commodity market.

Just as the highway system and electrical power grid were the infrastructure for the industrial economy, so our information networks will be the highways for the new economy. Without a state-of-the-art electronic infrastructure throughout organizations, no country can succeed. Organizations and societies that understand this shift have a chance of succeeding in this crazy, new, volatile, competitive business and geopolitical environment. Those that don't will be bypassed and fail.

The internet will enable the networking of intelligence as the pipelines for knowledge transfer and human collaboration become digital, vast, and of very high capacity. Some brief examples illustrate the concept. A rural doctor consults an urban specialist by sharing high-resolution images of a lab test or EKG over the internet. An auto mechanic checks with factory technicians on new models through interactive television, pointing to a 3D simulation of the part in a window on the screen. Aerospace researchers thousands of miles from one another instantaneously view and discuss sophisticated wind-tunnel computer models. A consumer shops at home for a new sweater through an interactive video catalogue, perhaps trying on the sweater to see how it looks on a computerized model of her body. A cluster of companies comes together on the Net to create and market a new set of products—previously not possible due to constraints of the physical world. A nuclear physicist studies a 1979 KGB document showing, prior to the disaster at Chernobyl, how the main reactor pillars are 100 mm out of alignment. A family plans its holidays by taking an interactive multimedia walk poolside at the Hyatt Caribe resort in Cancun—without leaving home.

The crowning achievement of networking human intelligence could be the creation of a true democracy. Technology itself is shifting from mainframe, host, centralized computers to *network computing*, whereby each computer has autonomy and functions as a peer of the others. Similarly, rather than an all-powerful centralized government, arrogating decisions to itself, governments can be based on the networked intelligence of people. Individuals can collaborate on networks to create processes and decisions that correspond to their real needs. People can become directly and indirectly involved in making important decisions. Government as centralized mainframe can be replaced by government as a network. And perhaps by combining their intelligence, people can create new levels of consciousness at the local, regional, national, and even international levels.

The internet is not some future dream. The garden paths, roads, onramps, and bridges (see sidebar on analogy madness, p. 32) are being built today and many are already working. Between now and the end of this decade, internet construction and use will grow like crazy.

Take the Internet. One fairly reliable method of measuring growth is to look at the number of host computers on the Net. Hosts are the computers that deliver information and services to users; users range in number from one to thousands. According to the Internet Society, which measures traffic, there were around 100,000 hosts in 1989; 1 million by 1992; and close to 10 million by the end of 1995. This number is projected to grow to more than 100 million before the end of the decade!

Although no one knows for sure, conservative estimates put the number of users of the Internet at around 10 million in 1993, approaching 50 million by the end of 1995 (Figure 1.2). There should be well over 1 billion before the end of the decade. By the end of the decade there will be more than 1 million networks connected. Traffic in the network will exceed telephone traffic. There has never been any technology or innovation in human history that comes close in speed of adoption, significance, and impact.

Back when he was still a senator from Tennessee, Al Gore was well ahead of the curve. In 1991, after 15 years of promoting federal policy that invested in information superhighways, Gore wrote: "Gutenberg's invention, which so empowered Jefferson and his colleagues in their fight for democracy, seems to pale before the rise of electronic communications and innovations, from the telegraph, to the television, to the microprocessor, and the emergence of a new computerized world—an information age."

When Gore became vice president, he began using that position as a bully pulpit to promote an electronic highway that would parallel the

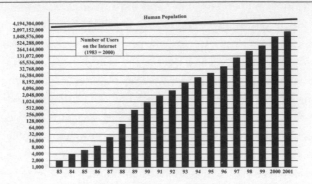

FIGURE 1.2 Estimated Number of Users on the Internet—1983–2001. SOURCE: © New Paradigm Learning Corporation, 1996.

postwar construction of interstate freeways and what those concrete links did for economic development. Gore is right, because in a global market there is an urgent need to eliminate—or at least reduce—time and space dependencies and to move to new forms of economic activity, learning, and social development.

What Is Technology to a Kid?

Apple fellow Alan Kay once said that technology is "technology" only for people who are born before it was invented. Twelve-year-old Niki Tapscott would agree. When asked if she would participate in a "consumer of the future" panel at a technology conference, she lectured her father: "Okay, Dad, I'll do it if you want me to. But I don't understand why you adults make such a big deal about technology. Kids just use computers to do stuff. We don't think of them as technology. Like a fridge does stuff. It's not technology. When I go to the fridge, I want food that is cold. I don't think about the technology that makes food cold."

Ironically, the Internet was created not by social visionaries but by cold warriors at the Department of Defense. The Internet was launched as a packet-switching system in 1969 for the Advanced Research Projects Agency (ARPA), part of the Department of Defense, so that ARPA research sites could share information and give access to computers elsewhere. The model of the network was highly distributed rather than the current vogue—hierarchical—to enable easy rerouting of communications in the case of an attack.

Electronic mail (e-mail) was a kind of add-on feature that allowed research-ers to send messages to one another, and it quickly became among the most popular aspects of the system. Other outgrowths included electronic confer-ences and bulletin boards where messages, questions, comments, and other types of information are posted for anyone to read and react to what's going on in what has become known as cyberspace.

What ARPA was trying to do was connect users without worrying about how many networks were involved or how the connections were made. It has become a network of networks that allows global access to computers and databases as diverse as the Library of Congress all the way to little-known pub-lishers. Because the Internet consists of local telephone systems, all of them interconnecting, it's particularly helpful when long distance lines are out. In the hours following the January 1994 earthquake in Los Angeles, the Internet and other online systems all reported high usage because they were working when other connections weren't. Prodigy (a joint venture between IBM and Sears Roebuck and Co.) had its second busiest day when users, hungry for up-to-date information, plugged in and worried relatives posted notes on electronic bulletin boards looking for loved ones. There were 813,000 log-ons compared with 890,000 on Bill Clinton's election day, about one-third more than a typi-cal day. Another service, GEnie, saw use double in the 24 hours following the first shocks. During the early days of the coup attempt against Mikhail Gor-bachev in 1991, the Internet offered the only accurate information.

An offshoot are "freenets," another way of thinking globally, acting locally. In their simplest form, freenets are just electronic bulletin boards, usually orga-nized to serve one city or small region, that let individuals send electronic mail to one another without going, in the jargon of the users, F2F (face-to-face). E-mail is already doing for the modern world what the British Post Office did in the eighteenth century when the rates were made standard. Could there be a modern parallel to the strength of industrial Britain as a result of regularizing the cost of communicating the written word?

Originally, the most popular use for the Net was e-mail and what might be called "chat," that is, practical pursuits. Corporate e-mail systems are now changing the way that many companies communicate and work. Scott McNealy, CEO of Sun Microsystems, says that Sun's 13,000 employees send or receive, on average, about 1.8 million electronic mail messages per day. That's an average of over 135 per person per day. People wasting time, you say? Well, somehow working this way works. Pound per pound, Sun is one of the most profitable companies on Earth. Now e-mail systems are being hooked up to the Internet, expanding the addressable population from a company's employees to the tens of millions of Net users. These days, a business card without a Net address is seen as a sign that you're some kind of Jurassic manager.

Beyond e-mail, a new world of applications is opening up. If a city agency has decided to put a contract out for tender, the specifications can be posted on the Net. That means a contractor doesn't need to dispatch an employee to pick up a thick document from city hall. The contractor can simply call up the contract, capture it in the company's own system, and read it whenever the need strikes. When the time comes for the contractor to put in a bid, the return trip is just as easy. Author Stephen King marketed a short story, *Utney's Last Case*, by putting it on the Internet, thus giving electronic nomads a free read. For the rest of the stories in the collection, *Nightmares and Dreamscapes*, the nomads phoned or sent a fax (with credit card number) to a designated bookstore.

Before the Gulf War, linguist George Lakoff placed some interesting new analogies on the Internet for discussion. He was concerned about the analogies being drawn between Saddam Hussein and Hitler, so he asked a series of questions about the Hussein-as-Hitler metaphor. His thinking quickly spread and became part of the fabric of the discussion, a way of elevating the tone of the debate and placing modern times in a historic context. Yet, there is another point here—access to the thinking was widespread. Lakoff's thesis wasn't published in some learned magazine with small circulation or delivered at a think-tank gathering of like-minded souls. The Internet set the tone for the debate.

Alex Finds Wayne Gretzky on the Net

When 9-year-old hockey player Alex Tapscott and his teammate Stephen Senders needed to solve a debate about their hero Wayne Gretzky, they interrupted Alex's dad to get access to the Net. Dad took a break from his Mac, and two minutes later the boys had found an NHL server in Hawaii containing a spec sheet on Gretzky. They printed it with a color photo of their hero and the debate was settled. They were both right. When Dad asked Alex why he went to a server in Hawaii, Alex replied: "We just thought it was so amazing that they would have information about hockey in Hawaii that we wanted to check it out." Alex and Stephen—Net surfers.

The new technology is penetrating our lives; much of this is happening through our children. Over one-quarter of American homes have a computer, but for many adults the machine is a mystery, or it is used for word processing, accounting, or home business applications. Children, on the other hand, are using machines for games, homework, communications, art, music, reference, and a host of emerging applications on the Internet. The average age of an Internet user is 21 and declining.

Such communications capacity doesn't mean an end to infojunk. When telegraph wires were first strung between Texas and Maine in the nineteenth century, writer Henry Thoreau wondered if the two states really had anything constructive to communicate. Maybe, Thoreau said, the telegraph system was nothing more than an "improved means to an unimproved end." Thoreau isn't the only writer to twit new ideas. Columnist Dave Barry has had similar fun with the information highway, wondering whether or not the whole thing isn't just "CB radio with more typing."

But already software "agents," or "knowbots," are in the marketplace. They go out onto the Net to find the information you want. Rather than drowning in data, agents will provide the structure to form data into information and the context into which to translate information into knowledge. When you apply your own human judgment and transhistorical insights, knowledge can become wisdom. Chances are the Net will enable us to move up this chain rather than down.

The World Wide Web

And how do you get on the Net? Various online services are available today including America Online, CompuServe, Prodigy, GEnie, and MicrosoftNet. Strangely, however, it was a freenet called the World Wide Web (WWW or "the Web"), as discussed earlier, that really got things going.

The WWW was developed at the European Particle Physics Lab as a vehicle by which to share information about high-energy physics among physicists working in a dispersed international environment. Led by Tim Berners-Lee, the developers rightfully reasoned that coming up with standards for hardware or software was a waste of effort. Instead, they developed a standard for representing the data. The standard was called the Hypertext Markup Language, or HTML. Using HTML, you simply attach a proper tag to a word or phrase causing it to become a link to another page. This link can be to a document on the same machine or on one across the world, exploiting the other major innovation of the Web, a universal addressing system. With this addressing system, nearly any Web document, optionally including sound, image, and even video, can be accessed and viewed effortlessly, without redialing another number, knowing any computer addresses, or entering log-in IDs.

A Net browser called Mosaic was the catalyst that got the WWW going. In February 1993, Mosaic was released by University of Illinois student Marc

Andreessen. This event catalyzed the explosion of information exchange now occurring. With Mosaic, a Mac, Windows, OS/2, or UNIX user with any level of Internet access could literally view the world of online information as a vast, seamless, interconnected universe. You entered at any point and began exploring, effortlessly visiting something called Home Pages and information-rich documents from around the world. Most with-it companies now have Home Pages—places where customers and others can go to learn about their products, services, and the companies themselves. Through the hypertext links called "hotlinks" you simply click on any highlighted word in a document and link to other computers, Home Pages, and documents anywhere. According to John Landry, "Mosaic 'energized' the World Wide Web."

Mosaic was the first wildly successful graphical browser for the Web. According to Landry, "Andreessen must have watched *Field of Dreams*. He believed that if he built it they would come—and come they did."

To get Mosaic, all you had to do was download it, for free, from the University of Illinois or numerous other "mirror" sites around the world. In 1994, every day nearly 4,000 people did. In the first two years since release, over 1 million copies were downloaded from Illinois, thousands more from the mirror sites, thousands more from sharing disks, yielding estimates of more than 3 million users before the end of 1994. In January 1993, when Mosaic was introduced, there were only 50 known Web servers. By October 1993 there were more than 500. By June 1994 there were 1,500 growing to 5,000 by the end of the year. By the end of 1995 there were more than 100,000 Web servers.

Now the market has shifted to a commercial product based on the Mosaic model called Netscape, which is provided by a commercial venture cofounded by Andreessen. The new company is able to offer the kind of support and quality expected of commercial software. And in a widely oversubscribed public offering in August 1995, Andreessen became an instant multimillionaire.

Adam Landry—New Information Publisher!

Adam Landry, 15-year-old son of Lotus chief technology officer John Landry, has built his own Home Page, complete with pictures (from a photo CD) and curriculum vitae (sports, music, travel, etc.). His CV highlights, in particular, those interests he feels would be attractive for consumption by browsers of the opposite sex. He's debating whether to put in "No Girlfriend, Yet!" And, of course, Adam can track interest in his Home Page. Of special interest to him is the number of hits from young ladies. (This gives a whole new meaning to "being hit on.")

According to Dad, "Adam is no geek, but he does know how to compose HTML pages because he downloaded the instructions off a server on the Net. Compose the page with any text editor, tag it with HTML, and link it to another page and voila, you're a Webster!"

So Adam Landry, sophomore at Wayland High, is now an information publisher, and his interests, opinions, image, and voice, as well as links to things that he thinks are "cool" on the Web, are available effortlessly to millions of people worldwide. And the value of that experience for him is incalculable, and for Dad, unforgettable. And although Adam hasn't realized it, he is an early example of an incredible worldwide phenomenon that will revolutionize learning, work, and living. As Dad puts it: "This is the new information publisher—Adam Landry."

One turning point for the commercial use of the Net was the formation in 1991 of the Commercial Internet Exchange (CIX), a group of commercial Internet providers that established cooperative agreements to let users communicate with others, regardless of which network provided their Internet connection.

But nobody owns the Net. Every participant owns it. The Net is about giving something back as much as it is taking advantage. Intrusive ads, gratuitous junk mail, and nothing-for-nothing attitudes will do a disservice to any organization that contemplates using these tactics on the Net (in fact, such users risk being heavily criticized and ostracized faster than they can say "I'm sorry").

Internet-related standards are truly global and are advancing at a rapid rate to meet the demands of the participants. The users of the Net are deciding the viability of Net services (voting by their use). We are entering a new era of truly open systems in which all technology platforms can participate and all users can have a say.

This is not to say that there are no problems. There are huge issues regarding security and authentication on the Net. The expression used to be, "Doing that is like putting it in the *New York Times*." Now it is, "Doing that is like putting it on the Internet." But the genius of tens of thousands of companies and hundreds of thousands of people from the converging industries of computing, communications, and content (entertainment and publishing) is being applied to transforming our nascent networks into a robust information highway. And every day the situation changes and improves.

Other concerns center on control of the Net. The introduction of Microsoft Network in late 1995 was seen by many as an effort to take over the Net, although arguably the company is now just another player (albeit a significant one).

Highway Analogy Madness

Bumper-to-bumper: Sex chat group.

Construction delays: When mergers fail and alliances peter out.

Drive-by shootings: Your competitor steals a client.

Easy rider: Ace on the Net.

Fastlane: Broadband communication networks, as in "Life in the Fastlane."

Firefighters: Those who attempt to douse flamers.

Gridlock: Network's down.

Guardrails: A way of imposing responsibilities on internet users.

Holiday Inn file: No surprises.

HOV lane: Bulletin board.

In the ditch: Where organizations go that aren't getting ready for the Net.

Mad drivers: Flamers (those who bury neophytes or traffic violators with abusive messages).

Minimum speed: A 286.

On-ramps: The computers, televisions, and other information appliances and their associated software providing access to the Net.

Out of gas: Information underload.

Pedal to the metal: Putting the boots to mainframes.

Photo radar: Videoconferencing gone awry.

Pothole: The Pentium chip goof.

Rest stations: MUDS—Multi-User Dungeons to pause for a respite. As in "virtual water cooler."

Road hogs: internet riders who load up e-mail addresses.

Roadkill: The companies that either through poorly conceived strategies or failed alliances end up as someone else's dinner.

Rush hour: A bad time to be on the Net.

Tollbooths: Devices that may be used to collect taxes to pay for services and enable the highway to be extended to underserved areas.

Tow trucks: Systems administrators who can rescue crashed systems.

Traffic jams: What happens at rush hour. See "Gridlock."

Out of control: internet analogies.

Such advances mean that time and space have become far different concepts than they once were for the 40% of Americans who do some part of their job each day away from the office. Some 8.8 million people were telecommuters in 1994, a 16% increase from 7.6 million in 1993.[19] The most eye-popping example of telecommuting must surely be Steve Roberts, who publishes *High-Tech Nomadness* while he rides the roads on a bike with built-in keyboard, computer, and Earth station. His motto: "Home is everywhere."

The future has arrived in Palo Alto, California, where citizens have been provided with full, two-way Internet capability. Access nodes in City Hall mean that the Palo Alto World Wide Web server accommodates 1,500 inquiries a day for information such as the city government directory, local maps and train schedules, local news, and access to the Stanford University server. "It truly opens up possibilities and potential we haven't even imagined yet," says Palo Alto mayor Liz Kniss.

The project is part of what's known as Smart Valley, Inc., a nonprofit organization that acts as a focal point for information infrastructure and applications projects on a regional basis—an electronic community that will include Silicon Valley, San Francisco, and Santa Cruz. Such high-speed networks can help business use distributed work teams, do two-way videoconferencing, deliver parts designs to fabricators, and reduce publishing and delivery costs. Telecommuting in particular may change the very makeup of the region; the project has a goal to make up to 10% of all area employees telecommuters by the end of the decade. "The public access phenomenon is sweeping the Bay Area and the nation," says Dr. Harry Saal, president and CEO of Smart Valley. "It is a wave we are all catching."

The future is information technology, and it isn't just for propeller heads. It's not just about bits and bytes and other jargon. Instead, the new technology is a real business tool that shakes up the basics of the game. Look at gains made possible by IT in the retail sector. After 10 years of going nowhere, productivity began to skyrocket at the beginning of this decade. "Information technology is suddenly making a difference," says Jerre Stead, former head of AT&T Global Information Solutions. "The collection, dissemination, and analysis of customer information has become an essential prerequisite of a modern retailing operation. Technology is no longer just an aid to retail strategy—it's at the heart of the strategy."

At its simplest level, IT can tell a retailer when and if expansion is required. Talbot's, the women's wear chain, collects the zip codes of all shoppers at the point of sale and uses that information to plan future stores. At a more complex level, Walmart is organized so that inventory is minimized, suppliers decide when to ship, and Walmart can pay for its goods with cash collected from consumers. Chase Manhattan Bank is using interactive video kiosks to supply product information to clients. Nordstrom, of Seattle, Washington, offers a direct mail catalog through online services like Prodigy, CompuServe, and America Online. The next step in the evolution will be an interactive multimedia application that will be the equivalent to an in-store personal shopper. The secret of Nordstrom's future success, according to Pat Adkisson, operations and business development manager, is "being where the customers want to be, whether that is in stores, in a catalog, hi-glossy brochures, talking to an 800 number personal shopper, on the road ordering through a dial-up on their laptop, or in the home."[20]

Now retailers are set for the really big changes as markets become electronic. Want a pair of custom-designed Levi's jeans? Click onto Levi's Home Page on the Net; watch the program about how to measure yourself; enter the data and your credit card number and within a couple of weeks the jeans arrive at your house, guaranteed to be a 100% perfect fit. The work of creating the jeans is done by many companies working on the Net that are coordinated not by Levi's but by a new company called Custom Clothing Technology. Many stores as we know them will be replaced by virtual stores and FedEx trucks. The bricks-and-mortar buildings that remain will have to become interesting places to actually visit.

For many organizations, however, their structure and the people within them are long out of date because the world has changed. The gap is widening between what is actually occurring and what we believe is going on. New leaders must be created with strategic visions that fit tomorrow. "When you come to a fork in the road," says everyone's favorite baseball pop philosopher Yogi Berra, "take it." The world is at just such a crossroads and must embrace change. The Industrial Age is over; the Age of Networked Intelligence is beginning.

And Who Will Build the Internet?

Because public coffers are empty and leading-edge innovation is desirable, the private sector needs to take the front-line role in financing, building, and operating the information highway, but there are many differing views on where the business opportunities lie. In the nineteenth century, when railways were built across the North American continent, investors found that the most profitable aspects turned out not to be passengers (the population was too thin) but the millions of acres of real estate that went with the right-of-way. The information superhighway may be just like that. As Joel Birnbaum of Hewlett-Packard puts it: "In a gold rush there are two ways to get rich—digging for gold and supplying the infrastructure for the gold diggers."

There are also vigorous debates regarding the nature of the highway. For example, will it be based on the telephone networks, cable systems, satellites, digital radio, or other transmission media? What will be the most important applications—business, education, entertainment, shopping, health care, interpersonal communications? What will be the economic model—that is, how will users pay for using the Net? And how can companies make money? Right now there appear to be more prophets than profits on the Net. What will be the structure of the internet—an open network of networks like the Internet, or some other model?

An emerging consensus is that more competition and less regulation are necessary to stimulate private-sector investment and innovation. In such a world, governments act as referees to safeguard the public interest rather than controllers of how technology will evolve. Perhaps the first inkling of this change came in 1984 with the government-ordered breakup of AT&T and the creation of the so-called Baby Bells. The resulting competition in the residential long-distance telephone market is widely credited with driving down costs, improving quality, and stimulating innovation.

For example, in 1987 AT&T said it would take more than two decades to convert its network to superior digital technology. But the competitive pressure from companies such as MCI and Sprint forced AT&T to achieve the conversion in just four years. In the past decade American residential long-distance costs have dropped 50%.

REENGINEERING: INADEQUATE FOR THE NEW ECONOMY?

If the main management tool of the past half dozen years has been business process reengineering (BPR), a far more comprehensive approach is urgently needed to handle the challenges of the new situation. What matters in every case is that the new technologies can transform not only business processes but also the way products and services are created and marketed, the structure and goals of the enterprise, the dynamics of competition, and the actual nature of the enterprise. "Virtually every business will find it possible to use these new tools to become more competitive," Vice President Al Gore said in his 1994 speech to the Academy of Television Arts and Sciences. "And by taking the lead in quickly employing these new information technologies, America's businesses will gain enormous advantages in the worldwide marketplace."[21]

Why isn't BPR making the grade?

The Four Problems with Reengineering As Practiced

1. *The cost reduction thrust.* BPR arose in the early 1990s, fueled by a recession and the beginnings of the restructuring of Western economies. Cost cutting was the focus of most businesses, and BPR fit in well with that goal. Downsizing, rightsizing, smartsizing, streamlining, working out, and reengineering became euphemisms for cutting costs—typically headcount.

As one CEO asked of the BPR manager in a bank, "How many heads are we gonna get?" Another was heard describing a project: "When we found redundancies everywhere, I had to bite the bullet and lay off a bunch of people." (The reference to biting the bullet is interesting. During the American Civil War, soldiers facing amputation were given a bullet to bite to help distract them from the excruciating pain. But here we have the amputator, rather than amputee biting the bullet.) One company was so obsessed by reengineering that to save money they turned off the light at the end of the tunnel ...

As the new economy gathers steam, companies in most sectors need to focus on growth and value-added objectives, rather than just cost cutting. Cost control will be important forever and in some sectors key to competitive success. But even in the most cost-sensitive businesses such as retailing, companies need to shift their paradigms—marketing electronically, for example, delivering goods rather than building actual structures. BPR is inadequate and in some cases diversionary from such out-of-the-box thinking. Whether reengineering is well intentioned or not, there is a danger of companies entering into some new corporate *anorexia*, to use the phrase made popular by management consultant Gary Hamel, whereby, in pursuit of cost control, they permanently downsize their market share, revenues, profits, long-term competitiveness, and viability.

2. *BPR focuses on business processes.* A business is more than a set of processes, so process improvement is an inadequate response to the challenges of the new economy. BPR projects typically miss opportunities to go beyond the streamlining of work to the transformation of business objectives and effectiveness. The starting point for transformation should not be the business process but the business model—the high-level abstraction of how the business can respond to and create markets, of what the business is and could be. The new economy demands that companies change their business model, and the new technology enables it.

The best impact of BPR itself occurs if it is done within the context of a higher-level model of the business. Says Dave Cox, CIO at Northern Telecom: "We found that we needed to get beyond the lower-level process modeling being done by many companies today. We found that when we did BPR we lacked the larger context of the business model. Having spent some time developing that model, our horizons have been widened and reengineering projects have far greater scope and creativity. Companies need to bring business modeling into prime time."

Furthermore, reengineering typically focuses on and results in creating relatively *structured* business processes. However, in the new economy much of the effort of the new enterprise is knowledge work based on teams, changing human networks, new types of jobs, serendipitous communications, ad hoc collaboration, and brainstorming for innovation.

Ron Ponder, CIO of AT&T, is responsible for the work of more than 25,000 information systems professionals. His message to all of them is to focus on the customer. "Reengineering doesn't cut it. Every company needs to make processes better, faster, and more economical—but this is really just continually fine-tuning your operating structure," says Ponder. "But you can't use reengineering to transform a business. You reengineer inside of a business, addressing operational needs of the business. But our transformation is coming from the outside in. It is market-driven, not process-driven."

3. *The human imperative.* In many situations, BPR projects have misunderstood the human imperative. Projects with a goal of massive cost cutting have often been resisted by workers; newly reengineered business processes are conducted by demotivated workers. Couple this with what Paul Strassman calls "the violence of reengineering" and you have a formula for fear. Finding the dark side of reengineering is simple. Here are just a few of the pronouncements by reengineering leaders. "On this journey ... we shoot the dissenters."[22] "What you do with the existing structure is nuke it!"[23] "[Re]engineering must be initiated ... by someone who has enough status to break legs."[24]

Furthermore, many reengineering efforts falsely assume that some senior czar or steering committee can, in a top-down way, comprehend business processes as well as opportunities for change and sell this vision down to the organization. Such approaches are contrary to modern thinking and practice about creating learning organizations, shared vision, and team leadership.

Reengineering theorists to date have also missed the broader implications of the IT-enabled transformation of business on virtually every other aspect of human work and social life. Huge issues need to be tackled—from quality of work life, retraining, and lifelong learning for the new economy, the changing nature of work and the end of the career as we know it, the danger of a haves and have-nots society, all the way to fundamental changes in the nature of the workings of government, the democratic process, and democracy itself.

4. *Old paradigm views of technology.* Many reengineering proponents assume information technology is critical to new processes. However, other than *Paradigm Shift,* none have really explained how the old paradigm in technology is ill-equipped for the new enterprise. As a result, many companies have thrown old paradigm technology at new paradigm reengineering problems. To bring about organizations that are high performance, integrated, networked, open, and client-service, companies need the new technology that is high performance, integrated, networked, open, and client-server. The old model of computing—low performance (traditional mainframe or minicomputer), unintegrated (based on islands of computing), host-based (rather than networked), proprietary (nonembracing standards), command and control (unlike client-server) computing—is the antithesis of the new enterprise.

The Power of Internetworking

As John Landry, chief technology officer for Lotus, told me: "I'm not talking about incremental change here. I'm talking about a set of technologies that will be as significant in impact as assembly-line technology was to mass production, and as mass-media technology was to mass marketing. But this internetworking technology will replace many advantages of mass production and mass marketing by allowing for mass customization ... creating, in some industries, custom goods better, faster, and cheaper than mass-produced goods and providing the framework for addressing individuals with custom marketing and messages and individualized customer service."

Rather than only quality or reengineering, companies need a new approach for business transformation. The differences among the three are outlined in Table 1.1.

Quality, Bpr, and Business Transformation: What Are the Differences?

TABLE 1.1 Differences Among Quality, Reengineering, and Business Transformation

	Quality	Reengineering	Business Transformation
Full-scale Deployment	1980s	1990s	Latter 1990s
Life Cycle	Mature	Midlife	Embryonic
Goals (in practice)	Reduce defects	Streamlining, cost displacement, and cost avoidance	Value creation, new products/services delivered through new distribution channels to new markets
Business Context	Globalization, new international competition, changing customer expectations	Recession of the early 1990s and pressures from the emerging economy for disaggregation, responsiveness, and strategic efficiencies	Rise of the digital economy, the national information infrastructure, new drivers for innovation
Targets	Incremental	Breakthrough	Breakthrough
Approach	Continuous improvement	Greenfield—start from scratch	Envisioning the future, modeling today, gap analysis, and migration plan
Investment Required	Relatively low	High (management attention, work redesign effort, information systems)	High (management and all other personnel involved, migration to enabling infostructure)
Impact	Long-term	Short- and middle-term	Short-, middle-, and long term
Success Rate of Those Undertaking	High (for those that stick it out)	Low	Moderate
Domain	Product	Process	Enterprise, extended enterprise
Competitive Differentiation	No. Quality is a necessary but insufficient condition for competitiveness.	No. Strategic efficiencies are required for competitive parity.	Yes, if done correctly.

The Dark Side of the Age of Networked Intelligence

There are significant perils for business in the new economy. Some companies that have delayed embracing the new media are already showing signs of falling behind. As Alliance collaborator Araldo Menegon says, "When we look back at the end of the century, companies will have fallen into two categories: those that did and those who did not." But the dark side extends beyond the business imperatives for change.

When Alexander Graham Bell invented the telephone, he thought he was creating a tool to help deaf people and that's how he wanted to be remembered. Thomas Edison thought the main use for the phonograph would be as a dictation machine. Johannes Gutenberg had no idea what the impact of his invention would be on society, but movable-type printing in the fifteenth century meant that books became more widely available. Knowledge was no longer the privilege of a very few. Gutenberg changed culture, science, power, economic structures, and the very fabric of society.

The early pioneers in the automotive business were equally unaware of the revolution they were unleashing. The car was a liberator that provided mobility to the masses and helped to create wealth and jobs, but there was a terrible downside, too: cities cloaked in smog, the alienation of suburbia, carnage on the highways, sprawling metropolitan areas, and streets choked by traffic. In the words of Joni Mitchell's lament, "They paved Paradise and put up a parking lot." At the same time, the automotive sector became the dominant force in the U.S. economy for the most part of the twentieth century, employing one worker in six.

At this point, it is unclear how the new media will affect the way society does business, works, learns, and lives. Yes, the internet is already evolving to provide the infrastructure for a digital economy. In the digital frontier of this new economy, however, old social norms, laws, regulations, institutions, education, and customs are proving to be inadequate and inappropriate. There appear to be more questions than answers regarding what is to come and how business and societies can successfully manage the transition.

There is widespread concern that life in the settlements of the new digital frontier and in the vast society to follow may not be entirely pleasant.[25] Fear lurks everywhere that technology will bring unemployment, numbing of the mind, and invasion of privacy.

Are we to become captive of the new technologies? Will a new technology imperative or market-driven determinism confound our ability to guide these new tools in responsible directions? Can we devise useful investment crite-ria, organizational structures, marketplace rules, and government policies to ensure that technology serves people?[26]

Revolution is usually the midwife of a new age. Violence, war, and social upheaval are all part of the transition from an old economy to a new one. How will the transition to the Age of Networked Intelligence be achieved? So far in the 1990s, the world has seen far too much violence. Nor has suffer-ing remained outside the realm of the developed world. The 1995 bombing in Oklahoma serves as a fearsome reminder that not all is right.

There are far-reaching management and social issues as we make the shift:

◆ Change will cause dislocations. Employment in agriculture went from 90% of the population at the turn of the century to 3% of the population today. Today, the worker displaced when the foundry in Nashville closes can't get a job in the Northern Telecom plant where the average plant worker has the equivalent of a community college degree. The fact that we're entering a new economy is of little consolation to that displaced worker and his or her family. How will we manage the transition to new types of work and a new knowledge base for the economy?

◆ The internet has the chilling potential to destroy privacy in an unprec-edented and irrevocable manner. Most of us believe we have the right to decide what personal information we divulge, to whom, and for what purpose. We accept that we must give government and corporations some details about our lives to qualify for services, loans, and so on. But such information should be used only for the purpose for which it was obtained and not sold to someone else. And if the demand for informa-tion seems unreasonable, we can always say "no." Left unchecked, the internet could render such thinking irrelevant. As human communica-tions, business transactions, working, learning, and playing increasingly come onto the Net, unimaginable quantities and types of information become digitized and networked. How can we safeguard privacy in an economy that is digital?

◆ Recent trends show a severe bipolarization of wealth in which the top 20% of households—those worth $180,000 or more—have 80% of the country's wealth. This skewing of income and wealth is happening faster in the United States—the leading new economy country—than any-where else and faster than ever before. Surely this is undesirable, but is this trend reversible? An ill-conceived information highway and transi-tion to the digital economy could foster a two-tiered society, creating a major gulf between information haves and have-nots—those who can communicate with the world and those who can't. As information technology becomes more important for economic success and social well-being, the possibility of "information apartheid" becomes increasingly real. Is there an emerging "revolt of the elites"[27] who will use the new infrastructure to further cocoon themselves—children in private schools, paying for their own social services, surrounded by high perimeter fences, identifying closer with friends and business associates in cyberspace, losing any sense of responsibility to others in their physical communities or country? (In 1995, the hottest real estate category was "secure communities" surrounded by walls and security systems and accessible only through guarded gates. However, the Oklahoma bombing indicates that the perimeters will have to be expanded.)

◆ What about other gaps caused by differential access to the new technology and the economy—between knowers and know-nots, men and women, old and young, cities and rural communities or inner cities, whites and minorities, skilled professionals and unskilled hourly workers, developed world and undeveloped world? A study on home ownership of computers in Canada points to the problem. By education: high school—27%; college—47%; university—63%. By income: less than $30,000—21%; $40,000 to $49,000—39%; over $70,000—66%. By gender: men—45%; women—35%. By profession: professional—62%; unskilled 27%. How will the new technology change the social fabric?

◆ What impact will the digital economy have on quality of life? Will telework create new, flexible, enjoyable working environments, or will it enslave people to piecework done in isolation? Will we, as some pundits argue, drown in data or amuse ourselves to death? As Alan Kay says, "Another way to think of roadkill on the information highway will be the billions who will forget that there are offramps to destinations other than Hollywood, Las Vegas, the local bingo parlor, or shiny beads from a shopping network!"[28] As technology invades our offices, homes, cars, hotel rooms, airplane seats, kitchens, and washrooms, is there a danger of the separation of work and leisure vanishing? Psychologists have already argued that multitasking is leading to new stress-related disorders. Or can the technology do the opposite—freeing us, stimulating us, relaxing us?

◆ What will be the impact of the new media on the family? The new media hold the promise of strengthening the family by moving many family activities dispersed by industrial society back into the home. These include some working, learning, shopping, entertainment, health care, caring for the elderly, and even participation in democracy. But are there other dangers? Despite its unhealthy impact on people, television at least brought families together around an electronic hearth. But in my family today, it's not unusual for the four of us to be clicking away on our keyboards in separate rooms. Further, some families will have better access to the new media than others.

◆ How will we deal with the sleaze and porn running down the gutters of the internet? How will parents protect their children from the exaggerated yet very real, unwholesome, violent, racist, sexist, and (for lack of a better word) disgusting experiences available on the Net? Rather than pulp fiction, how to protect them from violent offensive "bit" fiction, or worse from pedophiles prowling the Net for victims? Censorship and the purification of cyberspace as envisaged by the 1995 Communications Decency Act is neither feasible nor desirable. It won't work because, as Internet pioneer John Gilmore says, "The Net interprets censorship as damage and routes around it." Further, the Act doesn't differentiate between naughty behavior among consenting adults and obscenity. It makes the federal government a censor for communication between adults. As such it is an unprecedented attack on free speech. How should this problem be addressed?

Marilyn Ferguson was one of the first to popularize the notion of a paradigm shift in the *Aquarian Conspiracy—Personal and Social Transformation in Our Time*. In 1976 she wrote that a paradigm shift involves dislocation, conflict, confusion, and uncertainty. New paradigms are nearly always received with coolness, even mockery or hostility. Those with vested interests fight the change. The shift demands such a different view of things that established leaders are often the last to be won over, if at all.[29]

This is leading to a crisis of leadership in many organizations, in business, and in the developed world as a whole. Many businesses are falling behind because of old economy thinking. Corporate executives, blinded by cynicism about the poor payback from the old technologies, are unable to see the opportunities for the new.

Still, important changes are happening in the world of work. The contract between a company and those who perform work is being altered radically, for employee loyalty and job security are no longer acceptable bases for employment. Some people have mistakenly argued that the concept of the job is obsolete, but these new directions do not mean that all knowledge workers will become independent contractors. Rather, they will thrive from intense collaboration that is provided by an organization. Organizations can also provide an environment for trust and learning.

At the same time, the concept of supervision and management is changing to team-based structures. Anyone responsible for managing knowledge workers knows they cannot be "managed" in the traditional sense. Often they have specialized knowledge and skills that cannot be matched or even understood by management. A new challenge to management is first to attract and retain these assets by marketing the organization to them, and second to provide the creative and open communications environment where such workers can effectively apply and enhance their knowledge.

One of the most important emerging themes is trust. It is only when workers identify with the goals of the organization and trust its managers to act in mutual self-interest that effective knowledge work can be performed. As Riel Miller, OECD economist working with the Alliance says, "Netiquette is not, as some have implied, about being nice. It is about creating the norms and rules on a new frontier where trust between people is essential for functioning." Yet how can trust be created and maintained in molecular, virtual, ever-changing businesses where there are no guarantees of permanence?

Many governments seem slow to comprehend the shift; bureaucracies by definition resist change, thinking that heads-down is the route to survival. Can government become electronic, transforming the way government services are delivered? The so-called reinvention of government is not possible without reinventing the delivery system for government, and in doing so, dramatically reducing costs and improving the services government provides to its customers. And beyond changing the business of government, how can the new technology and the new economy change the nature of the democratic process itself? Will the electronic town hall become an electronic mob? Will cyberdemocracy become hyperdemocracy? Or can we craft a new age in which networked intelligence can be applied for the good of the people?

And what will be the role of the unions in the new economy? It is in the interests of working people to partner with business and government to help achieve transformation. Every nation needs competitive businesses or it will face structural unemployment; but national competitiveness cannot be achieved through a low-wage strategy. Such approaches are generally infeasible (reducing wages from $15 per hour to $1); undesirable (reducing purchasing power, motivation, and quality of life); and unnecessary. A low-wage strategy will not bring national competitiveness and success in the new economy. Rather, countries can attract investment and generate new wealth and high-paying jobs only through a value-adding workforce—one that is highly educated, motivated, disciplined, empowered, and equipped with state-of-the art knowledge tools and infrastructures. But will organized labor step up to a fuller role and help to change institutional structures or, in restricting ambitions to combating employers for the short term, will they become marginalized?

As for the mass media, they have an uneven appreciation of the challenge as well; the misunderstanding of many in the media is reflected in simplistic stories of computers killing jobs. Can the media shift to become full participants in achieving a national awareness of the transformation we are going through?

What about education? There's an old saying that war is too important to be left to the generals. In the new economy, learning is too important to be left to the schools. Besides, as knowledge becomes part of products, production, services, and entertainment, the factory, the office, and the home will all become colleges. As educational activity shifts from schools to firms, will businesses continue to emphasize social responsibility, humanism, liberal arts, and political and moral values, or will they shift values to competitiveness, profit, and materialistic goals?

Can the formal education system transform itself? Can we create a virtual college or university system for all the other faculties that eliminates the lineups of tens of thousands of prospective students across the country? Will teachers and administrators be able to reinvent education? Talk to the students; they're willing. As Geoffrey Bannister, president of Butler University, says: "Just wait till the generation of teenage Internet users hit the universities where the average age of a tenured professor is 50. Sparks are going to fly!"

The regulatory environment will have to change, too. In this intense, competitive environment we need an open, competitive domestic environment for telecommunications. We can't continue the current practices; they hobble progress.

Every company, hospital, school, publication, police force, local government, retailer, union, native band, and nation needs to find within itself the leadership for transformation. And with will, every person, regardless of position in an organization, can become a leader for change.

The easy route for businesspeople is to turn their backs on such complex challenges. Every corporation needs to grapple with these questions because they will deeply affect their customers, employees, and the environment for business transformation. Rather than passively observing or merely predicting these broader societal changes, businesspeople need to become actively involved in solving the problems and shaping the future.

The challenge is one of leadership for the digital frontier. Executives from all industry sectors are uniquely positioned to provide socially responsible leadership in resolving the myriad of emerging challenges the new technology is posing to the way society works, learns, and lives. We must forge common directions and strategies for a new economy and a new age. Businesspeople need to make a turn and do the right thing. Let the discussion begin.

NOTES

1. Nicholas Negroponte, *being digital*, Alfred A. Knopf, New York, 1995.
2. All part of remarks prepared for delivery by Vice President Al Gore at the International Telecommunications Union, Monday, March 21, 1994.
3. Nuala Beck, "Shifting Gears: Thriving in the New Economy," HarperCollins *World*, New York, 1995.
4. James M. Utterback, *Mastering the Dynamics of Innovation*, Harvard Business School Press, Boston, 1994.
5. Terence P. Paré, "Why the Banks Lined Up Against Bill Gates," *Fortune*, May 29, 1995.
6. *Harvard Business Review*, January-February 1994, p. 128.
7. Peter Drucker, "The New Organization," *Harvard Business Review*, January-February 1988.
8. Peter Senge, *The Fifth Discipline*, Doubleday, New York, 1990.
9. William Davidow and Michael Malone, *The Virtual Corporation*, Harper Business, New York, 1992.
10. Peter Keen, *Shaping the Future: Business Design Through Information Technology*, Harvard Business School Press, Boston, 1991.
11. Tom Peters, *The Tom Peters Seminar. Crazy Times Call for Crazy Organizations*, Vintage Books, 1994.
12. D. Quinn Mills, *Rebirth of the Corporation*, John Wiley & Sons, New York, 1991.
13. Charles M. Savage, *5th Generation Management: Integrating Enterprises Through Human Networking*, Digital Press, 1990.
14. Russell L. Ackoff, *The Democratic Organization*, Oxford University Press, New York, 1994.
15. James Brian Quinn, *The Intelligent Enterprise*, The Free Press, New York, 1992.
16. Michael Hammer and James Champy, *Reengineering the Corporation*, Harper Business, 1994
17. Gary Hamel and C.K. Prahalad, *Competing for the Future*, Harvard Business School Press, Boston, 1994.
18. Bob Allen, chairman of AT&T. From a presentation to the Networked Economy Conference, September 26, 1994.
19. Data drawn from a speech by Michael B. Greenbaum, vice-president, business development, Small Business Services, Bell Atlantic, at the Doing Business on the Internet Seminar, University of Delaware, January 17, 1995.
20. *Interactive Multimedia in High Performance Organizations: Wealth Creation in the Digital Economy*, case study by the Alliance for Converging Technologies, November, 1994.

21. Vice President Al Gore, from a presentation to the Academy of Television Arts & Sciences, UCLA, January 11, 1994.
22. Forbes ASAP, Summer 1993.
23. Mike Hammer, "The High Priest," *Site Selection*, February 1993.
24. R.M. Randall, "The Reengineer," *Planning Review*, May/June 1993.
25. The evidence for this view comes from recent media discussion; debate in the NII Advisory Council and its working groups; the creation of organizations such as the Electronic Frontier Foundation, the Aspen Institute and the Alliance for Public Technology; and the plethora of articles and broadcast programs appearing on related topics.
26. "The Promise and Perils of Emerging Information Technologies." A Report on the Second Annual Information Roundtable. The Aspen Institute, 1993. A thoughtful discussion of key issues by this high-powered think tank.
27. Christopher Lasch, "Revolt of the Elites: Have They Cancelled Their Allegiance to America?" *Harpers Magazine*, November 1994.
28. Alan Kay. From a speech given to the Superhighway Summit at the University of California at Los Angeles, 1994. As cited in WIRED, May 1994, p. 76.
29. Marilyn Ferguson, *The Aquarian Conspiracy—Personal and Social Transformation in Our Time*, St. Martin's Press, New York, 1976.

PART ONE

THRIVING IN A
NEW ECONOMY

Sometime in the middle of the next century we will move past software and hardware to wetware—the merging of digital and biological information into a ubiquitous and functional DNA. Before plunging into this "childhood's end," humanity will serve an arduous apprenticeship. Over the next few decades the Net, and the intimate relationship between producer and consumer invoked by personalized products, will shatter the anonymity of mass consumption, mass politics, mass media. It will be an age of "in your face" contact harkening back to village life. And it will also be an age of insecurity as the fixtures of daily experience such as going to school, going to work, and going on vacation are smashed. Old ways of working and learning will get as little respect as did the rhythms of the farm when people moved to the city and factory.

Yet the dividing line between social meltdown and successfully completing our apprenticeship will depend more than ever on our collective ability to create trust. Without trust, the intangible knowledge that is the life blood of an innovation-driven economy will not flow. And without the flow of learning we will be unable to overcome the fragmentation, polarization, and cultural homogenization that threaten the cherished dream of human self-determination and fulfillment.

Riel Miller
Alliance for Converging Technologies, 1995

20th Anniversary Edition Commentary on
Chapter 2: Twelve Themes of the New Economy

O F ALL THE CHAPTERS in *The Digital Economy,* first edition, this one received the biggest response. I remember Raymond "Ray" Lane, then-president of Oracle, saying that he required all of his senior management team to read the chapter.

In hindsight every one of the 12 themes holds up well today—with the topics of prosumption, immediacy, molecularization, discordance, and disintermediation along with its flipside "re-intermediation" standing out. Most organizations are still in the early days of trying to figure out how these themes apply to them.

The Architecture of the Firm

Probably the greatest contribution of the chapter was the first introduction of Nobel Prize–winning Economist Ronald Coase's theory about *the Firm*, as being critical to understanding the meaning of the Internet. Let me elaborate with a 2014 lens.

Ronald Coase died in 2013 at the age of 102. He was awarded the 1991 Nobel Prize in Economics, largely for his inspiring 1937 paper "The Nature of the Firm." The Nobel committee applauded the academic for his "discovery and clarification of the significance of transaction costs ... for the institutional structure and functioning of the economy."[1] However, Coase's enduring legacy may well be that his paper and theories, 50 years later, helped us understand the Internet's impact on the economy and all our institutions.

As a young economist, Coase was perplexed by large American companies run by titans such as Henry Ford and Alfred P. Sloan, Jr. If the free market was the best way to allocate resources, why did these capitalists run their companies in much the same way as Joseph Stalin ran the Soviet Union's economy?

Coase wondered why there was no market within the firm. Why is it unprofitable to have each worker and each step in the production process become an independent buyer and seller? Why doesn't the draftsperson auction his or her services to the engineer? Why is it that the engineer does not sell his or her designs to the highest bidder? Coase argued that preventing this from happening was "marketplace friction."

Coase argued that marketplace friction gave rise to "transaction costs"—or to put it more broadly, "collaboration costs" or "relationship costs." There are three types. First are "search costs" such as finding different suppliers and determining if their goods are appropriate. Second are "contractual costs" such as negotiating the price and contract conditions. Third are the "coordination costs" of meshing the different products and processes. The upshot is that most vertically integrated corporations concluded it was cheaper and simpler to perform the maximum number of functions in-house, rather than incurring the cost, hassle, and risk of constantly searching, contracting, understanding, collaborating, and executing transactions with outside partners.

It makes sense for a firm to expand until the cost of performing a transaction *inside* the firm exceeds the cost of performing the transaction *outside* the firm. This is why large and insular corporations prevailed in the Industrial Age economy.

This is no longer the case. Many behemoths have lost market share to more supple competitors. Digital technologies slash transaction and collaboration costs. Smart companies are making their boundaries porous, using the Internet to harness knowledge, resources, and capabilities outside of the company. From Google to Procter & Gamble—which now gets 60% of its innovation from outside corporate walls—firms set a context for innovation and then invite their customers, partners, and other third parties to co-create their products and services.

Today's economic engines are Internet-based clusters of businesses. While each company retains its identity, companies function together, creating more wealth than they could ever hope to create individually. Whereas corporations were once gigantic, new business ecosystems tend toward the amorphous.

Looked at one way, for example, Amazon.com is a website with many employees shipping books. Looked at another way, however, Amazon.com is a vast ecosystem that includes authors, publishers, customers who write reviews for the site, delivery companies like UPS (United Parcel Service), and tens of thousands of affiliates that market products and arrange fulfillment through the Amazon network. Hundreds of thousands of people are in the Amazon viral marketing network.

How has the Internet affected Coase's analysis? Strictly speaking, his thesis remains as valid as ever: A firm or any organization should still expand until the cost of performing a transaction internally exceeds the cost of performing it externally. But the Internet has caused transaction costs to plunge so steeply that it has become much more useful to view Coase's analysis in reverse. Nowadays firms should shrink until the cost of performing a transaction internally no longer exceeds the cost of performing it externally. Transaction costs still exist, but now they're often more onerous in corporations than in the marketplace.

This is leading to the biggest change in the corporation in a century and how we orchestrate capability to innovate, create goods and services, and engage with the world. From now on, the ecosystem, not the corporation *per se*, should serve as the point of departure for business strategists seeking to understand the new economy—and for managers, entrepreneurs, and investors seeking to prosper in it.

The Internet tonic does not apply only to corporations. With ubiquitous broadband, society now has the most powerful platform ever for bringing together the people, skills, and knowledge needed to ensure growth, social development, and a just and sustainable world. The Web enables new approaches to almost every institution in society from government, media, health care, and science to our energy grid, transportation systems, and institutions for global problem solving.

Governments can change from being vertically integrated, Industrial Age bureaucracies to become networks. By releasing their treasures of raw data, governments can now become platforms upon which companies, NGOs (non-governmental organizations), academics, foundations, individuals, and other governmental agencies can collaborate to create public value.

Media companies are becoming networks that collaborate with countless partners and where readers, listeners, and viewers co-create value. Universities are beginning to disaggregate into networks offering courseware through Massively Open Online Courses (MOOCs).

If we listen to the theories of Ronald Coase from almost 80 years ago, we can understand how the digital revolution helps us find the uniquely qualified minds and talent to create wealth, govern, and educate ourselves for the future.

Notes

1. http://www.nobelprize.org/nobel_prizes/economic-sciences/laureates/1991/press.html.

TWELVE THEMES OF THE NEW ECONOMY

Take a moment out of the heat of your current pitched battle and chew on the implications of this thought. We are right now in the very early stages of a new economy, one whose core is as fundamentally different from its predecessor as, say, the automobile age was from the agricultural era. If you grasp this premise it's much easier to understand a lot of what's going on around you, including why a seemingly unrelenting tsunami of change keeps washing over you and your business.

John Huey, 1994[1]

It is fairly widely accepted that the developed world is changing from an industrial economy based on steel, automobiles, and roads to a new economy built on silicon, computers, and networks. Many people talk of a shift in economic relationships that's as significant as the previous displacement of the agricultural age by the industrial age. There are new dynamics, new rules, and new drivers for success.

But as Alan Webber, former editorial director of the *Harvard Business Review*, has written: "[N]o one has asked the all important question ... what's so new about the new economy?"[2] His question is reminiscent of the time that Albert Einstein was monitoring an exam for graduate physics students and was told that there was a problem because the questions on the exam were the same as on the previous year's test. "That's okay," he replied, "the answers are different this year."

Well, the answer to Webber's question is different this year, too. And it will be different next year also. The new economy is all about competing for the future, the capacity to create new products or services, and the ability to transform businesses into new entities that yesterday couldn't be imagined and that the day after tomorrow may be obsolete.

The Twelve Themes of the New Economy

A dozen overlapping themes are emerging that differentiate the new economy from the old. By understanding these you have the precondition for transforming your business for success.

Theme 1: Knowledge

+ *The new economy is a knowledge economy.*

Information technology enables an economy based on knowledge. But notwithstanding the rise of artificial intelligence and other "knowledge technologies," knowledge is created by human beings—by knowledge workers (professional and technical workers now outnumber industrial workers by almost three to one) and by knowledge consumers. "Leveraged intellect and its prime facilitator, service technology, are reshaping not only the service industries but also U.S. manufacturing, the country's overall growth patterns, national and regional job structures, and the position of the United States in world politics and international competition," argues James Brian Quinn, professor at Dartmouth's Tuck School, in *Intelligent Enterprise*.[3]

To begin, the knowledge content of products and services is growing significantly as consumer ideas and information and technology become part of products. Take, for example, the new era of smart products that are beginning to revolutionize every aspect of society.

+ *Smart clothes.* Clothing manufacturers are placing chips in clothes that can contain information on where and when the item was made, who manufactured it, when it was imported, when it arrived in the store, and when it was placed on the rack. When the item is purchased, information can be added about who purchased it, the date, and the amount paid. The item has a memory that can provide useful information to everyone in the value network. This can help to solve return problems, or if the item goes out the store door before it has been paid for, it can communicate back: "Help," cries the jacket. "I'm being stolen!"

+ *Smart cards.* Credit card, debit card, an access card to the office—who needs so many separate pieces of plastic with various expiry dates and annual fees? Coming: one card for all these functions plus driver's permit, personal health information including drug interreactions and organ donor info, spouse's sizes for gift giving—all managed by a single microprocessor embedded in the plastic. As for the issues of security and privacy? They are significant. (More on that later.)

◆ *Smart houses.* Burglar and fire alarms, appliances, and lighting can be controlled from a handy keypad or by dialing up the system from an outside phone. You can check on the room temperature, get supper started in the oven, feed the dog, and monitor goings-on to ensure that your teenagers aren't breaking too many pieces of furniture at the party they're not supposed to be having while you're on vacation. Soon, the pantry will keep track of items you're running out of and automatically issue food and beverage replenishment orders for food that is delivered to your door.

◆ *Smart roads.* Pavement can do more than carry vehicles to destinations. Roadbeds will monitor traffic and weather conditions, then issue warnings about dangerous conditions ahead. There will be fewer accidents because sensing devices will alert drivers who are following other cars too closely or who have fallen asleep and are swerving out of the proper lane. Transport trailers will give you sufficiently wide berth. Potholes? Unheard of.

◆ *Smart cars.* Too drunk to drive? The car won't start. Passing an historic site? An audio and video broadcast explains what happened and when. An integrated system monitors both your driving performance and the car's operations, automatically scheduling service visits where the technician plugs in and knows immediately what's wrong under the hood. Maps and directions will be broadcast via global positioning satellites. No man will ever again have to admit to his wife that he's lost.

◆ *Smart tires.* Logging trucks in Alaska and Northern British Columbia have onboard computers linked through satellite to geographical information and weather systems, which link back to the truck dynamically adjusting (among other things) the pressure in the truck's tires. Because trucks can go faster and last longer with tire pressure right for the road conditions, the entire cost of the system pays back in months.

◆ *Smart pucks.* Hockey is growing in popularity, but aging viewers find it hard to see the puck on the TV screen. Coming soon are pucks containing a chip that will transmit data to the network computers. The puck on the screen can be bright, or pink, or change color depending on which way the play is going, or it can even contain sound effects for the viewing audience.

◆ *Smart radios and TVs.* Who wants one-way communication? What about personal, interactive radio and television where you can ask for and receive more information about the music, movie, or commercial, including the capability to order merchandise? Or if you don't like what you're getting, more bowling scores and bingo locations can be yours. A built-in agent will look after your individual programming preferences and personal interests and then play information about them on command. Commercial messages will be tailored to your buying habits; no more ads for personal products you never intend to use.

◆ *Smart telephones.* Already phones have built-in answering machines and come with faxes and caller ID, but there's more yet. The smart telephone will combine all known communications functions, offer mobility, plus handle voice, video, and data at the same time. Now, if only there were a function known as call backward, so that you could turn back the clock and speak the wonderful sentence that you thought of five minutes after you hung up from that important conversation.

In an economy based on brain rather than brawn, there is a shift toward knowledge work. In the new economy the key assets of the organization are intellectual assets, and they focus on the knowledge worker. This is causing companies around the world to develop new ways of measuring and managing their intellectual capital.[4] For Peter Drucker, knowledge is not simply another resource along with the traditional factors of production such as labor, capital, and land; for him, it is the only meaningful resource today. Consequently, the knowledge worker is any organization's greatest single asset.[5]

Consider Microsoft as a new economy company. When evaluating the assets of Microsoft, it is ludicrous to contemplate old-economy questions such as the following:

How much land does the company own?
What is the value of Microsoft's manufacturing facilities—its plants?
How much inventory does it have?
How many office buildings does it own?
How great is its stock of raw materials?

Rather, the only meaningful assets are contained in the crania of the managers and employees of the company. These assets walk out the door every night (or in the case of Microsoft, many leave in the morning and at other sundry times of the day).

But surely capital is still a critical asset? Isn't Microsoft's ownership of and access to money what enables it to invest in new products, to acquire companies, to throw tens of millions of dollars into marketing a new product such as Windows 95? True, capital is a key asset, but it is a fleeting one. Fifteen years ago Microsoft had virtually no capital. Now its market capitalization is greater than that of General Motors or IBM. In the new economy, capital will more and more become a function of knowledge.

The means of production is shifting from something physical to something human. As Robert Harris says: "The most visible differences between the corporation of the future and its present-day counterpart will be not the products they make or the equipment they use—but who will be working, how they will be working, why they will be working and what work will mean to them."[6]

Furthermore, labor is no longer a commodity. In the old economy, the workers at one car company were pretty well equivalent to the workers at another. Labor was only a commodity and was interchangeable. Now, labor is highly variable. The craft workers at the old-economy Mercedes plant in Germany, hand-sewing the seat covers, have a completely different knowledge base and skill set from those of the highly educated workers running robots at today's Lexus plant. And in the battles shaping up between Lotus, Microsoft, Oracle, Novell, and other software companies, there is almost no labor in the traditional sense. The knowledge and creative genius of the product strategists, developers, and marketers are the key. What counts is a company's ability to attract, retain, and continually grow the capabilities of knowledge workers and provide the environment for innovation and creativity.

So AlliedSignal spends millions of dollars annually training plant workers to use sophisticated statistical methods to drive toward six sigma (very high) quality levels. It is this shift to knowledge work that is behind all the discussion in academic circles, management seminars, and boardrooms of organizational learning. In such a world, an organization will be competitive only if it can learn faster than either its current or emerging competitors. Any firm can have the same technology as another company; any product can be copied. In the new race to the finish line, lifelong organizational learning becomes the only sustainable competitive advantage.

Because production is based on knowledge, there are vast new opportunities for improvements in quality of life for societies that can achieve a successful transition and effectively distribute the social benefits. In the old economy, workers tried to achieve fulfillment through leisure. The worker was alienated from the means of production that were owned and controlled by someone else. In the new economy, fulfillment can be achieved through work and the means of production shifts to the brain of the producer.

Theme 2: Digitization

♦ *The new economy is a digital economy.*

Throughout history, revolutions in a natural resource have enabled a new paradigm in tools (iron, bronze, steel), which led to new modes of wealth creation and social development. The new age could be aptly dubbed the *age of sand*. The affairs of commerce, business transactions, human communications, and the insights of science are all reduced to charges on particles of silicon or racing through glass fibers—both derived from sand.

The new media, the internet, and the new economy are all built on a strikingly simple thing. All information can be represented as either 1 or 0, which form the basis of the binary number system. Number 1 is represented as a 1; number 2 as a 10; number 3 as an 11, and so on. If all numbers can be described as 1s and 0s, early thinkers concluded that a combination of 1s and 0s could be used to represent the letter "a" and the letter "b" and the capital letter "A" and, for that matter, other kinds of information.

These 1s and 0s can in turn be represented in a computer as the presence or absence of an electrical signal. The first computers could encode or translate numbers and, later, letters into 1s and 0s by using vacuum tubes. When the tube was on, this indicated a 1. When the tube was off, this indicated a 0. Later, tubes were replaced by transistors that could be turned on or off. These were, in turn, replaced by silicon chips in which the on or off was represented by the absence or presence of a charge on a particle.

Over time, digitization was applied beyond numbers and letters. Bits could be used to represent more and more types of information such as graphs and photographs. Furthermore, time-based media (which are not static but which take time to present themselves) such as audio and video, could be sampled and translated into bits. If, for example, the analog waveform of a human voice could be converted into a digital signal by sampling it a sufficient number of times, these bits could be stored in a computer or a digital storage device like a disk (as in the case of voice mail) and reconstructed back into an analog wave that your ear can hear.

In the old economy, information was analog or physical (or as Nicholas Negroponte likes to say "atoms"). People communicated by moving their physical presences into a meeting room, talking over an analog telephone line, sending letters made of atoms to one another, broadcasting analog television signals to homes, showing pictures developed at the local photo shop, exchanging cash or checks, playing records by the guidance of a stylus through some grooves on a record, publishing physical magazines purchased at a store or delivered by the post office, or projecting light through a physical film strip at a movie theater.

In the new economy, information is in digital form: bits. When information becomes digitized and communicated through digital networks, a new world of possibilities unfolds. Vast amounts of information can be squeezed or compressed and transmitted at the speed of light. The quality of the information can be far better than in analog transmissions. Many different forms of information can be combined, creating, for example, multimedia documents. (If a picture is worth a thousand words, the right multimedia document retrieved at the right time is worth a thousand pictures.) Information can be stored and retrieved instantly from around the world, eventually providing instant access to much of the information recorded by human civilization. New digital appliances can be created that fit in your pocket (or smaller) and can have an impact on most aspects of business and personal life.

By comparing something as simple as the post office and its delivery of physical mail to the digital electronic mail systems of today (even though they are relatively primitive), you can begin to understand the effect of digitization on the metabolism of the economy. The benefits of e-mail are not just that messages move faster (approaching the speed of light compared to mail trucks). Nor that there is additional convenience in being able to send messages with the flick of a keyboard to a distribution list. Nor that there is a permanent searchable record of communications. Nor that "shadow functions," like walking to the mailbox or playing telephone tag, are reduced. Although all those benefits are real enough, the point is that e-mail is just the beginning of a whole new way of human collaboration. Product planners are working as a team from various locations. People can work just as effectively from home or their hotel room as they can in the office. Similar change is coming to every aspect of commerce, management, and learning throughout the economy. As text-based e-mail systems are replaced by multimedia mail—in which your message contains information in many forms, including video—the capacity of humans to communicate across time and space will be affected significantly.

Theme 3: Virtualization

◆ *As information shifts from analog to digital, physical things can become virtual—changing the metabolism of the economy, the types of institutions and relationships possible, and the nature of economic activity itself.*

In the new economy, there are (to name a few) the following:

◆ *Virtual alien.* People working and participating in one country's economy who are physically located somewhere else—for example, "virtual data entry workers" who live in India. Virtual aliens are often, technically, illegal aliens.

- *Virtual ballot box.* Any information appliance (TV, telephone, computer, kiosk, etc.) from which citizens can vote.
- *Virtual bulletin board.* Message Maestro, hyperlinked to other boards. Push pins not required.
- *Virtual business park.* "House" business resources on the Net to help companies rapidly create virtual corporations. As in Bell South's Media Park, which provides resources for the creative community.
- *Virtual congress (aka virtual hearings).* Legislative hearings held from multiple locations asynchronously (in multiple time dimensions).
- *Virtual corporation (virtual enterprise, extended enterprise, interenterprise).* The conjunctional grouping, based on the Net, of companies, individuals, and organizations to create a business.
- *Virtual coupon.* On the Net, encouraging you to buy, for example, Jiffy peanut butter.
- *Virtual government agency.* Many different government agencies that have a similar purpose are linked by networks to deliver services through a single window to the public, as in "entitlements" virtual agency.
- *Virtual job.* Individual contract work conducted on the Net. Not to be confused with unemployment.
- *Virtual mall.* An environment on the Net in which like things can be found, as in "virtual shopping mall" or "virtual shoe sale."
- *Virtual market.* Any place in cyberspace where people shop.
- *Virtual office.* Anywhere. The location of work for the nomadic office worker.
- *Virtual reality.* The overriding oxymoron for virtualization.
- *Virtual sex.* Interactive multimedia sexual experience with digitized partner(s), in the future involving kinesthetic feedback.
- *Virtual stockyard.* Electronic auction of stock using interactive workstations. Stock do not need to be moved to a physical yard to be sold. Now replacing many physical stockyards, as at Calgary Stockyard Ltd., which conducts two-thirds of cattle transactions electronically.
- *Virtual store.* The store on the Net that isn't there, routing consumers to suppliers (aka virtual retail, virtual wholesale, virtual distribution).
- *Virtual village.* The grouping of individuals, independent of location, who share a broad set of common objective and subjective interests. Extends to village life, main street, village square, village clown.
- *Virtual water cooler.* Places on the Net where people can engage in informal, even playful communications such as those that occur around the (physical) water cooler. Sometimes called a MUD (Multi-User Dungeon).

Theme 4: Molecularization

◆ *The new economy is a molecular economy. The old corporation is being disaggregated, replaced by dynamic molecules and clusters of individuals and entities that form the basis of economic activity. The organization does not necessarily disappear, but it is transformed. "Mass" becomes "molecular" in all aspects of economic and social life.*

The principal economic unit of the industrial economy was the corporation. The roots of the command-and-control hierarchy were in the church and military bureaucracies of the agricultural age but were extended to become the firm. The objective of every CEO and board was to increase the corporation's size, revenue, and profit.

The traditional hierarchy has been in deep trouble for years now because it was poorly equipped to respond to the new business realities. Conventional wisdom of the past decade has called for more responsive, flatter, team-based structures. The most significant movement to create such horizontal, process-oriented structures is business process reengineering (BPR). However, as Riel Miller, an economist working with the Alliance for Converging Technologies, put it: "The necessity of adding knowledge at every step in the value chain is beginning to call into question the familiar notion of the firm as an organizational unit. The Net may be, at one and the same time, the source of both the demise and salvation of the firm as we have known it."[7]

More than 50 years ago 1991 Nobel Prize–winning economist Ronald Coase asked why firms exist. Why are there groups of people working together under one organizational framework? He wondered why there is no market within the firm. Why is it unprofitable to have each worker, each step in the production process, become an independent buyer and seller? Why don't the draftspeople auction their services to the engineer? Why is it that the engineer does not sell designs to the highest bidder?

One of the main answers to these questions has to do with the cost of information. Producing a loaf of bread, assembling a car, or running a hospital emergency ward involves a number of steps in which cooperation and common purpose are essential to making a useful product. An emergency room, where each doctor bids for nursing services in an attempt to get the lowest price, while at the same time determining if the nurse is actually capable of assisting with the operation, might provide a fully functioning market but not a particularly useful product for a dead patient. Similarly, holding an auction before the axle assembler would pass along product to the chassis assembler might slow down the line. It would be even less efficient if the information on engineering viability and compatibility needed to be purchased on the shop-floor marketplace at every step.

What makes a pure market impractical is the time and cost of acquiring the information needed to undertake complex production processes. What is being sold? What is the quality of the labor? What is the quality of the raw material or intermediate input? What is the price for the final product? How will it be sold? By whom? With what kind of information or marketing? Who will finance the production process, and how much will financing cost? The ensemble of functions within a firm consist not only of a series of discrete products but also the infrastructure of collaboration.

A clear framework and strict regimentation worked on many battlefields and in many marketplaces of the past. The role of the overarching infrastructure of the firm or army was clear and indivisible. But today, as Miller puts it: "The Net does not change the rules, but it changes what is possible. It opens up new horizons for what is economically and practically feasible. The costs of information and coordination are dropping. More than ever we are in a position to create wealth by adding knowledge to each product at each step."

The industrial hierarchy and economy are giving way to molecular organizations and economic structures. The word *molecularization* is awkward but helpful. In physics, a molecule is one of the basic elements of matter. It is the smallest particle into which a substance can be divided and still have the chemical identity of the original substance. Molecules can be held together by electrical forces. In *solids*, attracting and repelling forces are balanced, holding the molecules in place. The molecules do not have enough energy to move to another part of the solid. In *liquids*, the molecules move about easily although they still have attractive forces among one another. Certain organic compounds called *liquid crystals* have properties of both liquids and solids—molecules form clusters that can move about and change rapidly, yet they retain a degree of structure. As conditions change (temperature), the state of the molecules changes as well.

The analogy is helpful in understanding the new economy. The new enterprise has a molecular structure. It is based on the individual. The knowledge worker (human molecule) functions as a business unit of one.[8] Motivated, self-learning, entrepreneurial workers empowered by and collaborating through new tools apply their knowledge and creativity to create value. Conditions may warrant a solid structure that tightly binds molecules together. More likely, conditions will require more dynamic relationships among molecules, causing them to cluster in teams, as in liquid crystals, or even to move more freely, as in liquids. The capacity for new relationships is profoundly increased through the new infostructure. There is still a role for the organization to provide a base structure for such molecular activity, but it is a far cry from the old hierarchy.

When such molecular activity is extended to the economy as a whole, we can see very different kinds of relationships that make discussion of the virtual corporation seem trite. For example, the mass media will become the molecular media, through which readers, listeners, and viewers become customers able to access and interact with millions of "channels." They do so when they choose, rather than according to the schedule of a broadcaster. Mass production becomes molecular production with production runs of one—rather than one million—pairs of jeans. Even products become composed of molecules linked together through standard interfaces. The software industry is becoming a parts industry in which companies build and market parts that work with others. Just as a modern wide-body jet is referred to in the industry as a "complex assembly of parts flying in close formation" because most of the parts are not manufactured by Boeing or Lockheed or McDonnell Douglas but by their suppliers, mass marketing becomes molecular marketing as marketers identify specific customer groups or individuals to receive sales information.

Theme 5: Integration/Internetworking

◆ *The new economy is a networked economy, integrating molecules into clusters that network with others for the creation of wealth.*

When Ron Ponder took over as the CIO of AT&T in 1994, his central challenge was to create the network infrastructure for AT&T to segment its markets, to create a molecular delivery system. "We're creating a new operating model for the business," says Ponder. "We're creating the ability for unique segmentation for a customer market of one. But, you can't do this transformation without the new technology—it enables you to go from one paradigm to the other."

The new paradigm in wealth creation is possible because of computer networks that are digital rather than analog, and because of a shift in the style of networking from the host computer, hierarchical networks of the past to peer-to-peer webs based on the Internet model. As the bandwidth of such networks grows to achieve full multimedia (integrating data, text, audio, image, and video media), the opportunities for such new institutional structures grow dramatically.

The new networked organizational structures are not simply the creation of process-oriented organizations in which "stovepipe" business processes are reengineered horizontally to save costs and improve responsiveness. Nor is the change simply a shift to team-based structures (although the business team is central to the new enterprise). Rather, it is a radical rethinking of the nature and functioning of the organization and the relationships between organizations. The new organization, dubbed by the Alliance for Converging Technologies as the "Internet-worked Enterprise," is a vast web of relationships including all levels and business functions in which the boundaries inside and outside are permeable and fluid.

The new technology networks enable small companies to overcome the main advantages of large companies—economies of scale and access to resources. At the same time, these smaller companies are not burdened with the main disadvantages of large firms—deadening bureaucracy, stifling hierarchy, and the inability to change. As larger companies disaggregate—become clusters of smaller molecules that can work well together—they gain the advantages of agility, autonomy, and flexibility.

The Internetworked Enterprise will be a far-reaching extension of the virtual corporation because there will be access to external business partners, constant reconfiguration of business relationships, and a dramatic increase in outsourcing. The Internetworked Enterprise will behave like the Internet, where everyone can participate and the total effort is greater than the sum of the parts.

The overall economy will act in the same way. Networks of networks along the Internet model are beginning to break down walls among companies—suppliers, customers, affinity groups, and competitors. We will see the rise of internetworked business, internetworked government, internetworked learning, and internetworked health care, to name a few.

Every economy needs a national information infrastructure. This is the utility of the twenty-first century—a broadband highway for a broadband, high-capacity economy. And every organization needs to plug into this utility with an enterprise information infrastructure. The new infrastructure will change economic activity as significantly as did electrification. Just as business and wealth creation would be unthinkable today without electrification, so the new economy would be impossible without the power of information.

Cybertalk
Ballistic: What happens to you when nothing works, as in "I go...."
Cyberspace: Where everyone boldly goes.

Digital: Stuff you can count on two fingers.

Flamed: Dead meat—what happens to you if you break the Net rules.

Icons: Helpful signposts if you worship them respectfully.

Luddites: Bosses who don't know the difference between stability and paralysis.

Obsolete: The system you just purchased.

Vidiots: Those who spend too much time riding the Net.

Theme 6: Disintermediation

◆ *Middleman functions between producers and consumers are being elimi-nated through digital networks. Middle businesses, functions, and people need to move up the food chain to create new value, or they face being disintermediated.*

If your company has in its midst agents, wholesalers, distributors, retailers, brokers, or middle managers, it's time to do some serious strategizing (or career planning if you are one of them). All these roles in the past have been in the business of executing transactions, brokering, or in general boosting the faint signals that passed for communications in a predigital economy. Disintermedi-ation is changing the signal pattern. Musicians and their producers won't need recording companies, retail outlets, or broadcasters when their music becomes a database entry on the Net. Food producers won't need wholesalers or super-markets when customers can replenish supplies weekly by accumulating entries in their shopping-list databases and take deliveries at home. Hotels won't need travel agents to execute booking transactions when everything can be done by would-be travelers "helicoptering" in a geographical information system (GIS) over their destination city.

Take the case of consumer goods manufacturers being squeezed by giant retailers like Walmart demanding consignment sales and razor-thin margins. Manufacturers could use the new infrastructure to sell directly over the net-work, thereby eliminating intermediary retail channels. An electric tool and small appliance company such as Black & Decker could provide video or interactive programs on, say, home renovations featuring their tools. Or they may develop a cooking series, this week discussing Italian cuisine that features their pasta maker, food processor, and microwave oven. As such, they become infotainment companies providing content (for a fee or not) on the Net. In the process, the large retailers become disintermediated. People still like to go to the movies, but the home video market is now bigger than the Hollywood movie industry.

Government is also a candidate for disintermediation. Customers of government (the public) must line up at 15 different places to deal with 15 different government agencies, each having an office, staff, subcontractors, and related costs, and each delivering various degrees of service effectiveness. Leadership at the state level could create a single window on government through the information highway that would be accessible from the home (computer, television, or telephone), place of work, information kiosks, or other information appliances. Taxpayers could interact with computer-based services as appropriate or contact a human being (by audio or video) if necessary. If managed effectively, disintermediation could not only save billions of tax dollars but bring government closer to its constituents and improve customer service.

Or look at commercial real estate brokers who are in the business of matching property owners with potential buyers or leasers. They are true intermediaries, acting usually on behalf of the property owner. The goal is to find an appropriate buyer or lessee for the property. Usually they work as part of a team putting a deal together. The team may involve the broker, the owner, the owner's lawyer, the owner's accountants, and possibly others. The broker does not attempt to replicate the expertise of others on the team but tries to be the facilitator, the deal maker. On the other hand, the broker needs information and knowledge in a number of areas, including the market, types of deals, leases, and current tax legislation.

As critical information comes on line and owners and buyers become wired, the intermediaries are in trouble. Disintermediation is raising questions regarding the role of the broker. As Belleville, Ontario, broker John Beach describes it:

> As technology facilitates the exchange of information between suppliers and customers, we need to find new ways to deliver value to our clients. Rather than being in the transaction or information exchange business we need to become value-added facilitators of deals and ongoing partners for commercial real estate advice and knowledge and help. In doing so, it will make more sense for sellers to partner with us rather than to try and do it themselves.

When leasing space in a new shopping center, the broker needs to understand not only the customer—the potential purchaser (their financial situation, their requirements for retail space, etc.), but in order to deliver high value the broker also needs to understand the *customer's customers*. If a broker is attempting to lease a shopping center facility, he or she can provide significant value by understanding the potential customers of the customer—the local population, their demographics, their income, employment levels, purchasing history, exposure to media, and so on. Additional critical information includes municipal bylaws such as zoning, environmental information, tax information, and creative deal arrangements.

This new way of thinking demands that the broker have instant access to extensive information. Coupled with strong human relations skills, solid knowledge of key variables, and powerful tools to package deal scenarios, the broker can move up the value chain to forge trusted partner relationships. Rather than being disintermediated, the broker can use the new technology to create new value. This is not a future challenge and opportunity. In 1995, the NARLINK system became available to many brokers. It includes information on regulatory issues, research findings, government legislation, and NAR (National Association of Realtors) positions on issues affecting real estate as well as access to the NAR library.

Similarly, travel agents are vulnerable and need to provide new value. Already more than 20% of air travelers purchase tickets directly from the airlines. Soon, tickets will disappear as the process becomes digitized. Agents need to become travel consultants delivering new services. Agencies specializing in business travel can become convention planners, helping to ensure a high-performance meeting, ensuring best discounts from hotels, and so on. Summit Travel of Winston-Salem, North Carolina, has decided if you can't beat 'em, join 'em. It has created a software package that helps travelers to search the Net for flights and make the transactions themselves. But the software also routes the reservation through Summit, which receives a rebate of 5% of customers' fares. Other travel agencies award frequent flyer points. Whatever the step, agents need to provide new value in the digital economy—to "reintermediate."

Theme 7: Convergence

◆ *In the new economy, the dominant economic sector is being created by three converging industries that, in turn, provide the infrastructure for wealth creation by all sectors.*

In the old economy, the automotive industry was the key sector. The dominant sector in the new economy is the new media, which are products of the convergence of the computing, communications, and content industries. In the United States, new media and their ancillary industries and services account for more than 10% of the GDP. Computer hardware and communications bandwidth are both becoming commodities. The profit in the new sector is moving to content because that's where value is created for customers, not in boxes or transmission. Many of the content companies—the entertainment companies, broadcast networks, and publishers—are slow off the blocks for old paradigms die hard. The more successful companies are those with a background in software, services, computer-based content, and digital telecommunications.

Depending which corner of the triangle they inhabit, companies can suffer tunnel vision. Some television networks view the sole opportunity as interactive TV. Some Hollywood producers think convergence is irrelevant. Computer companies tend to focus on business applications only. The games companies view convergence as the new digital playground. And some telephone companies focus on enhanced telephony or video conferencing. Who's right? The marketplace will decide. "What do you think of radio?" Fred Allen once asked Titus Moody. And Titus replied: "I don't hold with furniture that talks." So much for the experts.

Some companies are making significant progress embracing convergence. One of the new media's corporate leaders, Dick Notebaert, CEO of Ameritech, notes that the old name "telephone company" doesn't even fit anymore. "In fact," he says, "we quit calling ourselves that a long time ago."

Convergence is becoming the basis of all sectors. The new media are already beginning to transform the arts, the way scientific research is conducted, and the way education is delivered. They are on the threshold of transforming the firm as we know it and changing the way we do business, work, play, live, and probably even think.

Theme 8: Innovation

◆ *The new economy is an innovation-based economy.*

"Obsolete your own products." This theme is made clear to product planners, strategists, engineers, developers, and managers at Microsoft and is constantly reinforced in all aspects of their work, beginning with their first orientation on their first day at the job. If you've just developed a great product, your goal is to develop a better one that will make the first one obsolete. If you don't make it obsolete, someone else will. For example, Microsoft technologist Ken Nickerson is proud to say that it was Microsoft (with Windows 95) that succeeded in making obsolete the best-selling software of all time—Microsoft's own DOS.

Indeed, a key driver of the new economy is innovation, including a commitment to a continual renewal of products, systems, processes, marketing, and people. Compare this view to that held by many mainframe aficionados at IBM who early on fought against shifting IBM's massive resources to the PC, open systems, and client/server development. Their goal was not to obsolete or to innovate but to preserve and to resist. Rather than obsoleting their own products, they let their competitors do it for them, and the results soon became clear in the marketplace.

Ironically, in the preindustrial economy, innovation was very important. Each gun or shoe was different—crafted by an innovator. The number of produced units for each product was very small, often only one. If the gun or shoe needed fixing, the craftsperson would innovate a solution. In the industrial economy, the number of units per product type increased for mass production of standard goods. In the new economy, there is a shift from mass production to mass customization of goods and services—just like going from Henry Ford, for whom every car was black, to Henry Fonda, to whom every film was different.

In an innovation company, product life cycles collapse. Japanese auto manufacturers work on a two-year life cycle, and Japanese electronics consumer products manufacturers assume a three-month cycle. There are financial products in some markets that have a product life cycle of a few hours—by then the competition has caught up. Most medium- or large-sized companies in North America introduce more than one new product per day. Last year Sony introduced 5,000 new products. Microsoft group vice president Nathan Myhrvold (coauthor with Bill Gates of the book *The Road Ahead*) says, "No matter how good your product, you are only 18 months away from failure." According to IBM CEO Lou Gerstner, the number of IBM products has risen dramatically. At the same time, the life cycle of an individual product has fallen sharply. In concert with that change, the effort to manufacture a product has collapsed from an average of 2,500-person days per product to three hours. Even something as seemingly stable and low-tech as beer requires innovation; 90% of Miller's revenues come from beers that didn't exist 24 months ago.

It was only a decade ago that the steel industry in the United States was in deep trouble, uncompetitive with low-cost, high-productivity Japanese steel mills. Rather than giving in, the industry innovated by creating minimills like Chaparral Steel and Nucor. They reinvented the process of making steel with new production processes based on new technologies. This enabled smaller plants to produce higher-quality steel at lower cost. The plants were also located closer to markets, were able to create better relationships with customers, and used different models of employer-employee relationships. The result: The industry is again productive, competitive, and producing the highest quality steel in the world.

"In today's global economy, companies that take their leadership for granted soon find themselves bringing up the rear," said Frank Shrontz, chairman and CEO at Boeing when the 777 was successfully designed and introduced to market. "Clearly, the world is changing and we must change with it—by striving to better understand the needs and expectations of our customers, by becoming more efficient and productive, and by offering products and services that represent superior value. Information moves too quickly, and valued technologies are too perishable for Boeing—or any other company—to assume that its past is a guarantee of its future."

How was it that Rubbermaid placed number one in *Fortune* magazine's annual poll of the most admired corporations? This seemingly unexciting, low-tech product company also tied for first with Microsoft in the United States's most prestigious industrial design competition. Forget about continuous improvement, Rubbermaid is into continuous innovation—the constant generation of new products and the regeneration of old ones. Even with a majority of its products selling for only a few dollars, the company has been able to innovate to meet customer needs and create new ones. It turns out that customers will happily pay for a large garbage can that (unlike any others) is very light, has wheels, is an attractive baby blue color, is animal proof, and is virtually indestructible.

Innovation drives every aspect of economic and social life. In the arts, whole new art forms are emerging based on interactive multimedia. Multivolume encyclopedias are being replaced by a single CD-ROM that can hold 360,000 pages of text. Not so long ago, music videos were a promotional add-on for a singer; now, they are necessary for success. Along with the perennial Academy Awards there now exists the Academy of Interactive Arts and Sciences; its first annual award show was held in 1994. Innovation is also beginning to drive education curricula. In the old economy, a curriculum was good for years and careers. In the new economy, to be relevant the education system must constantly change content, instructional tools, and approaches.

In the innovation economy, human imagination is the main source of value. The critical challenge for any company in the digital economy is to create a climate in which innovation is prized, rewarded, and encouraged. Every country needs innovative workplaces and organizations that foster creativity. Growth in the innovation economy comes from small- and medium-sized businesses rather than large corporations or governments. What's required are educational systems that teach and motivate students to learn and to be creative, rather than to recall information. Governments and regulatory frameworks must help to liberate the human spirit for invention and creation rather than acting as a bureaucratic brake on change and breakthrough.

Product and service leadership is one way to win in the innovation economy, but it is not adequate to understand the customers and their concerns and desires. Given the pace of change and complexity of markets, customers often cannot articulate their needs. You must innovate beyond what your markets can imagine. You must understand the needs of your customer's customer. Your organization needs a deep-seated and pervasive comprehension of emerging technologies. And you need a climate in which risk taking is not punished, creativity can flourish, and human imagination can soar.

Theme 9: Prosumption

◆ *In the new economy the gap between consumers and producers blurs.*

As mass production is replaced by mass customization, producers must create specific products that reflect the requirements and tastes of individual consumers. In the new economy, consumers become involved in the actual production process. They can, for example, enter a new car showroom and configure an automobile on the computer screen from a series of choices. Chrysler can produce special-order vehicles in 16 days. The customer creates the specs and sets in motion the manufacture of a specific, customized vehicle. In the old economy, viewers watched the evening network news. In the new economy, a television viewer will design a customized news broadcast by highlighting the top ten topics of interest and specifying preferred news sources, editorial commentators, and graphic styles. Moreover, that same viewer will be able to watch that broadcast whenever time permits or the need arises.

Every consumer on the information highway becomes a producer by creating and sending a message to a colleague, contributing to a bulletinboard discussion group, altering the end of a movie, test driving a virtual car, or visualizing the brain of a patient across the country.

In the old economy, such tasks were done by individuals but only as one part of a job. The worker produced with a lathe, a trowel, chalk, or a scalpel. In the new economy, such production occurs throughout daily life. Similarly, as the information and knowledge content of products and services grows, organizations will shift from being only consumers of information and technology to the point at which they are infotech producers. Automotive companies won't just assemble vehicles; they'll produce everything from infomercials to driver navigational tools and programming about auto safety. Toyota is already appealing to the 40-something buyer with a 30-minute infomercial and the 20-something crowd with an interactive CD.

Theme 10: Immediacy

+ *In an economy based on bits, immediacy becomes a key driver and variable in economic activity and business success.*

Product life cycles are cratering. In 1990, automobiles took six years from concept to production. Today they take two years. Hewlett-Packard's Computer Systems Organization chief Wim Roelandts says that these days most of HP's revenues come from products that didn't exist a year ago. In the old economy, an invention (like the Polaroid camera, xerography) ensured a revenue stream for decades. Today, consumer electronics products have a typical lifespan of two months.

The new enterprise is a *real time enterprise,* which is continuously and immediately adjusting to changing business conditions through information immediacy. Goods are received from suppliers and products are shipped to customers "just in time," thus reducing or eliminating the warehousing function and allowing enterprises to shift from mass production to custom on-line production. Customer orders arrive electronically and are instantly processed; corresponding invoices are sent electronically and databases are updated.[9] Enterprises seek to "compete in time" effectively.[10]

Electronic data interchange (EDI) is a powerful, if badly misunderstood, example of how the internet is creating information immediacy.[11] Advocates of EDI argue that by linking computer systems between suppliers and their customers for purchase orders, invoices, billing, and recordkeeping, companies can save considerably over manual (nondigital) methods. In fact, EDI goes well beyond those possibilities. It's just the first splash in a tidal wave of electronic commerce that will shift the metabolism of business to real time and in so doing forever change the relationship between companies.

Theme 11: Globalization

+ *The new economy is a global economy.*

According to MIT professor Paul Krugman, author of *Peddling Prosperity,* there's nothing more to the global economy than trade in goods, services, capital, labor, and information. "That's it," he says. "There is no more mystical sense in which we have a global economy. We are living in a world that is about as integrated, give or take a few measures, as the world of the nineteenth century."[12]

Mr. Krugman, I beg to differ. The new economy is as different from the old economy as a Sea-Doo is from a penny farthing bicycle or e-mail is from the Pony Express.

Just as the bipolar geopolitical world has disintegrated, giving way to a new, dynamic, and volatile global environment, economic walls are falling as well. This phenomenon is related to rise of the new economy. As Peter Drucker says, "Knowledge knows no boundaries." There is no domestic knowledge and no international knowledge. With knowledge becoming the key resource, there is only a world economy, even though the individual organization operates in a national, regional, or local setting.

Linked to this, and despite the efforts of old paradigm warriors fighting for protectionism, free trade zones are growing in North America and the Pacific Rim. Global customers demand global products. Work is performed globally by exploiting cost advantages of traditional input factors such as labor and raw materials. New economic and political regions and structures (such as the European Union) are leading to a decline in the importance of the nation-state.

As the world economy continues to globalize, the need for stay-ahead management becomes even more crucial. Ad hoc alliances, strategic partnering, and, above all, information technology will be vital for the future. Collaboration is going beyond the old boundaries. "Collaboration in business is no longer confined to conventional two-company alliances such as joint ventures or marketing accords," says Benjamin Gomes-Casseres, associate professor at the Harvard Business School. "Today we see groups of companies linking themselves together for a common purpose. Consequently, a new form of competition is spreading across global markets: group versus group."[13]

Globalization is both chicken and egg. It is driven by and driving the new technology that enables global action. Computer networks allow companies to provide 24-hour service as customer requests are transferred from one time zone to another without the customer ever being aware that the work is being done on the far side of the world. Networks enable smaller firms to collaborate in achieving economies of scale. Software development can be conducted on networks, independent of location. The office is no longer a place, it is a global system. Technology is eliminating the "place" in workplace. Home may be where the heart is, but increasingly the office is anywhere the head can be connected.

"These connections will empower us and enhance freedom and democracy. Citizens will be able to communicate—both send and receive information—on a previously unimaginable scale," said Anne Bingaman, assistant attorney general in the U.S. Department of Justice. "When you think about this, recall scenes from Nazi-occupied Europe of women and men crouched around the wireless, desperate to learn and tell the truth. Or think of citizens behind the iron curtain, searching the short-wave bands for Radio Free Europe or the BBC. And imagine how much more difficult an oppressor's job is when people yearning for freedom have access to digital computer networks."

There are few better descriptions on how the new economy is a global one than that cited by former Citicorp chairman Walter Wriston. He's seen it all. As late as the 1960s, communications between bank staff in New York and their colleagues in Brazil were akin to an adventure. There were so few international lines that once they'd gotten one, they'd hang onto it even if there were nothing to say, so that when the time came to exchange information, they had an established connection. In Wriston's words, what happens today is "global conversation." More than 100 million telephone calls are completed every *hour*, using 300 million access lines the world over, and the number of calls will triple by 2000. "The entire globe is now tied together in a single electronic market moving at the speed of light," says Wriston. "There is no place to hide."[14]

Similarly, globalization is driving the extension of technology. The new geopolitical world is opening up new markets everywhere, demanding a global response. Global businesses need to be able to link with customers, suppliers, employees, and partners throughout the world. New opportunities in global financial markets require an information infrastructure for exploitation. All this is contributing to a rethinking of organizational structure and entire industries on an international level. Companies and academics are working to build "transnational enterprises," "answer networks," "boundaryless firms," "global organizations," and "international enterprises."[15]

Theme 12: Discordance

◆ *Unprecedented social issues are beginning to arise, potentially causing massive trauma and conflict.*

As we stand on the frontier of the new economy, we can also see the beginnings of a new political economy that will raise far-reaching questions about power, privacy, access, equity, quality of work life, quality of life in general, and the future of the democratic process itself. As tectonic shifts in most aspects of human existence clash with old cultures, significant social conflict will tear at the fabric of structures and institutions.

New social dialectics—the juxtaposition or interaction of conflicting ideas—are emerging.[16] Hegel developed the concept of conflicting forces leading to a synthesis of something new. Marx applied the notion to a view of the evolution of societies called *dialectical materialism*, but history did not evolve as Marx had planned. The new economy demands that the notion of dialectic forces be revisited. For example, there are strong pressures for the dispersion of economic and political power. These pressures conflict with old structures that seek to centralize economic and political power.

The nature of work and the requirements of the workforce in the digital economy are fundamentally different. The concept of labor is undergoing a radical redefinition. Just as the percentage of the workforce in agriculture has been declining since the turn of the century, the number of workers involved in the production of goods (the old economy) has been falling for a decade. The new economy is bringing high-paid, high-value jobs, but there is little job mobility between old and new. How will such a huge reorganization of the labor force and its skills occur?

There is a concurrent trend toward self-employment and the creation of small knowledge-based industries providing work on a contract basis. In the digital economy, as intellectual capital becomes the most valuable resource, the means of production shifts from the plant floor into the innovative minds of knowledge workers—those who create value. Compare their emerging power to that of the industrial worker, who could withhold labor by going on strike. Similarly, employers could lock out workers and deny them access to the means of production. Knowledge workers can exert their power in infinitely more complex and effective ways. Bosses can't deny them access to their own brains. If they are unhappy or feel unwanted, they are likely to set up their own business, as millions have done in the last half decade. A good brain, a telephone, a modem, and a PC are all that's required to produce. As Miller puts it, "Bosses can't say I want x tons of innovative ideas out of this group, as he used to do with steel." Knowledge workers require motivation and trusting team relationships to be effective. They have emerging power far beyond anything Marx ever imagined. These owners of the new means of production will be better positioned than ever to share in the bounty. Yet this growing power conflicts with traditional ownership and power structures, which are based on ownership of industrial age assets, specifically capital.

In the new economy, those workers with access to the new infrastructure can participate fully in social and commercial life. Those without access, knowledge, and motivation will tend to fall behind. If not managed properly, this will increase social stratification severely, creating a new underclass. The have-nots will become confronted with the contradiction between the magnificent potential of the new technology on the one hand and their declining quality of life on the other.

In the new economy, learning will more and more be provided by the private sector. This will come about not out of social responsibility but, rather, because working and learning are becoming the same activity for a majority of the workforce and because knowledge is becoming an important part of products. Moreover, the traditional educational institutions are failing to meet the needs of the economy, and there are huge and growing opportunities for learning products and services. This places a greater responsibility on individuals (those who can afford it) to achieve lifelong learning—potentially increasing social chasms. Furthermore, teachers and their unions need to participate and lead in the transformation of education if the old industrial-age type of schools are to have a hope of transforming themselves and surviving. But increasingly, learning can be done without formal institutions, and learning in schools can be done through technology, requiring fewer teachers. This leaves teachers in a Catch–22 situation—become irrelevant by resisting change or possibly become irrelevant by leading it.

Development consultant Phil Courneyeur, currently living in Nicaragua, points to the political impact of restructuring, destabilization, and the breakup of nation-states and the potential negative use of the new technology by dictatorial regimes and by the many private armies emerging from the breakup of states. "It is staggering to think of the potential havoc of nuclear technology falling into the hands of gangs; or of lethal gases such as in the Tokyo subways; or bombs such as in Oklahoma; or the likely use of new technologies by small states in localized and proxy wars."

NEW ECONOMY, NEW ENTERPRISE, NEW TECHNOLOGY—TWELVE CORRESPONDING THEMES

The new economy, the new enterprise, and the new technology are not unrelated; they are inextricably linked. They are enabling one another, and they are driving one another. If you can understand how the new technology corresponds to the new Internetworked Enterprise, you can begin to forge a strategy for competing in the new economy. See Table 2.1.

TABLE 2.1 Twelve Corresponding Themes

ECONOMY	ORGANIZATION	TECHNOLOGY
1. Knowledge		
There is a shift from brawn to brain. Knowledge becomes an important element of products. The gap between consumers and producers blurs.	Knowledge work becomes the basis of value, revenue, and profit. Knowledge is added throughout the value chain.	Knowledge technologies, expert systems, artificial intelligence proliferate. Management information systems and their predecessor, data processing, evolve into knowledge systems.
2. Digitization		
Human communication, delivery of government programs, execution of health care, business transactions, exchange of funds, etc., become based on ones and zeros.	Internal communication shifts from analog (memos, reports, meetings, telephone calls, whiteboard drawings, blueprints, models, photographs, designs, graphic arts, etc.) to digital.	Shift from analog technologies such as television, radio, photocopiers, cameras, tape recorders, PBXs, etc. to digital.
3. Virtualization		
Physical things can become virtual—changing the metabolism of the economy, the types of institutions and relationships possible, and the nature of economic activity itself.	Virtual corporations, teams, stockyards, government agencies, jobs, etc.	Visualization of data, real-time animation, and virtual reality systems that provide kinesthetic feedback.
4. Molecularization		
Replacement of the mass media, mass production, monolithic governments, by molecular media, production, governance, etc.	End of the command-and-control hierarchy, shifting to team-based, molecular structures. Individual employees and work groups are empowered or break free to act and to create value.	Object-oriented systems and technologies. Software separates data from programming (services) to create chunks or Lego pieces that can be reused and rapidly assembled.
5. Integration/Internetworking		
The new economy is a networked economy with deep, rich interconnections within and between organizations and institutions. Wealth creation, commerce, and social existence are based on an ubiquitous public infostructure.	The new enterprise is an Internetworked Enterprise. Achievable in the past only through monolithic hierarchies, the new technology now enables integration of modular, independent, organizational components—an integrated network of services.	There is a shift from host computing to networked computing. Islands of technology are replaced by client/server networks, which form part of an enterprise and public infostructure.
6. Disintermediation		
Elimination of intermediaries in economic activity including agents, brokers, wholesalers, some retailers, broadcasters, record companies, and anything that stands between producers and consumers.	Elimination of middle managers, internal agents, brokers, or anyone else who acts as boosters for the signals that pass for communications in the preknowledge organization.[17]	Shift from multilevel, hierarchical computing architectures to new networked models. Host computers, through the hierarchy, are eliminated as part of a peer-to-peer network computing model.

7. Convergence

Convergence of key economic sectors—computing, communications, and content.	Convergence of organizational structures responsible for the technologies of computing, communications, and content.	Convergence of the technologies of computing, communications, and content.

8. Innovation

Innovation is the key driver of economic activity and business success. Rather than traditional drivers of success such as access to raw materials, productivity, scale, and the cost of labor, human imagination becomes the main source of value.	Innovation is the key driver of successful products, marketing strategies, management approaches, organizational changes. Old rules and approaches fail quickly. The only sustainable advantage is organizational learning.	The enterprise infostructure provides a platform for innovation. New tools plumb the richness of the infostructure for multimedia information and knowledge bases, ubiquitous access to people and resources.

9. Prosumption

The gap between consumers and producers blurs in a number of ways. For example, consumers become involved in the actual production process as their knowledge, information, and ideas become part of the product specification process. Human collaboration on the Net becomes a part of the international repository of knowledge.	Consumers of information and technology become producers. Human collaboration on the Net becomes part of the corporate multimedia information resource. Users become designers, creating new software applications themselves. Many responsibilities for technology purchasing and implementation are dispersed.	New software development tools, object computing, software agents, etc., enable users to create systems and databases, replacing the traditional role of the specialist, much as spreadsheets replaced application development teams a decade earlier. Graphic user interfaces shift to multimedia interfaces involving voice entry and response, enabling natural interaction with tools.

10. Immediacy

The new economy is a *real-time economy*. Commerce becomes electronic as business transactions and communications occur at the speed of light rather than of the post office.	The new enterprise is a *real-time enterprise*— continuously and immediately adjusting to changing business conditions. Product life cycles crater.	The technology is applied to capture information online and to update information banks in real time—giving an accurate picture or enabling the management of a production process minute by minute.

11. Globalization

Knowledge knows no boundaries. As knowledge becomes the key resource, there is only a world economy, even though the individual organization operates in a national, regional, or local setting. New economic and political regions and structures (such as the European Union) are leading to a decline in the importance of the nation-state and increasing the interdependencies among countries.	The new enterprise enables time and space independence; it redefines time and space for its employees and stakeholders. Work can be performed from a variety of locations, including employees' homes. The network becomes a repository for the time-independent communications. Networks of business clusters cooperate globally to achieve business objectives.	The global corporate network becomes the backbone of the enterprise and the key delivery system for supporting business operations. It is based on standards and enables both real-time communications and store-and-forward communications required when people are not able to reach each other at the same point in time. It also enables, as appropriate, access to the collective information resource from any location.

Economy	Organization	Technology
12. Discordance		
Massive social contradictions are arising. New, highly paid employment versus the inappropriate skills of laid-off workers. Gulfs are growing between haves and have-nots, knowers and know-nots, those with access to the internet and those without it.	Profound organizational contradictions are arising. For example, employees are told to "work hard, create the corporation's value, identify with the team and the enterprise," but they receive no share in the wealth they create.	There is the growing conflict of contrasting computing architectures, competing standards, legacy systems versus the new technology paradigm. In many companies the information systems function is out of alignment with the rest of the business.

Notes

1. John Huey, "Waking Up to the New Economy," *Fortune*, June 27, 1994.
2. Alan M. Webber, "What's So New About the New Economy?" *Harvard Business Review*, January-February 1994.
3. James Brian Quinn, *Intelligent Enterprise*, The Free Press, 1992.
4. Thomas A. Stewart, "Your Company's Most Valuable Asset: Intellectual Capital," *Fortune*, October 3, 1994.
5. Peter F. Drucker, *Post-Capitalist Society*, HarperCollins, New York, 1993.
6. Robert D. Harris, *The New Paradigm of Business: Emerging Strategies for Leadership and Organizational Change*, Pedigree Books, 1993.
7. Our thanks to Riel Miller for his insights on this section.
8. The first to introduce the notion of a business unit of one were Stan Davis and Bill Davidson in *2020 Vision: Transform Your Business Today to Succeed in Tomorrow's Economy*, Simon & Schuster, New York, 1991. Subsequently, Tom Peters has taken up the slogan in his "Tom Peters Seminars."
9. Stan Davis and Bill Davidson, *2020 Vision: Transform Your Business Today to Succeed in Tomorrow's Economy*, Simon & Schuster, New York, 1991. According to Davis and Davidson, the "real time organization" does not yet exist. For a good popularization of the concept refer to the above.
10. Peter G. W. Keen, *Competing in Time: Using Telecommunications for Competitive Advantage*, Ballinger Publishing Company, New York, 1988.
11. *EDI (Electronic Data Interchange)* is a term referring to the computer-to-computer exchange of data and documents. Information remains in computers and networks and need not be printed out. A popular example is the electronic billing between suppliers and customers. EDI uses data interchange standards enabling different kinds of systems to exchange information between them. The biggest obstacles to EDI are management issues, not technological. Companies have had difficulty understanding how to reshape their business practices and relationships with other companies enabled by the technology.
12. *Fortune*, June 27, 1994, p. 98.
13. *Harvard Business Review*, July-August 1994, p. 62.

14. Walter Wriston, *The Twilight of Sovereignty: How the Information Revolution Is Transforming Our World*, Charles Scribner's Sons, 1992.

15. Stephen P. Bradley, Jerry A. Hausman, and Richard L. Nolan. *Globalization, Technology and Competition*, Harvard Business School Press, 1993. A good discussion of new global organizational structures and their relationship to technology; Mary O'Hara-Devereaux and Robert Johansen, *Global Work—Bridging Distance, Culture and Time*, Jossey-Bass Publishers, 1994. A stimulating and thoughtful discussion, especially regarding "The Anytime, Anyplace Global Workspace."

16. *The Random House Dictionary of the English Language*, 2d ed., Unabridged. New York, 1987.

17. To paraphrase Peter Drucker in *The New Realities in Government and Politics/in Economics and Business/in Society and World View*, Harper & Row, New York, 1991.

T WAS A NIFTY set of cascading transformations: from effective individual, to high-performance team, to integrated organization, to extended enterprise, to internetworked business. Companies would do well today to use this model for applying the digital revolution to their operations.

Today enterprises attempt to achieve these changes under the rubric of "The Social Business," a good term that I wish I had coined. I find it helpful to think of social businesses in three dimensions: Social Media and New Business Models, The Social Workplace, and Social Marketing.

Social Media and New Business Models

Thanks to social media and the new tools for collaboration, companies are beginning to conceive, design, develop, and distribute products and services in profoundly new ways. The traditional notion you have to attract, develop, and retain the best and the brightest inside your corporate boundaries is becoming obsolete. With costs of collaboration falling precipitously, companies can increasingly source ideas, innovations, and uniquely qualified minds from a vast global pool of talent.

Arguably social media is becoming a new mode of production. In a new kind of collaboration—call it "social innovation" or "social production"—peers can create value, often outside the walls of traditional companies. This is beginning to change the deep structures and architecture of the firm, and how we orchestrate capability to innovate and create goods and services. The end result is that the corporation may be going through the biggest change in its short history.

While some fear that these heaving communities and new business models will reduce the proportion of our economy that is available for profitable activity, leading firms are proving otherwise. Networked models of innovation and value creation can bring the prepared manager rich new possibilities to unlock innovative potential in a wide range of resources that thrive inside and outside the firm.

There are seven new business models as described in *Wikinomics: How Mass Collaboration Changes Everything.*[1] They are the Peer Pioneers, Ideagoras, the Prosumers (adapted from *The Digital Economy*), the new power of the Commons, Open Platforms, the Global Plant Floor, and the Wiki (Social) Workplace.

* *The Peer Pioneers.* The people who brought you open-source software and Wikipedia, while demonstrating that thousands of dispersed volunteers can create fast, fluid, and innovative projects that outperform those of the largest and best-financed enterprises.
* *Ideagoras.* Emerging marketplaces for ideas, inventions, and uniquely qualified minds enable companies like Procter & Gamble (P&G) to tap global pools of highly skilled talent more than 10 times the size of its own workforce.
* *The Prosumers.* As described in *The Digital Economy*, they are customers who produce. This is a dynamic world of customer innovation, where a new generation of producer-consumers considers the "right to hack" its birthright.
* *The New Alexandrians.* Named after the Greek library of Alexandria, they exploit the new science of sharing—that can rapidly accelerate human health, turn the tide on environmental damage, advance human culture, develop breakthrough technologies, and even discover the universe—while helping companies grow wealth for their shareholders.
* *Platforms for Participation.* Smart companies that are opening up their products and technology infrastructures to create an open stage where large communities of partners can create value, and in many cases, create new businesses.
* *The Global Plant Floor.* It shows how even manufacturing intensive industries are giving rise to planetary ecosystems for designing and building physical goods, marking a new phase in the evolution of peer production.
* *The Wiki Workplace.* Organizations can go beyond e-mail to transform their internal operations through the next generation of collaboration suites—essentially industrial-strength social networking for the enterprise.

The Social Workplace

The "Wiki Workplace," aka the "Social Workplace" is worth centering out. New tools such as corporate social networks, wikis, blogs, ideation tools, telepresence, tags, collaborative filtering, next generation knowledge management, decision dashboards, and RSS (rich site summary) feeds are boosting the metabolism of high-performance workplaces. New integrated suites of tools have been shown to improve the pace of an organization, speed up innovation, reduce internal transaction costs, and make work more efficient—not to mention provide a platform that helps with employee satisfaction and retention. Replacing primitive technologies like e-mail, there is evidence that the Social Workplace can become the operating platform for the twenty-first century enterprise.

Big data and analytics play large roles in the Social Workplace. Enterprises are just beginning to understand the data management and analytics implications of these new platforms, such as how these new tools can change decision making. Innovative tools and disciplines are required to make better decisions by harnessing the wisdom of human capital both inside a company and in its business networks. The new discipline of Collaborative Decision Management (CDM) provides software and processes that engage the "wisdom of many" needed to help solve today's truly difficult problems. This requires, among other things, software that encourages full collaboration, enabling all participants to see the same information, at the same time, in the format that makes sense to them, and to "be on the same page" as their input contributes to the ultimate decision.

To date though, many attempts to introduce social networking for employee collaboration have not been aligned with business objectives and have consequently failed. Some deployments demonstrate measurable improvements in overall performance but unfortunately most do not. Companies begin adopting social software without a clear vision of what is expected and what is necessary to succeed. Most have not addressed the complex people, process, and organizational issues of change. Many initiatives have simply died from neglect.

With some enterprises demonstrating transformational wins, how to effectively leverage the social revolution in collaborative software is now percolating up to the C-level (CEO, COO, CFO) as a strategy issue in business and government. Some deployments demonstrate measurable improvements in overall performance, but there are many false starts.

The main lesson learned is that companies need a strategy for the Social Workplace. They need to think through critical questions such as: Where do you get started? What steps are necessary to ensure deployments will stay on track? How do you ensure that these tools do not devolve into a forum for pointless personal updates and internal company banter? How can user adoption be ensured? How can positive change be measured and managed?

Social Marketing

As *The Digital Economy* explained, the Industrial Age paradigm in marketing was founded on traditional media. The old paradigm was one of control, simple, and unidirectional: firms market to customers. They created products and defined their features and benefits, set prices, selected places to sell products and services, and promoted aggressively through advertising, public relations, direct mail, and other in-your-face programs.

This was possible because print and broadcast technology were centralized, one way, one to many, and controllable. Marketers extolled the need to focus on customers: be customer centric, create great experiences, promote, and defend your brand. *Public Relations* (PR) was the business of communicating and controlling "messages." Customer input was achieved through solicitation, as in surveys and focus groups. Customers were outside the boundaries of the firm and not really engaged in actual innovation, let alone in ongoing product and service co-creation.

The *Brand* was an image, badge, promise, trustmark, or "word in the mind." Industrial Age–marketing models emphasized pushing images, messages, and other marketing content. All this is best summed up in the famous *"4 Ps" of marketing*: having the right *product*, being in the right *place*, with the optimal *price*, and effective (one way) *promotion*.

Many forces are changing this situation. Most pundits emphasize how the technology paradigm is no longer broadcast; it is interactive. The new media are distributed, one-to-one, many-to-many, difficult to control, and more neutral. Rather than a passive audience, the recipients are users, actors, and collaborators. They provide a platform for new kinds of engagement, communities, and customer co-creation.

However, there are other forces. The impetus for a new marketing model is also stimulated by a new generation of consumers. These "Digital Natives" of the "Net Generation" have a different culture than their Baby Boomer parents. They behave differently as consumers and are more effective scrutinizers of product value.[2]

These new consumers want to be engaged. This generation is transforming marketing for many reasons, the foremost being their relationship to media. Unlike their parents in the United States, who passively absorbed 24 hours of TV per week, today's youngsters are growing up interacting. Rather than being flaccid recipients of mass consumer culture, the "Net Gen" spend time searching, reading, scrutinizing, authenticating, collaborating, and organizing. Over half of the TV they watch they time shift—eliminating the advertisements. The old saw "Half my ads work; I just don't know which half" needs revision. Half of advertising is ineffective because it's not even seen.

Because the new media radically drops collaboration costs, the twentieth century vertically integrated corporation is giving way to focused firms working within business webs. As costs continue to drop and capability continues to grow, it is now possible to view customers and consumers as part of a firm's business web rather than being outsiders. Further, consumers can co-innovate value and become "prosumers." Peers outside corporate boundaries, using the principles of *Wikinomics*, can collaborate, sometimes on an astronomical scale, to create goods and services—including everything from encyclopedias and software to motorcycles. Social networking is becoming social production. The Web is becoming a new mode of creation.

Further transparency as a new force in the economy is shifting power toward customers. This is far more than the obligation to disclose basic financial information. Customers are gaining unprecedented access to all sorts of information about corporate behavior, operations, and performance. Armed with new tools to find information about matters that affect their interests, stakeholders now scrutinize the firm as never before.

As a result, customer centricity is being turned upside down. Rather than simply listening to customers, companies must and can truly *engage* them. Customers become value creators themselves through new forms of collaboration. Companies can use the Web to build rich experiences that endure. The Brand, rather than being just an image, promise, or "word in the mind," can become, in part, an actual relationship between a company and its customers.

Marketing 2.0

There has been some progress in using social media for effective customer interaction, but the old paradigm in marketing remains intact. Today companies need to build wiki brands,[3] and integrated customer experience platforms. There are important breakthroughs in mobile and geospatial technologies that change many aspects of the customer experience. Social analytics can pay off big time. However, firms need to show that they have integrity and consider the interests of their customers to privacy. I don't think it's an exaggeration to say that this combination of forces completely changes marketing.

Product. Today they are mass customized, service-intensive, and infused with the knowledge and the individual tastes of customers. Companies must constantly innovate, and product life cycles have collapsed. Customers now participate in creating products and services through business ecosystems. Products are becoming experiences. The old Industrial Age approaches to product definition and product marketing are dying.

Place. Every business competes in two worlds: a physical world (*marketplace*) and a digital world of information (*marketspace*). B-webs enable firms to focus on the marketspace by creating not a great website but a great B-web and relationship capital. Hearts, not eyeballs, count. Within a decade, the majority of products and services in many developed countries will be sold in the marketspace.

Today geospaciality is delivering what we might call the *marketface*—the intersection between place and space. With tools like GPS (Global Positioning System), Google Glass, or Layar, consumers can explore the physical world including the marketplace with their digital devices. Ask your device where to find a store that sells Prada shoes within half a mile of your location. Look down a street through the video camera on your device and ask it to point to the ATMs (automated teller machines). View the hotel in front of you and ask for room rates and availability.

Price. Enabled by online marketplaces, dynamic markets and dynamic pricing are challenging vendor fixed pricing. In these early days of new price discovery mechanisms, we question even the concept of a "price" as customers gain access to mechanisms that allow them to state what they're willing to pay and for what.

> As John Svoikla pointed out in *Red Herring* years ago, price is a crude measure. It reflects in a single number all the attributes that customers may value in a product—time, effort, craftsmanship, innovation, fashion, status, rarity, long-term value, and so on. Customers will offer various prices for products depending on conditions specified. If you deliver this afternoon I'll pay *A*. If I can buy this quantity I'll pay *B*. I'll accept certain defects and pay *C*. If someone else will pay *D*, then I'll pay *E*. Buyers and sellers exchange more information and pricing becomes fluid. Markets, not firms, will "price" products and services. New companies like Exchange Solutions now create markets where price and money are only one of the variables in value.[4]

Promotion. Advertising, promotion, publicity, public relations, and most other aspects of corporate communications are archaic concepts. They exploited unidirectional, one-to-many, and one-size-fits-all media to communicate "messages" to faceless, powerless customers. The Net Generation's "N-Fluence" networks are powerful new forces that marketers must engage. Even traditional broadcast advertising can be transformed, as was the case of the Doritos Super Bowl ad contest—whereby Doritos engaged their customers in creating product ads (by my reckoning to great success).

The Web upends control. Friction breaks down among customers and between you and your customers. They often have access to near-perfect information about products, and power shifts toward them. Customers, no longer external entities, participate in your firm's B-web through multidirectional, one-to-one, and highly tailored communications media. They control the marketing mix, not you. They choose the medium and the message. Rather than receiving broadcast images, they do the casting. Rather than getting messages from earnest PR professionals, they create "public opinion" online with one another.

Relationship Capital. I remember all the prognostications that the Web pioneers—including Amazon, eBay, and Google—were doomed because their competition was only a click away. What the doomsayers didn't understand was the power of relationships. When firms use the Web to truly engage customers, the relationships can be strong and lasting. I'm tempted to describe this as a new form of wealth, say "relationship capital," which firms need to develop and manage like other forms of capital.

Go back to the pioneers; a simple, prosaic comparison between a physical bookstore and Amazon.com is instructive. A customer buys a book from an online bookstore. She can request all books on a certain topic or author. She can indicate authors she likes and find out what other authors are enjoyed by customers who share her views. She can request a bestseller list in a category or ask for a book's daily sales status. Some neighborhood boutique stores deliver a few such value-added services, but many such stores have disappeared. The costs are too great relative to the revenue received.

In the physical world, these costs hinder personalized service and relationship creation. But in the interactive world, you can get to know your customer, educate her, inform her proactively, and deliver value-added services on a personal basis. You can engage in ways that are simply not possible otherwise—you can have a relationship.

The astute online bookstore e-mails her when a new book fits her personal profile. The relationship is mutual:

◆ She creates value for the seller and for other participants by contributing her views.
◆ She establishes her personal profile (makes a relationship investment) that includes registering gifts she would like to receive.
◆ She complains about something and receives a personal note within an hour, telling her how the problem has been fixed.

She and the vendor develop a relationship.

Both invest by exchanging customized information and knowledge. The more she invests time and effort, the more personal the bookstore becomes. She builds loyalty to this company, not just because of the services it provides, but also because of the effort required to re-educate another company about her. For both buyer and seller, this networked relationship constitutes capital. Astute companies extract as much value—return—from the relationships as possible.

As I explained in *The Digital Economy*, the wealth embedded in customer relationships is now more important than the capital contained in land, plant, buildings, and even big bank accounts. Relationships are now assets. This relationship capital accumulates and provides a new foundation for marketing and sales revenue. A firm's ability to engage customers, suppliers, and other partners in mutually beneficial value exchanges determines its relationship capital.

The customer-facing aspects of relationship capital cause a profound rethinking of marketing. For the first time, a company can forge two-way, interactive, personalized relationships with all its customers on a mass scale.

While the virtue of deep relationships was always self-evident in theory, in reality it wasn't practical. But now the ubiquitous, cheap, and interactive Internet coupled with enormous low-cost databases enables producers to develop a meaningful direct relationship with each customer. Customers expect you to tailor each iteration of your product to their needs and wants. Sellers and buyers create an ongoing dialogue.

Notes

1. Don Tapscott and Anthony D. Williams. *Wikinomics: How Mass Collaboration Changes Everything.* New York: Penguin Group, 2007.
2. Don Tapscott, *Grown Up Digital*, New York: McGraw-Hill, 2008.
3. Wiki Brands by Sean Moffitt and Mike Dover. http://wiki-brands.com/the-book/.
4. Denise Shiffman *The Age of Engage: Reinventing Marketing for Today's Connected, Collaborative, and Hyperinteractive, Culture*, Hunt Street Press, 2008.

THE INTERNETWORKED BUSINESS

The end result of the application of information technology to knowledge work will be increased organizational productivity and effectiveness. However, as the emerging technologies are introduced we will see many more far-reaching changes. An enterprise's entire organizational structure may be modified. One early example is the company which [disintermediated]—discovering that regional offices were unnecessary once a communication system enabled the head office to communicate with the branches. New functions and activities are being created. Career paths are changing. Reporting structures are changing. The nature of knowledge work is being transformed. Even goals and objectives of organizations are changing, as companies find their office information and communication systems open up new markets. One example is the credit card company which entered into the mail order business.

Don Tapscott, 1981[1]

Rise Up, Couch Potatoes!

Social commentator Neil Postman's acerbic 1993 syndicated article in the *Toronto Globe & Mail* titled "Future Schlock: 500 Channels and Nothing On" charges that the whole purpose of the information highway and new technology is to get people watching more sitcoms, sports, news, and game shows. Warns Postman, "Information has now become a form of garbage. We don't know what to do with it, have no control over it, don't know how to get rid of it." In the cartoon accompanying the story there's a farmer giving directions to a family in a car looking for the information superhighway. Says he, "Keep going till you hit Brain Dead Avenue, turn right on Never Read Lane, go three blocks to Illiteracy Boulevard, then turn left at Couch Potato Road, which will take you right to it."

Well, Wait A Minute, Mr. Postman

Is this the new technology's promise to business and society? We shouldn't be too surprised that people extrapolate from their dominant experience with information technology—the television—and conclude that the information highway is only about watching more TV. In fact, one's view of the dominant applications tends to correlate with the corner of the converging technologies triangle from whence you come.

- ◆ *Communications.* Many telecommunications companies and professionals think the opportunity centers on video dial tone and video conferencing. Cable companies focus on interactive TV and home shopping.
- ◆ *Computing.* Computer companies usually focus on business applications, and many software companies emphasize education.
- ◆ *Content.* The main thrust is entertainment, games, and video (movies) on demand, whereas database publishers argue that the electronic delivery of information will be key.

Other people focus on the opportunities to transform human communications through e-mail, computer conferencing, "telepresence," newsgroups, and MUDs (Multi-User Dungeons). Some emphasize social applications such as health care or the cost-effective delivery of government programs. Artists and the creative community emphasize the transformation of the arts through the likes of interactive music and art. Researchers are excited about the opportunity to transform the way research and professional collaboration are conducted.

Who is right?

Everyone and no one. All the foregoing will be important. But there's more to the future than that. The new media are leading to a fundamental change in the nature of human work, the way business is conducted, the way wealth is created, and the very nature of commerce and business itself. We are moving from an economy based on the firm to one based on networks. Let's look at the evidence for such an apparently outrageous claim.

We can understand this promise by extrapolating from our limited experience to date with the new technologies. Their effect is clearly transformative. And reengineering business processes is simply not going to be enough by itself to create successful enterprises in the new economy.

Paradigm Shift discussed three cascading levels of transformation enabled by the new technology. The subsequent birth of two phenomena—interactive multimedia and the public information highway—requires that we expand this

Enabling Technology	The Promise	The Change

FIGURE 3.1 *Business Transformation through the New Media.* SOURCE: © New Paradigm Learning Corporation, 1996.

view to five levels. There is a new hierarchy of promise—the effective individual, the high-performance team, the integrated organization, the extended enterprise—all cascading upward to create a new model for the creation of wealth: the internetworked business. For each of these levels there is an enabling technology. And for each of these levels there is a fundamental change in the nature of work occurring. This is depicted in Fig. 3.1.

THE EFFECTIVE INDIVIDUAL

The nature of knowledge work changed little throughout the industrial economy. It is true that for some specialists, such as doctors or engineers, there has been considerable improvement in tools throughout the twentieth century.

But for most people—managers, teachers, salespeople, and others—the nature and tools of their work have remained fundamentally the same. The host-based mainframes and minicomputers of the 1960s and 1970s automated existing business processes with the goal of reducing costs. A by-product of those systems was the printout (or the truckload of printouts). Such reams of paper may have provided management information and other side benefits but did little to improve overall individual effectiveness or individual job fulfillment. (Even today companies rely strongly on printed output—as Hewlett-Packard's vice president of research and development Joel Birnbaum says, ink from the inkjet printer is the "embalming fluid of information.")

Personal computing brought the power of computing to the desktop. But the tools of the early PCs were limited, and the usability was typically better described as user-vicious rather than user-friendly. In addition to the fact that the interface was text-based, you were subjected to the bizarre world of MS-DOS and the mystifying "A>prompt." Or semantics like "Kill," "Abort," "Execute," "System Dead" (Gee, I must have killed something), or "Illegal Entry" (a felony). In the early 1990s, Windows did little to improve this situation. The only substitute for a Macintosh computer was human perseverance and lots of spare time. Many knowledge workers were unable to integrate the new tools fully into their work, and others simply gave up.

Multimedia is changing this picture dramatically. Personal computing is becoming multimedia computing as the rich and natural power of audio, image, and video become more integrated into compound digital documents and humanized styles of computing. By 1995, most personal computers were being sold with a CD-ROM drive, which can store vast amounts of information in various media. Most new computers are powerful enough to handle new forms of input beyond the keyboard, such as microphones, scanners, and cameras.

The research and experience with personal multimedia to date show striking improvements in task and learning efficiency. That is, individuals can do more in less time. For example, using multimedia-based learning tools you can typically learn something complex in about half the time, retaining the knowledge for two to three times longer. This is the reason behind the explosion of CD-ROM educational titles into the home and educational markets. As learning becomes more integrated with work, multimedia tools will become the basis of lifelong learning. For example, Fred Meyer Stores, a $3 billion retailer based in Portland, Oregon, has already made a huge investment in interactive multimedia workstations using touch screens to provide employees with company knowledge and training in job skills.

Efficiency (doing things better) results in time savings which can in turn be reinvested in personal effectiveness (doing better things).

For those in the knowledge business who fail to embrace personal multimedia, punishment can be swift. *Encyclopedia Britannica* published the best-selling encyclopedia in the world for over 200 years. According to Joe Esposito, North American president for *Britannica*, who is spearheading the shift of the company to interactive multimedia, "The company succeeded so long because it identified something in the culture that was not ephemeral. People want a summary of the world's knowledge."

But in one year, 1994, it slipped to number three. But it wasn't the company's traditional competitors, such as *Collier's* or *World Book,* that knocked *Encyclopedia Britannica* off its pedestal. No, it was competitors from left field—Microsoft and Grolier. The new encyclopedias came on a CD-ROM. *Britannica* came in a heavy, costly, multivolume set containing words and static illustrations. As CD authority 9-year-old Alex Tapscott commented, "It doesn't even talk to you." The volumes are fully updated once every decade, and annual yearbooks aren't integrated with the rest of the volumes. The new CD-based encyclopedias, on the other hand, fit in your pocket. They are updated every three months, and the cost is less than one tenth of the book version. Moreover, the CD-based encyclopedias have words integrated with color illustrations, as well as sound and video.

But that's not the whole story. It wasn't really the CD encyclopedias that caused grief for *Britannica* and other book companies, but more generally PCs. Responsible parents with means used to buy a set of encyclopedias to assist in their children's education. Today, they buy a PC. It is the multimedia computer, not just the CD encyclopedia, which led to the demise of the old encyclopedia market.

In response, *Britannica* has taken a bold and innovative new strategy. It has taken the next logical step and put its encyclopedia on the Net, charging a daily fee for those who "subscribe." The set of books has become a subscription service. The potential impact (and opportunities for the company) go far beyond the CD-ROM model. Rather than updating every decade or every year—or even every three months as the competition does—the encyclopedia on the Net can be updated hourly! Obviously the amount of information available is much greater than can be held on a CD. In fact, the amount of information is limitless. But most important, because it is on the Net, *Britannica* becomes something much greater than an encyclopedia. There are "hot links" enabling the "reader" to instantly link to related subjects contained on other Web servers around the world. It becomes a directory to all human knowledge that is electronically stored!

For example, a certain reference to an obscure work of Beethoven may be hotlinked to another computer where the actual recording of that work is contained. The same reference may also take you to a Beethoven discussion group or to other data banks with historical information or relevant data regarding other contemporary composers. This is more than the sort of serendipitous learning that used to be an offshoot of looking up a topic in the encyclopedia—this is rich, deep, informed, and authoritative understanding. For the user of this new knowledge tool, the resulting task efficiency can become learning effectiveness. You can not only better understand Beethoven and a particular composition and period of his life, you can also be led to new insights by experts you didn't know existed when you began the process and couldn't in the past have contacted even if you had known about them. By embracing interactive multimedia, *Britannica* has been transformed from a mere publisher of books to a company providing access gateways to all human knowledge.

Yes, there is a CD version of the product, but it is just a snapshot of the complete online encyclopedia. According to Esposito, *Britannica Online* is now their premium product. The basic problem, says Espositio, is that CD-based encyclopedias are not going to make money for their creators. Because CDs have become bundled with PCs sold by companies like Compaq and Apple, the perceived value of an encyclopedia has plummeted. This has helped kill the 20-volume book market. According to Esposito, "Encyclopedias went from the world of publishing to being a premium to sell hardware. This has had a devastating effect on the value of an encyclopedia," he says. "We didn't miss out on the electronic revolution. We were hit by companies that had bigger agendas. If the furniture business had decided to give away furniture to sell bookshelves, that would have had a similar impact." *Britannica* also concluded that the CD market would resemble the trade book business and be a very tight margin. As Esposito says, "The economics of any business is based on the distribution channel and the retail channel favors the retailer."

Moreover, its customer base is changing as well. Rather than selling simply to individuals, *Britannica* is now making licensing agreements with institutions. For example, in the 1995–1996 school year, over two dozen universities were signed up to *Britannica*. A few dollars of each student's tuition goes to unlimited access to *Britannica*.

Britannica is a case of a company that changed their product (from book to subscription service to digital directory); they changed their distribution channels and marketplace (from physical to digital); and they changed their customers (from families to everybody, including institutions). This kind of corporate action goes far beyond business process reengineering. It is transformation for the digital economy.

THE HIGH PERFORMANCE TEAM

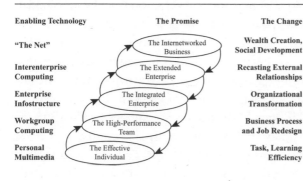

Enabling Technology	The Promise	The Change
"The Net"	The Internetworked Business	Wealth Creation, Social Development
Interenterprise Computing	The Extended Enterprise	Recasting External Relationships
Enterprise Infostructure	The Integrated Enterprise	Organizational Transformation
Workgroup Computing	The High-Performance Team	Business Process and Job Redesign
Personal Multimedia	The Effective Individual	Task, Learning Efficiency

For a decade, companies have been working to organize themselves into team-based structures. As Peter Drucker explained in 1988: "Traditional departments will serve as guardians of standards, as centers for training and the assignment of specialists; they won't be where the work gets done. That will happen largely in task-focused teams."[2] Some die-hard defenders of the old approaches have clung to hierarchy as "the most efficient, the hardiest and in fact the most natural structure ever devised for large organizations."[3] But most companies have chosen to work toward team-based approaches. Business teams can enable faster responses to changes in the business environment and increasing customer demands. Teams can help to bring the right people together from many disciplines and parts of the formal structure at the right time to battle competition at home and abroad. Business teams can help organizations to dramatically change their cost structure through the elimination of traditional bureaucracies or by avoiding the creation of new ones. Even reengineering theorists have been forced to recognize that teams are an effective way to execute horizontal business processes.

However, because of the power and capacity of the new media to open dramatically the channels for human communication and collaboration within an office, across geography, and across time, knowledge work is becoming collaborative work, taking place in teams on high-capacity networks. Such teams interoperate with one another, thereby enabling distributed team-based structures that are the antithesis of the old hierarchy.

In the traditional hierarchical organization with its multiple layers of management, accountability, and bureaucracy, information flow was vertical. Host-based islands of technology corresponded to the old structures. But through internetworked workgroup computing tools, the corporate pyramid can be replaced with internetworked teams. The focus shifts from the individual who was accountable to the manager, to teams that function as service units of servers and clients. Teams are both clients and servers for other teams who are both internal and external to the organization. As clients, they receive deliverables and other inputs from supply and support teams and add value to these for the purpose of serving others. This value-added output is consumed by other clients. The new model, first explained in *Paradigm Shift*, is derived from Michael Porter's concept of the value chain but extended into our notion of a *value network*. The provision of value is not something chained in a linear way but, rather, something that is generated through an ever-changing open network. It is a model designed to encourage flexibility, innovation, entrepreneurship, and responsiveness.

The "killer application" to launch workgroup computing was the software product known as Lotus Notes. Notes saved Lotus as a company after its previously popular spreadsheet application for the PC (1–2–3) had lost leadership—creating the value for IBM to justify its acquisition of Lotus. More important, Lotus Notes showed thousands of companies how technology could enable workgroups to form and be effective. The business team was a half-baked idea before Notes came on the scene. Notes has been applied to a wide range of problems from product planning to sales.

The team approach to designing automobiles used in Japan initially popularized the team concept. Each new car project was headed by a project leader with genuine power. The team consisted of people from all necessary disciplines—power-train engineering, body design, purchasing, marketing, finance, and manufacturing, among others. The project manager was more than a coordinator who traipsed from department to department making or collecting decisions; the project manager became a synergistic focal point, a leader for change. Better, faster, cheaper designs and quality Japanese automobiles devastated the competitive dominance of the American Big Three.[4]

However, the American manufacturers came to understand something beyond teams—the power of workgroup computing—and, as a result, are clawing back gains. Chrysler, for example, was the first to go beyond the Japanese approach to implement a technology-enabled team approach to design. Based on workgroup computing tools for designing an automobile, Chrysler created the "platform" approach—the Jeep platform, the large cars platform, the small-cars platform, and the minivan platform.

True, this approach embraced the Japanese system of empowered teams. For example, designers didn't have to go up the hierarchy to get key decisions made. But the Big Three went beyond the Japanese. In fact, when planning began for the Neon, Chrysler designers were simply given several criteria (mileage, cost, etc.) and told to create a vehicle. In the old world, Lee Iacocca was actually brought into design decisions. Because Iacocca liked cars with wire wheels and red seats, Chrysler vehicles always had these as options even though few buyers chose either of them. In the new world, designers were freed up to design without worrying about the boss's personal preferences.

Unlike the Japanese approach, the new basis of the platform is technology. Designers collaborate around workstations to engineer a new design concurrently rather than in a serial fashion. In simple terms, that means many functions can happen simultaneously; individuals aren't waiting for someone else to complete a task before they can add their input. Concurrency also enables better synergies across the various design teams. The technology is interactive multimedia—a computer-assisted design system that enables the creation of 3D designs.

Bottom line? Chrysler has reduced the time from concept to production of a new car from six years to two. The high-performance team structure has meant that they are beginning to take market share from Ford, GM—and the Japanese.

Ford Motor Co. responded with an integrated workgroup computing network linking engineers throughout the world to design the 1994 Mustang. Design chief Jack Telnack has dubbed the process "virtual colocation." Computer models take rough sketches and create realistic vehicles that can be viewed from all sides on the screen, as if the designer could actually walk around the vehicle.

Such activity goes beyond automotive design and manufacture. One of the most stunning examples is the Boeing 777, the first aircraft to be designed without physical models and blueprints. Although the story is told more fully in the next chapter, it's worth noting for now that the plane was designed by teams involving customers and suppliers on a workgroup design system. As with automobiles, the wide-body aircraft could be concurrently engineered, reducing the time dramatically. As the plane was being designed, it was tested in various performance situations and weather conditions. The final version had been "flown" through many tests before it was ever built. Again, the key is interactive multimedia that create workgroup computing tools for a whole new concept of the team.

THE INTEGRATED ORGANIZATION

Enabling Technology	The Promise	The Change
"The Net"	The Internetworked Business	Wealth Creation, Social Development
Interenterprise Computing	The Extended Enterprise	Recasting External Relationships
Enterprise Infostructure	The Integrated Enterprise	Organizational Transformation
Workgroup Computing	The High-Performance Team	Business Process and Job Redesign
Personal Multimedia	The Effective Individual	Task, Learning Efficiency

Business process reengineering (BPR) was useful because it highlighted the importance of designing business processes that are horizontal, that is, they cut across old organizational boundaries. However, in practice, most new processes are of a fairly low level; they are restricted to one department or perhaps span two or three departments. Because of the rise of standards and the feasibility of implementing something we call an *enterprise infostructure*, it is possible to think bigger—to create entire businesses that are integrated.

When asked to describe the main impediments to BPR, most change managers put legacy technologies high on the list. What's the problem here?

Enterprises of today are locked into the technology of the past; they are islands of technology that codify old business practices and old organizational structures. During the 1960s, 1970s, and 1980s, firms implemented computer systems when the technologies matured to the point at which cost-beneficial applications were feasible. Such systems tended to be planned within the context of the old structures—systems for production, marketing, financial management, or research. Technology was not used to change the nature of work but to automate old ways of working—in other words, paving the cow path, as described in *Paradigm Shift*. As a result, companies remain saddled with legacy systems that are an impediment to change, rather than a catalyst.

This problem is not trivial. Many of these legacy islands are old enough to vote and drink. They are not simply "code museums," as some pundits have said. They are operational systems upon which businesses run, so bringing the bulldozer into the data center is not a feasible strategy for fixing the problem. Worse, because they lack a vision for enterprise systems, firms perpetuate the legacy with each new investment. Every dollar spent makes the islands bigger rather than better for the future. Companies need to create the conditions that mean new investments contribute to a desired future rather than perpetuating the past.

The key to solving this problem is for business leaders to define a target information-technology architecture and devise a migration path to get there. Because of the maturity of technology standards, it is now possible to plan an entire enterprise architecture rather than just adding another room onto the farmhouse.

The new architecture is based on principles defined by businesspeople, not technologists. It includes models of the business, applications, information, and technology. The architecture also defines a number of standards for systems within the organization. As it becomes implemented, the enterprise has an *enterprise infostructure* upon which it can become an integrated enterprise.

The enterprise infostructure provides the backbone for the new enterprise. It enables an organization to move beyond the old hierarchy because layers of management are not required when information is instantly available electronically. An infostructure can enable the enterprise to function as a cohesive organization by providing corporate-wide information for decision making and new competitive enterprise applications that transcend autonomous business units or teams.

At the same time, such architectures provide a platform for entrepreneurial innovation in the use of computers by business teams while maintaining an enterprise capability. Business units can become viewed as networked clients and servers, working in a modular, flexible organizational structure. That's a very different concept from the stovepipes of the old hierarchy.

Chemical Bank and the Canadian Imperial Bank of Commerce are two of the first financial institutions to work toward an enterprise infostructure. Both have developed a principle that states that "all customers will be treated as a customer of the bank" rather than treating individuals as customers of one branch or users of one product or a single service. This principle will result in far-reaching changes to both banks—changes that will go beyond business process reengineering. This thinking involves new ways of interacting with customers, for example, through an information appliance; new virtual services that combine old ones; new customer-focused organizational structures; new roles for employees freed from the deadening bureaucracy of old redundant processes; and new ways of delivering new services to customers of the banks.

Union Pacific's nightmare was far-flung: knowing the location of each and every one of its 1,000 trains that were rolling on rail lines. Once the company built an enterprise architecture, it could transform business operations. Now, all cars are barcoded and can be tracked by using sensors that are in turn connected to fiber-optic cables along the tracks. What was once a boxcar business has been transformed into an information business that satisfies customers with an on-time delivery success rate that has doubled from 48% to 94%. "Fast info-movement is the only way to run a railroad," says Union Pacific CIO Joyce Wrenn.

One of the early examples of an integrated organization is Federal Express. Through pursuing and measuring quality, a strategy of innovation, and an enterprise infostructure, FedEx has become the dominant force in the package delivery business in North America with 50% of the market share. In this business, companies must strive to deliver packages correctly 100% of the time. If they fail once, they may never recover that customer. In 1986 FedEx changed its mission statement to reflect the importance of information technology in achieving quality. The mission includes the words: "Positive control of each package will be maintained by utilizing real-time electronic tracking and tracing systems." A service quality index was developed to define quality and an integrated computing architecture enabled its measurement. Such integrated systems placed FedEx on the ground floor of tracking parcels in real time. Detailed information regarding minute-by-minute parcel movements also enabled the proactive improvement of quality—service to the customer. Federal Express was able to build an integrated enterprise in which people work together across the organization with the tools to deliver customer service and quality. This is a far cry from reengineering business processes. Punishment is swift for those who fail to transform themselves through the new technology. While Federal Express revenue soared, the U.S. Postal Service was unable to break free from the old paradigm. The ultimate irony? From time to time the post office has been forced to subcontract overnight delivery to FedEx.

"The command-and-control organization that first emerged in the 1870s might be compared to an organism held together by its shell," says Peter Drucker. "The corporation that is now emerging is being designed around a skeleton: *information*, both the corporation's new integrating system and its articulation. Our traditional mindset—even if we use sophisticated mathematical techniques and impenetrable sociological jargon—has always somehow perceived business as buying cheap and selling dear. The new approach defines a business as the organization that adds value and creates wealth."[5]

THE EXTENDED ENTERPRISE

Enabling Technology	The Promise	The Change
"The Net"	The Internetworked Business	Wealth Creation, Social Development
Interenterprise Computing	The Extended Enterprise	Recasting External Relationships
Enterprise Infostructure	The Integrated Enterprise	Organizational Transformation
Workgroup Computing	The High-Performance Team	Business Process and Job Redesign
Personal Multimedia	The Effective Individual	Task, Learning Efficiency

Walmart and Target stores have transformed their businesses and become successful retailers through interenterprise computing—again by linking their computer systems with their most important suppliers. Interenterprise computing enables suppliers to forecast demand for their products as well as to help the retailers strengthen their supply networks, reduce inventory, and improve product availability on the shelves. Today when you buy a jacket at Walmart, a stream of computer bits is sent across the value network all the way to the factory that mills the cloth, putting in motion a series of events that results in the jacket rack being replenished. The new jacket, however, did not go into a central warehouse. It was sent directly to the store from the manufacturer, just as 97% of all Walmart's goods never pass through a warehouse. This enables what Sears new CIO Joe Smilowsky calls "the strategic efficiencies that have transformed the nature of retailing."

Just as the walls within organizations are falling, so the walls among organizations are falling too. The result is what's been called the *virtual corporation*. Rather than staff up, you partner. You understand your core competencies and unite with companies having other talents. You forge a series of ever-changing alliances to achieve competitive success. Most advocates say that information technology is the most important enabler of such virtual structures. But how?

The fact is that interenterprise computing is already beginning to blur lines among organizations, enabling new kinds of business relationships. Networks are extending the reach of companies in ways previously unimagined, transforming the nature of business interactions and raising far-reaching issues of business strategy.

For years, business schools and boardrooms accepted as conventional wisdom the notion of the "value chain." According to widely accepted management theory by leaders such as Michael Porter, organizations took inputs from suppliers and added value to create outputs that were in turn consumed by others. If you could manage suppliers and their costs, understand your company's core competencies, and effectively discern the requirements of customers, you could create products and services that could be successfully marketed. You could find your unique place to add value in the chain (see Figure 3.2). The value chain was also applicable to the relationships *within* organizations.

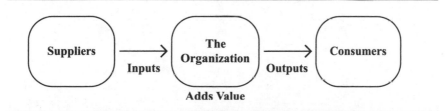

FIGURE 3.2 *The Value Chain (Information Flow Physical: Value Added).*

As mentioned earlier, during this era, organizations exchanged funds, information, and knowledge by physical means—through paper documents such as letters, reports, invoices, computer printouts, blueprints, proposals, checks, face-to-face meetings, and telephone calls. Consistent with this, computer systems were internal to each enterprise.

The new technology forces a rethinking of the value chain. Such transactions and communications are becoming digital on networks. Systems are extending outside an organization to customers, suppliers, other partners, and even competitors. The physical exchanges become virtual—they consist of charged particles from microprocessors on a network. Business transactions become bit streams on a global network of networks.

The result of this shift from physical to virtual does not simply reduce costs, speed up communications, or provide players with more timely information, although that's all true. Rather, when information exchange becomes electronic, a world of subtle and not so subtle changes in the nature of human and organizational communication occurs—changes that enable new kinds of relationships between organizations and people. The *value chain* becomes a *value network*, as new relationships become possible (see Figure 3.3). And rather than *value-added*, the technology enables the organization to create new institutional structures that can be *value-generative*. The provision of value is not something chained in a linear way but, rather, something that is generated through an ever-changing open network. It is a model designed to encourage flexibility, innovation, entrepreneurship, and responsiveness. The digital infrastructure sets the foundation for the creation of fundamentally new and different kinds of value.

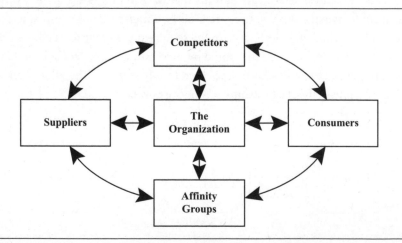

FIGURE 3.3 *The Digital Value Network (Information Flow Digital: Value Generated).*

The Boeing 777 was designed as a digital aircraft because it was more than a digital set of drawings. The 777 can fly in digital space, where its velocity, wind resistance, handling characteristics, and responsiveness can be tested. Because it was digital, customers, such as the airlines, could be effectively brought into the network to contribute to the design, helping to ensure that their requirements and innovative ideas were incorporated and that the digital plane worked.

Furthermore, most of the pieces of the plane were manufactured by suppliers to Boeing—hundreds of them—who were also brought onto the network. Because designs, specifications, and other information are bits rather than atoms, the cluster of companies was able to work together differently. By using a network, Boeing created an extended enterprise that ensured that designs met customer requirements and that the plane was manufacturable, largely by business partners.

Consortia and partnerships based on interenterprise computing are flourishing. The Insurance Value Added Network Services (IVANS) links a group of insurance companies with thousands of agents. In the auto-parts industry, used parts suppliers cluster around AUTONETWORK to exchange information and make their industry competitive against new parts manufacturers who have united to connect to retailers through MEMA/Transnet, a group initiated by the Motor Equipment Manufacturers Association. A number of electronics companies in Silicon Valley, California, are creating a virtual partnership called Commerce Net. Companies will be able to communicate, access product information, and exchange software and even consulting services over the network. In Toronto, a company called the Virtual Corporation provides a network and other services to enable independent consultants and software developers to partner on projects.

Interenterprise computing is causing new economic dynamics in many ways, as follows:

◆ *Accessibility of partners.* Information not previously available can become available when digitized, in turn enabling new kinds of access between partners. For example, computer databases of government information, ranging from land and geographic data to road safety information, provide various stakeholders with access to information that manual searches or manual communications may never be able to satisfactorily address. This enables governments to create new partnerships in providing such information as well as classes of information users.

Similarly, companies can conduct new product launches over a global videoconferencing network. Car rental customers are able to enter their destination on an airport computer and get a printout of a customized map. Computer-driven voice response systems grant customers access to information that previously was too expensive to provide. Hotel guests review their accounts on their in-room television. Vacationers learn about opportunities for holidays through an interactive screen that shows actual video footage about alternatives.

- *New interdependencies.* Early systems such as the American Airlines SABRE reservation system and the American Hospital Supply customer order system, have become legends in how to use technology to create mutually beneficial interdependencies. In each case the company provided customers with direct access to computer systems in order to strengthen relationships, thus locking in the customer.

  However, such systems were really the tip of the iceberg. Today insurance agents link electronically with insurers. Auto dealerships configure car orders on a screen, which in turn are transmitted to the manufacturer. Various companies cooperate to create frequent flyer, renter, buyer, user, and guest points. In each case, the technology is enabling new beneficial interdependencies.

- *Interorganizational metabolism.* The port of Seattle took business away from the port of Vancouver when Seattle began using electronic data interchange (EDI) to speed up the process of a ship clearing the harbor. The metabolism between a shipping company and the Seattle port was much faster because the voluminous information exchange activity between the two was electronic rather than through manual documents, forms, checks, and meetings. Vancouver has now caught up by implementing a similar system.

- *Cooperative competitiveness.* Sounds like an oxymoron, but every time you use a banking machine you are helping banks compete through cooperation. The banking networks, built through cooperation among competitors, currently handle billions of interbank transactions per month, enabling banks to provide new services and compete effectively with domestic and international rivals. Today, competing hotel chains have built a common reservation network. And competing research laboratories cooperate in the United States to implement a massive research network.

- *Interorganization value creation.* Interenterprise computing enables new kinds of partnerships to create new products and services. Later in the chapter we'll look at how a housing consortium has attacked the Japanese marketplace.

All this is being done by using the information garden paths of today. But consider what kinds of opportunities will exist as the network becomes a highway and its capacity—bandwidth—increases a hundred or a thousand times.

The value *chain* is becoming a digitally based value *network* for enterprises to reach out through technology to their customers, suppliers, affinity groups, and even competitors. Virtual corporations on the internet are competing in a digital economy.

Punishment is swift for the laggards. Walmart and Target transformed themselves for success. Sears—the greatest retail empire of all time—stuck with the old model and fell behind. The half-vacant Sears Tower is a monument to tradition. But Sears learned and is staging a comeback that threatens to leapfrog its new competitors. More on that later.

The Internetworked Business

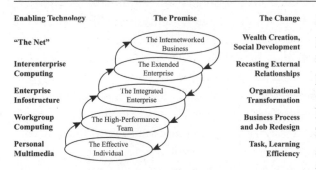

Enabling Technology	The Promise	The Change
"The Net"	The Internetworked Business	Wealth Creation, Social Development
Interenterprise Computing	The Extended Enterprise	Recasting External Relationships
Enterprise Infostructure	The Integrated Enterprise	Organizational Transformation
Workgroup Computing	The High-Performance Team	Business Process and Job Redesign
Personal Multimedia	The Effective Individual	Task, Learning Efficiency

Beyond the virtual corporation, commerce must move on to the public internet. For example, there's a huge housing market in Tokyo where the average age of a construction worker is 55 and there are no raw materials available. How could an extended enterprise exploit this opportunity? Create a cluster of companies on the internet. The cluster could include architects, forest products firms, appliance manufacturers, and various building trades such as plumbing and heating, carpentry and masonry, roofing and flooring, and all the other elves and shoemakers required to complete a family dwelling.

In the first step by an internetworked building group, the prospective home-owner and the architect create a house on a computer workstation. Working with aspects from several basic designs, the client chooses a floor plan, decides on the number of bedrooms and bathrooms, then picks the other main features such as a fireplace or rear deck. To test the "feel" of what's being created, they go for a walk together through the virtual house on the screen. The client can see how the dining room looks from various locations and can make changes to the ceiling height. Don't like the way the kitchen table is visible from the front hall? Alter the placement of the door opening. As the design is finalized, the cost of the end product is calculated in real time. The completed drawings are then transmitted over the Net to the other partners in the cluster who go into action and fabricate the structure in various locations where the expertise and materials exist. Three weeks later, the house is in a shipping container on its way to Tokyo for final assembly on site. Without the partnership, there would be no timely way to respond to this opportunity. And without the Net, it would take months rather than weeks to create the house. The technology enables this new interenterprise.

Far-fetched? Plans are underway to do exactly that. Such clusters are currently being organized in San Francisco and Calgary. The evidence is mounting that this type of technology-based arrangement is not a fad but, rather, a part of a fundamental change in the way we do business and work.

The final dimension of transformation is a new kind of internetworked enterprise that makes the virtual corporation look like child's play. We are on the threshold of a new digital economy in which the microprocessor and public networks on the Internet model enable fundamentally new kinds of institutional structures and relationships. The firm as we know it is breaking up. What's happening instead is this: effective individuals, working on high-performance team structures; becoming integrated organizational networks of clients and servers; which reach out to customers, suppliers, affinity groups, and even competitors; which move onto the public Net, changing the way products and services are created, marketed, and distributed. In economic terms, this means new models of wealth creation. In social terms, it means new systems for sustaining social development and improving quality of life.

As Alliance collaborator Carl Thompson puts it, "I think the ability to integrate internal and external information services with the Net represents the next major wave of change." He argues that the promise of widespread use of EDI, for example, will finally be realized through the simplified and more ubiquitous services on the Net. Transforming internal information and transaction-based systems to integrate with the Net represents a major opportunity for many organizations to transform themselves and their relationships with outside entities.

Buckle up—look where this is going.

Sung Park, a young Korean and a former IBM software engineer, was on a short business trip to Hong Kong. There he visited a suit shop and was asked if he would like to purchase a custom-made suit. When he explained that he was leaving that evening, the shop owner explained that an imminent departure was no problem—the suit could be ready before his flight. It was. He picked it up at 6 p.m.

Custom-made suits in short order are no surprise in Hong Kong, but opposite thinking has long applied in the United States. Clothing manufacturers create tons of goods that are shipped to warehouses, then transported on to retailers. Some of these goods are sold to customers, but leftovers remain that are returned to the warehouses and eventually dumped into discount markets, many in the Third World, for a fraction of their cost. In all, 75% of the costs in the clothing industry are in distribution, not manufacture.

In response, Park established Custom Clothing Technology. This tiny firm, now with big revenues, is an internetworked business that uses the internet to bring various players in the clothing business together to create mass customized goods. To begin, he tackled the hardest problem in clothing fit: women's jeans. (Only 27% of women who purchase jeans are happy with the fit.) Custom Clothing entered into a deal with Levi Strauss to provide the infostructure to electronically link retailers, cutters, stitchers, and washers together to manufacture Levi's jeans. A woman who wants to buy jeans can now go into a store and be measured by a clerk guided by touch screen software that requires no special computing skills (or she can use an information appliance herself either in the store or from home—with instructions on how to take the measurements). Those measurements are transmitted over the Net, using Lotus Notes, to the various other companies who will be involved in the creation of the jeans.[6] The jeans arrive at the store or are sent by Federal Express to the home within three weeks (soon to be within days). The customer happily pays $10 more for the jeans because there is a guaranteed perfect fit. There is also no inventory. No wasted distribution costs. Higher profit. Eventually, no retail store is required. This is mass customization on the Net.

The service, called Levi's Personal Pair Jeans, began in Cincinnati, Ohio, where sales jumped 300% over the previous year through use of this method. The service is being rolled out at 30 Original Levi's Stores throughout 1995. "Sung has built the quintessential virtual, mass customization clothing company," says Custom Clothing Technology board member John Landry. "The company raises big questions about the future of manufacturing and retail. This is the electronic store. Soon, you'll go to the Levi's Home Page on the Internet and get a clip on how to measure yourself. Ordering will be online. And the software creates a workflow process to create a pair of jeans." In an industry in which $25 billion worth of manufactured clothing remains unsold or sells only after deep discounts, preselling is revolutionary.

The history of the digital economy will note November 1994 as a watershed month and the painful experiences of Intel Corporation as seminal. At the end of October 1994 things were going well at Intel. The Pentium chip—Intel's strategic product—was getting rave reviews and selling like the proverbial hotcakes. Company revenues and profits were strong. Then, on October 30, Professor Thomas Nicely of Lynchburg College posted a message on the Internet reporting a flaw in the chip. Within days this message had been circulated in cyberspace to thousands of people, and an angry mob rivaling the largest protest demonstrations of the 1960s had formed. Intel had a crisis on its hands—more dangerous than any in its history.

Intel was slow to understand the dynamic of electronic markets, downplaying the problem using classic, one-way PR statements. CEO Andy Grove's November 27 statement on the Net caused the roar to increase, as did a statement on December 8 by Intel's software lab technology director Richard Wirt. On December 12, IBM, a minor player in the sale of Pentiums and a competitor to Intel with its PowerPC chip, announced on the Net and to the media that it was halting shipments of Pentium-based IBM PCs. A Web server with Pentium jokes appeared. The brouhaha spread to the mainline print and broadcast media, and by December 20, Intel conceded its error and agreed to a general recall of the Pentium chip.

The Pentium story marks a new economy watershed. Net discussions continue months after the events. James Barr and Theodore Barr describe the new realities of cyberspace marketing in which information is shared and sifted by thousands of knowledgeable people. They note that time is collapsed, facts are quickly checked, loss of credibility can be instantaneous, second chances are rare and harder to effect, grandstand plays had better be perfect, and the playing of one audience against another is far easier to detect.[7]

Digital markets are different from physical markets in a number of ways. Because physical constraints are eliminated, comparison shopping has no boundaries. Companies with truly different products or better price performance will more quickly rise to the surface and those without will fail. For example, what happens when a number of companies with the slogan "We will not be undersold" enter a digital market? Alliance contributor Steve Caswell says: "It's like the four service stations at an intersection launching a price war. Either they put themselves under or they decide [on] some rules regarding how to deal with each other." In digital markets, all companies are at the same intersection.

Every industry will be unrecognizable in a decade. Musicians who can't get their creations recorded by a record company can already place their song, or video, or score, or musical on the Net through the Internet Underground Music Association (IUMA). As a "listener" you simply download the file onto a CD or digital tape and play it on your information appliance or home stereo. Any website with music on it becomes a directory for other sites, effectively creating a new world of music accessible by anyone on the Net. Even a star like Madonna already has selections on the Net. Given that there will be a billion people on the Net by the end of the decade, why would anyone market any other way? What is the role of the retail outlet in such a world?

The IUMA is an example of a entire industry in which production, distribution, marketing, and sales are all moving from the physical world of bricks and mortar, big company organizational charts, and high-paid executives to an electronic world on the internet. In doing so they will, in the words of musician Bob Dylan, shake your windows and rattle your walls.

NOTES

1. Don Tapscott, *Office Automation: A User-Driven Method*, Plenum Publishing, New York, 1981.
2. Peter Drucker, "The New Organization," *Harvard Business Review*, January-February 1988. For a more complete presentation of Drucker's views, see Peter Drucker, *The New Realities*, Harper & Row, New York, 1989.
3. Elliott Jacques, "In Praise of Hierarchy," *Harvard Business Review*, January-February 1990.
4. James P. Womack, Daniel T. Jones, and Daniel Roos, *The Machine That Changed the World*, Rawson Associates, New York, 1990.
5. *Harvard Business Review*, January-February 1995, p. 62.
6. Lotus Notes is seen by most as a workgroup collaboration tool, but hundreds of companies like CCTC are using it as a delivery system.
7. James Barr and Theodore Barr, "The Pentium Bug War Ends PR As We Know It," © Omegacom Inc. 1994. See Omegacom's Home Page for a discussion of the topic.

20th Anniversary Edition Commentary on Chapter 4:
The New Technology: Say You Want a Revolution

THE INTERNET HAS developed through several periods: The first (early and mid–1990s) was the creation of the website, where the Internet was a platform for the presentation of content. As foreshadowed in *The Digital Economy*, by the late 1990s it had become a transactional platform for e-commerce. Then 2002 brought the crash of the dot-coms and "the dark period"—where business executives, investors, and the media (and readers of books) wanted nothing to do with the Internet. All this changed around 2005 with the rise of the mobile Internet, brought to us first by companies such as Qualcomm and BlackBerry and then by Apple and later Samsung, as hundreds of millions of new people joined the Web. Toward the end of the decade, social media took the world by storm, as the warm-up acts like MySpace were eclipsed by Facebook, Twitter, and other platforms.

Today there are six big themes of immediate relevance to most organizations:

1. *The Social Web.* These are websites and software that enable people to connect and interact. Facebook alone is approaching 2 billion members. The flipside of exploding social media is the exploding loss of privacy, as people disclose intimate details of their lives for the entire world to see.
2. *The Mobile Web.* The time spent on mobile devices such as smartphones and tablets continues to grow. The rate of growth of Internet users and smartphone users is growing less quickly than in previous years, but in 2014 mobile data traffic exploded by 81% with accelerating growth, driven in part by video. Laptop activities are moving to tablets, smartphones, and other mobile devices like watches.
3. *Geospaciality.* In the old Web we surfed websites. In the new Web, we surf physical reality with sound, video, graphics, or GPS provided by technology such as Google Glass. Augmented reality is usually done in real time, with the information about an object or place appearing on the screen while the user is there.

4. *The Internet of Things.* Soon mobile computing devices, broadband access, wireless networks, and computing power embedded in everything such as toasters, lightbulbs, bicycles, and factory tools will converge into a vast global network that will fuel exponential change in business model innovation.

5. *The Cloud.* The old Web was a platform for presentation of content, with a focus on websites, eyeballs, clicks, stickiness, and the like. Think of today's Internet as a computational platform—a global computer. Every time you do something—upload a photo, remix some music, or comment in a discussion—you are programming this computer. Human activity is now building a machine and creating value on this massive platform of computing power or data storage. Companies can move their internal information technology (IT) capabilities onto the Cloud and in doing so move from fixed to variable and much lower costs, better integration, instant access to more capability and, the best part—the world becomes your software development department. IT companies, rather than selling software, are changing to offer Software as a Service (SaaS), so users can log into a service or program remotely without having to install an application on their own computer. Amazon, Google, and Oracle Cloud are examples.

6. *Big Data and Analytics.* The massive amounts of data that once overwhelmed traditional data-processing applications have become a new asset. This data is produced by almost every facet of society, including billions of devices and sensors, hugely popular social media, and business processes such as retail and wholesale sales. An example would be Walmart analyzing all items purchased during a month to determine the buying patterns of its shoppers. The real-time costing of airplane tickets today (to achieve full flights) will become the real-time costing of bananas tomorrow, as computers ensure that demand and supply are perfectly tuned. A company will blend its proprietary data with public data from the Internet and social media. Huge data sets are also common in fields such as meteorology and genomics. Big Data is so important, and changing so fast, it's worth a more in-depth review.

Big Data and Analytics, in Depth

The practice of analytics is rapidly evolving. It used to be select analysts manipulated opaque spreadsheets based on data whose accuracy and timeliness were suspect. It has now become a broader ecosystem, where all team members (including participants from beyond the organization's walls) actively participate in collecting and acting upon information.

Today's volatile business environment rewards those who can innovate the most quickly, and understand and respond to changing consumer sentiment. The staggering amount of data being created is a daunting challenge. Research suggests that 2.7 zettabytes (the amount of data in 50 million Libraries of Congress) of corporate information was created in 2012, an increase of more than 48% from 2011. One thousand zettabytes is a yottabyte, which is the estimated amount of data U.S. government agencies have gathered on people inside and outside the country. This is the equivalent of 250 trillion DVDs. Dramatic reductions in storage costs means for the first time that the archiving of data is now more expensive than just leaving it where it is.

New analytics tools and capabilities are appearing in the marketplace. Leading companies and technology providers are rethinking the fundamental model of analytics, and the contours of a new paradigm are emerging. The new generation of analytics goes beyond Big Data and the traditional narrow approach of analytics that was restricted to analyzing customer and financial data collected from their interactions on social media. Today companies are embracing the social revolution, using real-time technologies to unlock deep insights about customers and others, and to enable better-informed decisions and richer collaboration in real time.

To take advantage of this data, firms need to deploy collective intelligence and build on information from many sources, far broader than simply historical sales and financial information. There are five main characteristics of the new analytics:

1. *Data is collected socially.* Innovative companies collect, organize, and exploit structured and unstructured data from as many sources as possible from inside and outside the company. The most interesting data is sourced from myriad social interactions of customers and prospects.
2. *Data is analyzed socially.* Rather than specialists accessing information as individuals, analytical tools penetrate through an enterprise and data is analyzed in a collaborative fashion. As information becomes more trusted, transparent, and dispersed, it enables the true collective intelligence of enterprises and their business ecosystems. With more voices comes more creative and holistic feedback. This builds a broader picture that results in better-informed decisions.
3. *Data and tools become mobile.* The personal computer used to be the main device to support analytics, but as technology improves and corporate information becomes more democratic, it is being replaced with apps running on powerful mobile devices such as smartphones and tablets equipped with intuitive apps and data-collecting capabilities, including video.

4. ***Data is more visual.*** Powerful new applications, as well as enterprise soft-ware suites, illustrate data through graphs, visuals, and interactive simula-tions. Such tools explain the data more fully, and enable better collaborative analysis and more innovative thinking, especially for "visual thinkers."

5. ***Data is more current, broadly available, and actionable.*** Just as work is con-ducted in real time, data can be collected, analyzed, and distributed faster than ever before—in real time. The implication of this phenomenon is that data is more accurate and complete, and more useful to support innovative real-time decision making and predictive modeling. When your best cus-tomers enter your virtual or physical outlet, they will receive the red carpet treatment.

Used properly, the new analytics empower individual workers and other contributors, and drive value in all areas of the organization. To extract maxi-mum benefits, companies need to plan carefully, invest in the right infrastruc-ture, and constantly iterate and innovate in a collaborative manner. At the same time, wider access to data increases risk, and risk management policy needs to be codified and enforced, and as a result of the financial crisis of 2008 its under-lying modeling assumptions must be better understood.

You Say You Want (Another) Revolution: Technology in the Next 20 Years?

It wouldn't be wise for me to predict the next 20 years because advances in technology will come at an ever-increasing pace. The digital revolution has moved on to "the second half of the chessboard," a clever phrase coined by the American inventor and author Ray Kurzweil. He tells an old fable of a gullible king being so delighted with the game of chess that he offered the game's inventor any reward he desired. The inventor asked for rice.

"I would like one grain of rice on the first square of the chessboard, two grains of rice on the second square, four grains of rice on the third square, and so on, all the way to the last square," he said. Thinking this would add up to a couple of bags of rice, the king happily agreed.

He was misguided. While small at the outset, the amount of rice escalates to more than 2 billion grains halfway through the chessboard. The final square would require 9 billion billion grains of rice—enough to cover all of Earth.

After decades of doubling and redoubling, we're achieving gargantuan leaps in all facets of information technologies, such as processing power, stor-age capacity, and bandwidth. Examples are everywhere, from Intel's computer chips to low-cost consumer electronics. The first microprocessor Intel built in 1971 contained 2,300 transistors. About every 18 months since then a new chip was developed with double the number of transistors. Now chips have billions. Massive parallelism of cheap processors is now driving everything from Google to IBM's Watson.

Computer chips are poised to take another huge leap in power with quantum computing. In place of today's transistors in silicon-based conventional computers, tomorrow's computing devices will use quantum bits, or qubits. Instead of storing information as 0s or 1s, as today's computers do, a quantum computer's qubits can be either a 0 or a 1 or both at the same time. A quantum computer can process a vast number of calculations simultaneously. The result will be computing devices many millions of times more powerful than today's supercomputers. With enough data, a quantum computer would have the processing muscle to accurately predict the weather around the world for a two-week period in real time.

Microsoft established a significant and well-funded quantum computing research effort in 2006, and since then other companies such as IBM and Northrop Grumman have begun their own programs. So has the U.S. government.

IBM is also exploring other technologies using a neurosynaptic computing chip. The chip is designed to function as a human brain. It is also looking at silicon photonics, which would use particles of light to replace the electrons on a conventional chip.

Data storage is another area where costs continue to plunge at an ever-quickening rate. Look to a future where multi-terabyte USB flash drives will sell for a dollar or two, and the cost of storing data will be so low that we won't bother to figure out what to keep and what to erase. We'll just keep it all. And new storage devices using tungsten will be virtually indestructible.

This has big implications when everything you do can be constantly monitored. All of the data collected about your targeted advertisements will move from being "dumb" to "smart" and from ads to orders. Let's say you surf the Internet looking for a new stereo and you order one online. Today's dumb technology will continue to inundate you with stereo advertisements for weeks. Close, but they are missing the mark. In the future, they won't. For example, say you are driving on Friday afternoon toward your cabin. The local general store will confirm by text that your standing order of milk, bacon, eggs, hamburger, and chicken will be ready for pickup. The size of the order will be increased as a result of the weight (of the passengers) in the back seat. Further, the Internet will know that you have forgotten to bring your bathing suit and that it is not in the vehicle and that the forecast is for hot weather. So the Internet will suggest that the general store add a bathing suit to your purchase. Knowing (from their smartphones) who is in the car may change the order because a passenger is glucose-intolerant. This, of course, is all happening as the Internet turns off your air conditioning at home and sets your alarm system.

When you walk down a store aisle, the company's inventory, your tastes, and psychological profile (including impulsiveness) may reduce the price for items that you have previously glanced at five times (camera and computers will track your eye movements) but you have been ambivalent about purchasing. The instant price reduction convinces you that it is time to put the item in your cart. Trying to outfox the store's computer and get discounts for items will be part of the shopping experience.

Not sure whether the store promised you an extended warranty for your dishwasher at no extra charge? Just call up the conversation you had with the salesperson when you bought the dishwasher. You know you recorded the whole transaction with your Google Glass, because you record everything you do throughout the day. However, revisiting your history over a disagreement with your spouse may be a high-risk undertaking.

This nonstop monitoring won't just happen in stores. When you go out in public, what you are watching, the mood you are in, the speed at which you are walking, and many other variables will be tracked and available for analysis. The early stages of such a world are already in place. In New York City, the police department has installed a new Domain Awareness System (DAS) developed by Microsoft. It links 3,500 cameras, 2,600 radiation detectors, and dozens of license plate readers in fixed locations and mounted on cars. When a 911 call comes in about a suspicious package, the police can immediately review past footage from cameras in the area to see who put the package there. If the police enter a car's license plate number, the system is able to tell police everywhere the car has been during the last four weeks.

The Brookings Institution released a paper titled "Recording Everything: Digital Storage as an Enabler of Authoritarian Governments." It is now feasible to record everything that is said and done by a country's citizens. It costs pennies to store the audio from a year's worth of a person's phone calls.

Many amazing "advances" are becoming technologically possible. Some of these advances may delight us, and some we may dread.

Digital Currencies

There is lots of controversy but I've concluded that few new digital technologies are as important as digital currencies such as Bitcoin. They have quickly gone from fringe curiosity to front-page news. Investor and Web browser pioneer Marc Andreessen told the *Washington Post* that "when we're sitting here in 20 years, we'll be talking about Bitcoin the way we talk about the Internet today. We just need time for it to play out."

Digital currency advocates point to the rapid adoption of Bitcoin, now accepted by thousands of businesses including Virgin Galactic, Tesla, WordPress, and Overstock, as clear evidence of a changing tide. Critics paint them as a speculative toy with little or no intrinsic value. To them, digital currencies are a tool used by cyber-criminals to launder money and avoid taxes. Lack of oversight and regulation—and the prevalence of fraud and hacking—make digital currencies volatile, opaque, and untrustworthy.

But digital currencies offer tremendous ease of use—no permanent address, bank account, or identification is needed. Simply owning a cell phone empowers billions of people living in poverty to take control of their limited finances and enter into transactions without a bank account or credit card.

Digital currencies have low to no transaction costs. As an example, Bitcoin has no enforced fees, unlike traditional payment systems such as credit cards, debit cards, and PayPal. This has caught the attention of financial companies, such as banks and credit card companies. They wonder if service fees will evaporate as quickly as long distance revenues did for the telcos when Skype appeared.

Yes, digital currencies involve risks. Lack of trust is at the heart of the risk to users of digital currencies and to the currencies' long-term viability. They can also be volatile. But I believe they can also serve as the foundation for an explosion of innovation and commerce. The current Internet is good for social collaboration and access to information. But it lacks many of the key capabilities needed for rich, trusted commerce. Imagine a new global platform where identity and trust are assured, where fraud is virtually impossible, and where appropriate payments are always made. To me this is the hidden promise of digital currencies.

The technology underlying Bitcoin offers more promise still. Andreas Antonopoulos is chief security officer at UK–based Blockchain.info, the world's largest Bitcoin wallet provider with more than 1 million registered users. He told the UK's *The Telegraph* that Bitcoin's digital foundation is one of the most important inventions of the twenty-first century.

> People think Bitcoin is just a better way to do PayPal, and it's not. Just like the
> Internet, it's a platform, and on that platform you can now build an incredible
> variety of things. We can't even imagine what things people are going to build.

But just in the last year, from watching the start-ups in the space, I've been amazed at the range of innovation that occurs when you combine Internet, the sharing economy, and crypto-currencies.[1]

We could see totally open services out of the control of any organization. Already a peer-to-peer Twitter-like messaging service aims to offer the same as Twitter but without a central point of control. Bitmessage wants to do the same with e-mail. Law enforcement agencies' subpoenas would be rendered impotent, since they wouldn't know to whom the subpoenas should be served.

Collecting personal information about your whereabouts, spending habits, tastes, and finances will become more invasive and more valuable. This information will help companies to more effectively target you and price products such as life and car insurance tailored to your circumstances and risk. Protecting what's left of your privacy will be a constant cat-and-mouse game.

Biotechnology/Medicine

It's hard to project future developments in digital technologies because increasingly they overlap with developments in other areas of science and human development. None is more significant than the concept of *biotechnology* (*biotech*)—the modifying of living organisms to meet our purposes. This involves breeding animals to meet human purposes, going back to domestication of animals and the cultivation of plants. But new technology involves multidisciplinary areas such as the environment, chemistry, microbiology, and genetics, which enable genetic engineering as well as cell and tissue culture technologies.

A lot of biotechnology research is focused on boosting the world's food supply. Since 1850, the global human population has grown sevenfold, from 1 billion to 7 billion. That's a lot of mouths to feed, and there will be many more mouths to feed in the years to come. A lot of food companies believe that the safest and most cost-effective way is through *genetically modified organisms*, or *GMOs*. This refers to plants or animals created by the gene-splicing techniques of biotechnology.

But the technology is controversial. Widely adopted in the United States, Brazil, and Argentina for the production of corn, soybeans, and cotton, GMOs are essentially banned in Europe and tightly regulated elsewhere. Opposition to GMOs can make some farmers seethe, since they believe using technology to boost crop yields is the only way to economically produce enough nutritious food to feed the planet.

Henry I. Miller, a physician, molecular biologist, and founding director of the U.S. Food and Drug Administration's (FDA's) Office of Biotechnology, wrote recently in the *Wall Street Journal*: "Perhaps the most illogical and least sustainable aspect of organic farming is the exclusion of 'genetically modified organisms,' but only those that were modified with the most precise and predictable techniques such as gene splicing."

Miller noted that "virtually all the fruits, vegetables, and grains in our diets have been genetically improved in one way or another, often through wide crosses, which moves genes from one species or genus to another in ways that do not occur in nature." To exclude genetic engineering "makes no sense. It also denies the consumers of organic goods nutritionally improved foods such as oils with enhanced levels of omega–3 fatty acids."[2]

Biotech can meet other needs. Promising T-cell therapy protects patients from infections when they've undergone a bone marrow transplant. Gene research with trees offers variations on existing trees that would make them better equipped for climate change. New forms of algae or other plants may be used as carbon dioxide sponges, to remove centuries' worth of the toxic by-product of combustion.

Once the genome is better understood, technology may give you options as to which sperm combined with which egg will produce a child free from regressive genetic anomalies. This technology may also be applied to height, weight, hair color, and intelligence.

Researchers are already exploring ways in which knowledge that has been trained into one rat is then communicated via computer to the brain of another untrained rat. The second rat learns the training faster than the original rat. If the trained rat is rewarded every time the second rat passes a test, the transfer of knowledge happens even faster. It is stunning to imagine a world in which the knowledge of one human can be passed on to another by connecting the two brains. What are the implications for education and society when you absorb the knowledge of college graduates or accomplished artists?

Robotics

Traditionally associated with factories and assembly line work, robots will soon walk out of the factory to perform myriad functions. These include making advancements in areas such as health care and education.

In health care, new prosthetics can take the place of lost limbs that offer the flexibility and precision similar to that of the actual limb. This can dramatically improve the quality of life for lower-limb amputees, and give them the unprecedented ability to walk and climb stairs. In addition to sophisticated physical technology, researchers have developed a chip that connects to the central nervous system so that mechanical and electrical devices respond to the thoughts of the human running them.

In state-of-the-art operating rooms, minimally invasive surgery uses computers, electronic equipment, and robotic instruments to perform "keyhole" surgery instead of traditional open-incision surgery. Instruments are inserted and manipulated through small incisions using remote optical or video guidance, greatly reducing patient trauma and recovery times. It will become standard practice for a physician to perform surgery on patients many miles away.

In the classroom, robotic devices are already helping teachers demonstrate math and science's core concepts. Without any prior experience in robotics or computer science, teachers can demonstrate abstract concepts like slope, sine, cosine, and vectors. Students find robots fun and engaging, and as visual tools they improve the information retention by up to 400% compared to traditional methods. Robots can also help educators meet the learning needs of children with learning disabilities, autism, and other pervasive developmental disorders. Robots can draw on infinite patience.

Intelligent Transportation Systems

With congestion and gridlock a problem in the cities of virtually every developed country, the impact of intelligent transportation systems will be enormous. Soon there will be autonomous vehicles moving around the streets and highways, guided by electronics and not the person behind the wheel. Google's autonomous vehicles have completed over 500,000 kilometers of road tests in the United States. The only accident was when a Google car was hit from behind at a red light.

Further, according to a University of California study, every car-sharing vehicle made available by companies such as Zipcar replaces 9 to 13 cars. So combine autonomous vehicles with new incentives for ride-sharing to exploit excess capacity in cars, along with low-emission vehicles, and we could have a "virtual" public transportation system for entire cities with almost no cost to government.

Artificial Intelligence

Siri, the personal assistant built into iPhones, and Watson, the IBM supercomputer that won a *Jeopardy* game against the show's most successful players, are often thought to be examples of artificial intelligence (AI), but technically they are not. The computer Watson essentially uses brute computing force to answer questions. It doesn't "understand" a question in the way a human person does. Watson applies a keyword search against an enormous database, much like Google does. But the distinction between artificial intelligence and Siri-like programs will grow less and less consequential as both computing power and the efficiency of data storage soars.

Decades ago, a wave of computer-generated automation wiped out blue-collar jobs. This was followed by a wave of outsourcing that affected some white-collar workers. Now a new wave of very clever machines will be displacing knowledge workers. What happens when a computer can analyze thousands of x-rays with greater accuracy than a physician?

Wearable Technology/Virtual Reality

Soon we will be wearing much of the technology that we use daily. This will include fitness and physical activity trackers, mHealth devices, smartwatches, e-textiles and clothing, and virtual reality glasses. Sony has even filed a patent application for "SmartWig." It can be worn "in addition to natural hair", and will process data and communicate wirelessly with other external devices. Stay tuned for "SmartBeard" to monitor your caloric intake.

The wearable technology that will likely have the biggest impact is the virtual reality headset. These headsets are usually thought of in the context of gaming, giving the game player the sensation of being immersed in a situation, such as driving a car or fighting a dragon. Facebook made headlines earlier this year when it bought a headset start-up, Oculus VR, for $2 billion.

"After games, we're going to make Oculus a platform for many other experiences," Facebook CEO Mark Zuckerberg wrote in a blog post. "Imagine enjoying a courtside seat at a game, studying in a classroom of students and teachers all over the world, or consulting with a doctor face-to-face—just by putting on goggles in your home."

Now that the smartphone and tablet market growth is showing signs of slowing, many companies view wearables as the next major wave of consumer electronics.

There is already a Wearable Technologies Innovation World Cup in which innovators from around the globe are invited to submit their contributions in wearable technologies in the categories Sports & Fitness, Health Care & Wellness, Gaming & Lifestyle, and Safety & Security.

Manufacturers are teaming up with fashion designers to make their devices chic and trendy. Manufacturers know that aesthetic appeal will be a large factor in driving consumer acceptance. Years ago, MedicAlert under-stood that its users would be more likely to wear the bracelet if it looked somewhat stylish. The same is now true for emergency devices such as those that can alert a caregiver if a disabled or elderly person falls and can't get up. Rather than look like clunky and utilitarian medical devices, companies are hooking up with designers to make emergency bracelets look chic and those worn around the neck look like jewelry.

In a few years, perhaps those looking for romance at a nightclub will wear a necklace or sweater that will glow to indicate a person's interest in a potential partner. When budding romantics make eye contact with their Google Glass, digital fireworks could occur.

Your smart toilet, doing chemical analysis, combined with your smartwatch that monitors your temperature, heart, and blood pressure, will make most regular checkups with your doctor obsolete. Even then, when abnormalities appear, a conversation with Watson or equivalent may be the next logical step in diagnosis.

Nanotechnology

Scientists are now able to deal with technology at an unimaginably small scale. A nanometer is one-billionth of a meter. At this size, even the most power-ful light microscope doesn't work. Nanotechnology is making advances in a wide array of fields, including electronics, construction, and medicine. In health care, nanotechnology opens the door to revolutionary new tools to diagnose patients, gene therapy, and drug delivery. Many illnesses take place at the cel-lular level and nanotechnology can deal with the illness at that level.

Researchers at Harvard Medical School have crafted a nanorobot from DNA that can carry a small number of molecules. It can precisely deliver beneficial molecules that cause leukemia and lymphoma cells to essentially commit suicide.

Television

In 20 years, most video entertainment will be on demand. Traditional television will no longer exist, and programming will become just another application on the Web. Just as today's consumers turn to the Web to book a hotel or down-load a song, soon we'll all look to the Web for our video content. The notion of gathering with family or friends to watch a certain program will apply only to live sporting events or shows such as the Academy Awards. And even these events have become interactive, as many viewers add commentary through Twitter.

All content will be delivered by the Internet to computer screens, iPads, smartphone screens and, of course, the large OLED 3D TV screen in the living room.

It's not just the delivery system that will change but also the content itself. The 20/20 version of *Monday Night Football* is an app, usable from any device. Chances are it would also be a 3D hologram playing out on your floor or table top. You could do your own instant replays from multiple cameras, get stats in real time throughout the game, or search for flashbacks from previous games. Stop the action and zoom in on the running shoes of your favorite player to find out about their brand, features, and price—and then execute a purchase.

You'll probably have input into the coaching. Others will have access to your views. If you consistently have good commentary, you'll be chosen by many as a broadcaster. If your audience is big enough, you'll generate your own advertising revenue for your punditry. Coaches and players will each have their own communities that you can join.

New Sources of Power

Enormous effort will continue to be expended in the quest for clean energy. One project is called "Solar Roadways." The project seeks to develop modular solar panels that are so cheap and durable that they could be used to transform every roadway, parking lot, landing strip, bike path, driveway, and playground into giant solar panels. A solar grid like this would generate clean power and among other things cut carbon emissions by 75%. Sure we may not pave America with solar panels anytime soon, but the 2014 Indiegogo crowdfunding campaign of "Solar Roadways" shows that a large number of people are enthusiastic about innovative approaches to energy.

There are those today who wish to live off of the energy that the sun supplies to the panels on their roofs. Self-sustainability, smart grids, and public networks may soon make such a dream a reality.

Promise and Peril

Technology has brought amazing benefits, and most people believe this will continue to be the case. In a study by the Pew Research Center, Americans were asked their general views on the future long-term impact of technology. Technological optimists outnumbered pessimists by two-to-one. Six In ten Americans (59%) feel that technological advancements will lead to a future in which people's lives will be mostly better, while 30% believe that life will be mostly worse. The optimists tended to have more education and a higher income.

While the general public is favorably disposed toward technology's advances, "experts" aren't so sure. Another Pew Research Center project surveyed 1,400 high-profile technology thinkers about the future and the results are sobering. They saw the potential for governments to curtail Internet freedoms and monitor the activity of citizens 24/7. They also worried about the commercialization of everything online and much of the control of the Internet being usurped by corporations. Lee Rainie, director of the Pew Research Center's Internet Project, told the *New York Times* that those surveyed had a "palpable sense of dread" about what may happen to life online. Rainie did note that the research was done when the news was dominated by the National Security Agency's (NSAs) spying on ordinary citizens.

As a society, we have only scratched the surface of the digital revolution. But clearly as the pace of change accelerates and explosive new technologies surpass our ability as a society to comprehend them, we must be vigilant that technology *serves us* and doesn't become a tool for our enslavement. We must constantly remind ourselves that the future is what we make it. More on this later.

Notes

1. Matthew Sparkes, "The Coming Digital Anarchy," June 9 2014, *The Telegraph Online*.
2. Dr. Henry Miller, "Organic Farming Is Not Sustainable," *Wall Street Journal Online*, May 15, 2014.

THE NEW TECHNOLOGY: SAY YOU WANT A REVOLUTION

One of the tools which shows the greatest immediate promise is the computer, when it can be harnessed for direct, on-line assistance, integrated with new concepts and methods .... Every person who does thinking with symbolized concepts (whether in the form of English language, pictographs, formal logic or mathematics) should be able to benefit significantly.

Douglas Englebart, 1962[1]

Four years after writing those words, Englebart had implemented a fully functional Augmented Knowledge Workshop at Stanford Research Institute. Knowledge workers were directly supported by networked workstations providing sophisticated communications, information handling, and decision support tools. The system contained a number of inventions. The users manipulated something called a "mouse" for cursor control. It went beyond data processing to use an innovation called "word processing." Electronic documents contained and were linked through a complete structure called "hypertext" (the basis of today's Internet). Users were "online" and could communicate with one another through something called "electronic mail." Most important, the system was used directly by knowledge workers, not just operators. It was not a data processing system to automate things. It was a communications systems to support people.

Some 30 years later, it is high time Englebart receive full credit as a great visionary. In many ways, he was the first person to get past the old data-processing mentality to envisage the new paradigm in technology. The Augmented Knowledge Workshop foreshadowed a number of shifts in technology that are just coming to fruition today.

The 10 Technology Shifts (and Why They Matter)

A number of shifts in the nature of technology itself are driving the convergence of the computing, communications, and content technologies and industries (Figure 4.1). These shifts are creating the power, capabilities, and price performance for new media, a new organization, a new economy, and a new society. You don't need to become a technology expert to win in this new economy, but you do need to understand the main shifts that are underway and to ensure that your organization achieves them.

Shift 1: From Analog to Digital

♦ *Digital technologies for the digital economy.*

According to Joel Birnbaum, chief scientist at Hewlett-Packard, the single most important change in technology leading us to the information highway is digitization of the media and networks. This one shift perhaps both creates and captures the interactive age more than any other. Digitization means that all information, including audio and video content, can be used in any order and can be rearranged at will. Digital content can also be transformed for use in another medium—for example, from text to voice or vice versa.

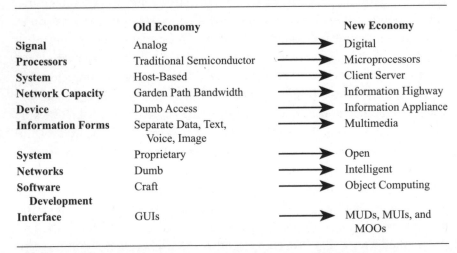

	Old Economy		New Economy
Signal	Analog	⟶	Digital
Processors	Traditional Semiconductor	⟶	Microprocessors
System	Host-Based	⟶	Client Server
Network Capacity	Garden Path Bandwidth	⟶	Information Highway
Device	Dumb Access	⟶	Information Appliance
Information Forms	Separate Data, Text, Voice, Image	⟶	Multimedia
System	Proprietary	⟶	Open
Networks	Dumb	⟶	Intelligent
Software Development	Craft	⟶	Object Computing
Interface	GUIs	⟶	MUDs, MUIs, and MOOs

FIGURE 4.1 *The 10 Technology Shifts.* SOURCE: © New Paradigm Learning Corporation, 1996.

Computer networks have been based on digital technologies since the beginning. That is, numbers and words were reduced to strings and packages of 1s and 0s and transmitted along networks between computers. Usually these data were modulated through a modem to run over an analog telephone system. Now the other two corners of the converging technologies triangle are going digital as well: telephone networks and entertainment broadcast networks. Once digitized inside a computer or network, all media look pretty much the same—whether it's a sentence, a photo of a child, a song by Pearl Jam, a 3-D image of the human heart, a Schubert symphony, a visualization of the stock market at 11:22 a.m., the design of an aircraft by an engineer, or a television show. For this reason, they can be changed and communicated, thus creating the new media.

Rather than being part of a schedule on a series of channels, television will become digital files in a multimedia database. "And what do I feel like watching tonight? Perhaps a program on refinishing antique boats ... hmm ... that bit on mahogany staining was complicated. I think I'll stop the program and ask for more information on matching stains."

Similar changes are underway with the third corner of the triangle—telephone systems—first with digital switches that route calls from one location to another and now with actual digital transmission over wires. As networks become fully digital, new kinds of applications, such as distributed voice mail, are possible. Using distributed voice mail you can send "voice" Christmas cards. Or pass a voice mail message received from one colleague along to a coworker. Digitization not only improves quality (compare a music CD to vinyl) and enables interactivity, it provides the foundation for a whole new world of computer- and networked-based applications as well as enabling fundamentally new approaches to finding and managing information.

SHIFT 2: FROM TRADITIONAL SEMICONDUCTOR TO MICROPROCESSOR TECHNOLOGY

◆ *High-performance processing for the high-performance organization.*

The first computers worked with binary numbers (1s and 0s) by vacuum tubes that were either on or off. They consumed vast quantities of power and generated vast amounts of heat. The 1947 ENIAC computer dimmed the lights of Pittsburgh every time it was turned on. Because the temperature in the room was 130 degrees, the operators worked in bathing suits. Today your child's video game has a capacity somewhere around four orders of magnitude greater (that's 10,000 times greater).

The greeting card that sings happy birthday contains more computer power than existed on planet Earth before 1950. Most home video cameras contain a more powerful chip than an IBM system 360 computer—the computer that changed the world. Genesis offers a game with a computer more powerful than a multimillion dollar 1976 Cray supercomputer. And Sony has a video game with a 200 MIPS (millions of instructions per second) processor that not so long ago would have cost about $3 million in mainframe form.

To get some idea of the incredible acceleration of computing power, let's review the reliability of the much-touted Moore's Law of Productive Technology. This law, named after Gordon Moore, former chairman of Intel in Silicon Valley and one of the founding fathers of the chip industry, asserted that available computing power quadruples every 30 months. Amazingly, Moore has turned out to be right, even though the prediction was made two decades ago.

The microprocessor—a computer on a chip—is at the center of the new economy. Traditional semiconductor technology that fills the massive cabinets of mainframes and minicomputers in corporate data centers is going the way of the dinosaur. If you open the door on a mainframe or minicomputer in your data center, you'll find boards with many different types of chips on them meant to perform the various functions of a computer. These boards are put together into racks gathered in a frame, and when you shut the door, you have a uniprocessor—that is, a computer. The microprocessor is a computer on a chip. Microprocessors have inherently better price performance than the traditional semiconductor technology.

Microprocessors now dominate leading edge computers of every size. Their computing power, measured in MIPS, cost hundreds of dollars or less on a microprocessor-based system compared to tens of thousands of dollars on traditional mainframe systems. And today, systems that combine many microprocessors into a single large computer can dramatically outperform mainframes in sheer power.

The growth can be expressed thus: 2 to the power of n where n is the current year minus 1986.

- In 1987, that meant 2 to the power 87 minus 85, or 2 to the power of 1, or 2 MIPs.
- In 1990, 90–86, so 2 to the power of 4, or 32 MIPs.
- In 1994, 94–86, it was 2 to the power of 8, or 256 MIPs.
- By 1997, 2 to the power of 11 or it'll be over 2 BIPs, or 2 billion instructions per second—all available on a desktop.

Some pundits have compared cars and microprocessors, saying: "If automobiles developed like microprocessor technology, the fastest car today would travel at 10,000 miles per hour and cost $2."

The analogy has problems. The car would be 2 inches long and, like a computer system, it would blow up occasionally, killing all the passengers. Worse, what applications would we use the car for? Who would drive this car? How would we train people to use it? What would be the implications of the car for the architecture of transportation, for policies in areas from policing to insurance?

Similarly, the microprocessor is changing everything we know about computing, about the applications that are possible, computer architecture, and technology policy, not to mention the IT industry.

Microprocessors are important not simply because they have spectacular price performance. They enable the powerful new applications that, for example, are multimedia—integrating data, text, voice, image, and video—and require massive desktop horsepower. They are also the basis for new concepts of the organization. They provide the *power to empower.*

Microprocessors also enable a new way of computing that (like organizational empowerment) moves intelligence out into the enterprise where the action is (for example, at the point of sale, customer service, R&D lab, or marketing department). As a result, information technology enables organizations to have empowered computing architectures that exploit the superior price/performance of microprocessor technology and in turn enable empowered organizational architectures.

SHIFT 3: FROM HOST TO CLIENT/ SERVER COMPUTING

* *Network centric computing for the Internetworked Enterprise. Client/server computing for the dynamic client/customer service organization. The network becomes the computer. The enterprise becomes a network.*

Strategy discussions a few years ago at John Hancock, the Boston-based life insurance company, often tended to come to a similar conclusion. Huge changes would be required in their approach to information systems if they were to achieve future goals for customer service and competitiveness. Like many other organizations, they concluded that the host-based islands of technology in the company would become unable to deliver the goods for corporate renewal.

According to Diane Smigel, vice president of the Corporate Information Services Group: "To create a customer-centric, empowered, flatter, and more responsive organization we needed a more empowered, distributed, and responsive computing architecture." In response, Hancock adopted the new approach of client/server computing, with "far-reaching implications and results."

The first era was one of "master/slave" computing. Each "host" mainframe or minicomputer had slave terminals attached to it. The terminals were typically "dumb" with a cryptic user interface made up of numbers and letters. The enterprise also became populated with islands of personal computers, some attached to local area networks, which enabled the simple sharing of files and devices such as printers.

Now, because of the spectacular power of the microprocessor and the maturity of networking technology and standards, a fundamentally different style of computing is emerging. It goes by different names such as network computing, cooperative processing, and client/server architectures. To confuse things slightly, the Internet contains a number of host computers linked together, because the Net predated the rise of the client/server. But for practical purposes, computers on the Net are not really hosts at all. They are servers and will no doubt eventually be renamed. Regardless of the name, the new approach provides the potential for users to access a wide range of information, applications, and computing resources without worrying about where they are or how they are connected.

Software is processed not only on a host but wherever it makes most sense. Software is not limited to one machine but can be processed cooperatively on various computers on the network. In client/server computing, software works on a client computer, like your desktop PC, and also on a server, which can be located anywhere. The computer becomes the network and the network becomes the computer.

To use a human analogy, in the new enterprise, thoughts are processed in the minds of many people in an office—not just in the mind of the boss. And processing of ideas, information, and knowledge is communicated as needed to meet requirements of the collective process.

The Federal Express PowerShip application, which enables customers to prepare and track packages without paperwork, is based on something called "client/server computing." As Cynthia Spangler, vice president of corporate headquarters systems, says: "As a client/server application, PowerShip allows us to get as close to the customer as soon as possible. Client/server gives us flexibility and speed which couldn't be achieved on the mainframe."

Many companies have mistakenly concluded that the main reason to adopt client/server computing is to reduce IT expenditures. However, companies often see only the opportunities for cost savings on hardware. A frequent term is "downsizing," referring to shifting applications from mainframes to smaller, microprocessor-based systems— with a typical objective of hardware cost-savings.

It is true that price performance gains of 10,000% in hardware over traditional mainframes is compelling. But it is important to look at the entire cost of ownership of a system—not only the hardware purchase price. The client/server approach demands new skills and complex software and represents a big change for most MIS departments to tackle.

When all is said and done, client/server computing can reduce IT costs significantly, but that isn't the best reason to use it. Rather, the new paradigm in computing, of which client/server is central, is the missing piece in the discussion of how to achieve the new effective, competitive, and productive enterprise.

The research shows that it is only through the new modular, powerful, networked style of computing that the responsive networked enterprise can be achieved. "A user only cares that there are islands if he has to navigate between them," says Dave Carlson, FTD Florists' CIO. "If you set up a good client/server environment, the client device provides the platform that allows users to move from island to island without worrying whether they're on open space or on land. One of the reasons why we're so passionate about client/server architectures is that you can change the server structure behind the client without affecting the client," says Carlson. "Or change the server without changing the database."

John Hancock has implemented about 30 client/server systems over the past 5 years. Planning is underway to integrate all these into an "institutional architecture" for client/server. One of the most far-reaching of these systems is a billing and accounting system in the employee benefits business (group insurance). This new business process has enabled the company to completely transform and is supported by a sophisticated client/server system. Once a new policy is booked, the information at the front end becomes part of the institutional database. But until the work is finalized, it stays out in the field. "We moved all of the thought process regarding obtaining a new case or customer out to the field offices where all the knowledge base and real client contacts reside," says Smigel.

Hancock had to revolutionize the operational support processes for systems in the complicated client/server world. Problem resolution, capacity planning, security, disaster recovery, and other operational support services that have been around for decades in the mainframe world had to be reinvented. "There is the same paradigm shift occurring in the technology and in the organization," says Smigel. "They are in lockstep with each other. The new technologies are enabling flatter, customer centric organizations where workers are empowered with the tools and knowledge they need to delight customers in every interaction—not just to meet their expectations, but to enable people to handle entire work processes rather than just being a step along the way or a hand-off in a serial process. The whole game is improving the delivery of service to customers—better, cheaper, faster."

Shift 4: From Garden Path Bandwidth to Information Highway

♦ *Broadband communications for the networked economy.*

Today's Internet is a garden path, a low-bandwidth network shipping mainly data and text. As MCI's Vint Cerf, one of the pioneers of the Internet, describes the VBNS (very high-speed backbone network service) of the Internet: "Eight years ago we were transmitting at a speed of two pages per second. The new network transmits at the speed of 'two small public libraries per second.'"

Translating the vision of broadband, multimedia networks into reality will be an expensive and contentious task. To understand the competing claims and criticisms, it helps to separate the internet's *carriage* from its *content*. Carriage is the physical structure of the highway, composed of networks, software, and switching devices. Content is the information that will actually flow over the system.

Many companies are vying for the prize of building and operating the carriage. Some of these also want to generate much of the content. The winners will reap billions of dollars in revenues. Two technical features of the proposed carriage make it far superior and much more costly than the communications systems we have in place today. First, it would be everywhere and capable, when necessary, of offering full-color, full-motion video. This is known as *broadband capacity*. Second, the highway would be fully interactive and offer a two-way flow of information, as telephones do.

Neither of the two most familiar communications systems, telephone and cable, can meet both criteria of interactivity and broadband capacity. The question is whether either can expand to meet the highway's needs, or whether they will be supplemented by totally new technologies. Telephone's advantage is that anyone can use any phone in the world and establish two-way communication with any other phone. This is possible because the systems contain switches at the hub of star-shaped networks that can direct a specific phone call (or transmission) to your specific location. The drawback is that the typical twisted copper telephone wires going into homes, offices, or factories are extremely limited in capacity, equivalent to a garden path whereas full-motion video signals require a freeway.

Capacity is cable's strength, effortlessly carrying dozens of video channels, but it is not interactive. The cable networks are not stars but loops or strings. Rather than individual transmissions to individual homes, a common transmission is sent out to all homes on the string and shared. Today there is no way a classroom can, for example, dial up a television picture from a distant museum. Nor is cable designed to send a video signal from this classroom to another classroom across the country. Right now cable is a one-way street, not a highway.

A decade ago, cable and phone companies were seen as totally different businesses, but technology has brought them into direct competition. This is because all information—audio, text, video, images—can now be converted or "digitized" into the same commodity (i.e., the bits of data that computers use). Depending on whom you talk to, this is enabling the phone companies to encroach on cable business and is enabling cable companies to poach in the phone business. In fact, in some locales the fight has already begun. The Vidéotron cable company in Britain is successfully offering local telephone service. In Canada, BC Tel snared an exclusive contract with the developer in Vancouver's Concordia Pacific complex to provide all communications services, including cable, to a proposed housing development for 13,000 people. No matter who builds the highway, the backbone of the system will likely be fiber optic cables running underground from coast to coast. Some of them are already in place—thin strands of glass using light pulses to convey 5,000 video channels or 500,000 phone conversations per fiber.

The spectacular growth in bandwidth possibilities is partially depicted in Figure 4.2. To give a little precision to the highway analogy earlier, the width, if you like, of the road is shifting from a three-foot garden path to a highway sixteen miles wide. But because the highway analogy is imperfect, Figure 4.2 doesn't tell the whole story. The issue is not just the width of the road but how tightly high-speed traffic can be squeezed on the road—the number of moving vehicles. Using compression technologies that squeeze more bits through the pipelines, the capacity of fiber is going up. Nicholas Negroponte points out that recent research results show we are close to being able to deliver gigabytes per second. This means that "a fiber the size of a human hair can deliver every issue made of the *Wall Street Journal* in less than a second" he says. "Transmitting data at that speed, a fiber can deliver a million channels of television concurrently—roughly 200,000 times faster than twisted pair … and mind you, I am talking of a single fiber, so if you want more, you just make more. It is, after all, just sand."[2]

Name	Bandwidth	Bits/second	Highway Analogy
1. POTS (Plain Old Telephone Service)		64,000	3 ft. Garden Path
2. ISDN (Integrated Services Digital Network)	2 x POTS	128,000	6ft. Sidewalk
3. T1	12 x ISDN	1,544,000	4 lane Roadway (72 feet)
4. T3	28 x T1	43,232,000	112 lane Superhighway
5. OC3	3 x T3	129,696,000	1 mile wide Superhighway
6. OC48	16 x OC3	2,075,136,000	16 mile wide Superhighway

FIGURE 4.2 *The internet (from Garden Path to 16-mile-wide Highway).* SOURCE: © New Paradigm Learning Corporation, 1996.

Telephone and cable certainly aren't the only players in this game. There are also direct-broadcast satellites, cellular television, low-orbit interactive satellites, and even high-altitude balloons, to name a few. Some electrical companies are assessing their possible role, because they have extensive fiberoptic systems in place to monitor their electrical grids. Technology is evolving so quickly that it would be rash today for any country to commit itself exclusively to just one or two systems. It is far from clear which technologies and strategies can most effectively deliver the content at the best price.

In the end, the real prize for suppliers will be in content, not carriage. Bandwidth will eventually become a commodity and be dirt cheap. The real value to be created for customers will come from the vast array of services and information—the content—available through the Net.

For customers, bandwidth is becoming an enabler rather than an obstacle.

SHIFT 5: FROM DUMB ACCESS DEVICE TO INFORMATION APPLIANCE

◆ *Smart on and off ramps for the information highway.*

Until recently, customers accessed the three technologies of communications, computing, and content through dumb devices (the telephone, the television, and the computer terminal). The first to change was computing, with the rise of the PC during the 1980s. In the case of computing, desktop intelligence was the prerequisite for mass use. The GUI (Graphic User Interface) of the mid 1980s and early 1990s made computers usable by normal, nonpropeller-head humans. Desktop (and lap and palm) intelligence also set the basis for client/server computing, the growth of new distributed and cooperatively processed software applications, and the empowered organizational structures discussed in this book.

But what about the other two technologies? Does this mean we'll soon start talking to our TVs, or our telephones will suddenly sprout video screens? The television has a long way to go to carry the mantle of "information appliance." Pound for pound, TV is one of the dumbest appliances in your house, ranking on the home appliance IQ scale at about at the same level as the toaster. Set-top boxes for the TV will initially provide intelligence and enable initial interactivity. Eventually, microprocessor technology will transform television into something unrecognizable, a multimedia information work-learn-play station. Ditto for the telephone.

But which will win? In many ways this is not important. It is a side question to the broader issue of which applications will drive the information highway. The big five on everyone's list are business applications, education, entertainment, home shopping, and videoconferencing. The rate of penetration will depend on many factors, including the capital invested by various players, consumer acceptance, the growth of standards and the effectiveness of marketing and partnering strategies in the new media industries.

As for the appliances, it is likely that there won't be just one standard information appliance. Instead, different areas in the house or other places may have appliances with a different twist. Clearly, the home office and students' rooms and other locations will have a direct extrapolation of the computer. Today, PCs are outselling televisions by far, and 70% of PCs are going into the home. The living or entertainment rooms may have a device with a larger screen and high fidelity sound that more closely resembles the TV and stereo. And your pocket may have a device that looks like a cross between a palmtop and a cellular telephone.

SHIFT 6: FROM SEPARATE DATA, TEXT, VOICE, AND IMAGE TO MULTIMEDIA

◆ *Interactive multimedia for complete human communications.*

In the first era, the immaturity of technology and digitization meant that the four forms of information—data, text, audio, and video—were separate, each with separate technologies to manage them. Data processing systems handled data. Word processing systems and telex handled text. Telephone and dictation systems handled voice. Photocopiers and microform systems handled image. Now each of these media is being swept by digitization into a multimedia stew. Multimedia computing is natural computing in which systems work the way people do by integrating these information media into business processes and daily life.

Roger Levian of The Document Company Xerox has explained why paper has lasted so long: good quality, portability, cost, and familiarity. However, technology is getting to the point at which these benefits are clearly out-weighed. Levian predicted more than a decade ago the rise of something he called Group Dynapaper—a portable workstation about the size of a piece of paper and about as thick as 100 sheets. Such products are now coming into the marketplace with all the advantages of paper as well as some new attributes. Two professionals in different parts of the globe can exchange (at the speed of light) computerized, or "digital documents," that contain data, text, audio, and video. A document on a workstation screen may have text surrounding a digitized photograph or film clip and a "live" spreadsheet with another's voice (requesting clarification from the recipient) attached to certain parts.

This compound document can be filed electronically, retrieved, altered, and communicated as appropriate without ever being transformed onto paper. And like the piece of paper, you can take it on the subway. Unlike the paper, it com-municates with other documents and people as you ride along, perhaps play-ing you a bar of your favorite song when a new message arrives.

In this scenario there are *static media*, such as data, text, and still images, and there are *time-based media*, including audio (voice and sound) and video. Real-time animation may look like video, but rather than being a series of frames that are stored in advance and displayed in rapid sequence, the content is software-controlled and rendered or created on the fly. With real-time ani-mation, users can fully interact with the moving environment—for example, turning the car to the left or turning to the right to walk up the stairs (all on a screen). Real-time animation enables genuine interactivity, 3D navigation, and photorealism.

Another time-based media is virtual reality—the extension of real-time ani-mation to surround the user, usually with clothing such as headgear or gloves. Yet another is kinesthetic feedback—the sensory experience derived from the nervous systems associated with muscles, tendons, and joints. Also known as *haptic experience*, this medium is often associated with virtual environments such as flight simulators.[3] And it's not unthinkable that smell and even taste will be integrated into the multimedia experience.

Shift 7: From Proprietary to Open Systems

♦ *Open systems for an open world.*

The information highway and the new media must be built on standards. But when it comes to computer-based systems (as with the king): "Open systems are dead! Long live open systems."

An explanation is in order. Standards have existed in the telephone industry for many years, enabling *interoperability* of telephone systems around the world so that your telephone can call any other. With computers it isn't quite so simple. To enable computers to interoperate (talk to one another) more than a mere physical connection is required. Compatibility in many areas of software is also necessary. In the early days of the computer industry, computers used software designed to run on one computer only—*one computer, one vendor*. When customers needed a larger computer, they had to rewrite their software to run on the larger computer. Such conversions were often as much effort as programming the computer in the first place. Even after the lengthy process of conversion, the sole accomplishment for all that upheaval was that the firm could now run its previous software programs on a different computer. Big deal.

In the 1960s, IBM introduced the famous 360 computer family (referring to 360 degrees around the world, addressing the universal needs of customers). For the first time, software applications were portable—that is, they could be moved or ported from one computer to another—*multiple computers, one vendor*. Also, computer companies were creating systems that enabled their computers to interoperate—but still, multiple computers, one vendor.

In the mid-1970s the computer industry (like the construction industry of seventeenth-century Boston, the railroad industry of the nineteenth century, or the electric bulb and automobile industries of the twentieth century) matured to the point at which it began to consolidate around standards. Standards such as the UNIX operating system began to enable both interoperability and portability—*multiple computers, multiple vendors*. Even though the UNIX operating system was owned by AT&T (and later Novell), its evolution was broadly controlled by many computer companies through vendor-neutral organizations developing standards and new directions.

Standards began to arise in all areas of computing, including communications, databases, user interfaces, computer operating systems, and software development tools. Some of these standards came from formal standards bodies (de jure standards) and many people thought that such bodies would be their main source—as with other areas of standards, such as the electrical code. The key defining factor of open systems for many was the notion of vendor neutrality. Standards by definition, it was said, cannot be controlled by any vendor. Vendor-neutral standards organizations were needed, it was thought, to determine the future of open computing. However, the reality has not unfolded according to plan.

It turns out that there are several dimensions of openness beyond vendor neutrality. That is, a number of factors are now determining whether software and information are portable, and computer systems of different size and brand interoperate fully. These include platform availability and market penetration. For example, multimedia user interfaces controlled by Microsoft, IBM, and Apple are each controlled by one vendor. Yet each works on computers of different brands and sizes. Software applications, such as the leading document creation tools, are portable to computers running each of these user interfaces. And computers using these three environments can talk to each other, exchanging information in standard formats. Most of the standards to make all this happen resulted from the marketplace rather than formal standards organizations.

Furthermore, openness is not black or white but, rather, a continuum. Standards and products have various degrees of openness. So open systems defined as "computing environments based on vendor-neutral standards" are dead.[4]

A new view is emerging: Net-based software environments based on standards (both de jure and de facto) that enable varying degrees of interoperability and portability of software and information. In other words, what counts is that computers of different sizes and brands talk to one another and that software and information are portable, not so much who controls the evolution of products.

It is the Net, not the standards bodies, that is finally turning the open systems dream into a reality. The joke, "On the Internet, nobody knows you're a dog," points to the shift. Well, on the Internet nobody knows you're a Mac, or a Windows PC, or an OS/2, or a UNIX machine either. The Net was designed using de facto standards which arose from the UNIX world and which increasingly enable interoperability of systems regardless of brand or size. In fact, many companies are applying Net standards and software to create open architectures internally within their companies—dubbed the Intranet.

It is true that there are many *competing* standards (an oxymoron), but leading companies have concluded that adequate clarity exists to embrace the concept.

Some people trivialize open systems by discussing their benefits. It is true that open systems have far-reaching advantages over the traditional approach. They are significantly less expensive due to their exploitation of microprocessors, have lower vendor margins due to customer freedom, and can use shrink-wrapped, as opposed to home-grown, software to name a few.

However, standards do not provide benefits only. Increasingly they are an imperative for customers, organizations, and suppliers as well. Standards are becoming necessary to be effective in the new economy. For example, standards are required to link with customer, supplier, or even competitor systems. Standards are required to achieve integration of information. Open systems are necessary to create open organizations.

As well, standards are transforming the computer industry. George Shaffner, formerly of the X/Open consortium, describes open systems as "the systematic elimination of low-value differentiation" in the IT marketplace. Open systems prevent the reinvention of wheels, as software suppliers include standards components and interfaces in their products. There is a new division of labor occurring in the industry as various companies compete, ironically through cooperating in areas of mutual self-interest. All this benefits the customer.

Open systems as originally conceived—based on formal standards arising from vendor-neutral consortia and standards bodies—have not come to pass. Those open systems are dead! But open systems based on industry standards and the Net are alive and well. They are shaping vendor products and customer architectures alike, enabling portability of software and the interoperable network of networks/that is the internet. Long live open systems!

Competing Standards

Here are a few other such oxymorons we've gotten used to: scented deodorant, programmer productivity, jumbo shrimp, fresh frozen, management science, deficit reduction, airline cuisine, male responsibility, nonworking mother, family vacation, accounting principles, legal ethics, mandatory options, and safe sex. (My international oxymoron database is accessible on the World Wide Web at www.mtnlake.com/paradigm.)

SHIFT 8: FROM DUMB TO INTELLIGENT NETWORKS

◆ *Hypermedia and letting your agent do the walking through the Net.*

Until recently, it was not only information appliances that were dumb—the pipelines that carried information had no intelligence built into them. This is not a problem when all the information and services you want are on one computer. But when you need to access thousands or, soon, millions of computers, and the only information on the network is your address (as sender) and the address on some computer out there (the recipient), this becomes a serious problem. Although Net surfing may be fun, it is not practical for most people to spend their lives on the surfboard looking for the fish they want.

The initial step to solving this problem is a mechanism called *hypermedia*, developed by Douglas Englebart, as discussed earlier, and articulated best by Ted Nelson. Hypermedia, or hypertext as it was called then, is a computer-based information delivery system that enables the user to jump around a document and between documents rather than creating or reading a document from beginning to end. On the Net, initially through the World Wide Web (WWW), this is taken further so that you can easily "hotlink" between documents on different computers around the world. For example, if this book were on the Net, you could click on the word *Englebart* and it might take you to a dozen other computers containing information about Douglas Englebart. The world of hypermedia is limited only by the number of links built into the documents. The software that enables such links is the hypertext markup language (HTML). (This book is not yet on the Net because the publishing industry has not yet developed a business model that makes digital books profitable.)

Now that hypertext has become hypermedia, a link can be a photograph, video clip, sound, or compound document that links you in turn to another such document. Hotlinks help to ensure that you, not some software designer, determine what information is important.

Using hotlinks, the following scenario is now possible: You go onto the Net and identify some information that is of interest to you. You select a portion of that data, hotlinks and all, and paste it into a document on your workstation— say, a spreadsheet. You send the spreadsheet to Japan, where your colleague opens the document on her workstation. She clicks on one of the hotlinks in the document and it is still active. It takes her to all the other documents around the world to which your document was originally linked!

As the Net grows and as new users come on by the tens of millions, each with the capability to link his or her information to other information, the web of links grows exponentially. (You can see why they called it the World Wide Web.)

However, there is still the danger that you will spend a lot of time surfing, linking yourself here and there in search of the key piece of knowledge. This situation is changing as a new era of "smart networks" appears. Intelligent software "agents," "knowbots," or "softbots," built into the network, can be recruited on your behalf. These tireless little workers surf the Net for you day and night looking for information you've requested, organizing your personalized daily newspaper, communicating for you and doing other jobs. As Andy Reinhardt of *Byte* writes: "The advantages of agents are powerful: Agents make data networks smarter about people, instead of requiring people to be smart about networks. They let you focus on getting your job done rather than on the details of how you communicate."[5]

A precursor to agents were the services that create a custom newspaper for you. A not-so-well-known daily, read by only one person, is called "Don Tapscott's Heads Up." I have been getting this for some time now. It summarizes daily the issues I care about from hundreds of sources and presents the results on the Net. If I want to get the original article on an item of interest, it is just a click away.

Rather than being browsers, agents are finders. Let your mind go on this one. An agent will be able to gather anything you might want on the Net. You might want all your faxes, e-mail, voice messages, and a directory of physical mail, telephone messages, and other notes to be available to you in a "universal in-box." No problem. Or you'll be able to write a letter containing a number of blanks. Tell your agent to take the letter on the Net and get the blanks correctly filled. Wall Street brokers already have systems that automatically search the Net to create profiles on companies of interest. Or an investment banker can be advised when a particular stock passes a threshold price level.

The more your agents get to know you, just like your travel agent, real estate agent, or investment broker, the more useful things the agent can do on your behalf. This does not necessarily involve artificial intelligence, but it will. The Age of Networked Intelligence will not only network humans and computers but silicon-based intelligence as well.

Agents will also transform the way commerce is conducted on the Net. You want to buy a leather jacket, so you list your criteria to the agent—style, color, measurements, designer brand, and so on. The agent goes onto the

Net and finds the best price, thereby transforming the jacket into something of a commodity. The electronic market will be a commodity market, because price and availability will be the main factors in sales. Furthermore, the price may change dynamically, depending on availability on the Net. A seller of jackets might send agents onto the Net to determine today's price, or this hour's price or this minute's price. Or the seller may decide that when there are 1,000 in inventory, the price is x. When there are 100, the price is y. Or there may be no inventory at all. The seller acts as virtual manufacturer, wholesaler, and retailer for a group of companies who together manufacture jackets on demand.

The old paradigm expression was "Let your fingers do the walking through the Yellow Pages." The new paradigm: "Let your agent do the surfing on the internet."

SHIFT 9: FROM CRAFT TO OBJECT COMPUTING

♦ *Rapidly deployable software for the rapidly changing world.*

There's a Fortune 500 company's head office war room that has a wall chart depicting more than 300 computer systems. The reason for the graphic representation is that the firm is changing each of these systems. The alteration requires an army of people working for more than 18 months, and it costs millions of dollars. The modification? The company is changing the number of digits in a part number from 8 to 10.

What's the problem here? Why is software so hard to alter? Why does software development take so long, cost so much, and produce results that are frequently inflexible and unsatisfying? There is a simple answer. Until recently, software development was a craft, just like the manufacture of guns was a craft until Eli Whitney and D. F. Winchester invented guns that were produced with interchangeable parts. Before that, when a gun broke, a craftsman had to fix it because there were no standard parts.

Some software development has been worse than a craft. It has been like an *art form*. Programs, like a musical symphony score, are complex and often huge (involving thousands or even millions of lines of code). Like a musical score for a symphony, a single mistake (one note in the second cello part) could mess up the entire thing. Finding the mistake and fixing it is typically a major challenge and (unlike a symphony) by changing the cello part you're likely to have a ripple effect that messes up the tuba.

Moreover, the size of these intricate programs means that they take a long time to create. Like a symphony, the software composer could labor for years creating the work of art. Unfortunately, many software works are never completed, leaving many latter-day Schuberts with at least one unfinished symphony to their credit. Adding something to the program is often a major problem due to the ripple effect. Each *part* of the software symphony is typically created from scratch, as is each *new* software symphony. The software created to alphabetize cash receivables can't be reused to alphabetize electronic mail messages.

This situation is coming to a head with something called "The Year 2000 Problem." Most information systems managers shudder when you mention the phrase because some systems did not anticipate the coming of 2000. To save space they dropped the "19" from the year, i.e., "65" instead of "1965." As much as $50 billion worth of software in North America that can't be reprogrammed will stop working on the last day of 1999 because the original source programs have been lost or destroyed and the original programmers have retired or died.

This model of building systems is inadequate for the new economy. Business users need software that can be built and changed fast in minutes, hours, or days, not months, years, or decades. Because of the old approach, there is limited reusability of software. Often the majority of funds spent on information systems goes to maintenance—just keeping things working or fixing and changing software—after it has been implemented. Symphonies don't talk to one another—they are standalone works of art. Users must make a huge personal investment in learning different, inconsistent, and poorly designed systems. And only programmers, not users, can create programs.

Just as the move to the industrial design and production of rifles was significant, software is going through a fundamental transformation. Developers use and reuse modules or parts that are standardized and that work together. The new approach is called *object-oriented computing*; rather than creating large, complex, tightly intertwined software programs, programmers create chunks of software called *objects*. Such chunks are developed in standard ways and have standard behaviors and interfaces. Such Lego-like pieces enable the rapid *assembly* of software rather than its laborious *crafting*.

The software industry is becoming a parts industry, and through standards software vendors create standard parts to enable customers to rapidly assemble computing environments. Object-oriented systems combine data and programs (previously separate) into chunks that are like objects in the real world. An object could be an invoice, a filing cabinet, a type of employee, or a computerized representation of a part in a jet engine. Each includes data about the object and logic enabling the object to do certain things. For example, the engine object includes data about the characteristics of the object and software that determine the kinds of things that object can do, such as rotate in a certain direction. The outcome of an object orientation to software is reusable elements that can be used for large numbers of applications.

Here's how object-oriented systems might work in financial services. A bank could have an object called "customer" that includes data as well as programming needed to do a wide range of operations such as calculate balances, evaluate credit levels, and send promotional material. This object could then be used to build capabilities related to handling various accounts: mortgages, life insurance, credit cards, cash management accounts, and ATM cards—all of which are also objects. A change in the customer's address would apply across the board. A change in one of the accounts that could affect credit risk could automatically apply that object to every banking relationship of that individual, and so on.[6]

Object-oriented systems and techniques are becoming viable faster than most pundits had thought, but leading companies have already made the commitment to shift. Northern Telecom, for example, is working to shift over hundreds of traditional programmers to object-oriented environments within the next year. Dave Cox, the chief information officer at Northern Telecom, is convinced that the company needs "rapidly deployable computing environments for a rapidly changing marketplace." Cox says: "I want to give management business simulators. Object technologies will allow us to move to business simulation rather than business reporting. I want to let the executive fly through the company visualizing and simulating various outcomes based on various decision scenarios. The goal is to ensure positive outcomes, rather than reporting on the past."

One of the most powerful aspects of the object approach is that the business can be modeled as objects. Objects can be placed in a hierarchy—some very high level and others very granular. As a company changes its business model, it can rapidly change its corresponding software. In the insurance business, a policy application process might be considered an object at the enterprise level. This object would be linked to a number of component objects. "The goal of object computing is that the user should be able to build the application right in front of them," says Cox. "Object technology will be vital to fast-track organizations in this competitive global economy."

It was the Net that gave objects the big boost. Rather than huge, complex applications, software is becoming chunked, with smaller "applets" that fly across the Net as the user needs their services. As with many things in the digital economy, software is becoming molecular.

Shift 10: From Guis to Muis, Moles, Muds, Moos, Avatars, and Vr

◆ *New collaborative environments for a new economy.*

A principal obstacle to widespread use of computers was the user interface. Prior to the Xerox Star of the early 1980s, the ill-fated Apple Lisa and the watershed Macintosh of the mid-1980s, computers had character-based interfaces. The user interacted with the computer using the alphanumeric character set—letters and numbers on the screen. To describe these as "unfriendly" is to be charitable. Terse, cryptic, incomprehensible—they were more often than not "user vicious."

All this changed with the GUI (Graphic User Interface), but the GUI was just a step in a broader progression toward what the Alliance refers to as the MUI (Multimedia User Interface). "The user's working environment will shift from icons and symbols to direct, dynamic depictions of and interaction with familiar living objects," says Alliance president David Ticoll. "The MUI will learn from the user and provide a natural dynamic work, learn, and play environment."

"There is more information available at our fingertips during a walk in the woods than in any computer system, yet people find a walk among trees relaxing and computers frustrating," wrote Marc Weiser, director of the computer science lab at Xerox PARC. "Machines that fit the human environment instead of forcing humans to enter theirs will make using a computer as refreshing as a walk in the woods."[7] Says HP's Birnbaum, "Information appliances must be consistent and predictable and they have to be idiosyncratic for particular people, particular cultures, and especially for particular applications."

The shift from the GUI is, ironically, articulated well by Michael Spindler, the CEO of Apple, the company that established the GUI. "The GUI is one size that fits all. It is a static user interface," he says. "I want a computer that recognizes me and works the way I do. You don't get up in the morning and say I want to compute today. You want to do things. You want a computer that is intuitive and that learns about you and from you."

Among the innovations of the MUI is a variety of input devices beyond a keyboard and a cursor control device like a mouse. The most important of these, voice recognition, is now feasible for single words and will be in full use for continuous speech this decade.

The mouse will also become the mole—defined here as a 3D mouse. I first introduced the idea of the mole in jest at a debate held in 1981 in Urbino, Italy.

Office automation authority Amy Wohl took the position that the mouse was not always an effective device compared to scroll keys, which was countered by James Bair (now of the Gartner Group) and myself who argued why it was and why it would triumph over scroll keys. I argued, however, that the mouse would need to develop a 3D capability as the world evolved into multidimensional, multimedia computing. In the animal world moles, unlike mice, are capable of three-dimensional travel because of their capacity for burrowing.

The immediate breakthrough in 3D computing is virtual reality, which promises to transform the user interface. As Jerry Michalski of Esther Dyson's Monthly Report *Release 1.0* says: "... the flat, document/desktop metaphor world we are familiar with so far is a warm-up exercise for more complex and useful virtual worlds to come that will find common use in business."[8] This evolved in concept from flight simulation systems that enable pilots to lose all their engines in a training situation without losing their lives. Virtual reality (VR) today usually involves some kind of clothing such as a glove, goggles, and headset. You find yourself sitting in hyperspace, experiencing a simulated world. At the beginning of the 1990s this sounded like science fiction, but VR is now in widespread use in everything from kids' games to theme parks. Imagine the future applications you might create with your VRML (virtual reality markup language), the VR equivalent of the hypertext markup language used to compose Home Pages. Petroleum engineers will penetrate the earth to the wellhead. Doctors will navigate through your cardiovascular system. Researchers will browse through a library. Students will stroll on the moon. Auto designers will sit in the back seat of a car they are creating to see how it feels and to examine the external view.

Eventually, 3D will not be on the screen but in the air through holograms. As Negroponte puts it: "Sometime in the next millennium our grandchildren or great-grandchildren will watch a football game (if they call it that) by moving aside the coffee table (if they call it that) and letting eight-inch-high players run around the living room (if they call it that) passing a half-inch football back and forth."[9] You may choose to have a replay, using your mole to reposition one of the defensive backs to see if he could have made an interception if he had been in a different position.

Another significant innovation is the MUD (Multi-User Dungeon, or Multi-User Domain, depending on whom you're talking to). Much of the innovation regarding MUDs is coming from the Xerox Palo Alto Research Center. A MUD is a "place" on the Net where users create their own dramatic adventures in real time. John Seely Brown, head of PARC, describes MUDs as "Dungeons and Dragons without weapons and monsters."

The MUDs were initially text-based virtual realities. You typed text to enter "rooms" such as ballrooms, offices, taverns, warehouses, prisons, or closets—each with its own entrances, objects, and written description. The users were able to walk around the rooms and do various things. The first MUDs were simply games that allowed people to move around an imaginary world while killing monsters and other players. But according to Seely Brown, "Talking to other players turned out to be more interesting than killing them, and now MUDs are intended as virtual hangouts—exotic worlds where people can gather and chat without leaving their chairs." MUDs are evolving into virtual meeting places on the Net.

Increasingly in MUDs, you take on a graphical image of yourself—an avatar—to facilitate your interaction with others. You become someone or something on the screen—a graphical interface. Avatars can also represent a process, such as an agent. For example, a computer process that finds information for you may look like a person, an animal, or a cartoon character. Avatars are yet another step away from the GUI with its menus and computerese prompts.

MUDs have now been combined with object-oriented programming concepts to create the MOO (MUD, Object Oriented). There are MUD programming toolkits that allow users to create objects, characters, and places. MOOs have already gone far beyond games and entertainment and are becoming powerful tools to construct virtual social realities—creating important opportunities for human collaboration such as enabling environmental scientists to meet in a troubled bioregion and share data, research, and solutions. We are also seeing the rise of what could be called MMOOs—Multimedia MOOs in which, for example, when a participant clicks on the object representing a person, a video stream of that person appears. Or the environmentalists click on a real stream and it appears, too. There are many new forms of human collaboration and discourse in cyberspace with potential we are just beginning to fathom.

THE INVESTMENT DICHOTOMY

Any organization that wants to succeed must adopt the new media. Although it is possible to discuss benefits of the new paradigm, the argument to embrace it is strategic. Yet the investment strategies of many organizations we interviewed or consulted too often focused on the wrong opportunities. Table 4.1 summarizes the results of a survey of approximately 400 chief information officers and other senior managers.

TABLE 4.1 Opportunities for the New Paradigm

OPTIONS	PERCENTAGE OF RESPONDENTS
Question 1: [a]**All things considered, where do you think the real opportunities for the new paradigm in information technology lie?**	
1. Cost savings in information technology through improved price performance of microprocessor-based systems, reuse of software, reduction of maintenance costs, reduction of systems costs due to flexibility, and so on.	7
2. Cost savings in the business as a whole through streamlining and reengineering business processes, reducing redundancies, saving overhead, and so on.	23
3. Value-added opportunities, including improved customer service, better quality, improving innovation, improving business responsiveness, increased revenue, market share, and so on.	70
	Total: 100
Question 2: **Thinking back on the business cases for the new technology that you have reviewed or presented, what was the main emphasis in cost-justifying investments in the new technology paradigm?**	
1. Cost savings in information technology through improved price performance of microprocessor-based systems, reuse of software, reduction of maintenance costs, reductions of systems due to flexibility, and so on.	55
2. Cost savings in the business as a whole through streamlining and reengineering business processes, reducing redundancies, saving overhead, and so on.	29
3. Value-added opportunities, including improved customer service, better quality, improving innovation, improving business responsiveness, increased revenue, market share, and so on.	16
	Total: 100

[a] Defined as client/server, multimedia, object-oriented, standards-based, networked computing.

The data show a powerful dichotomy. Most respondents believe the real opportunities are strategic but that investment strategies are in reverse order to the real assessment of opportunity. The explanation? Some said they found it more difficult to build a hard-dollar business case using strategic rather than tactical logic. As one said, "Saving money on hardware is easier to quantify than reinventing the company for success." Others indicated that in a time of cost cutting the only benefits management would consider were cost savings.

But for most, the problem was described as a cultural one. They felt their organization or decision makers were not equipped with the knowledge, skills, and motivation to intelligently evaluate the wisdom of shifting to the new technology. This challenge to achieve change by finding leadership for transformation will be discussed in Chapter 10.

Ten Reasons for Embracing the New Technology

1. When television becomes interactive, you can take revenge for years of vacuous programming.
2. Since account control died, there are no more tech tours to Hawaii anyway.
3. Because heavy metal is really popular only with a bunch of long-haired middle-aged degenerates.
4. It may provide an opportunity to communicate with your teenage kids.
5. Maybe if everyone is doing it there will be no time for hype.
6. Because you don't want to be without an answer when your 13-year-old asks you how to find the Jupiter MOO on the Net.
7. It's like drugs. If the users want it anyway, you might as well give it to them in a controlled program.
8. Cooperative processing is more politically correct than master-slave computing.
9. It beats sitting through another quality management program.
10. It will be so much easier when the next paradigm comes along.

NOTES

1. Douglas Englebart, *Augmenting Human Intellect: A Conceptual Framework*, Stanford Research Institute, 1962.
2. Nicholas Negroponte, *being digital*, Alfred A. Knopf, 1995, p. 23.
3. The Alliance for Converging Technologies, Toronto, Canada.
4. This definition is a hybrid of key industry bodies.
5. Andy Reinhardt, "The Network with Smarts," *Byte*, October 1994.
6. John W. Verity and Evan I. Schwartz, "Software Made Simple: Will Object-Oriented Programming Transform the Computer Industry?" *Business Week*, September 30, 1991. This article provides a readable explanation of object-oriented programming written for a business audience.
7. Marc Weiser, "The Computer for the 21st Century," *Scientific American*, September 1991, pp. 94–101.
8. Jerry Michalski, "Multi-User Virtual Environments," *Release 1.0*, EDventure Holdings, New York, August 3, 1994.
9. Negroponte, p. 123.

PART TWO

INTERNETWORKING

20th Anniversary Edition Commentary on Chapter 5: The Internetworked Business at Work

O NE OF THE MOST profound changes in the last few years is that, increasingly, it's inadequate to change your company to compete. The Internetworked Business is one that changes its whole industry, by itself or more likely in cooperation with its competitors.

In our 2006 book *Wikinomics*, Anthony D. Williams and I looked at dozens of companies that have used the Internet to transform their business models and achieve tremendous success. The Canadian mining company Goldcorp used mass collaboration to increase Its market capitalization from $90 million to over $30 billion. Procter & Gamble (P&G) is profiting handsomely from its use of open Ideagoras, and Amazon is exploiting open platforms. However, in the eight years since *Wikinomics'* publication, I've noticed something striking: the rate of business model innovation has not accelerated. Yes, some individual companies have achieved competitive advantage by exploiting the Web and networked business models. But overall the gains have been modest.

We're beginning to understand the reason. Increasingly, it's becoming difficult or even impossible for companies to achieve breakthrough success without changing their entire industry's modus operandi. Some disrupters like Google, UBER, Tesla, and Amazon are single-handedly disrupting various industries. But for most companies this is not achievable. Instead firms need to cooperate to make the structural changes to their industries that enable them to prosper.

Some Representative Industries

Let's take a look at five industries.

Pharmaceuticals Can't Fix What Ails Them One by One

Pharmaceutical companies are about to drop off what's called "the patent cliff." They will lose 25% to 40% of their revenue in the next 2 years as the patents for many blockbuster drugs expire. There is little that individual companies can do to recover from this crisis and instead need an industry-wide solution.

The global biomedical community is generating about 25 new medicines per year, but only a handful of these are "pioneer drugs" rather than "follow-on drugs"—variants, formulations, or combinations of existing therapies. Despite increased research spending, the impact on the number of new medicines approved is negligible. Pioneer drugs address societal needs, but their discovery will also allow pharmaceutical companies to grow because consumers are willing to pay for such innovation.

It is in everyone's interest that those involved in the quest for pioneer drugs share rather than hoard information. Unfortunately, the current structure of drug research encourages the industry to protect its ideas and material with intellectual property (IP) rights or restrictive collaboration agreements. The public sector too has been encouraged to secure intellectual property on early-stage discoveries.

In addition, the clinical trial process is not as open as it could be. The outcomes of these trials, particularly if they fail, are not published until several years after the termination of the projects, if at all. A corollary is that the pharmaceutical industry is downsizing research and focusing on less risky activities.

Instead, the industry should share some of its clinical trial data, such as results from failed trials or from control groups. "This will not undermine the competitive advantage of companies," says former Merck executive Stephen Friend, now a champion of the open source biology movement. "It will enable it, by changing the basis on which companies compete and setting a platform for a sustainable industry."[1]

Rethinking the Music Recording Industry

As I explained earlier, the Web always held the potential to deepen the bond between musicians and their fans. Instead, the music recording industry became the poster child of failed digital opportunities. Instead of clinging to late twentieth-century distribution technologies, like the digital disk and the downloaded file, the music business should move into the twenty-first century with a revamped business model that converts music from a product to a service—"Everywhere Internet Audio."

The new model of music as a service rather than product should eventually eliminate "illegal downloading" because the problem of copyright protection would vanish. Few people will want to take possession of the song. The record labels could still own the music industry if they joined forces and put all their music in an exchange, whereby they and artists get compensated each time a song is streamed.

Banks: Placing Risk Management in the Commons

The day-to-day gambles of Wall Street almost brought down global capitalism and yet, so far, nothing fundamentally has changed. Restoring long-term confidence in the financial services industry requires more than individual banks changing their behavior or even government intervention and new rules. The financial services industry needs a new modus operandi, whereby all of the key players (banks, insurers, investment brokers, rating agencies, and regulators) embrace principles such as transparency, integrity, collaboration and sharing of information.

For example, banks should open up financial modeling and make pertinent assumptions and data transparent to all interested parties. Financial modeling allows analysts to estimate the value of goods, ranging from a company's stock to a barrel of oil. The valuations, and associated risk estimates, are behind almost every financial instrument. Over time, both the products, and the underlying financial models, have become increasingly complex, and therefore, opaque.

In contrast, the Open Models Valuation Company (OMV) is one organization attempting to use the Web to create a global community of experts dedicated to establishing credible valuation and risk assessments for credit securities and contracts such as collateralized debt obligation (CDOs), credit default swaps (CDSs), and other derivatives. OMV rejects the current system's opacity, using an open process for academics, industry experts, quantitative analysts, banks, and investors to collaborate and determine the worth of such securities.

Craig Heimark, a long-time industry veteran and one of the founders of OMV, likens it to the scientific peer-review process: "In the scientific world when people publish something, they don't just publish their results, but also the steps in the process, their methods, and assumptions so that they can be vetted by others."[2]

Open Models Valuation Company's business model is designed to evaluate both existing assets, such as the problematic mortgage-backed securities (MBSs), as well as new offerings brought to market by investment banks:

> Asset holders or sellers would approach OMV for help in valuing the instrument. Open Models then uses an independent network of community modelers and experts who would come up with a value and more importantly comment on the underlying assumptions. The whole process is documented in a wiki-style format and open to the community.[3]

Whether or not this small company succeeds is not the point. Rather the financial services industry needs to change the industry business model.

Rethinking Manufacturing for Sustainability

Green technologies are being developed by traditional companies, but these ideas and technologies are not being leveraged to their full potential. Too often the activities are isolated and ineffective, in conflict, compromised, or diluted by duplication of effort.

For example, Nike spent an entire year creating an index to measure the sustainability of their products only to discover that companies ranging from Marks & Spencer and Patagonia to Adidas and Walmart had invested similar amounts of time and effort to develop their own proprietary indexes.

"Collaboration," says a Nike executive, "would not only have gotten us there quicker, it would have resulted in a better index."[4]

Collaboration is a better approach. So Nike worked with Science Commons, a nongovernmental organization (NGO), to develop a new model of patent licensing that would make it straightforward for companies to share sustainable technologies, and make them open for reuse and modification. It's called the GreenXchange and the idea is to create an online marketplace where companies not only share cutting-edge practices but also share the technology and underlying IP needed to make things happen.

Early adopters, such as Best Buy, have agreed to contribute their "green tech" assets to the pool and, in turn, they hope to benefit from innovations contributed by new participants as they join. Other disruptors, such as Tesla, have gone a step further and placed all of their patents in "the commons." This is "sharing" in the true sense of the word and, rather than being some kind of new socialism, delivers big advantages to the sharer. For Tesla, it helps build up the electric car ecosystem against its gas-guzzling competitors.

Shifting to Collaborative Health Care

Despite the advancements of modern medicine, health care's business model has remained unchanged for centuries.

It assumes that, medically speaking, physicians are smart and patients aren't. Doctors wait for sick people to come to them and tell their patients what to do, one-on-one, face-to-face. Patients play little or no role in deciding their own treatment plans. As one physician put it to me: "Today's health-care institutions are like the old media: centralized, one way, immutable, and controlled by the people who created and delivered it. Patients are passive recipients."[5]

The entire industry needs to reinvent itself around the Internet and recast the doctor-patient relationship.

Patients should use the Internet to become informed. Every citizen, including newborns, would have a personal health page. Think of it as a patient's personal window into his or her own health and the basis for participation in a broader health social network. Adults would own and control their own data, but health-care professionals (and perhaps family members) could access it, as required, with appropriate levels of privacy and security.

Much like Facebook, a patient could create a community or join medical "causes." And just like the App store, low-cost or free applications could help individuals measure their own health, do prediagnosis of a sick child, or test for possible drug interactions.

In this new industry model, patients become more like partners. This goes beyond the current catchphrase of "patient centric" health care. The patient co-creates health care and wellness, producing an outcome that is more evidence-based and costeffective (i.e., safer, better, and cheaper).

Other Industries

The list goes on and on. The auto companies should place fuel cell development in the commons. We need a new intelligent power grid for the production and distribution of energy. Codevelopment and collaboration within the industry, and sharing, is necessary.

Ironically companies from every industry seem to be prepared to share computing resources by increasingly placing their data and even applications in the Cloud. But when it comes to the really important exploitation of commonly held IP, we're still nibbling at the edges. And in almost every industry, everybody suffers.

If we are to get out of the chronic economic malaise in which we all find ourselves, we need to understand that the unit of correction is not the corporation. It's the industry, stupid.

Notes

1. Don Tapscott, "Business Models for Five Industries in Crisis," *Wall Street Journal Online*, July 10, 2011.
2. Tapscott, Ibid.
3. Tapscott, Ibid.
4. Tapscott, Ibid.
5. Don Tapscott and Anthony D. Williams, "Better Health Care at the Click of a Mouse," *Globe and Mail*, December 28, 2010

THE INTERNETWORKED BUSINESS AT WORK

The upheavals of the early 1990s—process reengineering, downsizing, and PC proliferation—were a tea party compared with what's coming next. Capitalism is about to be completely reinvented. As the Ice Age of the old economy comes to an end, cracks widen in the fault lines of crumbling business models. Intuition and creativity will blossom in organizations rooted in the fertile soil of the new media.

David Ticoll

President, Alliance for Converging Technologies

THE DIGITAL CARE OF HEALTH

A 40-year-old woman from Baltimore, vacationing with her family and driving in the family car through the southeastern desert of California, is seriously injured in an accident.[1] She is unconscious and unresponsive. Transported to a nearby rural hospital she arrives looking pale, with a pulse of 120 and blood pressure of 110/90. A breathing tube is inserted through her trachea, and she is placed on a ventilator.

The emergency physician at the rural California hospital, High Desert Hospital—conducts a teleconsultation with specialists from the University of Southern California/Los Angeles County Medical Center (USC/LAC). As a result of this consultation, the patient is immediately transported to USC/LAC for further evaluation and treatment. A computer tomography (CT) scan of the abdomen reveals a massive hematoma of the liver with no free blood in the peritoneal cavity.

The patient's health care identification card is swiped through a card reader that gives access over a national network to her medical records.

The patient's electronic records show two very useful facts: She had a triple bypass operation a year ago and she is allergic to certain drugs. The discovery of the preexisting condition eliminates the need to perform surgery on a possible ruptured aorta. The information about the drug allergy allows the physician to prescribe a nonallergenic alternative, and then to select a less expensive generic drug.

Next, the doctors at USC/LAC initiate another teleconsultation with the patient's personal physician located at Johns Hopkins University Medical Center in Baltimore. During the consultation both doctors view, manipulate, and analyze three-dimensional medical images of the patient's internal organs. They see that a segment of the small bowel has been ruptured. They then compare the previous CT scan with the new 3D reconstruction of the abdomen and agree on a very limited surgical approach that avoids the need for other invasive tests and more dangerous surgery.

This taste of the future occurred in September 1994 when the National Information Infrastructure Testbed (NIIT) demonstrated—on the basis of a real case—how internetworking could transform health care (see Figure 5.1). The NIIT is a nonprofit consortium committed to evolving the internet by demonstrating and testing a series of real-world applications. The organization's dozens of members include many of the most important providers of technology and networks, along with researchers and customers.

The preceding scenario includes the following:

◆ Personal multimedia (diagnostic and 3D visualization tools), thereby creating effective individuals. A vast array of new medical and general-purpose workstations can improve the personal effectiveness of medical and administrative personnel. Workstations should also include multimedia learning tools, communications tools such as electronic mail, document creation, and management tools for administrative functions.
◆ Workgroup collaborative computing environments that create high-performance health-care teams. These are generally referred to as clinical information systems. Patient-focused care, customer service, and community-based care models will require team approaches to delivering health care, linking specialists, family practitioners, and others.
◆ Integrated health-care delivery systems, which extend across an organization such as Johns Hopkins University Medical Center or a health-care maintenance organization (HMO). The islands of patient records that currently paint the health-care landscape in hospitals, clinics, private labs, provider offices, and pharmacies need to be integrated into a computer-based patient

record (CPR). This record would include demographic information, discharge summaries, operating room reports, pathology and lab results, medication profiles, radiology information, and hot links to information in systems outside the organization, such as access to medical reference databases, drug formularies, and anagrams.

◆ Community and regional networks linking the High Desert Hospital to USC/LAC. It is estimated that CHINS (community health care information networks) could save $20 billion in administrative costs alone, by making claims and payments electronic, thus avoiding duplication and making the system paperless. A big challenge here is to get various parties, some of them in competition, to share information.

◆ Links across the country on the national information infrastructure. As a patient moves through the system from office visits, to inpatient care, to ancillary services such as home health, practitioners have the tools and information to create high-performance health care.

The bottom line? Because the information is available through the accident victim's health card and the Net, an appropriate diagnosis is possible. She avoids unnecessary surgery or dangerous medication, thus improving her chances of survival. Administration and claims processing are all electronic, improving the metabolism of the system and cutting costs. Health care becomes digital.

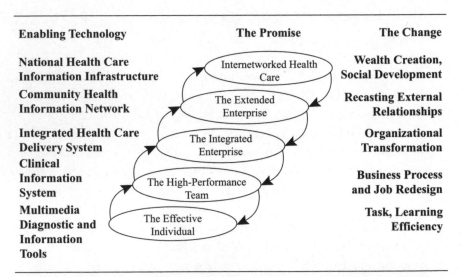

Enabling Technology	The Promise	The Change
National Health Care Information Infrastructure	Internetworked Health Care	Wealth Creation, Social Development
Community Health Information Network	The Extended Enterprise	Recasting External Relationships
Integrated Health Care Delivery System	The Integrated Enterprise	Organizational Transformation
Clinical Information System	The High-Performance Team	Business Process and Job Redesign
Multimedia Diagnostic and Information Tools	The Effective Individual	Task, Learning Efficiency

FIGURE 5.1 *The Transformation of Health Care.* SOURCE: © New Paradigm Learning Corporation, 1996.

This is not science fiction but an actual working prototype of how acute health care could work. Imagine the possibilities of moving all health care onto the internet! As Leslie Sandberg, executive director of the Institute for Telemedicine at the Center for the New West, says, "NIIT offers a dramatic glimpse of how a national health-care information infrastructure will transform medical practice as America enters the new millennium."[2]

"The demonstration shows we can save lives, improve health-care delivery and reduce costs simply by integrating information," adds Bill Murphy, chair of the NIIT. "If historical and current information is available, practitioners can be brought out of the dark." Or as one of the doctors who observed the testbed demonstration said, "People are dying because we don't have this technology today. I could save lives if we had this infrastructure in place."

No business is more important or will be more affected by the new technology than health care. Not only does it affect each of our lives directly, but health care as an industry is one of the engines of the new economy. It is currently a $1 trillion dollar industry growing at a 10% annual rate. The industry represents 14% of the gross domestic product in the United States (10% in Canada) and is larger than the auto, steel, and transportation sectors combined. As people age, they place escalating demands on the system. Diseases such as AIDS, cancer, and mental illness also put severe pressure on the system. Wage demands from a highly labor-intensive industry (80% of costs are directly related to salary), new expensive medical technology (such as MRIs, lipotripcy, and molecular medicine), and the high cost of pharmaceutical research will continue to drive up costs. The Congressional Budget Office predicts that, if they continue unchecked, health-care costs will be close to $2 trillion dollars—a whopping 18% of the GDP—by 2000.

Yet public expectations regarding health-care quality continue to rise. People want better health care. At a time when there are 35 million uninsured Americans, there is widespread support for the principle of universal health care as a basic human right. Clearly, tinkering with this problem is not the answer. We need to reinvent the business of health care.

What is the problem? Unlike the scenario just painted, the health-care industry in the United States has been and continues to be an unplanned collection of hospitals, physicians, and other practitioners. Estimates are that from 15% to 40% of health-care costs are unnecessary and that the infrastructure in place is underused. A key missing element in this system has been a lack of integration. In all but a few cases, hospitals, physicians, laboratories, and other providers operate with a minimal use of advanced information technologies and without coordination. This has led to a health-care system in which treatment decisions are made in isolation. Worse, they are based on clinical tests and on a physician's own experience, instead of calling upon the vast body of clinical experience that exists. Physicians are influenced by the opportunity to make insurance claims as well as by practices in their communities. As a result, doctors perform twice the number of tonsillectomies in some communities than in others.

In many ways, the term *health-care system* has become an oxymoron. It is currently not a system at all but a mishmash of interoperating facilities, payers, insurers, consumers, and providers, in which users are passed from one entity to another. Each entity is on its own—keeps its own records, measures its own quality, and once it's through with the patient, simply passes the patient along with no concept of effectiveness.

The idea of managed care was introduced by insurers, employers, and health providers to address the problem—to provide health care that has both good quality and managed costs. Regardless of whether there is federal health-care reform, the revolution in managed care continues unabated. Close to 50 million Americans belong to HMOs, a total that is growing at a rate of 10% per year. Through HMOs, insurers and customer organizations band with locally based networks of doctors and hospitals to deliver health care at agreed-on fees in return for a guaranteed number of clients. And because employers see HMOs as a way to keep premiums down, we can expect that HMOs will continue to grow, assuming they continue to deliver.

To survive, HMOs and any organization in the health-care industry must become internetworked businesses. The promise of managed care can be achieved through effective *individual* practitioners, working in *teams*, that *integrate* across a facility such as a hospital, which in turn *reach out* to health-care facilities across a community, then in turn become part of a regional, national, and international *information infrastructure.*

Other shifts are driving health care toward the new technology. There is, for example, a shift from inpatient care to ambulatory and home-based care. As health-care institutions disaggregate, networks and effective information will be required to move a patient through the system.

A second trend is what Paul Sulkers, managing director of consulting company Health Technology Management, describes as "illness management" becoming "illness prevention." Prevention of illness through education, nutrition guides, and other techniques is seen as the answer to controlling costs in the long term. One related form of cost control is capitation. Under this scheme, a group of providers contracts with state governments or insurance plans to guarantee health coverage for a population for a fixed amount per person per year, regardless of the actual use of the health system by the individuals involved. Says Sulkers, "Under this scheme, the providers are clearly encouraged to put in place preventative health-care programs, education, and other techniques to keep patients out of the system, or at least to intervene before any condition worsens. In this case, the public will require increasing access to reference database and medical guidelines, incorporating multimedia courseware and video-on-demand services. The patient becomes part of the high-performance team."

The third trend is vertical integration, a step that reflects the importance of the patient as a customer within the extended enterprise. Health-care organizations that once focused only on acute-care hospitals, clinics, and physician office services are now expanding into vertically integrated organizations that own or have strategic partnerships with long-term care environments, nursing homes, and home care, again requiring the internetworking of these institutions. The combination of both vertical integration and capitation will drive health networks and shared CPR. The public, as part of the high-performance team, will use high bandwidth services to their homes, which will deliver both multimedia treatment guides (provided in multiple languages), as well as preventative and other medical education. Physicians will now be able to join other industries that enjoy the ability to work at home, accessing multimedia continuing medical education, clinical records, and diagnostic images over high-bandwidth cable networks. The home becomes part of the health-care extended enterprise.

Some states are regionalizing health care and exploring the creation of regional health enterprises. Cardiac surgery, for example, might be centered in San Francisco for the entire northern California region. Neurosurgery and all the requisite and expensive diagnostic and treatment technology might be located in San Jose. The idea is that patients are moved to where the critical technology is located rather than attempting to have the key technology in all locations. Regionalization requires comprehensive patient information to treat the patient as a patient of that region and as part of the system as a whole.

The new technology is critical to fixing this situation. There is a need to measure the effectiveness of the complete treatment rather than of a component. The patient needs to be treated as a patient of an overall health-care approach rather than of a single facility. Going forward from here, NIIT chair Murphy says there are three issues. First, technology. "We proved that it can work, even though it is in its early stages. There is more work to be done on bandwidth, robustness, interoperability."

But second, there are even more challenging issues around public policy. For example, the scenario included physicians in two states telecommuting, in real time, to help a patient in real time. Technically, it is illegal to practice medicine across state lines because physicians are licensed by individual states.

Third, there are important personal privacy issues. "If I'm in an operating room, I want the doctors to have every possible piece of information about my medical record that exists," says Murphy. "If I'm applying for a job, I don't want such information made available. We need privacy and security approaches that ensure ready access to your information when you want it, but privacy when you don't. This will require private-public sector collaboration to create a regulatory environment that allows people to capitalize on the technology."

The key to privacy of health data and the effectiveness of security measures will be directly related to the degree to which the patient—the customer— becomes part of the solution. The customer, using a health card and PIN, will have access to his or her own shared health record, with the ability to lock and unlock portions of the record to general or restricted access. Once again, the customer becomes part of the high-performance team, and in many respects, becomes the key to digital health.

THE DIGITALLY SUPPORTED MOVEMENT OF THINGS

If organized chaos has a home, it is at the Federal Express SuperHub in Memphis, Tennessee. There, in a frantic four-hour period that begins just before midnight, more than 100 airplanes wing in bearing 1.2 million packages for approximately 7,000 employees to sort on 200 miles of conveyor belts. On the night in 1973 that FedEx was launched, the firm carried 19 items. Today, its more than 108,000 employees and 35,000 trucks mean that FedEx has captured half of the overnight delivery market.

In Chapter 3, we explained the five levels of transformation: individual effectiveness, the high-performance team, the integrated organization, the extended enterprise, and the digital economy. It's hard to think of a more effective organization or a more spectacular rise to industry dominance than Federal Express Corporation. But Federal Express is transforming itself again. It's changing from being a courier company into a logistics and networking provider for its customers. Says CIO Dennis Jones: "Even today, FedEx is not simply a transportation company which moves goods from point A to point B quickly. We are the logistics link between customers and merchants." Let's look at how FedEx is changing the business through the five levels.

Focused employee training has been going on at FedEx for more than 10 years, but in 1995 FedEx launched a new interactive training system using multimedia workstations made by Silicon Graphics, Inc. These screens combine TV-quality video with text, graphics, and voice to teach basic interaction skills such as customer-contact methods and features of service categories for its 35,000 couriers and customer-service agents. "People will be trained at a pace that's more personal for them and more customized than the stick-and-pointer classroom," says Jones. A certain amount of training will be required annually, but because it will be done using interactive multimedia, there is more flexibility than in the past when classroom time needed to be scheduled. Now training can occur at the beginning or end of a shift, or whenever the individual can best fit in what will be very personalized instruction.

FedEx has spent tens of millions of dollars on training through its automated system, which can also measure performance through a videodisk system that is updated monthly. The knowledge system, known internally as pay-for-performance/pay-for-knowledge, was just one of the reasons that FedEx was the first service organization to win the coveted Malcolm Baldrige National Quality Award.

 The core of FedEx's operations is what we would define as a high-performance team. A customer calls in for a pickup and speaks to an agent in a call center. The call center moves the request to a dispatcher in the designated local market who, in turn, passes the request along to the nearest courier in a truck. "Once the request has been received, nobody," notes Jones, "touches a piece of paper or says a word. It's a network-based company. Most transportation companies are in a point-to-point business. Teamwork is a tactic to support us being a network-based company."

Teams interoperate through electronic mail. The company has one of the largest single e-mail directories in the world—some 70,000 employees. For Jones, e-mail is as important an application as the company's customer services and parcel management systems.

 FedEx concluded that if you can't manage delivery, you can't measure it. For years the measures were all internal—operational measures of success or failure—primarily focusing on the percentage of on-time deliveries. What was needed was a system that actually measured every transaction—hundreds of thousands per day—according to the *customer's* satisfaction.

"From the viewpoint of product differentiation we knew that the movement of information was as important as the movement of packages," says Jones. "We also knew that the customer-service systems we were building could not only provide this product differentiation, but, more importantly, would provide us with the ability to measure precisely our service quality." They noted at the time that they had a successful delivery rate of 99.5% of all packages on time.

Federal Express didn't study its situation to death. If a company spends too long getting information technology people to create a strategic plan, the firm may end up with a document that sits on a shelf because the world will have changed while the research was done. "We've got 10 measurements of service (from a customer's perspective) which we report on a daily basis and distribute to the company on a weekly basis," says Cynthia Spangler, vice president of corporate headquarters systems. Each vice president is responsible for a separate category and can initiate actions to eliminate problems. "When the category has been eliminated, we move on to new categories. As soon as we achieve success, we redefine success," says Spangler. "The corporate philosophy is people, service, and profit. If you have a highly motivated workforce, they provide the service to the customer which in turn will ensure profit. This is done through teams and team building to break down the old administrative barriers. We need to have a good team for ourselves to have good teams that include our customers."

FedEx developed a mathematical way of measuring their failure rate, called the service quality index (SQI), which is based on 10 events that FedEx knows disappoint and frustrate their customers. Each of these is weighted from a customer perspective on a 10-point scale. For example, if they lose a package, this is rated as being 10 times more serious than if a package is 5 minutes late.

Calculations are performed on every transaction throughout every day. Often, the customer isn't even aware that FedEx has failed. For example, the company offers delivery by 10:30 a.m. the next morning to most locations in the United States. If the company delivers a package at 10:31 a.m., the system counts that delivery as a failure, even though the customer may not notice.

Measurement is based on integrated technology—in this case integrating the three classes of systems—physical systems that scan or monitor physical events, transaction-oriented systems that use database technology to manage financial and other information, as well as end-user systems that directly support customers.

"Federal Express is a series of networks, and it takes about 17 hours for a package to move from shipper to receiver," says Jones. "During those 17 hours we must do everything possible to keep this shipment from going astray as it moves from shipper to station, to airport, to one of the sorting hubs, and on to the destination customer. We must have a flawless set of events happen for 17 hours and we must track and measure every critical point along the way."

To understand the role of technology and the engineering of an enterprise around quality goals, it's worthwhile to review what happens to a parcel you send with FedEx. Every time that parcel changes status, information is recorded through sensors and entered into the COSMOS (customer, operations, management, and services) database. The database contains all the basic customer information—name, account number, address, package pickup location data—and it communicates with a number of other systems and devices to maintain a complete record of each shipment that FedEx handles, from the beginning to the end of the process.

When a customer calls in to have a package picked up, that call is taken by a customer service agent at one of the 42 call centers worldwide. The package pickup request is transmitted to the COSMOS system and then relayed to the dispatch center in the city closest to the shipper. Seconds later this pickup request is transmitted to a small computer (called DADS, or digitally assisted dispatch system) located aboard a FedEx van.

The courier then drives to the customer's location and picks up the package. It is at this point that service quality measurement begins. The courier uses the Supertracker—a small, portable, battery-operated, menu-driven computer having a barcode scanner—to scan the smart barcode on the package. As well, the courier keys in certain information such as the destination ZIP code. The Supertracker device is very smart. It knows its own ZIP code, which route it is on, who the courier is, and the time and date.

When the courier leaves the customer and returns to the van, the courier places the Supertracker into a port located on the DADS computer. The package information is automatically transmitted back to the dispatch center and to the COSMOS database, making the data available to all customer-service personnel worldwide.

At that point, less than five minutes after the package is picked up, FedEx has all the information required for the shipper and consignee about when the package was picked up, who picked it up, the location, the type of service, where the package is going, and the intended routing. As the package moves through the system and is scanned, this information is continually updated. Before the night is over FedEx will have scanned 2.4 million shipments, up to nine times each, as they move through the network.

All during this period FedEx is running comparison reports in all systems to determine if any shipments have gone astray. The idea is to be proactive—to spot and correct a problem before there is a failure from the customer's perspective.

After the package arrives at the destination city, it is scanned and sorted. When it is placed on a courier's van for delivery that morning, another scan is carried out so that the system knows which truck and driver has the package. Finally, when the van arrives at the customer's destination, a scan for proof of delivery is conducted by keying in the name of the person who signed for the package. The courier then returns to the van and places Supertracker in the DADS computer, and the final proof of delivery information is transmitted back to the main databases in less than four minutes.

The result is that FedEx has complete package information. "What is more important, is if that package was delivered five minutes late, if there was an exception, if it had been damaged, or misrouted, we would have been able to capture all of that information on a real-time basis," says Jones. By the middle of the afternoon, FedEx will know how many packages in the cycle have been misdelivered, delivered late, damaged, or lost.

The next morning the individual courier receives a quality feedback report giving details of all transactions that were not 100% correct. Other teams work to understand exactly why an error was made and to follow up if there is a dissatisfied customer.

The FedEx approach combines continuous learning and action. Information technology is no different from marketing. It is continuous and needs always to be taken into account. "It requires more expertise by people at lower levels to understand information technology. They need to know where the information is and where it's coming from. When technology is so integral, you've got to know more than just what's coming across your desk," says Spangler.

Federal Express has now taken its information systems and put the power into the hands of its clients. This is the extended enterprise. For example, the FedEx PowerShip network consists of shipping systems for shippers with up to 50,000 packages a day or as few as one package per year. It automates shipping by printing the mailing labels, does the cost calculations to the client's customers, and provides tracking and shipping. "The strategy is to bring internal and external customers more useful information to make timely decisions," says Spangler. "We're in the business of saving customers time and, hopefully, money if we can make them more efficient. We need to understand the needs and frustrations of our customers. We feel that customer service is a main factor that differentiates us. With each step closer to the customer, we can improve service. And the new technology is the backbone to achieve this."

PowerShip is the Federal Express trademark for the family of network-based products that it supplies to customers so that a client's PC is integrated with FedEx's client/server application. Three avenues are possible:

1. FedEx supplies a PC and software.
2. FedEx integrates the customer's system with the FedEx system.
3. FedEx supplies desktop software that can run on any PC equipped with a modem and laser printer.

"We've adopted open systems [because they] give us the greatest flexibility. We, not our customers, know what our future needs will be," Spangler says. The result is revolutionary: FedEx's customers are becoming part of the extended enterprise. And IT is a focal point. "We are no longer the critical path," she says, "we are now *the path*."

For customers, what it means is that they have a self-service customer service agent at their own site. Or, put another way, this is the consumer as producer, a theme that will be occurring more and more in the new economy as the gap between the two continues to blur. Customers can request a pickup over the network, generate their own shipping label, arrange their billing through the same system using no invoice, track or trace shipments by directly linking with FedEx, and create a manifest of shipments at the end of the day. Many customers even have a "hot key" that allows them to track packages that may have been ordered by *their* customers through FedEx. When catalog retailer L.L. Bean uses the PowerShip system, the shipping labels it creates act for both L.L. Bean and FedEx. "It's really a seamless flow. The L.L. Bean computers and the FedEx computers act as if they're one capability. We are caught up in the overall restructuring of the customer-supplier chain," says Jones.

L.L. Bean is just one of many catalog and direct marketing companies that have business alliances with FedEx. Another example of disintermediation is Calyx & Corolla, the San Francisco firm that sells fresh-cut flowers. Founded by Ruth Owades, who also launched the successful catalog company Gardener's Eden, C&C works with a dozen flower growers and sells their fresh-cut products directly to the end-user (the customer) using FedEx as shipper. As a result, the flowers stay fresher longer in the hands of the customer who buys them. "The customers we serve are really not the end customers; we serve the customers of our customers," says Jones. "Our role in the future will increasingly be to find ways to help our customers help their customers."

The next step beyond the extended enterprise alliance would be for FedEx customers with the PowerShip system to have the C&C catalog electronically embedded in their PowerShip software application. In that way, their PCs would become more and more of an information appliance, and FedEx would increasingly be a creator in the digital economy beyond the extended enterprise.

The FedEx clients are already there and waiting for such services. Two-thirds of all FedEx transactions are now handled using the PowerShip system. At peak pre-Christmas shopping time, up to three-quarters of all the courier company's business is via PowerShip. The walls between FedEx, its customers, and their customers are blurring. "People are trading off IT capability and transport for goods sitting on shelves, bricks, and mortar," says Jones. "You create value by reducing costs but you also create value by making your customers more capable to their customers. You make customers look good to their customers."

Another step in wealth creation will be the Net. "The Internet is certainly going to evolve and be the center of the universe," says Jones. "But there's a lot of networked-based business that can occur before the Internet reaches its full potential. What's happening now is a *Field of Dreams* approach—go on the Internet and people will buy. That's not necessarily correct. People have to have a reason to buy. They have to have a reason for changing how they buy. Putting goods on the Net doesn't necessarily create a change of practices. You need specific purposes and outcomes that create such an incentive for a customer that it's a success."

In preparation, FedEx has built a Web server on the Net. But this is more than a Home Page that provides information about the company. Customers can actually track packages on the Net by simply entering their ID number. This is one of the early interactive capabilities on the Net: providing customers with yet another way of interfacing with FedEx. According to Jones, within weeks of being available, the service was being used thousands of times per day: "We're not sure where this is going. In the past, any time we introduced a new service to the customers we saw 'S curve' growth. This will likely change many aspects of how we market to and interface with our customers. As buying becomes more prevalent on the Net, we will become an even more important component in the fulfillment chain."

"Federal Express is more than just an efficient and fast transportation company, but is an entrepreneurial enterprise whose success has been based upon combining sophisticated information and transportation networks to provide value to our customers by using our services to serve *their* customers more effectively," says Jones.

The Digital Creation of Ideas

You don't have to be a giant like FedEx to create an internetworked business. Sherri Leopard Communications, Inc., of Boulder, Colorado, is a 25-person public relations agency with annual billings of $8 million. The company is in the business of creating ideas to transform the marketplace image of clients. The way the firm is growing, it won't be small for long, all of it driven by Sherri Leopard who, in 1982, had crashed both personally and professionally. "My life was an absolute disaster," she says. "When the bottom fell out of the oil market, I found myself divorced and unemployed."

Her degree in parks and recreation wasn't much in demand, nor were there very many permanent jobs available in energy-dependent Colorado, so in desperation she turned to freelance writing and landed a few small contracts with IBM and Continental Airlines. Other lesser-light clients, a local barbecue restaurant and a dry cleaner, were neither as high profile nor as profitable, but they did offer some welcome barter possibilities for a struggling entrepreneur-to-be.

For the first six years, Leopard worked out of her house, slowly adding staff until there were six employees, enough to warrant real office space. She handled communications work for clients: press releases, slide presentations, direct mail, just about everything but advertising. In 1991 Leopard was drafting speech notes for an IBM executive and needed some examples to dapple through the text that described customers using IBM products, such as the firm's OS/2 personal computer.

 "I spent more time chasing those 15-second nuggets in the speech than writing the main themes," recalls Leopard. If only there were a central depository of such nuggets, she thought, others might find that sort of library a gold mine, too. And what if it were online, so potential users could have electronic access to it wherever they were and pull out instant, useful examples? But how to take such a leap into the technological unknown? Admits Leopard, "I didn't have a clue." What she did have, however, was a willingness to take a risk on her own idea and try to achieve change by using information technology. Leopard Communications ripped out its old system and installed a network of IBM OS/2 workstations and servers. The thinking was that the firm could get closer to its customers by using the same system they were. "We could understand them because we were using the same tools," says Leopard.

George Poirier, hired on contract and then named full-time MIS director, created the system Leopard needed by using Lotus Notes. Lotus Notes

(Level Two—The High-Performance Team) allows different employees to comment on the same situation. For example, a sales rep hears about a problem from a client and updates the account information with some suggestions for a solution. Her supervisor takes the file, adds some recommendations, and with a simple double click on the screen, sends the original note and her comments into a company-wide forum along with some charts and other graphics. Over the next 24 hours, another rep, and perhaps some R&D people, add more comments. The rep adds information about a possible responsive change to the product, then sends the whole proposal on to her boss and gets approval the next day. Clients across the country immediately receive on the network news about the change.

 There were no meetings. There wasn't even time wasted trying to set up a meeting, yet everyone added expertise to the project as time permitted. In the end, there was consensus and a solution was launched with the precision of a probe into space. Leopard Communications was creating an integrated organization. The new system caused an immediate impact. "We used to all manage files on our own desks. Now we've got a central file cabinet," says Leopard. Into that cabinet they poured details about specific product uses that they heard about from clients, trade magazines, e-mail chatter, and grapevines of every hue. A vast array of information on a variety of products, is important for a client like IBM. "IBM is attempting to have specialized marketing forces because product areas are getting so complex," says Poirier. "No matter where they are, they now have that database on their laptops."

 Sometimes, that means material that's not already in the database. At a recent Comdex show in Las Vegas (the huge computer trade show that annually attracts 130,000 attendees), a company rep wanted to show prospective clients a recent magazine advertisement. A copy of the magazine wasn't good enough—he wanted it on his laptop. So Leopard Communications scanned the ad in Boulder, put it into the database, and within two hours the rep was bedazzling clients.

Such access to information is essential when a potential client calls for a request for proposal (RFP). Clients usually want examples of other companies that are successfully using, say, the same client/server system they're considering. The capacity to find endorsements, an exercise that used to take several days, now requires seconds because the marketing rep has in the laptop examples that have been downloaded that morning from Leopard's digital document library. As well, there are videos of the product or service—all available for demonstration from this electronic library on the rep's laptop as part of the RFP (Level Four—The Extended Enterprise).

At the moment, there are 268 references in the database—focused on IBM desktop, LAN, and networking systems—and the number is doubling annually. Because the information is equally available to 15,000 IBM reps in the United States and an unknown number around the world through IBM servers in Cary, North Carolina, and Austin, Texas, "It's empowering people," says Leopard. "Who's the keeper?" Everyone and no one. "The infrastructure is in place now and with this information in their hands, they'll want more information," says Kathy Simon, the firm's technology director. As a former IBMer who joined Leopard Communications in 1984, Simon has seen how marketing has changed. For the recent launch of OS/2 Warp in China, everything needed was on two laptops, including video clips and audio. "I just smile when I think of the equipment cases we used to have to lug around the world."

Because the system is open and user-friendly, the newest employee at Leopard Communications can attain goals she or he didn't even know were possible. Patty Graff, 46, and the mother of 2 teenagers, started as a receptionist-secretary in 1991. She freely admits that she knew nothing about computers when she arrived, but after 18 months as receptionist she became an account assistant. "Two years ago I wouldn't have dreamed of … being in this job. Two years from now? The sky's the limit," says Graff. "You can't help but grow in this company. If you don't, it's your own fault. You just have to trust the technology," says Graff. "The more we learn about what we're doing, the more we can do. Organizations need to rely on each other as individuals and teams. No one person can achieve everything."

 Leopard's firm now offers clients a three-part service. First, there are the traditional, static PR agency items like direct mail. Second, are multimedia presentations beamed by satellite to trade shows, like the corporate ad to Comdex. Third, is the online communications database, or what Leopard calls "the future of the business."

The next step was to move everything onto the Internet, putting Leopard at the fifth level: the digital economy. "With our own Web server, we deliver to our clients via the Internet," says Simon. "We've changed our whole approach to clients because the big missing piece was content," says Leopard. And it means that more employees, like Patty Graff, can be as successful as the boss. "We've relied on Sherri to bring in the business, but her bandwidth is only so wide," says Poirier. With the database, every employee has access to all client account information, Leopard can monitor what's happening, and the whole team knows what's going on. "The trouble with empowering people is that they can all go and get business. Somebody's got to catch it all," laughs Poirier. Of course, that's better than not getting any business at all.

The database has become the core of Leopard's strength. After all, what's the point of hiring a PR agency if no one has anything to say? This way, everybody can use the same hymn book and anyone can reach even the highest notes. "Sherri can no longer do it all," says Simon. "As an entrepreneur, she has to believe in people's ability to get work done without her. We've seen people rise to the occasion. We can now form teams, then break them up and form new ones. At any given time, Sherri and I can be on three to four teams at once."

What IT has done, whether at giants like FedEx or small firms like Leopard Communications, is place decisions in the hands of people all the way down in the organization and create the capacity for firms to operate on all five levels of the internetworked enterprise—from individual effectiveness to the digital economy.

THE DIGITAL EXECUTION OF PROCESSES

 Paul Revere Life Insurance Co. set out, with fairly limited goals, to reduce costs and serve clients better using IT. Along the way, the company achieved a whole lot more personal mastery. When the process began at Paul Revere, a niche insurer specializing in disability income insurance to the high-end individual market, it took as much as seven weeks from the time of application to the point at which Paul Revere, the market-share leader in individual disability insurance, could issue the policy. The time was cut to two weeks by changing the data islands into connected networks. The objective was to create leaders at all levels of the organization, or "empowerment of employees," as information systems vice president Gary MacConnell puts it, by "giving them everything they need to do their jobs, to be followed by giving them additional authority."

A related goal was improving customer service, and the result was getting beyond reengineering to change fundamentally the way products are marketed. "Like many business processes, policy acquisition has grown topsy turvy, and the process has had various activities tacked onto it in an unplanned manner," MacConnell says. What Paul Revere did was to create workgroup computing that supported the teams in the underwriting department. Each underwriter now has a workstation that can integrate data from various sources; the entire department will become better integrated through an integrated computing architecture. Client signatures will even be captured electronically. According to MacConnell, "At the same time we are reengineering the business processes, we are retooling the systems infrastructure. Data processing systems are disjointed islands, and data are often entered redundantly multiple times."

The new integrated architecture is based on client/server computing and the distribution of databases. "We are reducing lower-level jobs and upgrading them to include more authority and a broader perspective on the function," says MacConnell. "Today we have people performing individual functions like an assembly line, but for the most part, they don't have a perspective on the broader process. In the new process, people will have an interest, view, and accountability for the total process, with the goal of reducing the size of the workforce, speeding up the process dramatically, and closing business."

"Dramatic change is hard for people to get their heads around," says MacConnell. "We are disturbing the status quo and asking the sales department, disability organization, and mail department, for example, to change. We are crossing the vertical lines of the old organization with these new horizontal processes such as acquisition. We need a new structure that can manage these horizontal processes. People will be losing some of the control they had in the past. People need to cooperate in new ways. My own feeling is that we are just scratching the surface today. If we go ahead 10 years and look back we will likely observe that we fundamentally changed the way we do business through the new technology."

THE DIGITAL DESIGN OF THINGS

The new Boeing 777 began in 1990 with a handwritten memo. Signed by James M. Guyette, executive vice president, operations, United Airlines and two officials of Boeing Commercial Airplanes Group, Richard R. Albrecht, executive vice president, and Phil Condit, executive vice president and general manager, it reads:

Although this preamble to the agreement took on a mantra-like meaning for everyone working on the project, it was just about the last handwritten document in a paperless process that created the world's largest twin-engine airplane. What Boeing Co., of Everett, Washington, accomplished was equal parts transformation of its corporate culture and an evangelical exercise in consciousness raising, for it altered the basic way an airplane had been built since World War II (see Table 5.1).

Once Boeing chairman and CEO Frank Shrontz authorized development of the 777, the company took the unusual step of calling in the airlines who would buy and fly the airplane. In the past, Boeing had manufactured its products on a "come and get it" basis. Now the firm was open to customer preferences. Even more revolutionary was the design-build process. Boeing set out to create a "paperless" airplane using digital design, cross-functional work teams, and advanced techniques in manufacturing. "It was a paradigm shift for everybody," says Larry Olson, director of information systems at the Everett site of Boeing Commercial Airplane Group. "We're in real competition with Airbus

TABLE 5.1

THE OLD ECONOMY WAY	THE NEW ECONOMY WAY
Build an airplane and deliver it.	Customer participates in design.
Make paper drawings and full-scale mockups.	Paperless, no mockups.
Test fly to discover blunders.	Computer simulation removes bugs.
Separate all work functions.	Design–build teams.
Write maintenance manuals last.	Mechanics involved throughout.

and we want to maintain as large a market share as possible. Our products have been around a long time and Airbus was delivering some of the newer products, so we wanted to improve our processes so that we could give better value and higher reliability to the airlines."

The process cost $4 billion, took five years, and resulted in an airplane that weighs about 550,000 pounds and, at 209 feet long with a wingspan of 200 feet, is only one foot narrower than a 747, can fly as far as 8,000 miles, carries up to 375 passengers, and costs about $125 million. When the first aircraft was delivered to United in May 1995, there were 144 orders and 99 options from fifteen airlines on four continents. "Engineers who had been with the company 10, 20, 30 years simply didn't think it would work," says Olson. "It was tough to change."

To create a team approach to designing the new aircraft, Boeing used the CATIA (computer-aided three-dimensional interactive application) and ELF-INI (finite element analysis system), both developed by Dassault Systemes of France and licensed in the United States through IBM. Designers also used EPIC (electronic preassembly integration) on CATIA. The workstations reduced or eliminated hand drawings, drafting tables, full-size metal mockups, and master models. Because every step was concurrent, engineers working together had simultaneous access to the design; they didn't have to wait while drawings ambled their way from place to place. CATIA's digital accuracy and three-dimensional checks at the preassembly stage allowed designers to see whether parts would fit or how adding new systems altered stress in the structure. That's because Boeing was able to create, in effect, an electronic mockup of the aircraft and focus on any of its 130,000 parts. So workable were the "drawings" that CATIA even had a computer-simulated mechanic who could demonstrate whether a human could get inside a particular area to carry out repairs.

"It's changed the whole way of building airplanes at Boeing," says Olson. "All of the digital data ... created by the engineer goes to make the tools that assemble the airplane. It means much higher accuracy in assembling. That means less drag and less fuel. Parts 'snap together,' as the mechanics say. If we had to go do this airplane on paper, it would take at least 30% to 40 % longer."

As a result of concurrent engineering and CATIA, changes were possible late in the procedure. For instance, aerodynamics was only one of the considerations in the wing-tip design. In the past, the process would have called for aerodynamic considerations first, followed by the later addition of such required items as visibility lights. The 777's design–build teams allowed everything to be built in at the same time.

The heart of the system included 1,700 individual computer workstations in the Puget Sound area, linked to four connected IBM mainframes that provided the capacity to carry out complete checks prior to assembly. This meant that misalignments could be spotted, tolerances confirmed, and weights analyzed. Access to the system went beyond Boeing itself to include many of the more than 500 suppliers in a dozen countries. A new computer-based control system made data available about production as well as offering updates on the status of the aircraft. Fully 20% of the 777 was produced in Japan, and key Japanese subcontractors working on the fuselage were connected via dedicated cable under the Pacific Ocean.

About 230 cross-functional teams, with up to 40 members, were organized around parts of the aircraft rather than according to function, as they had been in the past. The teams brought together engineering, procurement, manufacturing, operations, customer services, and marketing. "The biggest driving force for success was the 'working together' agreement not only with the airlines but all the employees. They could openly and honestly discuss all their problems," says Olson.

The result was as follows:

+ Sharing of knowledge and identification of problems before anything is manufactured
+ Reduction of engineering changes at the early stages of production
+ Lower manufacturing costs because parts have been integrated before production
+ 60% to 90% less scrap and rework than when using previous methods

In many ways, what Boeing did was return to its 1920 roots when the company was small enough that design engineers, the manufacturing group, and administrators could all sit around the same conference table and solve problems. As time passed, Boeing grew, departments became huge, and stages became separated. As each department finished its part of the project, it would throw plans "over the fence," in the jargon of Boeing, to the next department.

The new workgroups included not only Boeing staffers from every corner of the company but also key representatives from customers and vendors. The process meant joint problem solving, error reduction, and improved creativity. Coordination of the teams themselves resulted in fewer surprises. In the past, one function area might complete its work, then pass the results on without further communication. Now, manufacturing could immediately let the design team know the problems that had to be taken into account.

The teams did more than create the 777; they transformed Boeing by replacing bureaucracy and departmentalization with synergy and stimulation. The engineers also returned to the strength of the team process because they were able to collaborate over long distances on the same three-dimensional design just as if they were all brainstorming in the same room.

Critical to the process was the involvement of advisors from four of the airlines buying the 777 (Cathay Pacific, Japan Airlines, All Nippon Airlines, and United). The groups started counseling Boeing designers in 1989. The suggestions from the airlines influenced such basic considerations as the width of the fuselage, and they were particularly helpful on reliability and maintenance aspects of the aircraft. Other airlines were also involved. In all, they made more than 1,000 suggestions ranging from the size of operating buttons through the configuration of overhead baggage compartments to the speed with which toilet seats fall.

There were other advantages to the "paperless design." Among them was the fact that Boeing had twice as much time for testing before delivery. That was an important consideration because Boeing's previous effort, the 747–400 transport, was such an embarrassment to the company that it became famous in the trade. People would say, "The 747–400 is a terrific airplane. I can't wait until Boeing finishes it." The expense of that extra effort and time spent on the 777 will be offset by the fact that the aircraft won't come back for modifications once they're delivered.

Another advantage is the reduced production costs that result from the advanced design and manufacturing techniques. Boeing's rationale is that lower initial and operating costs will mean that more people can fly; in turn, such increased load factors will spark more orders.

In the past, the last aspect of any airplane to be created was the maintenance manual. Engineers wrote the tome and it was delivered to the airlines after delivery of the plane. With the 777, mechanics were involved throughout the process and the 30,000-page manual is supplied with the aircraft on a CD-ROM for quick access. Training is done on interactive computers. "People won't tolerate the old way any longer," says Olson. "It's a major breakthrough." Moreover, the Boeing 777 has secured 75% of the market in competition with the A–330 and A–340 Airbus models.

The digital economy reaches travelers in the 777 as well. Each seat location has a digital display that allows passengers to do things now available on other airplanes (such as play video games or make telephone calls), but eventually passengers will be able to use a bank or credit card to transfer funds, buy tickets, send faxes, transmit computer data, even gamble.

The Digital Design, Manufacturing, and Marketing of Things

Chrysler has adopted a new set of company values and a new technology platform that has combined to reduce the turnaround time for a car—from concept to production—from six years to less than two years. The results in the market add up to nothing less than a spectacular turnaround.

Chrysler's heyday came with the 1959 DeSoto Firedome with its fins that seemed to rise higher than the car roof itself. Throughout the 1960s and 1970s, the auto manufacturer went into a long, slow decline. Its factories produced poor-quality cars, forced them on dealers for customers who hadn't placed orders, and stockpiled the rest by the tens of thousands. The Big Three all suffered, but Chrysler was in the worst shape, and by 1982 Japanese imports had captured 30% of the North American market. Lee Iacocca, who joined Chrysler in 1978, had emerged by then as the new industry spokesman even though Chrysler's annual losses ran to $1 billion. He bravely told consumers if they could find a better car than a Chrysler, they should buy it. Many did. Chrysler was all but bankrupt, even though a government bailout of $1.2 billion in loan guarantees had rescued the mismanaged firm two years before. The bleak recession of the time did not bode well for increased sales and restored profits.

Iacocca pushed Chrysler to bring out a convertible, then in 1980 the minivan. This policy turned out to be prescient. Suburban families were looking for a change from the station wagon of old; the minivan remade Chrysler's reputation and bolstered profits. By March 1983, Iacocca had made a difference, and to cap the turnaround he appeared on the cover of *Time*. The Magic Wagon came out that fall, three years after Iacocca had given the go-ahead, seven years after it had first been promoted within the auto giant and even more years after it had been discussed at Ford but always postponed. But since Iacocca's retirement, there are even bigger developments underway.

Today, Chrysler is not only the most productive automaker in North America; it is the most profitable. The new Chrysler is based on a set of five core beliefs and values that are widely internalized across the company. The senior management training in these values was personally conducted by chairman Bob Eaton. They include the following:

- *Customer Focus:* Delighting customers stands above all other values.
- *Inspired People:* Success will be achieved only through inspired people operating in an environment based on mutual trust and respect, openness and candor, empowerment and teamwork, innovation and risk taking, encouraging and valuing diversity, and integrity.

- *Continuous Improvement:* Embracing constant change and creating a culture based on constant reinvention of the company and core processes make for continuous improvement.
- *Financial Success:* To pursue other values, the company must make enough money to ensure vitality in good times and bad.
- *Reputation:* Reputation is determined by the standards and behaviors of all Chrysler people.

Chrysler is relying on CATIA, the same Dussault-designed system used by Boeing for the 777—which enables, among other things, reusability of previous useful designs. Initially, these were intelligent terminals connected to a mainframe to provide 2D and 3D modeling for design and engineering of new cars, but a program is underway to replace these terminals with multimedia workstations. According to Gene Crombex of the technical computing center, "There are many advantages to the workstations, including their capabilities, a growing list of features, and systems performance, which is particularly bad on mainframes during the day."

Personal multimedia is used to create what Sue Unger, Chrysler chief information officer, describes as a "virtual car." The idea is to create a car made of bits before creating a car made of atoms. For example, the workstations allow computer simulation both in design and manufacturing. Testing for noise, vibration, and crashes can be carried out on the system before cars are assembled.

The same is true for designing plants. The computer simulation of manufacturing enables plant designers to create a "virtual plant." The goal is to get first-time capabilities 100% of the time—that is, 100% of the vehicles go through the plant with no defects. Simulation has led Chrysler to rearrange lines, thus challenging suppliers' assumptions. "We reconfigure plants before they are ever designed. It is important to do it right the first time," says Unger.

The real power of personal multimedia comes from its role in creating high-performance teams. Chrysler's most recent success was the Neon, the first small car designed and built in North America. The Neon was created by using a team approach called the *platform*. Everyone involved in the design and engineering of the car worked together as a team. But unlike the old teams, the new platform teams were empowered to make the key design and engineering decisions, rather than having to go up through the old management hierarchy. As well, the teams cut across the organizational lines. "It used to be that the engineers weren't allowed in the design studio," says Dennis Pawley, executive vice president of manufacturing. "Now they ... influence the design as it is being developed."[3]

Similar platform teams were used to develop the Cirrus, again reducing the time to market. The result? More up-to-date technology because everything can be changed on the fly, thus bringing a new generation of technology to market ahead of the competition.

The platform approach is more than a computer system; it is an organizational and management concept. Designer engineer, advance manufacturer, and supplier all work hand in hand on one platform. As in the case of Boeing, there is concurrent engineering. And because suppliers and manufacturing are involved, the vehicle can be designed for manufacturability.

"All the right parties are working together as a team, considering all aspects of the vehicle. That has made a huge difference. It's like everyone is in the same room working on the same idea even though they're not," says Unger. "It's a team approach which not only speeds up the time, but we get better designs. Because all the key people are involved concurrently, there is improved collaboration, teamwork, and better ideas."

The team approach improved the quality of worklife and motivation for the players, too. The shift is from being a task worker, along the old Taylorist model, to having a whole job in which you can see how what you do relates to the rest of the process. For example, the company used to have single-task jobs such as "checkers," people who performed a single task: checking the accuracy of blueprints. Those kinds of jobs are replaced by "whole jobs" that involve many different kinds of knowledge activities.

 The concept of platform teams has broken down the old hierarchies, leading Chrysler to take steps toward being an integrated organization. The team transcends traditional organizational boundaries, by, for example, linking design and manufacturing, which enables the designers to create things that can in fact be manufactured. Engineers now rub shoulders with assembly line employees. Executives and designers trade ideas. Union leaders work with techies. The old system caused attitude and quality problems. The platform team means that corrections can occur before full-volume production."[4]

To achieve integration, Chrysler is working to create an enterprise info-structure. MOPAR (Chrysler's parts division) was organized by country. If someone from Chrysler Corporation in the United States were looking for a part they would be able to see only U.S. inventory. This would create bizarre situations wherein the company in Mexico might be scrapping parts needed in the United States. "Now," says Unger, "we've taken an enterprise approach—one architecture across the whole company." A five-person executive team meets on a regular basis to oversee this thrust toward enterprise thinking.

Once the physical plant is up and producing, there are now factory information systems and performance feedback systems in which computers monitor manufacturing equipment and the production line problems. The integrated performance feedback systems also do manpower scheduling, provide information regarding what is to be built, supply quality indicators and SPC (statistical process control) charting—thereby providing any key messages to the workforce in the plant.

The integrated organization, as exemplified by Chrysler, holds lessons for much smaller firms as well. "Small companies need to work in teams and streamline just as much as large companies," says John Miller, general manager, large-car platform engineering. "To get competitive with the Japanese we've got to have four middlemen for their five. If they've got five and we've got seven, we lose."[5]

 Platforms reach out to suppliers. Vertical integration in the car industry is long gone. Seventy percent of a new car is manufactured by suppliers. It is therefore critical to fully involve suppliers in the design process. "We are trying to reduce the number of suppliers. They actually do more and more of the design and testing work," says Unger. "Some are located in the technology center itself and some are resident in the design center—some for a short period and others come for a year or more. Wherever they are they can simultaneously work on the same design on the screen."

 Chrysler is also reaching out to dealers through the new technology using DIAL (dealer information access link). Dealers register warranty claims on the system, which automatically verifies information and even transfers funds to the dealer. Other capabilities inform dealers of service bulletins and sales policy changes.

And where is all this headed? Onto the Net. Already Chrysler monitors automotive discussion groups on the Net and finds the Net an invaluable source of knowledge about customer opinions and about the problems and pluses of Chrysler vehicles. Like the other auto manufacturers, they are already marketing on the Net through devices such as the Chrysler Home Page.

Moreover, videoconferencing with dealers is in place. In the past, the company had to fly in engineers for dealer visits if there were problems. Now the dealers can show engineering the defective part via video. Down the road, such videoconferencing will be available directly from desktops. Multimedia are also being used for marketing through CDs. Today, potential customers can receive a CD that explains the Neon's features and benefits.

And in the future? Consumers won't have to go to a dealership to purchase a car. They'll be able to shop in the digital marketplace, evaluate financing alternatives, simulate a test drive, configure a car, and execute the transaction from their own PC. Chrysler isn't talking but we can expect, before the end of the decade, the three-day car will be here—the specific vehicle you customized to your need, built and delivered to you in three days.

The Digitally Supported Selling of Things

As commerce comes on the Net, the marketplace for many goods and services becomes digital. But on a more mundane level, traditional bricks-and-mortar retailing can be transformed for success by the new technology.

 Some people have made the extended organization look like a piece of cake. But as actor Henry Fonda put it, when describing his craft, "Nobody knows how hard I work to make sure the wheels don't show." Take Walmart Stores, Inc., the world's largest and most successful retailer, with 1994 sales of $80 billion from stores in the United States, Canada, and Mexico. As a strategy, Walmart decided to offer quality goods at low prices where the customer wanted them—a deceivingly simple mission statement that hides a complex structure.

For Walmart, the key is something called *cross-docking*, an inventory system that means goods arrive at the warehouse from suppliers and are dispatched to stores without dawdling in inventory. The result? An extended enterprise approach to stock replenishment. The right goods come from suppliers and are available at the right price when the customer wants them. Cross-docking means that items are continuously delivered to Walmart receiving docks at the company's two dozen distribution centers. There they are repacked and sent to individual stores without spending any time at all under Walmart's warehouse roof, crossing from one loading dock to the next in 24 to 48 hours. That savings in time and money means Walmart can buy at the lowest prices, keep a regular flow of goods to its stores, and reduce handling costs—a savings that goes right to the bottom line. Even better, the order process responds to consumer demand. Sales in the stores drive the order process, not the wild idea of some buyer presented with a one-off special.

At Walmart, every store's layout for the 36 departments is individually planned by using computer models so that shopping traffic goes first through softlines (such as ladies apparel or household paper goods) to hardlines (like toasters and anything else that won't bend) because profit margins on softlines are one-third higher than on hardlines. Walmart's designers want customers to see potential impulse items before they find what they came looking for.

As for individual effectiveness (Level One), employees are armed with a handheld Telxon gun that scans the product barcode on each item and gives sales information on the display readout. Sales for the day, week, and five weeks back give the associate, as Walmart staffers are known, the sales history of the item. There's also an instant readout of the number of items on the shelf, in stock, in transit, and on order—all the information needed to place an order. And that's exactly what the associate does, right in the aisle. "That's empowerment," says Bill Woodward, vice president and chief administrative officer for Walmart International. "It is the link to life at Walmart. If you expect people to do things and you give them the tools, they'll do it even better than you expected."

"There are basic human needs: the need to be liked, the need to be needed, and the need to be empowered," says Bill Redman, Walmart's senior vice president, store planning, Bentonville, Arkansas. "Nobody works for any company just because of the pay. It's probably not even in the top three. You can't have a company unless *you* feel empowered. There must be respect for everyone, no matter what their job is. Happy people equal customer service." That's why fun is always a part of Walmart, a concept started by founder Sam Walton, who died in 1992, and was always ready to clown around. In 1984 he did the hula in a grass skirt on Wall Street over a bet and always said, "When all else fails, sing a silly song and laugh at yourself."

Yes, employees are empowered by the technology for individual effectiveness, but they are also doing inventory right in the aisles (the high-performance team) where they can respond to customer's questions, thus doing two roles at once. Using barcode information flashed via satellite to Bentonville, Arkansas, headquarters (the Integrated Organization), Walmart can purchase truckloads of goods, split the items for redistribution, and not have to worry about the cost of carrying those goods in inventory. The satellite system in turn is linked to Walmart's more than 4,000 suppliers so that fully 85% of the 70,000

SKUs (stock-keeping units) in each store have come through the Walmart distribution system compared to 50% for its competitors. The sales stream is so fast that Walmart can use cash from the customers to pay suppliers, a step that moves Walmart up the ladder to Level Four, the extended enterprise.

The whole process is managed by using a satellite communications system that means information from checkout goes immediately to Walmart's suppliers. This is an example of the kind of disintermediation discussed in Chapter. 2. As one of the main themes of the new economy, disintermediation occurs when the middleman functions are eliminated through digital networks. The techniques used at Walmart, a clever combination of people and technology, work. Walmart's more than 2,000 stores, 105 SuperCenters, and 435 Sam's Clubs do $80 billion a year in sales, making it the world's largest retailer. A 100-share investment in the company in 1970, worth $1,650, is now worth $2.7 million. Not bad for an outfit that opened its first store in Rogers, Arkansas, in 1962. Contrast Walmart's individualistic client/server approach with Sears, saddled for years with host-based systems, and you'll begin to understand why Walmart succeeded while Sears was stuck in the past. Which of them is ready for the digital economy?

Other large retailers such as Levi-Strauss have implemented electronic data interchange (EDI) to link directly with suppliers by electronically communicating shipping advisories, invoices, messages, and in the case of Sears, for example, 21 million purchase orders annually in North America. McKesson Corp., of San Francisco, has become the world's largest distributor of pharmaceuticals and health and beauty aids by connecting its stores in the United States and Canada to one database ordering system. Called Econolink-Pharmaserv, the database responds, when a pharmacy orders items, by sending a plastic blue shipping box onto the conveyor belt in the nearest of the firm's three warehouses.

Barcode scanners run by computer direct the container through an automatic picking process that collects the desired items. Less common products are cherrypicked by employees wearing gloves equipped with infrared scanners. When the order is complete, a printer automatically generates an invoice and a label, then the box is sealed and the conveyor takes it onto a truck.

In the McKesson system, orders are filled at the rate of 12 per minute, mistakes are said to be nonexistent, and delivery is the next day. The system helps customers run their businesses, get instant turnaround, and carry little inventory. McKesson, obviously, achieves a competitive advantage in the marketplace.

Today, for a retailer not to train workers is tantamount to giving competitors an advantage. At Fred Meyer Stores, a hypermart chain based in Portland, Oregon, multimedia workstations are used to train sales staff for individual effectiveness. "Because the market supply is characterized by uniform pricing and availability of goods, the firm's profit margin is influenced by the customer service variable," says Pat Ogborn, assistant vice president of employee development. "The success of the workstations is due to the collaborative effort between the firm and all vendors in developing the courses."[6] Just another way that the enterprise can be extended.

THE DIGITAL SELLING OF THINGS

Bill Murphy, a Bay Area executive, and his wife Brenda LaChance, have set up a hobby winery called Clos LaChance Vineyard. Faced with the prospect of being empty nesters, they decided to enter the wine business, small time. Says Bill, "We are really a virtual winery. We buy grapes from other vineyards. We lease space at a production winery. We contract with talent for wine making and label design. We acquire materials like bottles and corks from other sources. We lease warehouse storage." This is done through the Net. They use information technology to communicate and monitor everything.

The marketplace for Clos LaChance Vineyard is an electronic one—they also sell through the Internet. Clos LaChance Vineyard has a Home Page explaining their product and showing how to order their products electronically. Efforts are underway to make available audio clips of authorities saying how much they like Clos LaChance Vineyard wine. Says Murphy, "We're really intrigued by the possibilities for leveling the playing field by marketing through the information infrastructure. Mondavi has a zillion dollars of advertising money and we have zero dollars. If we do a better job than Mondavi in positioning our company on the Net, we may be able to compete."

A PRINTING PRESS AT YOUR FINGERTIPS

When consultant Pat Mullen wrote a nasty note to Dollar Rent-A-Car about the bad service he had received, he advised them that he could have chosen to post the note on the Net instead, which would have had farther-reaching implications than the private note he had chosen to write. In the digital economy you risk losing not only Pat Mullen's business but an unknown and infinitely larger group of customers—those reading about Pat's problems via the internet.

Sun Microsystems was one of the first companies to establish a Home Page on the Web, and it is one of the more active sites. Sun and many of Sun's business partners publish information such as marketing literature, press releases, product announcements, and "bug fixes" on the Net. According to Sun CEO Scott McNealy, "We use it as a source of information for the Sun community in a very aggressive way. Today, we don't do a lot of transactions over the Internet because of the security and authentication problems. You don't want people ordering a bunch of pizzas like people used to do in college. The pizzas would be delivered to the person next door and the delivery guy would decide to leave it rather than take it back. That kind of stuff will happen if you don't have security and, most importantly, authenticated communications so you can be sure who sent you that pizza." McNealy says that security concerns will be eliminated and insists that he was never personally involved in such pizza scams in college. Duly noted here for the record.

The electronic market is no small potatoes. For example, CUC Home Shopping Services, of Stamford, Connecticut, already provides more than 30 million consumers with access to computerized shopping services such as auto insurance, travel, and dining through an online network. "In order for there to be a successful digital marketplace, more vendors need to be successful," says Rick Fernandez, senior vice president of financial services. "Vendors can learn from one another and pool research and development resources to create a supply of successful applications."[7]

In the next chapter, I examine a special example of the Internetworked Enterprise—Government.

Notes

1. Based on the description by Leslie A. Sandberg who is the chair of the NIIT Health Care Working Group. "Reflections on Building a Transnational Telemedicine Demonstration Network," *Vision Becomes Reality*, The Journal of the National Information Infrastructure Testbed, January 1995, Vol. 95, No. 1, Washington, D.C.
2. Ibid., p. 13.
3. Fred Langan, "Driving Change," *Ways*, November/December 1994, p. 27.
4. Ibid, p. 32.
5. Ibid, p. 32.
6. Case study courtesy The Alliance for Converging Technologies.
7. Ibid.

20th Anniversary Edition Commentary on Chapter 6: Internetworked Government

"AROUND THE WORLD, the public sector is under siege: Taxpayers everywhere want better, cheaper government. The message is simple: Tinkering with the system is not good enough. What's needed is a complete reinvention of government."

I wrote these words 20 years ago, and they foreshadowed today's crisis of government. Back then, I highlighted the problem—Industrial Age government bureaucracy—and the opportunity to create a new model of government for the networked world.

To be sure there has been progress, but the crisis is deeper than ever. Perhaps there is finally a burning platform for such a reinvention to occur.

Today, the big theme is "Open Government." But the idea is misunderstood. Three elements are typically muddled.

1. *Government Transparency.* This is often expressed in the so-called "Freedom of Information" legislation. Transparency is good for sure, as sunlight is the best disinfectant for everything from inefficiency to corruption.
2. *Citizen Engagement.* This is when governments undertake programs to engage citizens in sometimes radically new ways. This holds the promise of reinventing democracy. (See Chapters 1 and 14.)
3. *Some Fundamental Changes to the Business of Government.* These are far-reaching and involve a new division of labor in society regarding how we create public value. This idea is explained below.

Governments today face incredibly complex challenges. Most people refer to the *fiscal crisis*—government debt is crushing economies and whole societies. In some countries, most notably in Europe, governments are in danger of defaulting on their sovereign debt. There is no end in sight, as tax revenues just can't keep up with basic expenditures.

However, the challenges are even greater. Sustaining societies and economies in the face of climate change, energy shortages, growing income inequalities, demographic shifts, and security will test the ingenuity of those who wish
to see, do, and participate in the public good.

The first wave of digitally enabled "e-government" strategies, which were
described in *The Digital Economy*, delivered some important benefits. It made
government information and services more accessible to citizens while creating
administrative and operational efficiencies. But too many of these initiatives
simply paved the cow paths—that is, they focused on automating existing processes and moving existing government services online.

Still today these so-called "e-government" initiatives are mired in old thinking such as the creation of "government portals," "joined-up government," and
"one-stop government." As such, they are missing the much bigger opportunity
to change the way governments orchestrate capability to create and deliver
services—ultimately changing the division of labor in society for economic and
social development, and social justice.

Until now, governments were modeled after the command-and-control
industrial organizations that dominated the landscape. If it was good enough
for General Motors (GM) it was good enough for bureaucrats. *The Digital Economy* described this problem well. But today in the private sector, mammoth,
vertically integrated industrial corporations have started to unbundle. Today's
most successful corporations aren't just speeded-up versions of the old industrial behemoths. Instead, we are seeing the rise of the "business web," a much
more supple and effective form of wealth creation.

An equally dramatic innovation is starting to happen throughout the public
sector, paralleling the new forms of commercial value creation. Just as customers in the private sector have moved from passive consumers to active consumers, becoming value-added participants in successful digital age business
models, there is a similar transformation in governance.

Governments are more and more dependent for authority on a network of
powers and counterinfluences of which they are just a part. Whether streamlining government service delivery or resolving complex global issues, governments are either actively seeking, or can no longer resist, broader participation
from citizens and a diverse array of other stakeholders. Just as the modern
multinational corporation sources ideas, parts, and materials from a vast external network of customers, researchers, and suppliers, governments must hone
their capacity to integrate skills and knowledge from multiple participants to
meet expectations for a more responsive, resourceful, efficient, and accountable form of governance.

Partnerships between governmental and external organizations, which were previously impossible, are beginning to materialize. They use the Internet to share power, forge new relationships, and partner on service delivery. These initiatives deliver a bigger bang for the taxpayer buck and create the opportunity for injecting private-sector innovation.

I call these new multistakeholder networks "governance webs." The big wins are not achieved simply by taking the status quo online, but instead by transforming the Industrial Age model into digital age governance.

The digital age allows the age-old question of "who does what" to be answered more creatively than ever before. "Public" value no longer needs to be provided by government alone. It can be provided by any combination of various public agencies, the private sector, a community group, or citizens themselves, using the Internet as a mechanism for collaboration, process management, and conducting transactions. The result is greater value and lower cost for the customers of government.

It is the next wave of innovation that presents an historic occasion to fundamentally redesign how government operates, how and what the public sector provides, and ultimately, the appropriate division of labor in society as we create public value. A growing number of governments understand the need to distribute power broadly and leverage innovation, knowledge, and value from the private sector and civil society.

Franklin Delano Roosevelt (FDR) and Winston Churchill wanted stronger government; Ronald Reagan and Margaret Thatcher wanted less government. Thanks to the Internet we can now have it both ways. Governments can become a stronger part of the social ecosystem that binds individuals, communities, and businesses—not by absorbing new responsibilities or building additional layers of bureaucracy, but through their willingness to open up formerly closed processes to broader input and innovation.

In other words, government becomes a platform for social innovation and the creation of public value. The idea of "government as a platform" was first introduced by academics at Princeton and Yale and then explained more thoroughly in the book *Open Government: Collaboration, Transparency, and Participation in Practice*, published by writer and thought leader Tim O'Reilly,[1] who had been developing the concept for the previous two years. The idea is a new role for government whereby it provides resources, sets rules, and mediates disputes, but allows citizens, nonprofits, and the private sector to do a lot of the heavy lifting. The idea is a simple one.

In the past, governments collected tax dollars from citizens. Government employees, inside the boundaries of government, created services that were delivered back to the citizens. This exchange of tax dollars for services will continue, but courtesy of the Internet, there's an expanded model of government whereby government acts as a platform.

There is an enormous amount of data inside government such as data about climate change, the success of entrepreneurs, radon gas, bicycle accidents, and so on. With governments starting to make this raw data available to citizens, people will self-organize to use the data to create value. This is not about outsourcing or privatization. This is about a new division of labor in society with respect to how we create public value. The results are better government services and a government that costs less.

The province of British Columbia (BC) is a leader in this thinking. It recently challenged programmers to create innovative Web-based and mobile apps that would raise awareness of climate change and inspire BC residents to take action. As an incentive, the private sector chipped in $40,000 in prize money.

One of the winning apps helps students track their carbon footprints. Users record activities such as bathing, eating, and transportation, and the app calculates an "impact statement" with annualized kilograms of carbon dioxide equivalents generated. Another winning app, targeted at small- and medium-sized businesses, lets a business measure its emissions and then benchmark its score against industry peers.

None of the initiatives spurred on by the contest required new rules or new legislation to move forward. The "BC Challenge" created millions of dollars of public value but cost the government virtually nothing. And it took a small step toward becoming a data platform on which private companies, civil society organizations, and individual citizens can collaborate to create public value.

There is a new kind of public sector organization emerging—one that opens its doors to the world; co-innovates with everyone, especially citizens; shares resources that were previously closely guarded; and harnesses the power of collaborative innovation. I'm hopeful that there is finally a burning platform for change.

Notes

1. Daniel Lathrop, and Laurel Ruma, (eds.) and Don Tapscott (Foreword), *Open Government: Collaboration, Transparency, and Participation in Practice,* (Sebastopol, California, O'Reilly Media 2010). In particular Chapter 2 "Government As a Platform," by Tim O'Reilly, explains the concept.

INTERNETWORKED GOVERNMENT

The megastate that this century built is bankrupt, morally as well as financially. It has not delivered. But its successor cannot be "small government" (as the so-called conservatives want). There are far too many risks domestically and internationally. We need effective government—and that is what the voters in all developed countries are actually clamoring for.

Peter Drucker, 1995[1]

Government bashing has become everyone's favorite sport, but governments are central players in the new economy. They set the climate for wealth creation. They can act as a deadening hand on change or be a catalyst for creativity. They can cause economic stagnation through runaway deficits, or they can set a climate for growth. They can be blind to the challenges of transformation—for example, addressing issues that cannot be left to the market—or they can provide leadership.

THE PROBLEM: THE INDUSTRIAL AGE BUREAUCRACY

Around the world, the public sector is under siege: Taxpayers everywhere want better, cheaper government. The message is simple: Tinkering with the system is not good enough. What's needed is a complete reinvention of government.

The federal government initiated the National Performance Review in 1993. A team developed a report and set of accompanying documents that addressed key issues of reinvention. Since then, by most accounts, overall progress has been uneven in implementing the approaches developed.

The report notes that public confidence in the federal government has never been lower. The average American believes 48 cents of every tax dollar are wasted. Five of every six want "fundamental change" in Washington. Only 20% of Americans trust the federal government to do the right thing most of the time—down from 76% 30 years ago. The national debt now exceeds $4 trillion—$16,600 for every man, woman, and child in America.

There is enormous unseen waste. The Department of Defense owns more than $40 billion in unnecessary supplies. The Internal Revenue Service struggles to collect billions in unpaid bills. A century after industry replaced farming as America's principal source of wealth creation, the Department of Agriculture still operates more than 12,000 field service offices, an average of nearly four for every county in the nation—rural, urban, or suburban.

The performance review goes further:

> And yet, waste is not the only problem. The federal government is not simply broke; it is broken. Ineffective regulation of the financial industry brought us the Savings and Loan debacle. Ineffective education and training programs jeopardize our competitive edge. Ineffective welfare and housing programs undermine our families and cities.

> We spend $25 billion a year on welfare, $27 billion on food stamps, and $13 billion on public housing—yet more Americans fall into poverty every year.

> We spend $12 billion a year waging the war on drugs—yet see few signs of victory. We fund 150 different employment and training programs—yet the average American has no idea where to get job training, and the skills of our workforce fall further behind those of our competitors.[2]

The conclusion was that the United States is suffering the deepest crisis of faith in government in memory. In past crises—Watergate or the Vietnam War, for example—Americans doubted their leaders on moral or ideological grounds. They felt that their government was deceiving them or failing to represent their values. Today's crisis is different: People simply feel that government doesn't work.

Calls to "reinvent government" often originate from the lack of control, accountability, and visibility of centralized, macrolevel initiatives. It is no wonder that depersonalized programs aimed at the "average citizen" spawn alienation. People criticize a faceless bureaucracy that is unable to accurately meet expectations of personalized services that recognize differences and uniqueness.

The weaknesses of the public sector reflect in large part the continued reliance on mass-production methods.

A Canadian government report, *Blueprint for Renewing Government Services Using Information Technology*, written by public servants, candidly recognizes the public's rising frustration: "Many consumers of government services appear to have lost their tolerance for bureaucracies. They feel they receive better service from banks, car rental companies, even supermarkets, which have transformed business with innovative information technology. The government increasingly appears to be out of date. Many want to know why they have to spend their precious time finding answers to their questions, after being bounced from department to department, when sometimes it is easier to get satisfaction from customer-hungry private companies." The *Blueprint* says that taxpayers are rightfully demanding to know: "Why do I have to call so many places? Why do I have to wait so long? Why can't [the bureaucrats] solve my problem right here, right now?"[3]

In defense of the bureaucrats and government leaders, 10 years ago such complaints largely defied solution. Governments are Industrial Age organizations, based on the same command-and-control model of the enterprise that was created for the industrial economy. Bureaucracy and the industrial economy rose hand in hand. The economy needed roads, sewers, electrification, railways, and a sophisticated military. As government got bigger, and thereby the revenues of government increased, it became necessary to have more elaborate procedures, structures, and controls than were appropriate for an agrarian economy. These helped to ensure some degree of accountability, the reduction of overt patronage, and the use of a government job as a payoff for political support.

As a result, different departments or agencies were created, run by new layers of professional managers. Hiring practices not controlled by politicians, pay scales, procedures for making appointments, financial systems, audit processes, and the like were put in place. Such agencies grew in size and funding, applying new rules and procedures to ever-increasing layers of staff. All this was judged to be state of the art at the time. (Bureaucracy was a very positive term 100 years ago.)

Such bureaucracies have therefore traditionally operated like individual "stovepipes"—with information flowing only vertically and rarely between departments.

During the last 35 years, governments applied computers to their work as each agency acquired and built data processing systems to meet their automation needs. Old procedures, processes, and organizational forms were encoded in software. Huge, unwieldy mainframe beasts not only cemented old ways of working, they added additional levels of bureaucracy to plan, implement, operate, and control them. In the 1970s, this practice was extended to minicomputers and in the 1980s to PCs and LANs. Spending grew to the point that by 1994 the U.S. government alone spent over $25 billion per year on information systems, excluding "embedded" military systems. The result? Government organizations today are locked into old structures and ways of working, each with corresponding islands of technology. This is creating a demand-pull for new approaches to technology.

This problem today is compounded by the political nature of government bureaucracies in which everyone is oriented to avoiding mistakes that could by picked up by the opposition to embarrass the party in power. As described by the National Performance Review report:

> The budget system, the personnel rules, the procurement process, the inspectors general—all are designed to prevent the tiniest misstep. We assume that we can't trust employees to make decisions, so we spell out, in precise detail, how they must do virtually everything, then audit them to ensure that they have obeyed every rule. The slightest deviation prompts new regulations and even more audits.

> Before long, simple procedures are too complex for employees to navigate, so we hire more budget analysts, more personnel experts, and more procurement officers to make things work. By then, the process involves so much red tape that the smallest action takes far longer and costs far more than it should. Simple travel arrangements require endless forms and numerous signatures. Straightforward purchases take months; larger ones take years. Routine printing jobs can take dozens of approvals. This emphasis on process steals resources from the real job: serving the customer.[4]

INTERNETWORKED GOVERNMENT FOR THE AGE OF NETWORKED INTELLIGENCE

As Osborne and Gaebler write in the landmark book *Reinventing Government*, we need governments that are catalytic—steering and sparking action rather than doing things themselves; community-owned—empowering rather than serving; mission-driven, results-oriented, and customer-focused. Governments, they say, should inject competition into service delivery; focus on earning rather than spending; shift from hierarchy to teamwork and participation; and focus on prevention rather than cure.[5]

Academics and pundits discussing the reinvention of government have given lip service to the notion that the new information technology is the key enabler of government transformation. But progress has been slow on how technology can achieve the new paradigm in governance. Interestingly, the leadership, with few exceptions, has come from government itself, not its critics and analysts. Such leadership is occurring at the national, state, and local levels, in particular in the United States and Canada.

The notion of electronic government is sweeping across the North American public sector like a prairie fire, sparking interest in many other countries. The electronic government is an internetworked government. It links new technology with legacy systems internally and in turn links such government information infrastructures externally with everything digital, and with everybody—the taxpayer, suppliers, business customers, voters; and every other institution in the society—schools, laboratories, mass media, hospitals, other levels of government, and other nations around the world.

Internetworking is the vehicle to not only reduce the costs of government but also to radically transform the way government programs are delivered and the very nature of governance (see Figure 6.1). Internetworked government can overcome the barriers of time and distance to perform the business of government and give people public information and services when and where they want them. Governments can use electronic systems to deliver better-quality products to the public more quickly, cost effectively, and conveniently. The result will be programs designed primarily around the needs of citizens, rather than just the old structures or the convenience of civil servants.

As Jim Flyzik, chair of the Government Information Technology Services (GITS) Working Group of the U.S. National Performance Review, says:

It is an opportunity to use the power of information technology to fight the war on crime, to deliver entitlement benefits to the needy in a secure and efficient manner while eliminating fraud and cheating, to improve health care delivery, to find missing children, to improve privacy protection for all citizens—in short, to completely reshape how government delivers its services to its customers.

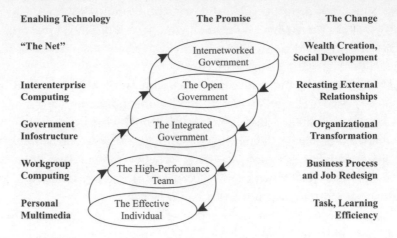

Enabling Technology	The Promise	The Change
"The Net"	Internetworked Government	Wealth Creation, Social Development
Interenterprise Computing	The Open Government	Recasting External Relationships
Government Infostructure	The Integrated Government	Organizational Transformation
Workgroup Computing	The High-Performance Team	Business Process and Job Redesign
Personal Multimedia	The Effective Individual	Task, Learning Efficiency

FIGURE 6.1 *The Promise of Internetworked Government.* SOURCE: © New Paradigm Learning Corporation, 1996.

1. *Effective individuals.* Personal multimedia computing will provide government employees with the tools they need to dramatically enhance task and learning efficiency. Time saved can be reinvested to create effective individuals. For example, rather than attending long training courses, such skills development can be integrated into the worker's job and done at home. Because the learning tools are multimedia, the student learns faster and retains information longer. There are no disruptive, time-consuming, three-day refresher courses because the student is constantly "refreshed" through the working-learning environment that personal multimedia provides.

2. *High-performance teams.* Such workstations can be combined into workgroup computing environments to create high-performance teams. Tools for workgroup collaboration, information handling, time management, and decision making can lead to new team-based structures and high performance. For example, social assistance workers who save time through using the technology can reinvest that time delivering life skills counseling with the goal of reducing client dependency on social assistance. This is achieved through a new division of labor for the team, the redesign of business processes, the retraining of the workers involved, and new market positioning to the clients.

3. *Integrated Governments.* Enterprise-wide government information infrastructures, based on standards, set the precondition for the new

organizational structures that cut across traditional government lines. Of course, governments were not alone in operating like a collection of separate fiefdoms. Many first-time shoppers for a mortgage know the frustration of having to demonstrate to the mortgage officer that they have been good customers of the bank for the past 20 years. But today's smart banks are striving to treat their customers as people instead of a bunch of separate accounts, and they're using internetworking to do it. And smart governments are starting to think along the same lines. Horizontal internetworking can create such integrated governments.

There is growing recognition of the need for this change in attitude. For example, in a speech on government organization, Marcel Massé, Canadian minister of intergovernmental affairs, noted, "There are now virtually no departments where problems are self-contained or where solutions do not involve more than one traditional sector of government activity. As a result, there is a greater need for new and more horizontal ways of studying problems and finding solutions. Horizontal coordination is now essential, requiring new mechanisms and new approaches to systems."

Government-wide information infrastructures also enable new forms of *disintermediation* (as middle layers of duplication across departments are eliminated). They also facilitate *molecularization*, as governments move certain functions into smaller more dynamic units or even non-governmental forms.

"We need to think outside the box and look at tearing down the walls that exist between government and others. In the past we have been constrained by the traditional lines of demarcation ... we would think 'what are the benefits to my agency,' rather than 'what are the benefits to the customers of government,'" says Flyzik.

4. *The open government.* As governments reach out electronically, delivering services to suppliers, customers, and others, the value of those services is transformed. The federal government and governments at many state and local levels are already implementing electronic procurement for suppliers. The documentation to procure a fleet of trucks, a large computer system, or a building is handled with bits rather than atoms. Requests for proposals are online rather than in large paper documents. Likewise, proposals are submitted online. Projects are managed on networks involving the suppliers and their government customers. Funds are dispersed electronically using EDI. And information about the project is made available to the public electronically.

5. *Internetworked government.* Finally, as more and more human communications, flow of funds, accessing of information, and execution of transactions move on to the Net, lines blur, not only within government agencies, but between government and those that touch it. New models and even goals of government begin to emerge. Communities can be empowered to execute functions previously performed badly by governments. Internetworked governments can deliver services to the public around service themes such as unemployment assistance rather than around organizational stovepipes from various levels of government addressing unemployment payments, welfare, job counseling, food stamps, and the like. Virtual agencies can be created and disbanded as the needs of the economy and society dictate. Governments can catalyze networked-based partnerships and contribute to wealth creation—for example, between government and the major auto manufacturers—to generate a new generation of automobile. Governments can generate new processes for citizen participation with "electronic hearings" to examine possible government initiatives; "electronic brainstorming" on critical issues; "electronic straw votes" to assess public views; and foster the launching of "virtual interest groups," which can contribute to societal well-being. Accountabilities can be achieved in an ongoing way rather than every four years. A fuller democratic process can be forged—a real-time, participatory democracy—if we want it. See Table 6.1.

TABLE 6.1 Shifts to the Internetworked Government

FROM: INDUSTRIAL AGE GOVERNMENT	TO: INTERNETWORKED GOVERNMENT
Bureaucratic controls	Client service and community empowerment
Isolated administrative functions	Integrated resource services
Paperwork and file handling	Electronic service delivery
Time-consuming processes	Rapid, streamlined response
Explicit controls and approvals	Implicit controls and approvals
Manual financial transactions	Electronic transfer of funds
Awkward reporting mechanisms	Flexible information inquiry
Disjointed information technologies	Integrated network solutions
Election of governors every few years	Real-time, participatory democracy

Seven Themes of Internetworked Government

We have identified seven classes of opportunities for internetworked government. Aspects of these are underway at various levels in the United States, Canada, and Europe.

Theme 1: Administrative Renewal

Scenario:

In the offices of different suppliers, sales managers are watching the clock and their computer screens. In 10 minutes, and for the following hour, a federal government procurement team of professionals from various agencies will be holding an electronic auction-style competition for the right to provide a year's supply of optical disks, magnetic tape, and computer disks. A bit like electronic trading on the stock market, it beats shipping a five-pound document by courier every month to the government bidding center. Because the products are to be delivered to agencies across the country, there is a good chance that most suppliers will get some business. And, of course, because bids are made in electronic form, payment is made directly to the supplier's bank account as each shipment is being made. The result is reduced costs for government and suppliers, faster delivery of products, better procurement decisions because of the team approach, and faster payment to the suppliers.[6]

Initiatives can be taken to radically change the business of government— the way agencies manage themselves and government employees work and work with one another and suppliers. Although there have been many problems with business process reengineering, government is today just beginning to be fertile ground for technology-enabled BPR initiatives. The thrust of such initiatives can be to shift from multilevel bureaucratic stovepipes to distributed team structures and the horizontal processes of the integrated government. Many government programs, for example, share common clients with a number of governmental agencies. Government programs may also have interdependencies among them. For example, there are relationships between federal unemployment insurance and job training programs and in turn with state-run programs having to do with social assistance.

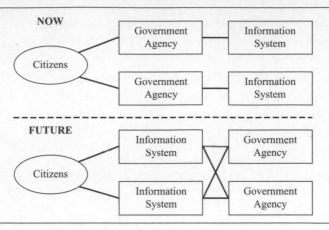

FIGURE 6.2 *Reinventing Government.* SOURCE: Washington State Department of Information Services.

To achieve renewal, governments need to achieve the 10 technology shifts outlined in Chapter 4. Of particular importance are standards to achieve technology internetworking and thereby organizational internetworking. Most savvy governments are implementing government-wide electronic mail as a critical precondition for internetworked government.

The result can be a more supple bureaucracy, with fewer rungs in the bureaucratic ladder (see Figure 6.1). Databases can be shared rather than duplicated. Information can flow much faster, paperwork bottlenecks can be unplugged, and civil servants can make decisions today instead of tomorrow. Knowledge-based or expert systems can eliminate the onerous approval procedures and replace them with responsive, guideline-based processes and supporting technologies. Basic operations can be restructured to meet customers' needs. There can be a shift from systems in which people are accountable for following rules to systems in which they are accountable for achieving results. Those who work on the front lines can be empowered, through empowering technology, to make more of their own decisions and respond on the spot to customer problems and needs.

Theme 2: Integrated Digital Benefits Transfer[7]

Scenario:
A single mother, twins in a shopping cart, checks out groceries at the local supermarket, showing her ID. When all items are scanned into the system, the clerk states the number of required food stamps, which in turn are automatically

deducted from the mother's account in a government database. Rather than three billion physical food stamps being printed and sent to government distributors, who send them to households, who give them to retailers, who take them to financial institutions, who credit store accounts and send redeemed stamps to the Federal Reserve Bank, who count them and credit the banks, bill the U.S. Treasury and destroy the stamps, there are zero stamps. The government alone saves $400 million per year in administrative expenses. Fraud and abuse are eliminated.

Most countries in the developed world spend more money on social assistance than anything else, including the military. In the United States, almost 30 million people receive food stamps and another 30 million receive monthly authorization for Medicaid. Four million workers draw monthly disability benefits, and the Social Security Administration is expected to distribute over $450 billion annually to 44.3 million beneficiaries by 2000.[8] Application for, distribution of, and management of such programs are all paper-based, costly, cumbersome, frustrating for providers and clients alike, and subject to fraud and abuse. Electronic benefit transfer can significantly reduce these problems.

Tulare County, California, is a small farming community highly populated with refugees from Southeast Asia. About one-quarter of the population receives government assistance. The Department of Social Services administers government programs with 4,500 rules elaborated in more than 6 feet of documents. Applications for public support are as long as 32 pages. However, the county has now implemented an interactive, multimedia touch-screen system that guides applicants through the process. The system cost $3.2 million to develop but will save $108 million. The real impact will come once electronic delivery of benefits is implemented.

The most ambitious program will be the efforts of the federal government to deliver electronically and nationwide "fast and efficient government assistance—including food stamps, Social Security benefits, and veterans benefits." The goal of this effort is to integrate benefit programs from such diverse corners as the USDA, the Department of the Treasury, the Social Security Administration, the Office of Personnel Management, and the Railroad Retirement Board. Electronic government is internetworked government.

"We can view government on functional terms rather than agency terms, for example creating the virtual department of government entitlements," says Flyzik. "Today a customer of government could be getting half a dozen different entitlements—foods stamps, aid for families with dependent children, Women, Infants and Children, Social Security, etc. This creates a nightmare in terms of administrative costs, not to mention fraud and inconvenience to the customer. To change this situation we could use the power of information technology to tie together all those agencies involved in entitlement benefit distribution. This virtual agency would tie together affinity groups—which are not a formal structure but people working in similar functional areas. Geographical boundaries and hierarchical structures would no longer matter. The customer should be dealing with one agency. He or she should be treated as a customer of government."

THEME 3: INTEGRATED DIGITAL ACCESS TO GOVERNMENT INFORMATION

Scenario:
An unemployed worker visits an electronic kiosk at a nearby shopping center, instead of trekking across town to a government office. He scans jobs that match his computerized skill profile that is contained on his "smart card," and prints out the jobs that seem promising. He then scans new training courses available at a local high school. He decides to apply for one course and receives almost instant approval from the government and school. It's all as simple as an automated teller.

The new technology holds the promise of open government. Access to government information may be a right in many countries, but practically speaking it is usually cumbersome and often not achievable. Most citizens have little knowledge about what information is held within government coffers, let alone how to find it. Finding information can be time consuming, costly, and frustrating. If more than one agency is involved, the citizen can become a pinball, bouncing from one source to another.

All this is about to change. For example, the reference documents in this chapter of the book were pulled directly from the World Wide Web. A wealth of information can be made available, including information about you, your company, and your dealings with government. The U.S. federal government has established the government information locator service (GILS) to help the public and agencies access government information. The GILS will use standards to open access to information held in computers and in other forms.[9]

Access to this world of information will be made through various information appliances—the computer (at home, work, office, or kiosk), the telephone (which is getting smarter), and the television (which is becoming interactive).

Bob Woods, who is in charge of federal government telecommunication systems, says that government needs a customer-oriented retailing model. "The government is like the restaurant that closes at lunch and dinner time," he says. He questions why someone should have to take off work in order to apply for a driver's license. "We need a retailing model that makes government services and information available 24 hours per day."

This is not science fiction. Such initiatives are already operational today at federal, state, and local levels. Indianapolis and Marion County were among the first. In 1994 they implemented CivicLink, which allows, anyone with a PC and modem to access public government information. Initially the system was of unique value to lawyers, realtors, insurance companies, financial institutions, and others who needed information from the Marion County Clerk of Courts, Recorders Office, and other city and county agencies. According to Marion County officials, up to 70% of information requests in the past had come from business customers. They concluded that by making such information available they could create better, cheaper government. Now a wider range of clients are getting their information in digital form.

CivicLink is being operated by the regional bell operating company Ameritech, through a joint venture with the British Columbia Systems Corporation. In 1995 it was extended into Los Angeles County and also Prince George County, MD, making online information available to residents of Washington, D.C. By all accounts the program is and will have a significant impact. For example, Los Angeles lawyers no longer have to manually file and retrieve paper documents for a case at the county courthouse. With the Interactive Client Services tool in CivicLink, they can do it all digitally. As information systems manager Daniel Roper puts it, "Prince George County is a progressive community that wants to proactively respond to the information needs of our residents. CivicLink offers us a convenient and more efficient way to deliver access to public information."

THEME 4: GOVERNMENT FOSTERED INFORMATION INITIATIVES

Scenario

A CEO is planning a branch office in the Pacific Rim. From his workstation, he accesses the complete multimedia mapping of planet Earth, zooming into cities, across mountains, or up fishing streams. For three alternative cities, he examines aspects of the local economy, the skill levels of workers, wages, strike histories, and the unemployment rate. He checks local climate, vegetation, health risks, demographics, water temperature, and political history and then accesses an interactive video capability to discuss plans with local government officials. In minutes he builds a complex decision support tool—a knowledge-based system that applies rules and criteria from his and others previous experience to help him analyze the information.

The information access opportunity extends beyond providing government information (open government) to governance for the digital economy. That is, governments can catalyze partnerships and efforts that result in the creation of multimedia databases previously unimaginable. Eventually it will make sense to change the G in GILS from "government" to "global," for GILS could provide the standards and interfaces to help make available information from around the world. This could include information on virtually any topic, from public or private sources, and in traditional or multimedia form.

Sound farfetched? Already initiatives are underway that are putting pieces of the picture together:

◆ *The National Environmental Data Index.* Steps are being taken by the National Oceanic and Atmospheric Administration to coordinate the development of environmental data collected by many sources. These include the Department of the Interior (biological surveys), the Environmental Protection Agency, NASA (satellite data), and private sources. Data are usually collected for a single purpose but can be applied to a myriad of other purposes.

◆ *International Trade Data System.* The National Performance Review has recommended the establishment of an all-inclusive database for disseminating trade information to government and businesses. Over 40 federal agencies collect, process, analyze, and disseminate vast amounts of international trade data to accomplish various trade-related government functions. Couple this with the reams of private sector information held by the banks, manufacturers, and other corporations and there is a big opportunity to equip business to compete better in the global economy. However, strong governmental leadership will be required to make this happen.

Theme 5: Intergovernmental Tax Filing, Reporting, and Payments Processing

Scenario:

In early April a citizen receives her completed tax form in the mail (or by e-mail) from her state tax office. She has no forms to complete. Her state and federal taxes have been calculated from records submitted electronically by her employer and her bank. She is one of 60 million Americans for whom the IRS has had access to all necessary information required to calculate her taxes. She verifies the bill and either dials an 800 number or replies by e-mail, paying her taxes through a credit card.

The National Performance Review pointed out that the IRS and state tax agencies still require taxpayers to compute what the IRS already knows. If the IRS computed those taxes, combined with electronic filing for the remainder, 75 boxcars of tax forms would be unnecessary.

This is the stuff of good government for a new age. Rather than making citizens file repetitive reports or jump through hoops to obtain services, the government is restructured to make its vast resources available in the most efficient and effective means possible—from the consumer's point of view.

Theme 6: National (and Global) Law Enforcement and Public Safety Networks

Scenario:

A massive earthquake hits San Francisco. Among the tens of thousands of situations is a family trapped in the stairwell of a building, a rail car with potentially lethal chemicals derailed, and a fire raging in an outskirts neighborhood, extending into the local brush. In each case, local, state, and federal agencies, including police and fire units, state highway units, and the National Guard, along with volunteer groups and private organizations, are able to cooperate to resolve the problem. Their collective efforts are marshaled over the Net, which has rerouted much activity to wireless transmission. The family is evacuated, in part through electronic access to building plans and effective Net-based teamwork. The chemicals in the rail car are quickly identified, along with weather patterns, and evacuation plans are drawn and executed. These include instant mobile printing of evacuation notices in four languages. The fire is extinguished by the effective routing of crews around broken highways and coordination with aircraft water bombers, and emergency medical crews arrive with the right equipment to save lives.[10]

Law enforcement and public safety workers need to effectively communicate and access one another's information. Computer databases have, however, been developed by different agencies at different levels of government. This problem is compounded as databases become multimedia. Internetworking is required to enable appropriate sharing of information. For example, the Royal Canadian Mounted Police can now communicate mug shots and composite drawings of suspects to enforcement personnel at the provincial and municipal levels, with the capability of aging the photographs coming online. The new technology enables new enforcement capabilities.

Most emergency communications occur over tactical land mobile radio systems. Such systems are poorly integrated because each is different, in local, state, and national governments in the developed world. The division of the radio spectrum to various agencies further complicates the problem, as do encryption algorithms designed to make communications secure.

"In the past, all law enforcement agencies ran their own tactical networks. You may have 200 radio networks of federal, state, and local agencies—none of which interoperate—some in the same building. Today we handle the interoperability problem by having five radios in one car," says Flyzik.

There is a clear solution—the adoption and implementation of digital wireless technology. But to avoid the problems of the past, this needs to be done in a coordinated manner. As a result, every country needs to achieve cooperation and leadership to build a national law enforcement and public safety network. And cooperation between countries can make such a network global. The huge cost-saving benefits pale in comparison to the opportunity to create a safer and more secure world.

To achieve this in the United States, the Law Enforcement Affinity Group has been established. "Instead of having hundreds of antennas on top of the World Trade Center, we'll have one or two," says Flyzik. "We'll save a lot of money, but more important, have the ability of law enforcement agencies to share information such as fingerprints and mug shots."

THEME 7: GOVERNMENT/CLIENT COMMUNICATION INITIATIVES

Scenario:
A Saskatoon businesswoman pops into a local business service established by a private company in partnership with government. She is looking for advice on how to market her patented new building panels. The researcher says he will

consult some databases and prepare a report that he will e-mail to her. Two hours later, it's ready. Page 1 has a list of coming trade conferences, buttressed by an Ottawa specialist's comments on which ones have been most success- ful in the experience of other manufacturers. Page 2 gives details of a recent Request for Proposals by an aid agency that needs such material for an African housing project. Page 3 lists construction companies with expertise in market- ing such material. And a note from a trade official in Tokyo says the embassy will keep the material in mind during discussions with Japanese officials on Canadian building materials suitable for the Japanese market. Page 4 includes preclearance approvals for exports."

In addition to providing a new world of information to its clients, internet- working opens up new channels for communication and delivery of new ser- vices. In the foregoing scenario, government catalyzed the creation of a new service based on the Net combined with access to government information. A private company, acting on behalf of government, provides a critical new service while creating jobs.

Given the soaring growth of e-mail, governments have an exploding oppor- tunity to communicate with citizens electronically. E-mail systems are also metamorphosing into new tools for collaborating, sharing ideas, informing. The various discussion groups on the Internet are just the beginning of new ways of communicating that promise to tear down the walls between govern- ment employees and leaders and the rest of us.

To achieve this new promise, every government needs a strategy to imple- ment e-mail for every government employee that will be accessible from his or her place of work or elsewhere. Unfortunately, e-mail has grown up on propri- etary computer systems. Many government agencies, like private sector orga- nizations such as banks, often prevent interconnection between their systems and the Internet. Some even prohibit their employees from having Internet e-mail addresses. Fortunately, the momentum behind internetworking is so strong that the defenders of the old ways will not be able to resist much longer.

ACHIEVING INTERNETWORKED GOVERNMENT: THE CANADIAN BLUEPRINT

To make the transition to electronic government, every government needs an architecture—a guiding set of principles, models, and standards. Canada was one of the first nations to address the problem when, in 1994, the government released a landmark discussion paper: *Blueprint for Renewing Government Services Using Information Technology.* The document is a taxpayer's dream, proposing a "government-wide electronic information infrastructure to simplify service delivery, reduce duplication, and improve the level and speed of service to [the public] at a lower cost to the taxpayers."[12] No other national government has published such a far-reaching approach to government-wide architecture to restructure the public sector around the information highway.

Some elements of this "customer first" philosophy are starting to appear:

◆ The federal Human Resources Development department has launched a comprehensive program to restructure the delivery of social services. Services are being integrated for delivery on a common information technology platform.

◆ Revenue Canada is introducing a single business registration number, which will provide one-stop service for corporate income and other taxes, source deductions, and importer accounts.

◆ The Department of Public Works is introducing a new electronic procurement and settlement system to eliminate the need for duplicate departmental systems. Paperwork will be reduced and suppliers will be paid faster.

◆ British Columbia Online allows public electronic access to government databases such as land titles, motor vehicles, land tax registries, and rural property tax. It is a single point of contact for payment, problem resolution, and account management.

TOWARD INTERNETWORKED GOVERNMENT IN THE STATE OF WASHINGTON

In the State of Washington, nothing less than a revolution is underway in how citizens deal with the state. "In the past, information systems have been sitting in the back room. Citizens came to government and talked to bureaucrats who in turn talked to information systems so that services were provided or information transmitted. What we see happening now is that information systems are coming out of the back room and talking to citizens directly," says George Lindamood, director, Department of Information Services for the State of Washington. "In the same way that automated teller machines have revolutionized banking, we hope that the Washington Information Network will revolutionize the way state government delivers service to its people," says Lindamood.

The first of what is now a network of 11 public information kiosks has been online since 1994 in what's called the Washington Information Network (WIN). Through the kiosks, citizens can have direct access to state information on a wide range of issues touching 20 agencies, including vehicle registration and licensing procedures, child immunization requirements, student loan information, and small business assistance. Most of the units are in high-traffic areas of shopping malls, but there is also one in the Seattle Public Library and one in the legislature in Olympia. The units were supplied by IBM and North Communications, Inc., in a creative joint venture in which the state and private sector split the initial $1 million cost of the kiosks.

"The information systems we have were designed for a more bureaucratic era in which the typical model was the industrial model with factory workers like cogs creating product. In government, we're now moving slowly to what the private sector has done with empowered workers and flattened organizations where quick response may even be more important than low price," says Lindamood. "The word efficiency doesn't seem to appear very often in books on competitive advantage and slowly it has been leached out of government lexicons as well. It doesn't matter so much at this point whether the cost of the driver's license is the lowest among the 50 states, it's a question of how much hassle is involved in getting the driver's license and whether or not you have to drive 500 miles to get it. That is gradually being taken into account in determining if citizens are getting what they want in more of a service-oriented exercise."

About 1,000 English- and Spanish-speaking citizens a day use the kiosks with their colorful graphics and stereo sound. The most popular information retrieved from the interactive touchscreen units is about job availability in the state. An individual can search for job openings on a statewide basis or right down to a regional or local basis—connected directly to the Department of Employment Security mainframe in Olympia. Once the user matches skills with a job opening, he or she obtains a printout from the kiosk describing that job, takes the printout to the state employment office, and jumps the queue for quick counter service. In the first 18 months, 150 people found jobs using the kiosks. The next most popular use, according to Lindamood, is the section that lists $150 million of unclaimed property such as abandoned bank accounts, payroll checks, deposits, stocks, and bonds. "The chances of finding a match on that are better than the state lottery," he says.

Initially, the state was concerned that there would be a high usage only so long as there was a novelty aura to the kiosks, but the intervening months have shown continued popularity. A survey of users shows 50% found the information they sought; 70% say they would use the kiosks again. "At a time when we're getting government-bashing, what we're seeing is the beginning of a trend when government is more responsive," says Lindamood.

Plans call for the number of kiosks to grow to 60 units by 1997, but the kiosks are just a modest beginning. "We've only come about 5% of the way; we're just scratching the surface," says Lindamood. A new feature, the Washington State Information Exchange (known as InfoX), provides an electronic information exchange through the Internet among agencies and between agencies and the public. In the future, interactive television, now being used for videoconferencing among state officials through 13 two-way sites, could also be used by citizens.

The system could also change the very nature of democracy itself. "Rather than have everyone in the population step into the ballot box every year or so and transfer a small amount of information, or a slightly smaller number of people attend a town meeting where everybody gets a 30-second sound bite, we're looking at giving an even smaller portion of the population a two-week dose of information and then asking them to give representative opinions," says Lindamood. "The problem is that there are so many issues that are so complex. Why not use specialization and say 'Why not form a jury here on this environmental issue?' and 'Why not form a jury there on this social issue or this tax issue?'"

Says Lindamood: "It's a question of tinkering with alternative forms of democracy."

THE FUTURE

What if an election brings a new administration? Aren't all the initiatives described in jeopardy? Not according to Flyzik. "If these ideas are acceptable to the American people, then they will become immune to the political process," he says. "If the customers find life with the government better than before, the political environment will become less relevant. Eventually we'll need some institutional structure for cross-government coordination. The trend to electronic government is really unstoppable."

Notes

1. Peter Drucker, "Really Inventing Government," *The Atlantic Monthly*, February 1994.
2. *Creating a Government That Works Better and Costs Less*. Report of the National Performance Review, Washington, D.C. 1993.
3. *Blueprint for Renewing Government Services Using Information Technology*, Treasury Board of Canada Secretariat, Ottawa, 1994.
4. *Creating a Government That Works Better and Costs Less*.
5. David Osborne and Ted Gaebler, *Reinventing Government: How the Entrepreneurial Spirit Is Transforming the Public Sector*, Addison Wesley, 1992.
6. Based on an example from *Blueprint for Renewing Government Services Using Information Technology*.
7. The term "Electronic Benefit Transfer" has been popularized through the National Performance Review initiative in Washington. See the Accompanying Report on *Reengineering through Information Technology*, September 1993.
8. *Reengineering through Information Technology*.
9. *Application Profile for the Government Information Locator Service (GILS)*, NIST, FIPS PUB 192, December 1994.
10. This scenario is based on a very effective video presentation of the power of interactive multimedia. In the film, over 50 emerging technologies and their effects are shown. Hewlett-Packard, Cupertino, 1995.
11. Based on an example from *Blueprint for Renewing Government Services Using Information Technology*.
12. *Blueprint for Renewing Government Services Using Information Technology*, Treasury Board of Canada Secretariat, Ottawa, 1994.

20th Anniversary Edition Commentary on Chapter 7: Have Network, Will Travel

W RITING IN 1994, it made sense to focus on the topic of travel, as the movement of people for work and vacation was clearly an early target for transformation by the digital economy. But there is some irony in this. I discussed industry opportunities and also the dangers of disintermediation, arguing that everyone in the middle (such as travel agents) were in danger. In explaining re-intermediation (creating new value in the middle), I cited the case of Rosenbluth International, the innovative 111-year-old Philadelphia travel agency. Despite their heroic efforts to reinvent themselves, they were forced into an asset sale to American Express Travel a decade later, in 2003.

Many travel industry leaders have suffered from the onslaught of digital, and, perhaps as much as in any industry, new players have emerged to dominate the industry. The hottest travel and leisure companies today didn't exist a decade ago, let alone in 1994.

Many of these companies exploit excess capacity. Rather than staying at a hotel, travelers can stay with Couchsurfing or Airbnb. Couchsurfing, founded in 2004, is now a for-profit company with more than 9 million members. Airbnb was only founded in 2008, but as of today it has more than 500,000 listings in 33,000 cities and 192 countries.

Want a traditional hotel? TripAdvisor, Expedia, and Hotels.com can help. If you're a luxury traveler, find your boutique hotel on Tablet (tablethotels.com). Need to book a dinner reservation? Go to OpenTable and choose from over 30,000 places. In a strange city and want a rating on almost anything? Go to Yelp, the online urban guide with close to 2,000 employees. Need tickets to a game or show, StubHub will hook you up—processing a ticket sale every second of the day. Need to get to the game? Uber will pick you up in a flash. Or go to Lyft to find "your friend with a car." Want to actually purchase a residence? Zillow, founded in 2005, is one of the hottest real estate platforms on the planet.

Many of these ventures are described as "peer-to-peer initiatives" or they have been referred to as part of "the sharing economy." However, they are more aptly called "commercial aggregators." If *sharing* is the act of giving something to others with no direct compensation, there is no true "sharing" occurring in these businesses. Regardless, together they are shaking the foundations of the travel industry and providing strong evidence for the re-intermediation law I presented in *The Digital Economy*: "New entrants are more likely to create the new middle than leaders of the old middle."

Looking forward to the next 20 years, there will be countless new players but expect much of the most important digital transformation to happen behind the scenes. For examples, hotels have been victims of the digital revolution and the rise of the online travel agents (OTAs)—the new intermediaries who control the industry. The entire industry is suffering and could be permanently damaged unless it gets innovative and begins to control how its product is marketed. Permit me to dig into this, as it's instructive for every industry.

These online agents were among the first to fill a market desire: a place where people could search a multitude of options about travel. Those who were there when the Web went mainstream, undoubtedly, recall the intoxicating sense of freedom and opportunity in surfing and discovering new places around the world. The world seemed to be at the traveler's fingertips.

As online booking became the norm, consumers celebrated their release from the "iron grip" of intermediaries that charged for services the Internet could now provide for free. These savings were, apparently, passed on to consumers in the form of lower prices. Marketers proclaimed the democratization of knowledge. But what actually happened was that a new model of trade emerged, one that hurt travelers and hotel owners.

In a little over a decade, the dominant business model in the travel industry evolved into one driven almost entirely by predatory data access and control. After traveler demand dried up in the wake of the dot-com implosion in 2000 and 9/11 in 2001, hotels turned in desperation to websites to offload rooms that would otherwise remain empty. Sites such as Hotels.com offered fabulous rates, which were often below rates offered by the hotels on their own websites. Consumers may have been perplexed as to how the OTA prices were cheaper than the hotels' prices themselves, but they liked the discounts.

Consumers began to start their travel shopping process on the online travel agent's site—a new behavior that triggered a cascade of negative effects. Buyers became accustomed to reduced hotel prices, and massive price erosion occurred. Value-added travel services were cut out entirely or framed as redundant, and customers were in effect "trained" to accept this new practice as standard. By the time the travel industry recovered from 9/11, the public had put their full trust in the OTAs. What consumers didn't realize is that the hotel industry had morphed into a high-stakes data game. Only the richest OTAs that could buy access to, and control, online search data flourished. People were accustomed to going to websites such as Hotels.com or Expedia.com. Consumers who started their hotel search on Google, would be immediately greeted by the OTA sites. These sites grew to dominate the travel industry, creating a debilitating dependency for hotels wanting to sell their rooms.

In the early days, a key word search on Google such as "Paris hotels" could be purchased for a moderate price. This gave the hotel a means to appear high enough in search results to enable users to "click through" to that hotel. But that cost today is exponentially higher, driven by the complexity of the purchase process for the search term. Although any hotel or hotel chain is welcome to bid on specific search terms made available for purchase by Google, the OTAs have developed sophisticated automated bidding processes that ensure their top placement in the search results.

The amount of money involved is staggering. OTAs will spend $4.15 billion on digital advertising in 2014 just in the United States. More than half of this is spent by the top two companies: Expedia and Priceline.com, which owns Booking.com. A big winner is Google. Expedia and Priceline.com account for close to 5% of Google's advertising revenue.

The upshot is that hotels can't rank on Google, since aggregators of hotel listings continue to outbid hotels. The idea that a hotel can use the Internet as an advertising billboard to capture search traffic is fine in theory, but impossible in practice. OTAs have replaced yesterday's travel agents, the difference being that OTAs add enormous cost but minimal value to the hotel booking process.

To make matters worse, many OTAs now also have the right to track a user right up to the point at which he or she books a hotel, even though he or she likely doesn't realize he or she has given explicit permission to do so by accepting the online agreements to use the search tools. Users are tracked by small pieces of browser data that inform the OTA of user behavior. So, whether the person books through the OTA—or backs out and books through the hotel directly—the OTA gets its stiff commission. Hotels are forced to hand over revenue that would be otherwise applied to benefit the consumer, such as rate offers to loyal guests, upgrades, renovations, and more targeted marketing efforts to attract the right mix of clientele.

The bizarre outcome is that hotels and other properties are prevented from participating effectively and fairly in their own marketplace. One can't fault consumers, since they believe the market is functioning optimally and that whatever commissions the OTAs receive for nominal service are justified. Consumers believe they are getting the lowest rates, but hotels must inflate prices to compensate for the migration of traffic through OTA channels. To make matters worse, consumers are not valued in these channels. Each inquiry is "atomic." Nothing about the consumer is revealed to the hotel purchasing the traffic, so the opportunity to provide personalized or tailored service is lost. Consumers are hurt in this scenario too because it would be possible for hotels to offer guests a lower price than they could get through an OTA while still coming out ahead substantially—because there's no 10% to 30% commission. Whether hotels would actually pass along such prices is another matter, although market pressures suggest they might.

So You've Been Disintermediated. How Do You Fight Back?

You'd be right to be unsympathetic toward the hotels and the old travel industry as a whole, as they were slow off the mark and basically missed the opportunity to rebuild the industry. For them, the trading model for the industry has been broken and usurped by the new intermediaries and consumers suffer.

Hotels want to take back control of the relationship they once had with their guests. But functional real-world marketplaces don't just appear out of nowhere. The infrastructure to support them needs to be built from the supply side out. Much the same way a fruit "market maker" in the 1800s set aside a patch of land and some tables and tents, today's market makers in the digital economy need the technical infrastructure and tools to build a compelling "place" for demand to go. As this happens, we will see not only the reallocation of existing value but also the materialization of new, previously untapped value. The travel industry will take back more control, and property managers will be delighted with the lower commission rates, greater market share, and the abundance of information about their own guests that comes from a direct relationship.

But there is hope. A great example of a new intermediary that is working to get control back to the travel industry is Demeure, a Waterloo, Ontario–based commerce technology company.[1] According to Chairman and Founding CEO Peter Schwartz:

> Demeure is rewiring the travel industry by creating functional support for the construction of branded, purpose-built travel marketplaces. This is in the same spirit as etsy.com, eBay, and so on. With a travel marketplace, large hotels, boutique hotels, vacation property rentals, yachts, cruises, and timeshares can take all that excess capacity and trade it together more directly in a new kind of marketplace.[2]

Schwartz says that Demeure "creates marketplaces by logically linking supply and demand, promoting collaboration, and providing the means to achieve a critical mass for a new trade model in the travel industry."[3] The way it works is that participants in these newly constructed marketplaces can opt to remain closed if they have everything they need or strategically link to "push out" unused capacity or "pull in" previously inaccessible options to extend the value they offer. Owners of vacation properties can even trade empty nights for buying power that lets them pay for travel to other destinations.

In *The Digital Economy*, I discussed the American Airlines Sabre reservation system and the concept of "yield management." Today, drawing inspiration from the success of yield management in the airline industry, Demeure's systems bring proficient "revenue management" to any type of property. Most existing revenue management systems are in fact simply "channel management" systems that provide the ability to connect hotels to OTAs. Yield management is the reason the person in the next seat may have paid three times more for the ticket; the airline uses the Sabre reservation system to optimize price for the right person at the right time.

Demeure's goal is to enable proficiency in total revenue management— channel management along with the ability to draw on insights into additional revenue sources such as food and beverage, conference and banquet space, tours and excursions, and spas and branded products. The difference between their approach and that used by airlines is that the value is constructed and shared according to the "value propositions" of the involved parties. As marketplaces form, they amplify the value they offer to their participants. Something much more powerful than Sabre can emerge from this model: what Demeure calls a "meta-marketplace." Meta-marketplace suppliers can exchange relevant supply, purchasing, and demographic data to transact directly and travelers can be valued for their buying power, including associations with other marketplaces, organizations, and loyalty programs. The goal is maximization of yield.

The story suggests that meta-marketplaces will achieve optimal yield in this and other industries by exchanging data and building long-term relationships that not only leverage the principles of commerce, but also evolve naturally based on the real-world experience and expertise of the participants. The new aggregators illustrate the opportunity to *monetize* in the industry—create trading models that value capacity and make it fungible with cash. Home-based travel agents and service providers can insert themselves into this movement and reappropriate the value that was disrupted with the shift to OTAs and their focus on data monetization to the detriment of the pure principles of commerce. Given the prevalence of contemporary online social networking and unprecedented connectedness in the new economy, the social nature of commerce will reestablish itself, as it has done throughout the ages. The mutual exchange of value—which can be apprehended by all trading partners—can flourish.

The story is instructive in that it shows the sophistication behind the scenes in the next generation of digital marketplaces—in this case, where the property owners strike back against the digital re-intermediaries. It also shows how transformation of your company alone may be inadequate. Transformation of your industry is required. Going 20 years forward, expertise in algorithms and bold actions to disrupt your industry again and again will determine who survives and wins.

Notes

1. Yes, I have decided to invest in new companies that I love, and Demeure is one of them.
2. Not to get too technical here, but the company seeks to provide access to prospective customers of a property for both public and private channels, that is, across all the usual online OTAs, but also across direct connections with private marketplaces, such as a timeshare company where members spend points on options such as a hotel owner's property. The idea is that these marketplaces represent a huge opportunity for hotels (and private properties) to reach large demand audiences through more direct, and thus profitable, channels.
3. Peter Schwartz, interview by author.

HAVE NETWORK, WILL TRAVEL

If your systems are difficult for your employees to use, the only people who are going to suffer in the long run are your customers. They're going to go elsewhere. We try to make sure that the systems are easy to use, that they work for the customer, and that they present things in a way that makes the customer like the experience.

Gordon Kerr

Former CIO, Hyatt Hotels, 1994

Hal Rosenbluth, president and CEO of Rosenbluth International, a Philadelphia-based travel agency, has a vision for tomorrow's travel. His version of a virtual reality voyage is called "The Vacation Chamber" and is aimed at two markets: those who have money but no time and those who have time but no money. In Rosenbluth's future, either person could climb inside the "chamber" and enjoy the sights and sounds of a destination holiday without the expense or time involved in actually getting there. His own particular dream destination would be a spa without the low-cal lunch or the pain of aerobics. "You'd go in with an anesthetist, get knocked out for five days, and lose weight," he says with a twinkle in his eye. "My gut tells me there is a market."

THE DIGITAL MOVEMENT OF HUMANS

When Kate Patterson, industrial relations manager at 3Com Corporation found out that her husband had landed a job in Phoenix, she decided she had to quit her job. After all, her husband was a promising attorney; the Phoenix opportunity was one that they both agreed he couldn't pass up. Furthermore, 3Com had no offices in Phoenix, and all her work was centered on the employees at the company's headquarters in Silicon Valley. When she sat down with

3Com CEO Eric Benhamou to tell him the bad news, Benhamou replied, "You're not quitting, you're just moving to Phoenix." And he was right. Kate Patterson, the new teleworker.

At the turn of the century, an employee sent on a mission away from the head office could be out of touch for weeks or even months. Whether it was a silk buyer to the Orient, a ship captain at sea, or a pony express rider across the plains, each functioned as a single combat warrior who had no regular contact with the employer who dispatched him. The arrival of the telegraph and telephone by the turn of the century forever altered the loneliness of the long-distance worker. The traveling salesman could call in orders once a week. Branch offices no longer had to rely on the post office to exchange information. Real-time transatlantic conversation was possible.

For decades thereafter, however, there was little technological change. Even when the 1980s brought cellular telephones and fax machines into the workplace, the actual nature of an employee's work wasn't much altered. Information exchange was still physical—the movement of atoms—including the movement of people from here to there and back again.

Information may have flowed more freely and a sales rep with a car phone might have become more efficient, but for most employees life went on as usual. Then came the modem and the proliferation of PCs and notebooks, a potent combination that allowed individuals to work at home or wherever.

Now that one-third of all households have a personal computer, telework has gone far beyond fad to function. When a modem's all that's needed to connect to the outside world, the barriers become nonexistent. The walls come tumbling down as millions of Americans are wired—working at home. But working at home is just the beginning.

To move into the digital economy, we need to rethink the concept of telework and get beyond the old view. In the old view, there were a number of postulated advantages of telework. These included the reduction of office costs, energy savings, environmental benefits, reduction in commuting traffic, increased opportunities for the disabled, single parents, and so on, and the tranquillity to actually get some work done. Postulated disadvantages included the social problem of creating alienated, isolated workers; the danger of piecework; issues of security (passkeys, security guards, and surveillance can't be readily used in the home); the issue of privacy (and the complications rising from introducing work into the home); and problems of managing people you can't see in telework environments.

What is emerging is a whole new digital economy in which the microprocessor and networks enable fundamentally new kinds of institutional structures and relationships. The value *chain* between individuals and organizations is becoming a digitally based *value network* as people and enterprises reach out through technology to their customers, suppliers, affinity groups, and even competitors. This demands a redefinition of telework.

The term *telework* comes from the Greek "tele," meaning afar. Telework has been viewed as simply "work from afar." True, in the digital economy, consumers, educators, and medical personnel can be at any distance from the place of work, retail outlet, classroom, or operating room. Yet telework is not just about working, watching, or participating remotely from the office, source, or the customer. In fact, all knowledge work is becoming telework, because more and more knowledge work is becoming based on digital communication networks that enable people to work anywhere at anytime. In the digital economy, the firm as we know it will be transformed. Just as the organization is changing, so are the job and the nature of work itself. As the world of work shifts from the hierarchical corporation to the new extended structures, there is a shift in the potential for work location. The office is no longer a place, it is a system. The roles of individuals in that system are no longer just jobs but fundamentally new working relationships. Regardless of the location of the information appliance the physician is using, she is not "afar" from the place of work. The place of work is a system, involving human components. Those involved *are* the place of work.

Examples of the new telework include the following:

- ◆ A mortgage loan officer can be part of a distributed team in banking physically located in the suburbs and can still interact directly with potential customers wherever they are; the bricks and mortar of the branch system are unnecessary.
- ◆ A life insurance agent supported by a nomadic networked workstation can visit customers in their living rooms.
- ◆ A university professor can walk through an archeological dig describing what she sees and feels via a direct-feed broadcast to students in 20 different locations.

In the recent past, the implementation of new work systems usually occurred within the reengineering context, in which the focus has been on downsizing, cost-cutting, and streamlining business processes. Traditional approaches to reengineering do not suit the new telework, where much work is serendipitous and the focus is on the value that is added, not on cost displacement. The successful implementation of the new telework also requires a full sense of ownership and support, not just compliance of the individuals involved. There is also the issue of the personal and organizational challenge that comes with managing the separation of work and personal time. Because people will be able to work anywhere at anytime, the traditional separation of the 9-to-5 workday from private time tends to blur for anyone with, say, a home computer connected to the Internet.

Travel Substitution: Moving Bits Instead of People?

The travel, tourism, and hospitality industry is one of the largest business sectors in the new economy; it already accounts for 10% of the world's economy. Travel, then, is worth a closer look because it gathers together the themes of this book and demonstrates how the industry is getting ready to ride the digital economy.

Within 10 years, travel and tourism, sales will have more than doubled to $7.9 trillion; all that growth will have been driven by new technology that will transform not only every enterprise in that field but also all travelers. Vast new opportunities are available to change the way that marketing is done as well as to reduce the distance between customer and supplier. Powerful new multimedia databases will enable customization of travel and tourism products. Moreover, "reach technology" will improve and transform "service," thus resulting in changing roles for everyone involved. Many futurists agree with Rosenbluth and say that the new technology may provide some people with a substitute for travel, rather than become a part of the process itself. In such a scenario, otherwise slow human voyages would be replaced by electrons moving at the speed of light across vast global networks. Travelers will substitute multimedia workstations for air miles and face-to-face meetings; they will enjoy sights around the world from the comfort of their armchairs. The "vacation chamber" will certainly exist in some form but so will international travel for pleasure. In fact, virtual reality travel will only increase the demand for the real thing.

In fact, the past relationship between advances in telecommunications and changes in transportation have tended to grow in parallel to support each other. Advances in telecommunications have led to more travel; advances in transportation have led to greater use of telecommunications systems. Direct-dial telephones enabled new communications to take place and led to an interest and demand by people to travel so they could meet each other directly. In the same vein, as the railways expanded across various countries, they were accompanied first by telegraph wires and then telephone wires strung beside the tracks.

That parallel development will continue. Travel will remain part of the intercourse of business for the future. Anyone who has ever attended a convention knows that being able to monitor the speakers through video is no substitute for serendipitous meetings at lunch or in the hallways with other delegates who are also physically present.

There is, however, evidence of a substitution effect in a number of specific areas. The first is routine business travel. For example, the new infrastructure of fax, PCs, and teleconferencing has already reduced the commute for some teleworkers in such sprawling urban areas as Los Angeles and New York. Other individuals have opted out of the hurly-burly and retreated to home offices in the city and country. Individual access to the world through the modem-equipped PC will also enable the sales force of a company to communicate orders, understand new products, and serve clients without ever showing up at the office.

Moreover, substitution is also occurring for certain types of nonroutine communications. For example, the new collaborative technologies of workgroup computing are enabling distributed teams to function together in ways previously unanticipated, thus reducing the need for travel. Technologies integrated across an organization and extended out among organizations have connected individuals who can then function together as a team. In fact, although part of such disbursement involves travel substitution, it also enables communications that couldn't occur even with travel.

However, as these new global relationships are forged on the network, certain destinations will become even more inviting. If young family members spend time visiting the San Diego Zoo through CD-ROM, interest in actually visiting the zoo and seeing the animals live is intensified. The search for authenticity will drive tourism in the future.

In addition, the new technology is creating technology-based travel destinations. It's one thing to play with a flight simulator on a home computer; it's quite another experience to pilot a jumbo jet in a multimillion-dollar flight simulator at an entertainment complex in Las Vegas or Orlando. As well, technology is making the actual experience of travel much more enjoyable and entertaining. Individual multimedia screens on airplanes already enable a traveler to select from a number of games, movies, television shows, or other information-based programming.

What about the impact of the new technology on the business of travel? In the old economy, a hotel had organizational stovepipes and islands of computing that corresponded to marketing systems, inventory systems, point-of-sale systems, reservation systems, property management systems, restaurant systems, or back office systems. In the digital economy, computing will focus on being able to treat a customer as a customer of the hotel, rather than of a specific department, says Gordon Kerr, former chief information officer of Hyatt Hotels.

> Everyone believes that they are ahead of their competition. If you ask any of the players, they'll say, "We're better than the other guy." Part of that is illusory or self-delusion, part of it is a real misunderstanding of what "ahead" might mean to the only people that count—and that's the customer.
>
> With that as a qualifier, I believe that the reason that Hyatt has an advantage in how it uses technology is that its technology is able to respond more rapidly to customer requirements. In the end, the only people who really care if you're ahead or behind are the people at the front desk or on the telephone making reservations. In a typical 500-room hotel, how many times in the course of a day do you think you have a chance to thoroughly annoy a guest by not doing something correctly or not doing something you should do? There might be a hundred times a day—and with 500 guests I have 50,000 opportunities a day to make mistakes. What we try to do is recognize that this is one of the quality metrics for a hotel, whether or not we are able to avoid making mistakes like not cleaning a room. We try to take that metric, or measure of our quality, and remove, as much as possible, the ways in which we can make mistakes.
>
> We try to position all our technology with the goal of making it as responsive as possible to our customers and because of that, responsive to our employees. But also, something that can change as rapidly as possible to meet changing requirements. Because if there's one rule that people discovered in the last 20 years, it's that the business requirements in the marketplace absolutely do not stand still. If any technology environment doesn't allow you to change quickly, it's going to drag you down and, possibly, run you out of business.

The Digitally Supported Movement of People

Another industry that has made the leap to the integrated organization is the car rental business. Think about what happens when you fly into San Antonio, grab your bags, and climb onto the Avis bus waiting at the curb outside the terminal. The driver asks for your Wizard number and enters the digits into a keyboard on the bus. The information is whisked by something called Ardis (a nationwide, two-way wireless communication network that's a partnership between Motorola and IBM) to a computer in Garden City, New Jersey. Before the bus has even left the terminal area, information comes flashing back to the driver about the car that's waiting for you, right down to the model, color, and location in the Avis lot.

Meanwhile, the Avis agent is receiving a copy of the rental agreement that, along with the keys, goes in the car. The bus pulls up behind the car, the trunk's already open, the engine's running, and the bus driver calls you by name. "What do I do now?" you ask the driver. "You drive it away," he replies. You clamber down, get into the car, and begin to wonder, "Where's the catch?" There's no need to go into the building, no need to stand in line while some-body ahead of you decides between two and four doors, no need to identify yourself and give all the same information you gave three weeks ago when you last rented a car. It's all been captured and—more important—saved and used to speed you on your way.

As you roll toward the exit, you check the rearview mirror a couple of times to see if police with flashing lights are chasing you, all the while feeling a little like the driver of the getaway car for Bonnie and Clyde. The return is equally simple. As you park the car in the lot, an attendant checks the number on the dash, enters that into the handheld computer, greets you by name, and makes eye contact. Fuel level and mileage are added to the information, and the computer then prints a receipt on the spot and you're finished. That's an integrated computing platform and an integrated organization that weren't possible so long ago. Think of the previous islands of technology that have been brought together: reservations, human resources, finances, and inventory.

THISCO: COOPETITION FOR MUTUAL SUCCESS

Since the first airline reservation system was installed, the volume of hotel bookings made through such systems has risen steadily. In the beginning, however, the system was both primitive and awkward. Replies were slow in coming and just as often the answer was frustrating—a denial rather than a confirmation. As airline systems, known as global distribution systems (GDS), improved, speed didn't. Travel agents became more computer literate, and they expected quicker response time. Soon airlines and car rental agencies adapted.

Travel marketing has always been about creating, integrating, and com-municating information. Previously, hotels had to build individual network interfaces to the various airline GDSs so that travel agents could book hotels through their GDSs. Such proprietary connections were costly, cumbersome, and difficult to change. Up to a half dozen such GDSs and a number of major hotel chains were faced with the prospect of more than 200 complex systems development projects in the industry. Moreover, each GDS kept a separate database of information about hotel room rates and availability that was infrequently updated.

The hotels decided they could expand the range of rooms available to travel agents, present a unified view to those agents, and shift business toward the members of their consortium by working together, thereby avoiding the massive costs of each developing its own interface to each GDS. The result in 1989 was THISCO (The Hotel Industry Switch Company). Membership includes Best Western International, Choice Hotels International, Forte Hotels, Hilton Hotels Corp., HFS Brands, Inc., Hyatt Hotels Corp., InterContinental Hotels Corp., ITT Sheraton, LaQuinta Inns, Inc., Marriott Corp., The Promus Companies Inc., Reed Travel Group, Utell International, and Westin Hotels & Resorts.

This system enables what John Biggs, president of Regency Systems Solutions, Hyatt's wholly owned technical support company, describes as "last room availability." That is, the last room is available for booking from all distribution outlets, rather than the previous situation in which a travel agent would have to bypass the GDS and telephone the hotel directly to see if rooms were available when they didn't appear in the restricted GDS. Biggs says, "I wanted to make the latest possible information available electronically through every possible delivery channel. I also wanted to be able to provide the best possible rate information through the same channels."

THISCO provides additional benefits. The travel agents do more of the bookings, reducing Hyatt's reservations costs. And Biggs believes they are providing a much better service to their distribution channels. "We just recognized that it makes sense to band together." THISCO meant that the companies could move beyond the islands of technology to begin to have integrated data that also enabled direct-mail campaigns targeting certain market profiles and segments. "It is not an association, it is a for-profit organization that is rather unique," says John Davis, president of THISCO of Dallas. "Most of the time, when you get a bunch of people together in an association they talk a lot but nobody makes any money. This is different; we do make money." The cooperation wasn't always obvious.

Initially THISCO enabled each hotel to develop only one connection—to the THISCO switch—which in turn connected to the various GDSs, some 340,000 airline terminals, and 24,000 hotel properties in real time. The reservation made by a travel agent was communicated to the GDS database and arrived electronically at the hotel looking the same as any other reservation. Subsequently, a second phase was implemented that provided direct online access by the travel agent to the reservation system in each hotel chain.

THISCO uses a system called UltraSwitch, which operates on a multiple-CPU, AT&T system 7080 computer in Phoenix. Dedicated phone lines link UltraSwitch to each GDS as well as to the central reservation system of THISCO's member companies. A travel agent searches for available properties and when a "sell" is done, a customer name record is created. Once the decision is taken, the whole transaction, including a confirmation back to the agent, takes two-and-a-half seconds. That sense of association is an example of the internetworked enterprise that is becoming the way of the future. "Everybody has to change the 'me' theory to what's best for the industry without going down to the lowest common denominator. You always have to be raising the bar," says Davis.

The THISCO system is now available directly to individual travelers without their having to go through agents. In late 1994, Hyatt was the first hotel chain to put its hotels on the Internet. The descriptions of facilities attracted 120,000 inquiries a week, 10% of them from Japan. Best Western, InterContinental and the other THISCO members are following throughout 1995. Although Net users can't yet do their own bookings, they can "cruise" the listings and see what's available and what amenities are offered. Soon, booking will be possible on the Net. "Technology is forcing hotel chains to compete. They always competed on check-in, the restaurants, bars, and amenities, but now it's different. The new system also means that hotel reservation systems will become more user-friendly," says Davis. "You've got an industry that grew up building pretty properties—now they have to compete electronically." If a hotel is going to use jargon like "rack rate"—a term that means the basic charge for a room—ordinary consumers won't understand. "Mom and Pop don't know what a rack rate is," says Davis. "They don't want to rent a rack."

THE DIGITAL TRAVEL MARKETPLACE

You've been charged with organizing a convention for your trade association. You "helicopter" on a multimedia workstation around three target cities on two continents. In each you ask for all the convention facilities that can accommodate your meeting of 6,000 people. You ask for all the five- and four-star hotels within a radius of two miles of the convention center. You "go for a walk" through selected hotel properties to examine the look and feel of the conference facilities and rooms.

You check the vacancy rates, ask for availability information on rooms, and check prices for a convention of this size. That positioning will include 24-hour availability and detailed information such as exact sizes of rooms, views, wheelchair access, bed configurations, business services, and other features. There could also be helpful comments from recent guests, comparisons with other hotel chains, and graphics that attractively display the hotel. You continue your "helicoptering," looking for interesting entertainment activities and local historical sites. You check flight schedules and airline vacancies to the city, along with local transportation.

Based on all of this information, you select the location for your convention. You then zoom in to the target hotels, requesting bookings and additional discount information for blocks of rooms plus proposals from the hotel regarding rates for additional meeting and event facilities.

The Net will create new clusters in tourism and new partnerships that will deliver customized products, cross-sell services, and have the ability to attract and retain new business. "You'll be able to stroll around San Juan on the Net," says retired American Airlines executive Max Hopper. But since the physical world is constantly changing, Hopper warns, "You've got to create huge digitized databases and maintain them. It's not like the movies."

Disintermediation at Work

The Condé Nast magazine publishing company plans eventually to create Web versions of all its 14 core magazines. The first was a version of Condé Nast Traveler called CondéNet, which offers detailed reports on more than 250 islands and 1,000 hotels. Eventually, users will be able to make airline, hotel, and dinner reservations, check local conditions, and have online discussions with travelers who have visited the sites they're considering going to. The president of Condé Nast says that CondéNet is "a serious seven-figure investment," which will "be an enormous business for us someday."[1]

ROOM SERVICE, PLEASE

New technology is also affecting the way individual hotels in the chains serve customers once they've checked in. The Hyatt in Buenos Aires uses Northern Telecom's Meridian switch (the usual equipment for Hyatt Hotels) and the Maxel software program (also used Hyatt-wide) for reservations, front office, housekeeping, and engineering. And they have added a PC that allows their communications center attendant to send and receive messages.

In this integrated organization, all guest requests flow through the communications department. As a result, a guest establishes a relationship with one member of the staff, no matter what service the guest has in mind. The system also means that other staff roles become more focused. The telephone operator, for example, is freed up to deal with customers looking for specific phone services rather than becoming bogged down handling a wide array of other requests from guests who don't know whom else to call.

"We can also create a daily report on the requests," says Ianni Massimo, general manager. "We can learn about problems, proactively improve quality, measure turnaround time and alter the menu because we know what people want. There's a daily measurement of productivity and efficiency. The customer shouldn't have to know that we have a laundry department that takes care of laundry and a housekeeping department that delivers sheets. We should treat the customer as a customer of the hotel."

Teams were important and so was employee understanding of the outcome. "People thought that this program was going to be like the police department, like the Gestapo watching all the time," said Anibal Marcote, the hotel's communications manager, who became a leader for this shift. "Once we began implementing it, people saw how it could help them work better and serve the client better. People needed to come to understand that I wasn't there to hurt them or punish them but to help them be more successful."

The search for a new way of operating began as a cost-cutting exercise, and indeed the hotel did save money by eliminating middle layers. However, the benefit of using technology properly went well beyond the savings. People were empowered and felt more motivated. "Now that the system is implemented fully, it will define our training needs and the basis of our quality control systems," said Massimo.

"In order to implement Business Plan," says Kerr, "we had to quickly go in and change the way the folio management [customer billing] gets done, change the way some of the other events in the hotel get done, change the way the reservation system for the hotel works, to create different categories for Business Plan, and do all that on a very tight timetable—probably six weeks. Five years ago, that would have taken three to six months, or we would have had to have people to do it manually. These kinds of marketing programs, these kinds of changes in the way we do business, more closely match what we sell to what customers want— the more rapidly we can do that the better, and [it matters] whether or not my computer system is getting in the way of customer-oriented changes."

Avoiding Disintermediation

There are some obvious opportunities for disintermediation—that is, the direct interaction and transaction between you, the customer, and the travel agent or provider of travel and tourism services. Approximately 25% of hotel bookings and 90% of airline bookings are currently done by travel agents, but more and more these transactions will be done by the customer. The travel agent's function will move from high value to low value. Initially, hotels paid the 10% commission for four keystrokes—the execution of the transaction. Hotel chains will clearly want higher value from travel agents in the future. Travel agents will need to become a true high-value intermediary—that is, an IT-enabled, trusted advisor to the customer—in order to succeed.

For travel agents to stay alive, they will need to move up the food chain and become partners for event planning rather than agents who simply execute travel-oriented transactions that any individual can do. Advises Davis of THISCO, "Find a niche that makes sense; add value. If all you're doing is taking orders, you're in trouble." Similarly, the implications for any travel industry business that fails to get its products and services into these new multimedia databases are clear. A hotel that doesn't appear on the multimedia map will be in trouble, because a customer will prefer to deal with a hotel chain that has transparent access. Those travel industries best positioned on the network will also be best positioned for business. Says Davis, "All of a sudden, the loners who thought they were building a competitive advantage are at a competitive disadvantage because they're not on the Internet search."

Rosenbluth International: Forging the New Travel Agency

Rosenbluth International, Inc., was founded by Hal Rosenbluth's grandfather in 1892, a booking agent for immigrants coming to America. When airline deregulation occurred more than a decade ago, Hal Rosenbluth embraced computers and leased two reservation systems, American's SABRE and United's APOLLO, so that his firm's agents would have direct access to reservation information. But every other travel agency had the same capacity. How to set his firm apart? Rosenbluth's realization: "We were no longer in the travel business so much as we were in the information business." With simple fare structures replaced by complex arrangements offered by several airlines, Rosenbluth made a specific promise to corporate clients: His firm would guarantee them the lowest fares. In 1978, corporate travel was less than 3% of the firm's $20 million in annual bookings. Today the firm has 3,000 associates at 825 locations in the United States and a dozen other countries. Corporate travel accounts for more than 90% of the firm's $1.6 billion in annual sales.

Along the way, Rosenbluth reinvented travel technology. "There are three perpetual business puzzles—change, people, and technology—and the trick is figuring out how to get them working for you instead of against you," he says. "The companies that have been using technology over the years are the same ones that know the benefits you get from that," he says. "That in itself creates the environment for new businesses to do things differently." At the same time, Rosenbluth realized a home truth. The mission at most companies is to put the customer first. He decided to put his employees first on the grounds that a happy staff would mean happy clients. "That meant giving people the right working environment, the right tools, and the right leadership. It meant eliminating fear, frustration, bureaucracy, and politics."

The focus on staff has played a role in the firm's capacity to stay technologically ahead. In 1992, Rosenbluth wrote a book called *The Customer Comes Second (and Other Secrets of Corporate Service)*. His central belief: "Attracting the very best people who listen awfully well, read a lot, and spend a heck of a lot of time not only with your clients but your suppliers and from that create new uses for technology that allow us to sustain a competitive advantage. At some point in time, someone's going to catch up but we've already used that time to create new businesses."

The early versions of airline reservation systems were independent of one another, and each had a built-in bias toward its own flights. Rosenbluth's niche was to create his own reservation data system that went beyond the low-price promise. It allowed corporations to link directly with the Rosenbluth system as strategic partners and make travel a more manageable expense. As the travel firm expanded nationally through the 1980s, all offices were tied together electronically. Software was developed that reduced by 75% the number of keystrokes required to book a reservation, thereby reducing both employee stress and the chance for mistakes.

The core product available from Rosenbluth is called Dacoda (short for discount analysis containing optimal decision algorithms), a statistical system that allows his 1,000 corporate clients to sift through the deals offered by various airlines and build a model for their own firm that takes into account travel patterns and corporate policies. Yield management systems as practiced by the airlines are complex mathematical models that predict how much money they'll get for a seat in the future based on history, the number of flights between the two points under consideration, size of the aircraft, and a host of other variables. Companies usually have deals with airlines that offer price discounts, upgrades, and other bonuses if certain targets are met. But every airline offers deals based on use during a certain period and the airline's market share; comparisons with other airlines are impossible since every deal is different. "Corporations are almost hostage to the airline yield management system. Dacoda is changing the playing field. It's like the Rosetta Stone of the airfare industry," Rosenbluth says.

Rosenbluth's software works like program trading on the stock market and allows corporations to create their own yield management systems that automatically display negotiated airfares, policy, preferred suppliers, and lowest fares. Firms can usually negotiate 45% reductions on airline fares, but with Dacoda, says Rosenbluth, they can achieve additional savings of 10% to 19%. Rosenbluth says that Dacoda keeps tabs on daily conditions and suggests preferred routings for the best deal. Trip Monitor is a system that checks the specific schedules for the lowest possible fares, constantly canceling and rebooking if it finds a better deal hours before the departure time. According to Rosenbluth, Trip Monitor finds additional savings opportunities averaging $170 per ticket. For Rosenbluth, controlling change in his industry means that you are constantly adapting and staying ahead. "What technology has allowed us to do is to create new businesses," he says. "We like to create the very businesses that will put us out of business because somebody else will if we don't."

Rosenbluth is a great example of how to beat disintermediation. In the digital economy, intermediaries need to move up the food chain to find new ways to create value for customers. Being in the middle between providers and customers doesn't necessarily mean you're toast. You can be disintermediated only if you don't change. In the travel industry, executing transactions provided value for decades. In the digital economy, new value is required.

NOTE

1. *New York Times*, May 1, 1995, C8.

'VE WRITTEN a lot about how the digital revolution could transform the schools. Progress has been slow. Let me comment about higher education in which, because of the burning platform there, has become a conflagration.

Twenty years ago, encyclopedias, record labels, and publishers in the business of producing unique content that generated big revenues. All are being bludgeoned by the digital age, which brought abundance, mass participation, democratized production, and the rise of a new delivery channel—the Internet.

A similar fate could soon await many universities, though they may appear at first glance to be in good health. University enrollment throughout the world is at an all-time high, competition to enroll is fierce, and campuses are awash with young, tech-savvy learners. Still, deep anxieties exist, and for good reason.

Universities are starting to lose their monopoly on higher learning. If all that the large research universities have to offer to students are lectures that students can get online for free from other professors, why should those students pay today's hefty tuition fees? This is especially true if third-party testers will provide certificates, diplomas, and even degrees. If institutions of higher education want to survive this challenge, they need to change the way professors and students interact on campus.

In 1998, none other than Peter Drucker predicted that big universities would be "relics" within 30 years. Increasingly, Drucker's seemingly hyperbolic and apocryphal predictions seem less shrill and even prescient.

I hope Drucker is wrong. I believe there are good reasons for students to attend university or college.

First, you get knowledge, know-how, and capability. Universities are places where students can learn and develop their capacity for thinking. Universities contain knowledge in their libraries (still one of the most important variables in rating universities). Universities have faculty who have knowledge, who encode this knowledge in courses (collectively the syllabus), and communicate this knowledge through lectures and (with help from their teaching assistants) through answering questions and stimulating discussions. It is presumed that students develop not only skills required for the workplace but also knowledge required for a knowledge society.

Second, you get a campus experience. Universities are places, period. Students partake in a campus experience, socializing and maturing with other students and faculty. The university campus has been "a wonderful place for young people to go for four years to get older," as Princeton sociologist Marvin Dressler told me a decade ago, joking: "While they're there they're bound to learn something." Students have a chance to meet people of similar social status, couple up, and create friendships and connections that will be helpful in future life.

Third, you get a degree. Universities are institutions that credential and certify people conferring social and economic value to each. Graduates can say they have achieved certain proficiencies, knowledge, evidence discipline, and so on. This usually pays off well, as university graduates do better economically than those who are not. Universities play an important role in the sorting of individuals in society, through the admissions process and the awarding of degrees. Universities screen human capital for future employers, graduate studies, and more broadly help stratify society. Those who get good marks in high school and on their Scholastic Aptitude Tests (SATs), who are proven to be hard workers, and have other talents, get into the best universities. Those who graduate—better still with distinction—have a credential to get the most desirable job or entrance to a graduate program. They have proven they have discipline and that they're prepared to play by the rules.

So there are good reasons for university campuses to exist. But in the digital era, I believe these reasons alone are insufficient. Educators need to reinvent the educational model. In the Industrial Age model of pedagogy, education was about absorbing content and being able to recall it on exams. Unfortunately the traditional lecture, with the professor standing in front of many students, still happens on many campuses. It's teacher-focused, one-way, one-size-fits-all, and the student is isolated in the learning process.

Most educators cling to this model, which I've called "broadcast learning." It was designed for an age when industry needed workers who did what they were told. The teacher was the sage who delivered knowledge, and pupils were expected to write down the sage's utterances and deliver them back if they wanted to score an A. As I often say, "the definition of a lecture is the process by which the notes of the teacher go to the notes of the student without going through the brains of either."

Not all universities function this way. The small liberal arts and science colleges are doing a wonderful job of stimulating young minds. With big endowments and small class sizes, students can have more of a customized collaborative experience. If you're fortunate enough to get into Amherst College, Williams College, or Swarthmore College, you're in good hands. But the same cannot be said of many of the big universities that regard their prime roles to be centers for research, with teaching as an inconvenient afterthought, and class sizes so large that the only way to "teach" is through lectures.

As the model of pedagogy or teaching is challenged, inevitably the revenue model of universities will be too. If institutions want to survive the arrival of free, university-level education online, they need to change the way professors and students interact on campus.

Many will argue: "But what about credentials? As long as the universities can grant degrees, their supremacy will never be challenged." This is myopic thinking. The value of a credential, and even the prestige of a university, are rooted in its effectiveness as a learning institution. If these institutions are shown to be inferior to alternative learning environments, their capacity to credential will surely diminish. How much longer will, say, a Harvard University undergraduate degree, taught mostly through lectures by teaching assistants (TAs) in large classes, be able to compete in status with the small class size of liberal arts colleges or the superior delivery systems that harness the new models of learning?

Educators must acknowledge that for today's students, the "broadcast model of learning" makes no sense. Most of today's students have grown up immersed in digital technologies, and as a result their brains are different. Schooled on Google and Wikipedia, they want to inquire, not rely on the professor for a detailed road map. They want an animated conversation, not a lecture. They want an interactive education, not a broadcast one dating back two or three centuries.

Potential employers want changes in the university as well. A recent study by Hart Research Associates noted that "more than three in four employers say they want colleges to place more emphasis on helping students develop five key learning outcomes: critical thinking, complex problem solving, written and oral communication, and applied knowledge in real-world settings."[1]

Research shows that mutual exploration, group problem solving, and collective meaning making produces better learning outcomes and understanding overall. A report by the Brighton Central School District in Rochester, New York, put it well: "If the factory was the model of the typical twentieth-century American school, the craftsman's shop or artist's studio is the model for a twenty-first-century educational delivery system."[2]

Yes, some material needs to be committed to memory. But it is almost always a gross misuse of the educator's many talents to simply teach routine and memory-based work. Today's sophisticated multimedia education software running on laptops, tablets, and smartphones can do a much better job, and at a time convenient for the learner. The software responds to the progress the student makes. If a student has trouble understanding chemical formulae, the computer can go back and cover the material again. This frees up the educator's time in class to deal with more substantive matters, either with students individually or in small groups.

In a similar vein, educators can "flip" their classrooms. They can make video recordings of their lectures, which students can watch online before the class. Class time is then devoted to the educator listening and conversing with the students, and encouraging students to discuss the material among themselves.

There are shining examples of such learning. I know an educator who practices "just-in-time teaching." It combines the benefits of Web-based assignments with an active-learner classroom. Warm-up questions, written by the students, are typically due a few hours before class, giving the teacher an opportunity to adjust the lesson "just in time," so that classroom time can be focused on the parts of the assignments that students struggled with. This technique produces real results. An evaluation study of 350 Cornell University students found that those who were asked *deep questions* (questions that elicit higher-order thinking) with frequent peer discussion scored noticeably higher on their math exams than students who were not asked deep questions or who had little to no chance for peer discussion.

I have some recent personal experience about the importance of projects in postsecondary education. My daughter Nicole Tapscott and her best friend Joanna Griffiths did their master of business administration (MBA) studies at INSEAD, the famous business school outside of Paris, France.

Joanna had thought of a business idea a few years prior and took advantage of being at school to test the idea's validity—collaborating with professors, fellow students, and leveraging the alumni network. The MBA program hosts an annual business plan competition and so Joanna, along with Nicole and two other classmates, formed a team and entered the competition, with the goal to create a new product—the next generation of women's underwear.

While developing the business plan, they simultaneously began rapid prototyping. By the competition finals, they had a solid strategy in place and working prototypes. They won the competition, along with $20,000 to start the business. Joanna moved to Toronto, Canada, to become the founder and CEO of what is now known as Knix Wear and Nicole is an adviser and shareholder helping to build the brand's presence south of the border. According to Joanna:

> Without INSEAD and the business plan competition, Knix Wear likely wouldn't exist. It was the perfect opportunity to test an idea and gain invaluable feedback in a supportive and risk-free environment so that by the time we went to market, I knew we were on to something big.

Today, Joanna continues to lead Knix Wear based on the principles she learned in school and it is working. In under a year, the company has secured distribution across North America, sold tens of thousands of pairs, been featured by hundreds of media outlets including *Forbes, Fast Company*, and *Entrepreneur* magazine, and is the first brand to secure a major retail partner through crowdfunding, when Canada's largest department store, the Hudson Bay Company, prepaid for product via crowdfunding in exchange for becoming the brand's first retail partner.

Global Network for Higher Learning

In a world of unparalleled connectivity, especially among today's youth, universities still operate as largely autonomous islands of scholarship and learning. For universities to succeed, I believe they need to cooperate to launch a "Global Network for Higher Learning."[3] It would have three levels or stages.

The first is *content exchange*. Professors park their teaching materials online for others to freely use. Massive Open Online Courses (MOOCs) would fall currently into this category. The second is *content co-innovation*, whereby teachers collaborate and share ideas across institutional and disciplinary boundaries to co-create new teaching materials using wikis and other tools. By level three, the university changes from being a place to a node in the global network of faculty, students, and institutions learning collaboratively, while at the same time maintaining its identity, campus, and brand. The Global Network for Higher Learning is not a pipe dream. Leading scholars are implementing elements of all three levels today. They know that universities and their faculties cannot continue to operate as islands, constantly reinventing the wheel.

The lowest level of collaborative knowledge production is simple *content exchange*: universities post their educational material online, putting into the public domain what would have traditionally been considered a proprietary asset and part of a university's competitive advantage. Massachusetts Institute of Technology (MIT) pioneered the concept, OpenCourseWare (OCW), and today more than 200 institutions of higher learning have followed suit.

OpenCourseWare came about when MIT asked its faculty in 1999 how best to leverage the Internet to advance knowledge and educate students. The faculty's reply was to publish as much as possible of the faculty's teaching materials, such as lecture notes or exams, on the Internet. The online content may be freely used, copied, distributed, translated, and modified by anyone.[4] MIT's OCW initiative is probably the single-most important and cost-effective contribution to the world's knowledge base in the past 10 years.

In addition to helping students study, the OCW material is being reused by teachers around the world. Consider what a change this offers to a typical professor's life. Prior to OCW, faculty members were largely isolated in the content creation process. Say you were a psychology professor assigned a second-year course on behavioral psychology. You chose a textbook written by an isolated author and published by a traditional publishing company. You created your own course outline and then painstakingly went through each module filling in the blanks. Slowly you built up the lecture presentation materials, reading lists, and so on. You developed material such as essay topics, tests, and exams, including the concepts of reliability and validity of multiple-choice tests. This was hard work, because as a professor you knew it was going to take multiple tests to get the instrument right. Sometimes you could rely on the work of other professors but, in general, this was discouraged as being unoriginal. You might run your course idea by a few colleagues, but the only people who really benefited from all your diligent work were the students who took your course. Once you had the whole package, if you were a good professor, you upgraded it every year or even every semester, adding new research and examples, and discarding ideas that didn't work. You were a professor as an island.

The better and more conscientious you were, the worse it got. If you wanted to foster enriching discussions and have students work in teams to solve problems, you needed to invent a framework, methodology, and of course, the content. If you decided to create computer-based learning modules for certain sections of the course—to enable students to learn about, say, different types of Skinnerian procedures—the effort and cost of finding the right technology and hiring programmers to develop the courseware could be pretty prohibitive. OpenCourseWare solves the problem of isolation and provides a wealth of materials that others can use and even build on, regardless of their university affiliation.

MOOCs were the next logical step for the OpenCourseWare concept. At the 2013 World Economic Forum in Davos, Switzerland, the big three companies that provide the free online learning technology—Coursera, Udacity, and edX—were all represented. Coursera had just announced it would be offering more than 200 free MOOCs at more than 33 universities. Having opened for business in the autumn of 2012, the company had more than 1.3 million students in a matter of months.

The presidents of Harvard University, Stanford University, and MIT were also at Davos, and they readily acknowledged that the experiments in new models of online learning would soon radically disrupt higher learning. One expert said we were in the early days of bankruptcies for many universities. Another predicted there may only be 10 universities that survive.

MIT President L. Rafael Reif talked about the university's OpenCourseWare project. Reif said the material had been accessed by more than 100 million individual learners and that the number of learners was growing by almost 1 million per month. But Reif said that he felt that university involved more than just watching videotaped lectures of university professors online. Many had predicted a similar transformation of education with the arrival of educational television decades ago. Rolling a TV into the classroom or having students watch lectures at home was thought by many to portend a revolution to existing pedagogical models. Of course, almost nothing changed.

Reif thought that the university experience had three components. The first was life on campus, living in dorms, and hanging out with other students. The second was the classroom lecture. And the third was the smaller group discussion in projects and labs, where he thought "the real education occurs." Reif said he saw a future where educators were viewed less as fountains of knowledge and more as mentors.

One can easily see a day when students treat all the universities as one big a la carte menu that can lead to something we could call a "MOOC degree." Take some law courses at Harvard, economic courses at McGill University, some engineering courses at MIT, and round out the degree with courses from Queen's University, Yale University, and the London School of Economics. The result will be students acquiring a better education by shopping around then they could have acquired at just one institution. And it won't take long before employers recognize this.

The second level in collaborative knowledge creation goes beyond discussing and sharing ideas to the actual *co-creation of content*. In the same way Wikipedia's editors collaborate to create, update, and expand the online encyclopedia's entries, professors could co-innovate new teaching material (based on work already in the OCW and other repositories) and then share this newly synthesized content with the world. Or consider the approach taken by the Wikiversity, a project of the Wikimedia Foundation. Rather than offer a set menu of courses and materials, Wikiversity participants set out what they want to learn, and the Wikiversity community collaborates to develop learning activities and projects to accommodate those goals. Imagine what a platform like Wikiversity could do if it had the muscle of the world's universities behind it. These are the sorts of projects that should be invigorating the worldwide academic community.

Once again, take the example of the behavioral psychology course. Psychology professors would work together to design the "perfect course" that pools the collective knowledge of the world's leading thinkers. Of course there can be no complete agreement as there would be various perspectives, schools, and teaching techniques.

But as in Wikipedia, the professors could work globally to create core modules that were not controversial and then subnetworks of like-minded teachers could form to develop ancillary elements to complete the course. For the ultimate course, the teachers would need more than course materials; they would need course software enabling students to interact with the content, supporting small group discussions, enabling testing, and so on.

These can be developed using tried-and-true techniques and tools of the open source software movement. If thousands of people can develop the most sophisticated computer operating system in the world (Linux), they can certainly develop the tools for a psychology course. Indeed, there are already many well-known open source software projects underway in the academic community, and there should be more. One of the most popular is Sakai. Built by educators for educators, Sakai facilitates collaboration in and across courses, research, projects, administrative processes, and multidisciplinary and multi-institution efforts. Creation of the software itself is a product of content co-innovation, and then the product in turn helps co-innovate content that can be taught to students.

Used properly, wikis and other social media should be used to co-innovate content directly with students too. Rather than simply being the recipients of the professor's knowledge, the students co-create knowledge with light supervision, which has been shown to be one of the most effective methods of learning. Matt Barton, a professor of English at St. Cloud State University in Minnesota, recently enlisted his students to help build a living, breathing resource on English rhetoric—including its history, uses, and meaning—on Wikipedia. "I could sit down and take days, weeks, even months to find all the terms," says Barton, "but with Wikipedia, I can start the list with three or four definitions and then kick back and let the community chip in a little."[5] Barton figures that the more eyes on his work the better, so he blogs about his work and, beyond students, he invites his peers to get involved too. "I might make a mistake that I'm not seeing, so having those people watching over it is a good thing." There is a growing contingent of scholars like Barton who sees the value of a dynamic, evolving body of knowledge that students are active in shaping as part of the learning experience.

The digital world, which has trained young minds to inquire and collaborate, is challenging not only the lecture-driven teaching traditions of the university but the very notion of a walled-in institution that excludes large numbers of people. Why not allow a brilliant ninth-grade student to take first-year college math, without abandoning the social life of his or her high school? Why not encourage a foreign student majoring in math to take a high school English course? Why is the university the unit of measurement when it comes to branding a degree? In fact, in a networked world, why should a student have to assign his or her "enrollment" to a given institution, akin to declaring loyalty to some feudal fiefdom?

Luis M. Proenza, president emeritus of the University of Akron, asks exactly these questions, challenging the notion of the ivory tower itself as the fundamental unit of higher education. True, students can obviously learn from intellectuals around the world through books or via the Internet. Yet in a digital world, why shouldn't a student be able to take a course from a professor at another university? Proenza thinks colleges and universities should use the Internet to create a global center of excellence. In other words, an institution should choose its best courses and link them with the best at a handful of other institutions around the world to create an unquestionably best-in-class program for students. Students would get to learn from the world's greatest minds in their area of interest—either in the physical classroom or online. This global academy would also be open to anyone online.

Of course, such open platforms could provide a means to address the needs of all learners, not just 20-somethings. For today's knowledge workers, remaining truly competitive in fast-moving fields of research and innovation means constant retraining and retooling to begin and/or continue their working lives in a modern, dynamic, and technology-focused environment. The cost of building new continuing education programs from scratch could be prohibitively high, but new models of collaborative education can help bring greater efficiency and creativity to the efforts to help school leavers and aging employees update their skills.[6] Indeed, why not allow companies and governments to participate in this global network for higher learning too?

Notes

1. "It Takes More Than a Major: Employer Priorities for College Learning and Student Success," Hart Research Associates, Spring 2013, Vol. 99, No. 2, http://www.aacu.org/liberaleducation/le-sp13/hartresearchassociates.cfm
2. Don Tapscott, "Education Should Open Pupils' Minds, Not Impart Facts," *The Sunday Times*, January 11, 2009.
3. As explained in Don Tapscott and Anthony D. Williams, *Macrowikinomics: New Solutions for a Connected Planet*, (Portfolio, 2012).
4. MIT OpenCourseWare at MIT. See: http://ocw.mit.edu.
5. Matt Barton, "The Matt Chat Blog," http://mattchat.us.
6. Paul Hofheinz, "EU 2020: Why Skills Are Key for Europe's Future," The Lisbon Council (2009), www.lisboncouncil.net/publication/publication/54-skillseuropesfuture.html.

LEARNING IN THE DIGITAL ECONOMY

I'm only attending school until it becomes available on CD-ROM.

Anonymous sixth-grade student

When we think of learning, we think of schools. In 1926, the great Finnish composer Jean Sibelius produced *Tapiola*, a most austere work that speaks mightily of the natural forces of the long and dark winter in that northern clime. To say the least, not everyone likes the work. Sibelius was unconcerned. "Others can provide the cocktails," he said. "I serve only plain water." Learning was once a plain-water process conducted by educational institutions. Teachers and professors shared what they knew. Students discussed the issues, then prepared papers by doing their own research in libraries, crammed for exams, and then graduated.

The digital economy requires a far-reaching rethinking of education and, more broadly, learning and the relationship between working, learning, and daily life as a consumer. Six themes are emerging.

THE SIX THEMES OF THE NEW LEARNING

Theme 1: Increasingly, Work and Learning Are Becoming the Same Thing

Because the digital economy is based on knowledge work and innovation, there is a convergence between work and learning. While you perform knowledge work, you learn. And you must learn minute by minute to perform knowledge work effectively.

In the old economy, the basic competencies of the industrial worker, bricklayer, or bus driver were relatively stable. True, you might have applied those competencies to different situations such as different construction sites, but the learning component of your labor was small.

In the new economy, the learning component of work becomes huge. Consider the researcher looking for a genetic basis for schizophrenia, the software developer creating a new multimedia application, the manager responsible for corporate planning in a bank, the consultant assessing a client's markets, the entrepreneur starting up a new business, or the teaching assistant in a community college. Think about your own work. Work and learning overlap for a massive component of the workforce.

Harvard's Shoshana Zuboff asks her audience: "What's the first thing you do if you are sitting back in your chair with your feet on the desk and you see the boss coming down the hall toward your office?" The audience replies, "Feet off and look as if you're working." She then makes the point that for many knowledge workers, thinking (regardless of where your feet are) is working. Thinking and collaborating are required to perform knowledge work effectively.

Theme 2: Learning Is Becoming a Lifelong Challenge

In the old economy, your life was divided into the period when you learned and the period when you worked. You went to school and maybe university and learned a competency—trade or profession—and for the rest of your life your challenge was simply to keep up with developments in your field. In the new economy, you can expect to have to reinvent your knowledge base throughout your life. Nobody knows what a career plan is any more.

Consider the words of Louis Ross, Ford Motor Co.'s chief technical officer, to a group of engineering students: "In your career, knowledge is like milk. It has a shelf life stamped right on the carton. The shelf life of a degree in engineering is about three years. If you're not replacing everything you know by then, your career is going to turn sour fast."

Learning has become a continuous, lifelong process. An expert is no longer someone who did something right once. An expert is a person who keeps up because knowledge doubles every 18 months. Amidst such hyperspace change, some people prefer to be oblivious about what's going on in the real world. "I don't need the news," said football coach Bum Phillips. "If they have a war, someone will tell me."

Others have greater insight. In the new organization of the digital economy, where leadership will exist at all levels, learning will be a lifetime art. Here's what Robertson Davies, the celebrated author of *The Deptford Trilogy*, said in 1993 when he was 80 years old: "I'm always trying to move on to something else. If possible, I want to be less stupid. Of course, the less stupid you are, the more you realize just how stupid you really are! If you give up the struggle, you give up life. You've got to be perpetually taking in what's happening. The world I live in is so much different from the world in which I was born that if I didn't pay attention, I'd be a fossil."

Richard Soderberg of the National Technological University puts it well: "People mistakenly think that once they've graduated from university they are good for the next decade—when they're really good for the next 10 seconds." If you graduate with a four-year science or engineering degree, half of what you learned in the first year is likely to be obsolete.

Theme 3: Learning Is Shifting Away from the Formal Schools and Universities

Because the knowledge economy requires lifelong learning, the private sector is having to shoulder a growing responsibility for learning. This view is becoming widely held and is best articulated in the stimulating book *The Monster Under the Bed* by Stan Davis and Jim Botkin. The book argues that education, once the purview of the church, then government, is increasingly falling to business because it is business that ends up having to train knowledge workers. Say Davis and Botkin, "With the move from an agrarian to an industrial economy, the small rural schoolhouse was supplanted by the big brick urban schoolhouse. Four decades ago we began to move to another economy, but we have yet to develop a new educational paradigm, let alone create the 'schoolhouse' of the future, which may be neither school nor house."[1]

Because the new economy is a knowledge economy and learning is part of day-to-day economic activity and life, both companies and individuals have found they need to take responsibility for learning simply to be effective. The enterprise becomes a school in order to compete. So McDonald's has Hamburger U., which according to CIO Carl Dill, Jr., provides credit-level education to more than 10,000 employees per year. In 1995 alone, more than 700,000 McDonald's employees received some form of structured training. There are Motorola U. and Hewlett-Packard U. and Sun Microsystems has Sun U.

Davis and Botkin present data to show that in 1992 the growth in formal budgeted employee education grew by 126 million additional hours. This represents the equivalent of almost a quarter of a million additional full-time college students—13 new Harvards. This is more growth in just one year than the enrollment growth in all the new conventional college campuses built in the United States between 1960 and 1990. "Employee education is not growing 100 % faster than academia, but 100 times—or 10,000 % faster," say Davis and Botkin.[2]

Take a look at the top half dozen jobs in terms of growth in 1994: home health aides (138%), computer scientists (112%), systems analysts (110%), physical therapists (88%), paralegals (86%), specialized teachers (74%), medical assistants (71%). In each of these jobs the technology of work and the content of the job change profoundly on a regular basis.

As a consumer, you must continuously change your knowledge base: learning how to use the navigational screen in your rental car; setting up Windows 95 on your home computer; working with your daughter in searching the Net for information about her project on acid rain or on her CD about the San Diego Zoo; using the interactive training package that comes with your new home telephone system; programming your home entertainment center; shopping for groceries on the Ameritech Peapod network. The providers of these knowledge-based products and services must build learning into their offerings, not as a peripheral but as a central capability. And as you enter the digital economy, you become not only a knowledge worker but also a knowledge consumer. This places a considerable responsibility on each of us to invent our curriculum. We need to plan our lifelong learning and how, through self-paced learning, on-the-job learning, and formal education and training, we can stay robust in a changing economy.

Theme 4: Some Educational Institutions Are Working Hard to Reinvent Themselves for Relevance, but Progress Is Slow

Pundits have been complaining about formal education for decades. Humorist Will Rogers put it this way: "Schools ain't as good as they usta be and they never was."

The intense pressure of the volatile business environment has forced many firms to step up, if only partially, to the learning challenge. Formal educational institutions have been slower to respond. With tenured professors, teachers threatened by technology, less competition, and teaching traditions dating back centuries, many educational institutions have become mired in the past.

At a dinner conversation of educators hosted by Ameritech, a university president complained to his peers at the table that the model of teaching in universities today dates back to the *post-Gutenberg* period. He was corrected by Geoffrey Bannister, president of Butler University, who argued that the model was closer to *pre-Gutenberg*, with professors working from handwritten notes and transferring them to a chalkboard. Even the printing press is not a central element in the learning paradigm.

At River Oaks Elementary School in Oakville, Ontario, business has been a partner in bringing IT to the classroom and creating a learning curriculum for the new, rather than old economy. Principal Gerry Smith has a pair of simple questions that send a surprising message. If a doctor from 75 years ago suddenly traveled by time capsule and arrived in today's hospital, would that doctor be able to function? Not a chance. But how about a teacher from that same era in a contemporary classroom? The chalkboard, desks, and multiplication tables would probably look all too familiar. "We live in an information-rich world and not all learning takes place within the four walls of the classroom," says Smith. "The world is a classroom and it's up to us educators to make that possible."

This situation is changing as many progressive institutions are working hard to reinvent themselves. The Canadian province of New Brunswick has a program called Unite, in which every student in the province has access to the Internet. Computers have penetrated classrooms in the United States—with more than one computer per 10 students. Computers are required tools in most universities, and many institutions provide access to the Net and a range of services such as the digitized *Encyclopedia Brittanica* for all students. But overall, there is little progress in using technology to fundamentally change the way formal education is delivered.

Theme 5: Organizational Consciousness Is Required to Create Learning Organizations

It was Peter Senge who popularized the notion of a learning organization that he described as a place "where people continually expand their capacity to create the results they truly desire, where new and expansive patterns of thinking are nurtured, where collective aspiration is set free, and where people are continually learning how to learn together."[3]

Despite Senge's thoughtful attempts and the success of his books, one of the basic problems with organizational learning is that the concept is still not well understood. Here are just a few of the attempts to define it:

- "Organizational learning means the process of improving actions through better knowledge and understanding."[4]
- "An entity learns if, through its processing of information, the range of its potential behaviors is changed."[5]

- "Organizations are seen as learning by encoding inferences from history into routines that guide behavior."[6]
- "Organizational learning is a process of detecting and correcting error."[7]
- "Organizational learning occurs through shared insights, knowledge and mental models ... [and] builds on past knowledge and experience—that is, on memory."[8]

Notwithstanding differing views, the basic idea is a sound one. There is no sustainable competitive advantage today other than organizational learning. That is, your company can compete only if it can learn faster than its competitors. To be successful in a knowledge economy, firms need to overcome their organizational learning disabilities and create learning organizations. And organizational learning occurs within teams. The team basis of shared vision and learning, however, leaves unanswered questions regarding how organizational learning can be achieved at the level of the entire organization or enterprise.

In the Age of Networked Intelligence, teams can be networked to achieve broader consciousness. Just as client/server computing distributes and integrates processing—the network becomes the computer—so internetworking can both distribute and integrate human intelligence to achieve a new form of organizational consciousness.

The network becomes the basis for the enterprise to think and thereby to learn. Organizational learning can be extended beyond teams. Team wisdom can become enterprise wisdom. Organizational consciousness is a prerequisite for organizational learning. And internetworking may be the missing link in organizational learning.

Theme 6: The New Media Can Transform Education, Creating a Working-Learning Infostructure for the Digital Economy

There are already more than 2,000 courses available over the Net. More significantly, the information base and culture created by humanity is becoming accessible through the internet. For example, the *Urbino Bible* (one of the books of antiquity that predated Gutenberg) was, until recently, available to only a handful of people. Kept in the Vatican and restricted to 200 people who could view it at the rate of four pages per day, the *Bible* is now on the Net. A hundred times more people saw it during its first few days on the Net than had seen it in the previous half millenium.

Increasingly, products have interactive learning built into them and consumption of them involves learning. Sun University and the National Technological University deliver formal courses and accreditation on networks, without classrooms. At River Oaks, education has been transformed using IT. Most students have a Macintosh computer on their desks, networked across the class, the school, and beyond. The results are spectacular and the lesson for business is simple. Computers have reached the point at which they can help youth and others learn. These students feel empowered. As workers, they are more likely to be able to take on more responsibility, act more efficiently, and become members of lifelong learning organizations.

Powerful machines are training people in their quest for new languages, skills, and insights. Moreover, the location of learning has exploded beyond the classroom; learning can now take place in the workplace, car, or home. The Discovery Channel, The Learning Channel, and video-based learning packages are only the first wave because they are neither digital nor interactive.

In addition to transforming learning in the private sector, the new technologies can transform schools. Education and health care are draining taxpayers' wallets, but the information highway offers cause for hope. New communication technologies that enable free-flowing information and knowledge can dramatically boost the value of education and health care tax dollars. Educational institutions can reinvent themselves if they will it, exploiting the enabling effect of the five levels of technology as depicted in Fig. 8.1

The MIT Media Labs now operate a test-facility school, in cooperation with sponsors Lego and Nintendo, in which games explore the relationships between playing and learning. What they're finding is that the best learning comes from

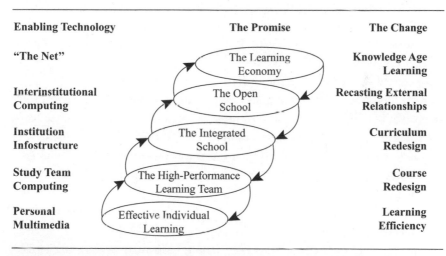

FIGURE 8.1 *The Transformation of Formal Education.* SOURCE: © New Paradigm Learning Corporation, 1996.

passion, passion instilled by teachers, passion felt by students. LabNet, created by Technical Education Research Centers of Cambridge, Massachusetts, has developed a communications network for hundreds of teachers around the country. Working first with Delphi, a commercial network, then America Online, the project includes e-mail, bulletin boards, and sharing of data among the schools, the teachers, and the students.

As access to information increases, students will have an advantage over teachers who are rooted in the past. Technology is now redefining the role of teachers as it assists them to become motivators and facilitators, not fact-repeaters. As Tony Comper, president of the Bank of Montreal, says: "Kids doing a random walk through all information in the world is not necessarily the best way for them to learn. Teachers can become navigators providing meta-learning—crucial guidance and support regarding how to go about learning." No school can afford to have an oceanographer on staff to teach children about dolphins. But through the new media every child in every school or at home should be able to get a private tour of the world of dolphins conducted by Jacques Cousteau. The teacher doesn't compete with Cousteau but, rather, is supported by him.

Youth view technology differently from adults. Adults may use a computer application with the goal of learning. But as Comper says, "For kids, learning *is* the application." The ease with which children embrace new technology is fueling the multimedia explosion.

Retail sales of home-learning software are increasing almost 50% a year and could hit billions of dollars by the end of the decade, a spending spree that is being largely fueled by the new multimedia computer. CD-ROMs, which store data, images, audio, and video, exploit these capabilities and make learning fun so that children are soaking up knowledge as they play. Some programs are deliberately structured as games, requiring children to answer geography or history questions as they try to track down some nefarious villain. Early studies of such interactive technology show great promise. Children are able to learn the three Rs faster, and they are more motivated to explore new subjects. "The use of computers in education is the most important single advance in pedagogy since the invention of grandmothers," says Tom Stonier. "Grandmothers are the oldest information retrieval system in the world."

Multimedia adds a richer, more compelling texture to a learning process that everybody agrees needs help. Still, school curricula can be more responsive to the child's needs and interests, making information more accessible. The information highway will allow teachers to take the techniques being shown by CD-ROMs to a much higher plateau. As the UNESCO report said, "Teachers armed with chalk and a blackboard are no match for these powerful new media."[9] The National Information Infrastructure would promote collaborative learning between students, teachers, and experts. Everyone could access online "digital libraries" and be able to take "virtual" field trips to museums and science exhibits without ever leaving the classroom.

Doctors are typical of professionals facing an enormous struggle in trying to keep pace with new developments. The American Medical Association is already publishing custom CD-ROMs, compressing 100,000 pages of medical advancements and news onto a new CD every three months. CD-ROMS are becoming popular in the home, too. Parents who once bought the multivolume encyclopedias from a sales rep at the door are now more likely to spend $2,500 for a CD-ROM-equipped multimedia PC bundled with an electronic version of the encyclopedia complete with animated footage and audio clips of animals in the jungle. Already, some 5 million units are in use in the United States, and a similar number were sold in 1994. In all, home learning will hit $1 billion annually by the end of the decade.[10]

But CDs have their limitations. Although the media are digital, they are still physical artifacts. The true power of the new media is when it comes over a network. In his book, *Life After Television*, George Gilder was one of the first to explain that the era of broadcast has given way to interactivity.[11] Two-way "telecomputers" will put any book, film, software, or public event in the hands of children. "By radically changing the balance of power between the distributors and creators of culture, the telecomputer will forever break the broadcast bottleneck. Potentially, there will be as many channels as there are computers attached to the global network ... [the creator] will be able to command a large audience without having to worry about mass appeal."

The Clinton administration has been advocating the National Information Infrastructure arguing that computer-based instruction is cost-effective, enabling 30% more learning in 40% less time at 30% less cost. More effective, faster, and cheaper teaching are benefits that administrators of the creaky North American educational systems—and beleaguered taxpayers—cannot afford to ignore.

Although the effects would be dramatic for all pupils, they would be truly spectacular for students in rural or isolated communities. They don't have the reference libraries, museums, zoos, or science centers that many urban children currently enjoy. When the information highway is everywhere, then for the first time we could have a first-rate education system that is truly universal.

Cyberspace Tutor

Clare Mullen, who tutors students with learning disabilities in Lincoln-Sudbury High School in Sudbury, Massachusetts, had a student who came in one morning with all his math homework correct. Surprised and delighted, she asked who gave him help with his work. It was not his parents or an older sibling. The boy had posted his math problems on a discussion group on the Net and received help from a math teacher somewhere out in cyberspace. The teacher saw a student in need and provided critical help.

An education system that fully integrates the information highway would be much better equipped to keep pace with the accelerating growth in knowledge or advances in technology that are occurring in almost every field. The job of classroom teachers will become more like that of a coach. They won't have to handle the rote learning, so they'll have time for mentoring, advice, and one on one—one teacher, one student. The highway would also be the best tool to enable graduates to continue the learning process once they have left school.

RIVER OAKS: A SCHOOL FOR THE DIGITAL ECONOMY

Since River Oaks opened in 1990, principal Gerry Smith has created a technological learning environment that is among the best in North America and serves as an inspiring example of what one committed person can achieve. "Anyone can do this," says Smith. "If you dream it, you can do it." Driven by a concern for the future of his own two school-aged children, Smith began in 1988 to redesign the curriculum into four areas: literacy, life skills, arts, and creative applications. First, there were board of education hurdles to overcome (such as the foolish rule that limited each school to three telephone lines and seven phones). Smith wanted a telephone in every room so that the students would have easy access to outside databases. "Peter Drucker says we spend too much time putting Band-Aids on kids rather than building their strength," says Smith.

The traditional school is an island; when the classroom door closes, the teacher and students might as well be stranded with whatever learning nutrition they brought along. At River Oaks, telecommunications create links with the world. But how do you fund such bridges to the outside? The traditional source for funds would have been public funds from taxpayers, but Smith is no traditional thinker. Rather than relying solely on public funding and spending all his time juggling budgets and trying to establish new priorities for what funds were available, Smith went to Northern Telecom Ltd. and proposed a business partnership. Northern agreed, and River Oaks now has a Meridian One telephone system. Not only is it more than the school requires, it's big enough to handle the needs of the entire school board in this bedroom community. As a result, the students have eight lines, jacks in every room, and a fiber optics link to Toronto's York University that allows students access to the Internet so they can do projects on spiders with their peers in Japan.

Smith expanded his horizons and went searching for more business partners. River Oaks now has 10 business partners including Northern, Sony Corp., Husqvarna AB, Claris, Microsoft Corp., Perceptrix, and Apple Computer, Inc. The school had no more money available than any other school in the local system, but Smith spent the funds more wisely and within three years acquired $500,000 worth of computers, scanners, CD-ROM players, and desktop publishing and video equipment.

Typical of the deals he struck was an arrangement with Apple to buy computers that, say, had slightly damaged exteriors and could not be sold for full retail price through the usual distribution chain. River Oaks got them at marked-down prices even though the innards worked perfectly. For its part, Apple has received the benefit of its equipment being visible to the thousands of visitors annually drawn to gawk and learn from the ongoing experiment that is River Oaks.

Smith's philosophy is simple: If you always do what you've always done, you'll always get what you've always got. For the school's 670 students and 36 teachers, the results have been nothing short of amazing. They collaborate more effectively and suffer fewer discipline problems than in the past. By the sixth grade, students are writing well-organized essays up to 3,000 words long. "Writing is no longer drudgery for them," says Ronald Owston, associate dean of education at Toronto's York University, who spent three years studying students at River Oaks as they progressed from the third grade through the fifth grade. "The maturity of their writing is remarkable. In terms of preparation for the future marketplace," says York's Owston, "these kids have a definite advantage."

Nor are these gifted children from high-income families or the "right" homes. Most are just average middle-class kids; some of them live in government-assisted housing. They happened to luck out by living within the school's jurisdictional boundaries. Kindergarten begins with the usual cut-and-paste and sandbox to teach dexterity and social skills, but there's also a computer available, and by the second grade, they're computer literate. In one exercise, seven-year-olds use a computer to state a problem they've faced, offer solutions, then write a story about the incident. Using a Sony Mavica, they add photos to make a multimedia demonstration of what happened. "The problem is a bully pushing me in the park," writes Gareth. Solutions he suggests? "Get up and walk away" and "Count to 10 and call an adult."

By the fifth grade, students are producing five-page, well-plotted stories that are rich in characters and vocabulary. In the seventh grade, students form a business, choose a president, decide what they'll make, create, and print a logo for the firm, and use computer-assisted design to produce items for sale at the annual craft show. In the music room, the screech of neophyte embouchures has been supplemented by synthesizers and software that help teach a 12-bar blues program or swing styles on the drums. In shop, where kids used to learn how to do things for car engines that had been rendered obsolete years ago, River Oaks students work in teams using computer-aided design on such real-life needs as a faster soapbox for the seasonal races.

The computers do not push individual students into screen-staring isolation. On the contrary, the technology combined with the curriculum promotes collaboration. For example, a group of students in the eighth grade might be told to produce a multimedia study on videodisk about an endangered species. "They have to synthesize, analyze, then communicate," says Smith. "That's a higher order of thinking." Everything is done in a context. Smith says that computers improperly used are a waste. Instead, he preaches a curriculum that engages, enables, and empowers. Technology is not an end in itself; it must be integrated into the day's activities and lifelong learning.

River Oaks is perhaps one of half a dozen centers of excellence in North America that has attracted a constant stream of visitors from Japan. Education using computers is an area in which Japan has fallen behind. The Japanese Education Ministry and prefectural governments want to spend $2.6 billion to place 22 PCs in each primary school and 42 in each junior high school by 2000. The Ministry of International Trade & Industry (MITI) and the Science & Development Agency have projects to develop "friendly" computer interfaces that respond to voice commands and gestures. Business in Japan is also behind in its use of computers. Only 10% of Japanese businesspeople use PCs, and only 13% of those are connected to networks, versus more than 50% in the United States.[12]

"This is an outstanding school compared with U.S. schools," says Kentaro Ohkura, research associate at Tokyo's Tamagawa University, who visited schools in several states before coming to that conclusion. "The computer will be necessary for future society."

NTU—Toward a University for the New Economy

In his book, *Crazy Times Call for Crazy Organizations*, Tom Peters mentions the National Technological University (NTU). He describes it as a "crazy" organization where "crazy" equals excellence. Says Peters: "We have disembodied enterprises for producing things (recordings), disembodied enterprises for coping with the knowledge revolution per se (individualized lifelong education as delivered by NTU). In fact, dispersed, ad hoc networks are becoming the new, if ephemeral, spine of enterprise based on knowledge—knowledge gathered from whomever, wherever, and instantly packaged to meet customers' fickle demands. Tomorrow's economy will revolve around innovatively assembled brain power, not muscle power."[13]

The NTU is a classroom-on-demand. Students can be anywhere and can participate interactively as the best professors lecture on the most up-to-date topics. Or the students can tune in on their own time by watching delayed versions of the lecture when their personal timetable permits. "American corporations have undergone substantial change and restructuring in the past 5 to 10 years," says Karl Reid, NTU chairman. "The emphasis has been on being the best in their business and not just on being one of the best. The result for many has been a strengthening of their competitive position."

The NTU was launched in 1984 in Fort Collins, Colorado, when six corporations—Digital Equipment, Eastman Kodak, General Electric, Hewlett-Packard, IBM, and NCR—invested $1 million in start-up capital. Ten other corporations paid individual site fees totaling $144,000, and all the firms encouraged their engineers to enroll in the computer engineering courses offered by nine universities via videotape delivery. The concept was simple: Use the best professors at universities throughout the country, videotape their lectures, and send the tapes to firms around the nation so that their young employees had access to the latest information from the brightest in the business. So many professional people are now involved that more than one-third of all U.S. engineering computer science faculty can walk across the hall and network with more than 400,000 engineers and managers in their workplaces.

In 1985, the NTU leased satellite time and the member universities added the necessary uplink facilities to put their lectures on the satellite. There were 16 sites and 5 students, and the first graduate completed the program for the master of science degree in computer engineering in 1986. Today, 47 universities (from Arizona State to the University of Wisconsin-Madison) offer 1,200 academic courses and 400 noncredit courses—some 25,000 hours annually—to more than 100,000 technical professionals. Master of science degrees are available in engineering, hazardous waste management, health physics, and computer science at 439 sites in the United States and other countries, such as China and France. The total alumni count has reached 625, and there are more than 1,700 students registered in degree programs. On average, graduates require 2.7 years of study before sitting for the same exams as their full-time university peers.

Chairman Reid describes Lionel Baldwin, the NTU president, as the "coach of the NTU Dream Team … [with] the vision, the courage to innovate, and the leadership ability to mold the team." For his part, Baldwin credits the flexibility of the programs for their success. "Students on campus started demanding access to tapes because they were concerned that off-campus students had an advantage," says Baldwin. "There were raging debates about whether or not students had to be there at the time of delivery." Word of mouth helped the NTU's growing reputation. "It wasn't like there was a national movement—there was diffusion. Engineers would move to a new firm and ask why it wasn't available at their new location."

Companies supply sites for learning and the average "classroom" is eight students. Each location has a microphone so that they can pose questions; the system is fully interactive. Moreover, students find that programs are useful; 85% of them say that they immediately use on the job what they learn. When asked, "Is this one of the best teachers you've ever had?," fully 55% of students say "yes." "Since they're highly motivated 33-year-old adults, you can take their word for it," says Baldwin. There is value in the program for professors, too, because the NTU offers a high-profile way of creating interest in new ideas. "Faculty come to the network to pioneer new classes," says Baldwin. "If it's popular in the workplace, it's easier to get it going on campus."

The network consists of 43 uplinks and more than 400 receivers linked by a state-of-the-art 2.9. Mbps compressed digital video system. In 1994, the NTU moved onto AT&T Telstar 401 where it operates fourteen channels of compressed digital video. For the future, the NTU is testing direct satellite delivery to a 30-inch antenna as well as a new single-channel decoder that is addressable. A Pacific Rim extension is now being tested; a Latin American network is next. Interactivity between the students and lecturers will continue as will the flexibility to watch the live broadcast or tape it for later when time permits. "Learning will be squeezed in around the job and the family. People need the flexibility this provides. They know the programs are current—it's not an old videotape." Nor is it a CD-ROM with no potential for student-teacher contact. Says Baldwin, "That human being at the other end is essential."

Although most programs have so far focused on engineering, some masters' degrees in business administration are also now being offered. Better yet, state education officials who were hostile or indifferent in the past are coming around to a more positive point of view because of budget constraints and more pointed regional interest. "Ten years ago, state educators were concerned about how they would regulate this," says Baldwin. "Now they're on the edge of their chairs. Their governors have all discovered the information highway and they're asking educators 'What are you doing on the network?' The whole thing has flipped 180 degrees."

SUN UNIVERSITY, SUNTALK RADIO: REAL-TIME LEARNING FOR THE REAL-TIME ENTERPRISE

How can you keep a company of 13,000 up to date on a daily or hourly basis about important developments that affect every employee? Sun Microsystems has come up with a digital multimedia fireside chat—Sun Talk Radio—as part of the answer.

Once a quarter Mike Leyman, Sun's CFO, does a two- or three-minute video on the financial results of the Palo Alto-based company, complete with a slide show. More frequently, whenever he thinks it's appropriate, Sun CEO Scott McNealy records a program on SunTalk Radio, which is likewise placed on Sun's internal network. McNealy, who describes himself as the Rush Limbaugh or Howard Stern of Sun, communicates important information or his opinions on developments in the industry (such as a deal with Microsoft). An e-mail that includes a SunTalk radio icon is sent to everybody, indicating that there is a new edition of SunTalk Radio. When employees click on the icon, Netscape software is evoked, accessing a Home Page on the server where the radio program is located. Employees can store it or forward it to someone. McNealy describes it as "an outstanding little fireside chat communication tool to all employees worldwide. In fact, it is better than a radio show that goes live because this is radio-on-demand. We can also find out exactly how many people listened to it, and who. It is really very effective."

"This is changing the way we do communications. People are feeling a lot closer, and I am not such a stranger to them," says McNealy. "I walk through the halls and I am recognized immediately. Everyone is learning together and feeling part of a team. I think we have a much higher alignment from the management team perspective. People know what we are doing."

The Net is particularly effective for situations where the competition has just come out with a new product and Sun employees need "a one-liner or a couple of knock-offs on it." On a day-to-day basis, people get the knowledge they need to be more proactive in dealing with the day-to-day competitive situations."

Such a learning infostructure is especially important for Sun given the strong leadership style of senior management—in particular McNealy—introduced at one Sun event as "Mr. Command and Control."

McNealy says it is at the heart of his efforts to flatten the organization, reduce the amount of management overhead and bureaucracy in the organization, and improve the lines of communication. The network is an alternative to "having to whisper from the CEO down the table to the president of the business, down to the vice president, to the director, manager, junior manager. By the time that message gets there, it is like whispering a secret around a dinner table after 14 beers."

McNealy has a theory that about 60% of what you try to communicate down through each level of management gets through. "So if you think about a four-level organization, .6 to the fourth power is a stunningly low percentage. People think they know and they feel empowered and enabled with less than 10 % of the complete story so they become absolutely dangerous. They think they know but they don't. It is not their fault. It is just that we have to find more effective communication tools."

Sun has other ways of creating opportunities for lifelong learning. "We believe the traditional notion of bringing people together in a classroom and training them is about as ineffective and inefficient as you can possibly be," says Ken Alvares, vice president of human resources. "People need to have information *when they need it* on their workstations. That will be a much better way of being able to give them the detectable information they need to be able to do their jobs."

As a result, Sun University is studying the difference between traditional video learning, face-to-face learning, and learning through accessing information on workstations. "People pull up programs on their machines, start to watch them, and in a very short period of time they are doing other tasks simultaneously. They'll be working on their e-mails, answering their phones, and talking to people in the office." Clearly, their attention is not fully focused on learning, but, says Alvares, "We think there may be a phenomenon there that we can build on."

In addition to the experimental processes, Sun has more traditional information sources such as a library and classroom format programs. But, there's also a software package called Forum that enables the instructor to teach and interact with everyone on the system.

Although it's in its early days yet, the technology in place at Sun has already changed not only the way but the where of work. The spouse of a Sun employee took a new job in Austin, Texas, so she moved to Austin with him—and relocated her job by carrying on with the same function she was doing when she was in the Sun building. E-mail can always find you.

Although Sun admits it has lots yet to learn, the organization has discovered one important lesson: "The office is a system rather than a place. That is a significant change in the way individuals think when they try to balance life, the conflicts of family and their ability to do individual jobs," said Alvares. "I think that technology will provide all of those kinds of advantages."

LIFELONG LEARNING IN THE LAW

Queen's law students Lisa Mendelson and Barry Hutsel ignored the library and turned to the Internet when their professor assigned them a project to negotiate a contract for a popular Detroit Red Wings ice hockey player. The students asked for advice from other online hockey buffs as to what sort of money and perks their theoretical client should demand when compared to other players. The lawyers-in-training were swamped with suggestions from ardent hockey fans, including strategy advice from a lawyer who actually negotiates player contracts for another NHL team. The modem-equipped computer is quickly becoming the legal community's most potent tool.

Particularly popular are huge databases of legal decisions from courts and tribunals that lawyers can access over ordinary phone lines. It now takes only a couple of minutes for lawyers to zip through tens of thousands of cases, looking for precedents or arguments that could buttress their clients' cases.

The giant in the Canadian legal database market is Quicklaw, a firm that mushroomed from a small pilot project started by IBM and Queen's Law School, of Kingston, Ontario, into a private company with offices across the country, offering more than 1,000 constantly updated databases for use by lawyers, accountants, and others. Whether you're in Inuvik or Toronto, their computers can give you the full text of Supreme Court of Canada judgments within two hours of their release. Quicklaw boasts that it has the full texts of judgments from the federal court, the tax court, and the courts of the provinces and territories, and leading administrative tribunals months before they appear in printed law reports. It can even offer the federal government's budget the day it's released, along with commentaries from leading accounting firms, businesses, law firms, and consumer organizations.

Not surprisingly, lawyers love it. Highly specialized lawyers can closely monitor developments in their field and can use Quicklaw to gain access to similar databases in other countries. Over lunch, a Vancouver trade lawyer can brief you on tribunal decisions handed down that morning in Washington or London. Neighborhood storefront lawyers use the system to quickly become *au courant* on subject areas they handle infrequently. When you phone from the police station demanding to know your rights, even the lawyer who handled the sale of your house will need only a couple of minutes on the computer to know what the courts are currently saying.

In a burst of marketing genius, Quicklaw makes its databases available free of charge to every Canadian law student. The result is a generation of lawyers totally hooked on thinking about the law in bits. Says law student Mendelson, "The only time I ever go to the library is to make a photocopy. Almost everything else I need I can get through my laptop at home." Such students are quite willing to pay the going rate when they graduate. Quicklaw is also free of charge to all Canadian judges, which Quicklaw says is its way of thanking the system that provides the company with its raw material. This also boosts the chance that some cranky judge might caustically inquire why your lawyer didn't take into account the obscure *Regina v. Blotz* decision four years ago.

NOTES

1. Stan Davis and Jim Botkin, *The Monster Under the Bed: How Business Is Mastering the Opportunity of Knowledge for Profit*, Simon & Schuster, New York, 1994.
2. Ibid.
3. Peter Senge, *The Fifth Discipline*, Doubleday, 1990.
4. C. Marlene Fiol and Marjorie A. Lyles, "Organizational Learning," *Academy of Management Review*, October 1985.
5. George P. Huber, "Organizational Learning: The Contributing Processes and the Literatures," *Organization Science*, February 1991.
6. Barbara Levitt and James G. March, "Organizational Learning," *American Review of Sociology*, Vol. 14, 1988.
7. Chris Argyris, "Double Loop Learning in Organizations," *Harvard Business Review*, September-October 1977.
8. Ray Stata, "Organizational Learning—The Key to Management Innovation," *Sloan Management Review*, Spring 1989.
9. GUEP, p. 19.
10. *Business Week*, February 28, 1994, p. 81.
11. George Gilder, *Life After Television*, W.W. Norton & Company, 1992.
12. *Business Week*, The Information Revolution, 1994.
13. Tom Peters, *The Tom Peters Seminar: Crazy Times Call for Crazy Organizations*, Vintage Books, New York, 1994.

PART THREE

LEADERSHIP FOR TRANSFORMATION

20th Anniversary Edition Commentary on
Chapter 9: The New Media Industry

I REMEMBER A COUPLE of years after *The Digital Economy* was published I was asked to do the opening speech to a large conference of broadcasters on the topic of "The Transformation of Broadcasting." I stood up and said:

> Good morning. I've been asked to speak about how the digital revolution is transforming broadcasting. Here are my views. Broadcasting won't be broad and it won't be casting. Are there any questions?

I thought I was being very clever, but I was greeted with dead silence. The opening did not go over very well. So I proceeded to explain the many shifts outlined in the book and in the end I did receive a nice applause. The broadcasting association brought me back a decade later to open their annual congress and I went through the exact same slides to scrutinize my previous projections. Flash-forward, the changes described in this chapter are still unfolding.

In the computer industry itself we've seen several massive waves of destruction. It's helpful, in a stunning kind of way, to review a little history—sort of like walking around a graveyard with rows of tombstones representing waves of wars.

In the beginning, there was the "mainframe" behemoth IBM and its handful of competitors: Burroughs Corporation, UNIVAC, NCR Corporation, Control Data Corporation, and Honeywell. IBM's five competitors were known as "the BUNCH," and the BUNCH's market share added together was less than IBM's market share. During the 1960s, RCA and General Electric joined the industry, which then became known as "IBM and the Seven Dwarfs." IBM is the only company that remains in the computer business, and even then most of its earnings (as forecasted in *The Digital Economy*) are software and services.

During the mid–1960s a new computing device arrived: "the minicomputer." Minicomputers sold for much less than mainframes and each had their own operating system and software architecture. Minis were designed for control, instrumentation, human interaction, and communication switching as distinct from calculation and record keeping.[1] About 100 companies entered the mini-computer market during its 20 years of existence. Hewlett Packard (HP) was pretty much the only one that survived—in part because it figured out it wasn't a minicomputer company.

Then came the "personal computer" (PC), specifically the IBM PC in 1982. Although ubiquitous today, the PC back then was a radical concept—a relatively low-cost computer designed for use by a person rather than a data-processing department. The first PC was the Programma 101 made by Olivetti. It was launched at the 1964 New York World's Fair. This was followed by high-profile devices from companies such as Commodore, Tandy, Apple, and, of course, IBM in the early 1980s. Eventually IBM sold its PC business to Lenovo because PCs had become a commodity. There were also powerful Unix workstations offered by companies such as Sun Microsystems, another company to bite the dust. Sun Microsystems created the Java programming language, and played a large role in the development of Unix, RISC (Reduced Instruction Set Computer) processors, thin client computing, and virtualized computing. Oracle bought Sun Microsystems in 2010 for $7.4 billion.

As computers became able to manage graphics, audio, and eventually video, they were increasingly viewed as communication tools and not just for data crunching. Companies such as America Online (AOL) and Compuserve could be accessed through modems with plodding communication speeds. AOL was founded in 1985 and franchised its services to other countries. It was famous for its "walled garden" of content, meaning users couldn't suddenly stumble across salacious material. At its peak, AOL had 30 million members. There was much discussion about the "information highway" and what it would look like. Would AOL and its competitors conquer the world, or would the little-known Internet, used mainly by academics, become popular? Many dismissed the notion of the Internet serving the needs of for-profit enterprises, saying the staid Internet community wouldn't allow it.

When the popularity of the Internet and particularly the World Wide Web began to explode, many companies vied to become Internet service providers (ISPs). Initially only available through dial-up modems connecting to AOL–style companies, telephone and cable companies suddenly found themselves in direct competition, as each sought to be the dominant means to bring the Internet to homes and businesses and connect users directly.

In the late 1990s, the private sector became transfixed with the belief that "the Internet changes everything." Economists spoke of the "long boom" and that the Internet would introduce a period of ongoing economic expansion.

Endless new digital business models were dreamed up, each promising to crush the old economy's "brick and mortar" dinosaurs. Most failed. The biggest disaster: Webvan.com, which is now owned and operated by Amazon. Other notable failures were Pets.com, fashion retailer Boo.com, eToys.com and delivery service Kosmo.com.

During the dot-com run-up period, the NASDAQ stock market more than doubled, reaching a peak of 5,048.62 in March 2000. It then began a hard downward spiral, hitting 1,695.38 on September 10, 2001, and falling even farther when the markets reopened after 9/11. No, I didn't sell any of my technology stocks prior to the crash. I figured a correction was coming, but not so soon. Bad figuring.

During this period the telco (telephone)/cable battle continued, with cable companies starting to offer VoIP (Voice over Internet Protocol) phone service. The massive consolidation of the telco industry occurred, wiping out a number of the cool companies that had given me jacket quotes for *The Digital Economy*.

Telco consumers wanted increasing download speed so they could stream content, particularly video. Soon attention turned to wireless connectivity, as "smartphones" began arriving, which combined the features of cellular phones and personal digital assistants (PDAs) such as the Palm Pilot. Qualcomm introduced the pdQ and Nokia released the Nokia 9000. In Japan, the telco NTT DoCoMo ("do communications over the mobile network") released the first smartphones to achieve widespread adoption. BlackBerry's popularity soared in the United States, and by 2006 it was dubbed the "CrackBerry." Then came the tremendously popular iPhone from Apple. iPhone competitors appeared, running on the Linux-based Android operating system developed by Google. BlackBerrys were quickly abandoned, and Android devices grew to dominate the market. Microsoft was caught flatfooted, and eventually bought Nokia just to ensure that phones were available that ran the Windows Phone system.

It's a staggering tale of creative destruction. I'm sure you can hear the chuckles of delight coming from Joseph Schumpeter's gravesite.

I won't give a detailed account of the changes that are turning the media industries upside down today as the impact of the digital revolution on newspapers, television, film, radio, and the music industry are each discussed at length in my book (coauthored with Anthony D. Williams) *Macrowikinomics: New Solutions for a Connected Planet.*[3] But in review, more than any other industry, it is striking to note how the statement "leaders of old paradigms are often the last to embrace the new" applies to the technology and media industries themselves.

The reaction of many mainstream media (MSM) companies has been good and bad, but mainly ugly. As they scramble to address the new economics of the digital world, many have attempted to create the equivalent of a movie by filming a stage play (minus a few notable exceptions discussed below). In hindsight, their record is pretty predictable, and even pathetic. Why didn't Rupert Murdoch create *The Huffington Post*? Why didn't AT&T launch Skype? CNN should have created Twitter, as they are all about the sound bite, no? Yellow Pages could have built Craigslist or eBay. Microsoft had the resources to come up with Google's business model. Why didn't NBC invent YouTube? Sony should have preempted Apple with iTunes. Kijiji would have been a perfect venture for the *New York Times* or any regional newspaper.

For sure Silicon Valley has come under lots of appropriate criticism for not building meaningful innovations that improve the state of humanity. The expression "where's my fucking jetpack?" was coined to express disappointment about the amazing technology that was supposed to happen in the future, but is nowhere to be seen. Urbandictionary.com reports the expression (also known as just "wmfj?") often refers to the endless lame announcements, gadgets, and events that only distantly resemble their hype. For example:

"Did you watch the new Apple keynote? Now you can, like, use your phone as a compass."
"Oh yeah, fuck Apple. Where's my fucking jetpack!?"
In 2014, the TV show *Silicon Valley* was launched[3]—a parody on the culture of the Valley.

As the media becomes democratized and as those vested in the old paradigm fight change, an historic period of calamity is in the making. At the same time, there are fresh, sometimes breathtaking new innovations in every medium—experiments and juggernauts that show us the way forward. Buckle up because the pace of innovation is accelerating.

Notes

1. http://en.wikipedia.org/wiki/Minicomputer
2. Don Tapscott and Anthony D. Williams, *Macrowikinomics: New Solutions for a Connected Planet* (New York: Penguin Group, 2012).
3. http://www.imdb.com/title/tt2575988/

THE NEW MEDIA INDUSTRY

The new rules [of the new technology industry] require more than ingenuity, agility, and speed. They call for redefining value in an economy where the cost of raw technology is plummeting toward zero. Sooner or later this plunge will obliterate the worth of almost any specific piece of hardware or software. Then, value will be in establishing a long-term relationship with a customer—even if it means giving the first generation of product away.

Neil Gros and Peter Coy, 1995[1]

The businesses of computing (hardware, software, and services), communications (telephony, cable, satellite), and content (publishing, entertainment, advertising) are converging or collapsing to create a new industry sector. This new media industry is the engine of the new economy and will be critical to leading a successful transition. The rise of this new sector and the transformation of corresponding markets is forcing every company to rethink its very existence. The urge to merge, the new alliances, the failed acquisitions—all are evidence of the turmoil. This convergence is changing all the rules. For example, things that cost money in the old economy are now available free. And things that were once free are costing money.

Examples from the three corners of the triangle (as seen in Fig. 9.1):

- Telephones used to cost money, but after a monthly charge their local use was free. Today, cellular phones are free but cost (a lot) to use locally.
- In the old economy, computer hardware was the big cost of computing and the source of profits for the industry. Today, general-purpose hardware is becoming dirt cheap. Cost (and profits) have shifted to software and services (which used to be bundled for free). Some major computer companies have had serious discussions about giving away hardware as part of a services contract.

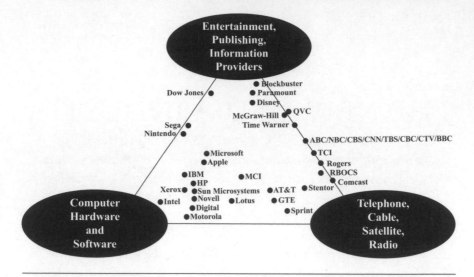

FIGURE 9.1 *Converging Industries*. SOURCE: © New Paradigm Learning Corporation, 1995.

◆ Magazines in the old environment cost money and advertising was free. Today, major magazines such as *Time* and *BusinessWeek* are free in their online form. And shoppers are showing willingness to pay for advertising if its informational content or entertainment value is high enough.

How will convergence affect key industries?

Publishing Goes Digital

The twelve drivers of the new economy are transforming the business of content. The industry has traditionally defined itself in terms of print media (newspapers, magazines, books, custom printing) rather than in terms of content. Gone are the halcyon days when clear lines separated the business of publishers, electronic information companies, games companies, broadcasters, film makers, record companies, and creative artists. The truck and trade of all of them is becoming bits. More and more their customers will purchase bits rather than books, movies, newspapers, and physical records. These bits have a funny tendency to intermingle—to become multimedia bits—and an uncanny capability to move at the speed of light through the air and through glass fibers.

So when *BusinessWeek* has a special advertising section on doing business in Baltimore, the publication decides that rather than simply publishing it in atoms (on the page), they publish it in bits (an interactive section—on the Net). This is not exactly a big technological leap, because the copy was created on computers, the page design done on computers, and the layout done on computers. But it is a huge cultural leap for the print media. Using the interactive advertising section on the Net, the reader can access the section and hot link to the various advertisers as well as to other databases about Baltimore. Says Michael Hehir, senior vice president, The McGraw-Hill Companies, "Publishing is being transformed by multimedia in ways that no one yet understands."

"Publishing is becoming electronic, especially Internet interaction," agrees Peggy Bair, director of administration technology for the Knight-Ridder Information Design Library in Boulder, Colorado. The library is working on software that will run on a flat-panel screen tablet that is 9 inches wide, 12 inches high, and 1/2 inch thick. Weighing about one pound, the flat-panel tablet will be connected to news and entertainment sources around the world and will be interactive. For print publishers, such tablets will eliminate central manufacturing and printing plants, thereby cutting delivery costs to customers by half. In theory, Knight-Ridder could save $700 million a year. "We are talking to a lot of people in the industry, particularly Japanese companies like NEC, Toshiba, Sharp, and Sony, who are developing the flat panels, to work toward a global standard for platforms. We can't do it alone."[2]

But forays into electronic publishing and online services have been uneven, however. One of the best examples of hindsight being 20/20 is the online providers who developed a pricing model based on the long-distance telephone business—that is, pay for use. Users paid for the number of minutes they were logged on to the service. In a nascent industry this was a mistake, inhibiting growth and the creation of a critical mass of users. Along came the World Wide Web with a different business model. Customers access the Net, essentially for free. You pay only when you "purchase" the use of it. This is similar to a book store: You can browse for free; you pay when you buy the book. Result? Both the Web and Internet exploded in use.

A company on the cutting edge of the shift to interactive use is CMP, the Manhasset-based publisher of more than a dozen trade magazines and newspapers for the computer and telecommunications marketplaces. One of CMP's publications, *Interactive Age*, was launched in September 1994 and is believed to be the first publication to be launched in both print and electronic versions (over the Net) simultaneously. A year later the company decided to place most of its emphasis on the digital version of the publication, shifting the print version to become an insert in one of its other print publications. Moreover, the foray into digital publishing had a huge impact on the other CMP publications. "Here we were launching a print publication called *Interactive Age*, dealing with all aspects of the Internet and the move to an interactive world. We had to do things differently—as will publishers of the future," says publisher Charles Martin.

During the transition years between print and digital, many publications will be both. Martin, for example, challenged many of the old print models. "Why should letters to the editor always refer to stories in a previous issue? Who is really going to go back to a past issue and check a story to see what a letter writer is talking about?" He created (and *Interactive Age* trademarked) a regular feature called "Real Time Letters." Some articles are published on the Net or distributed via e-mail in advance of the paper's publication. Letters are solicited on these articles and published in the magazine—letters referring to articles in the same issue! The page on which the story is carried is highlighted in the letter. Hundreds of readers asked to participate within weeks of introduction.

In another example, newspapers and magazines often generally published in parts, called "forms." Because some forms are printed earlier, there sometimes are errors that are noticed before distribution, but it's generally not possible to discard hundreds of thousands of copies. Once, when the editors noticed an error in an early form, they decided to place a correction in a late form, so it would appear in the same edition. They headlined it: "Real-Time Corrections," and referenced the page and error. The Internet version was corrected immediately. So, although there was one error in a story on one page, the information was correct on the Internet, correct in the electronic archives on the Net, and corrected in "Real-Time Corrections." Martin describes this practice as "a new kind of cyber-thinking and a new service to readers."

"Publishers must look at the Internet as much more than a place to just distribute an electronic version of their print publications," says Martin. Within the *Interactive Age* Home Page on the Net are photos and bios of the staff members as well as the latest news. In addition, advertisers have messages in various forms. There are the logos, but there are tied audio and video messages also. "When we started, AT&T wanted to have their ad on the Internet. We digitized it and realized there was far too much text for anyone to read off a computer screen. We decided to have someone read the text, so we converted the traditional print ad to multimedia," says Martin.

"In the case of MCI, they already had a well-known Home Page called Gramercy Press, so we wanted to capitalize on that. We created a hot link and on our Home Page provided a photo of President Gerald Taylor and included several audio clips from him," says Martin.

The publication got the BPA, the main auditing group of the computer press, to accept subscriptions over the Net, thus opening the door for other publishers to take electronic subscriptions.

"The speed of evolution on the Net is quite rapid, not only from an external growth standpoint, but from an internal infrastructure standpoint as well," says Martin. "In September 1994, we had to tap all the top experts there were to get our Home Page created. Now my assistant Christine creates them during downtime right at her desk."

Other publishing shifts are highlighted at *Interactive Age* as well. "Since we were all connected from the beginning, it seemed very natural for us to get all our correspondence electronically. It only dawned on us three months into the publication that virtually all our correspondence from readers had come to us via e-mail. Paper correspondence gets a very, very late look."

"This is opening a totally different dynamic in publishing," says Martin. "When we want to do an electronic roundtable with industry leaders, we simply send an e-mail to the chief executive. There are no filters." There was just such a roundtable discussion on the cover of the first issue. Participants were Reed Hundt, FCC chairman; John Malone, chairman and CEO of TCI; Richard McCormick, chairman and CEO of US West; Edward McCracken, CEO of Silicon Graphics; Gerald Taylor, president and COO of MCI; and James Trybig, president and CEO of Tandem.

"What was different about this discussion was that it was done totally electronically," says Martin. When the issue was distributed at the Networked Economy Conference in Washington, D.C., Reed Hundt's "handlers" didn't even know he had participated. Hundt even later sent an e-mail to the editor with some additional comments.

"This is a big change. We have the e-mail addresses of the CEOs. The pipelines are direct. We don't waste their time, but this is new in publishing where we can reach a chief executive of a technology company anywhere, anytime, through e-mail and get a comment on deadline. Plus, with electronic response, there is time for a thoughtful answer. The obvious downside is the potential careful crafting of the verbiage, but that hasn't seemed to be a problem yet. Most of the execs using e-mail really do it themselves."

There were several other ways that CMP's *Interactive Age* integrated its electronic and print properties. "At the bottom of every page, next to the page number, we list our Internet Home Page address," says Martin. "The week we added that, our Home Page visits went up 45%. We have found a direct correlation between the print version and the electronic version, from a readership standpoint." If this holds true across print publishing, the Net could provide ancillary products and even be integrated with the print version. *Time* gets a purported million "hits" a week on its Internet site, called Pathfinder.

One month after launch, *Interactive Age* introduced a daily news service on its Home Page, not as a print-product extension but as a separate product. The publication could then break news either electronically, in print, or simultaneously. "We put the content of the publication on the Net and within a couple of days it seemed old," says Martin. "People are used to having a publication sit around for a few days and it doesn't bother them to read what is essentially dated news. It is expected. On the Net, freshness is everything." CMP then extended the premise one more step, creating an e-mail version of the news service, delivered to customized lists. Basically the same information was then packaged and distributed in three different media. "In the traditional publishing model, advertisements were sold to appear in a print publication and the value was in reaching a certain number of people. In the electronic model, there are no established rules," says Martin.

A short time after launching the daily news service, MCI became its exclusive electronic sponsor for several months. The MCI advertising messages hot link to MCI's own Home Page. In the news stories on the Net, reporters routinely include hot links to other Internet sites. By early 1995, this had become common practice.

By February 1995, the *Interactive Age* daily news service was drawing more visits than any of the other 15 CMP Home Pages and was listed as part of the well-known Internet browser Netscape's section of "What's Cool." The paper pioneered several other "interactive" features, including a detailed index of every Home Page mentioned in an issue.

This CMP effort started in September, and by November, all 16 CMP publications—including *Information Week, CommunicationsWeek, NetGuide, Windows*—had Home Page locations on the Internet. The company formed a new division—the Interactive Media Group—to spearhead the efforts, reporting directly to President Michael S. Leeds. The group instantly included a full-text search feature, so that all the publications can be searched back one year on the Net.

Like other major publishing companies, CMP has made a serious commitment to the electronic future, to protect its past and its print publications, but also to position itself for its future and to capitalize on it as it is getting here.

In a fully digital world, readers or subscribers can create their own publications or at least request a certain kind of information. The role of the publisher changes. The reader has been the passive recipient of information in printed form. In the digital age, the reader can proactively decide very quickly what information is desired and when it is desired. Why does *Time* have to be delivered on Monday? What is so magical about weekly or monthly publishing cycles? Martin says: "With hypertext links and intelligent agents on the Internet, readers will be able to regularly and repeatedly select various sources and create their own publications. The consumer could become a quasi-publisher."

Print publications are simply snapshots in time, and in the case of publications such as *Interactive Age*, specific information is targeted to one group of people with a common interest, such as how to conduct electronic commerce. "As publishers, we have decided when the snapshot is taken, since we have the physical constraints of paper, mail, trucks, and all that. In the digital world, everything is instant and the reader can decide when is the best time to consume the information. The future presumption will be that the information desired will *always* be up to date—to the moment," says Martin.

And more than words will be provided. Publishers will be expected to deliver full audio and video to the desktop or home as part of the package. The case studies that trade publications write about will show the actual person talking—in his or her words—about business wins and losses, problems and solutions. Publishers will be able to link buyers and sellers instantly. It will be expected. That's what publishers do now, to some extent, but it will become more of a relationship and service to the consumer. "Just as CNN covers all major news events live, publishers in the digital world should be planning to provide the same kind of full, multimedia feeds of their specific information to their specific readers. Simple words on paper won't cut it," says Martin.

At this point in publishing, the unknowns far exceed the knowns. For example, publications are changing to become directories because of hotlinks on the Net. The business model for this is unclear. As one executive at Oracle (a company whose main products are database software) said to a publisher attempting to sort this out: "I won't pay you to put up an Oracle ad in your (electronic version of the) publication. I will pay for qualified hits on our ads from prospective purchasers of database software in Fortune 500 companies."

Other issues are very subtle. For example, in the print world it is not uncommon for four editors to handle a story. Publishers have found that on the Net less care is taken, and that leads to problems of syntax, grammar, and accuracy. In the print and broadcasting media you know how important a story is by its page placement and the font size of the headlines. Both are determined by an editor who has a sense of the news, importance, balance. On the Net it is hard to tell importance of information.

Clifford Stoll, the scientist and computer security expert who once tracked down an international spy ring by using the Internet, says: "The information highway is being sold to us as delivering information, but what it's really delivering is data.... Unlike data, information has utility, timeliness, accuracy, a pedigree." He says that what's missing in cyberspace is "anyone who will say, 'hey, this is no good.' ... Editors serve as barometers of quality, and most of an editor's time is spent saying 'no.' "[3]

THE BROADCASTING INDUSTRY GOES DIGITAL

Broadcasting and the mass media are in their final days. Major shifts are occurring in the technology, the customer, and the business of broadcasting. The first major shift is occurring with the technology itself. See Figure 9.2.

The Changing Technology

Signal: From Analog to Digital. Anyone who doubts the power and rapidity with which the digital revolution can storm a market need only look at the impact of CDs in revolutionizing music and publishing. But CDs are a pioneering phase, because the digital data are still stored and distributed on a physical medium. The next wave of digitization will truly transform the music industry as well as both television and radio. The issue here is not quality (distortions

	Old Economy		New Economy
Signal	Analog	⟶	Digital
Time	Synchronous	⟶	Asynchronous
Carriage	Air	⟶	Multiple
Device	Dumb (TV/Radio)	⟶	Intelligent (Information Appliance)
Quality	Low	⟶	High
Direction	One-Way Casting	⟶	Two-Way (Interactive)

FIGURE 9.2 *Shifts in Broadcasting: Technology*. SOURCE: © New Paradigm Learning Corporation, 1996.

can be eliminated) or capacity (so much more data can be sent over a given amount of bandwidth). Rather, digital transmission and digital networks will revolutionize everything about broadcasting as profoundly as radio and television transformed the nature of their predecessor—publishing.

Time: From Synchronous to Asynchronous. Television and radio need no longer be synchronous or simultaneous media. Rather than the viewer or listener receiving the transmission in real time, entire programs can be transmitted in seconds and come under the control of the user. The user can access that information in various ways that can include fast-forwarding, searches, or linking information from one news story to other information from other sources.

Carriage: From Air Transmission to Multiple Transmission Media. In television, there has been a strong shift from through-the-air broadcasting to wire-based transmission. Notwithstanding the impact of death stars (transmission from satellite to a dish on the window sill), this trend will continue. From a technological standpoint, this shift will happen in the long term as telephone companies come to transmit programming through optical fiber; in the short term, it will occur through asymmetric digital subscriber loops (ADSLs), the technology that allows high-quality video over copper wires with some interactivity.

Set-Device: From Dumb TV or Radio Set to Intelligent Information Appliance. Well before the end of this century, the television will be dead—replaced by an information appliance. Microprocessor technology will transform television into something unrecognizable, a multimedia information work-learn-play station that will enable the customer to interact with a vast array of information-based services as well as have access to multimedia data and numerical text voice-imaging video forums. The appliances in various rooms may have different peripherals and features, but they will all essentially be the same. "Why would I take this low resolution, dumb, obsolete appliance and stick a set-top box on it?" says David Ticoll of the Alliance for Converging Technologies. "I already have computers at home that can do way more than the TV with a set-top box."

Quality: From Low to High. This technology has already improved sound and image quality dramatically just as CDs have improved the quality of music. However, in the television world, this doesn't necessarily mean high-definition television (HDTV). Most home color computers already have better quality resolution for television than analog HDTV ever will. High-definition television will likely be overtaken by bit-mapped computer screens, which are dropping in cost and improving in quality almost weekly. This is true even considering the recent conversion of the HDTV movement to digital. The pace of innovation in television is so slow compared to that in the computer industry that HDTV is unlikely ever to get off the ground.

Direction: From One-Way Casting to Two-Way Interacting. One of the most important shifts enabled by digital technology is, of course, the shift to interactivity. To date, much of the discussion has been about shifting from broadcasting to narrow casting and may have missed the point. The future won't be about "casting" at all.

In the future, it will be the customer, not the broadcaster, who will do the "casting"—the searching and accessing of multimedia databases for appropriate information, content, programming, and services. This may involve person-to-computer interaction when, for example, a customer accesses a database of television programs, encyclopedia entries, movie listings, or traffic reports. It could also be person-to-person, mediated through the computer; for example, a person sends a piece of video mail that is switched through and stored on a computer. By the end of the decade, consumers will have access to personalized, interactive on-demand service, and random access to anything they want through digital radio and TV as well as through cable and computer networks.

Digital audio broadcast (DAB) receivers will be addressable, leading to customized advertising such as restaurant ads for a specific neighborhood. To really add value for listeners and advertisers would mean reaching interested, core audiences with features such as "Song of the Day" contests right down to details of happenings at the local country club aimed at members only.

The Changing Customer

These shifts in technology are causing a number of shifts regarding the customer. See Figure 9.3.

Role: From Viewer Listener to User. In this new digital world, the listening or viewing audience vanishes. The customers are no longer recipients of programming but users of interactive multimedia services and information. As a business, broadcasting begins to look a lot more like publishing.

Stance: From Passive to Active. Rather than being the transfixed passive recipients of broadcast programming as stereotyped by media critics, customers become much more active users. Yet many will say, as does Frank Biondi,

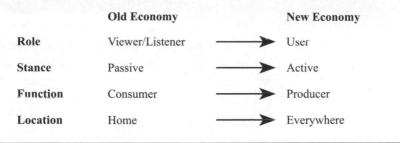

	Old Economy		New Economy
Role	Viewer/Listener	⟶	User
Stance	Passive	⟶	Active
Function	Consumer	⟶	Producer
Location	Home	⟶	Everywhere

FIGURE 9.3 *Shifts in Broadcasting: Customer.* SOURCE: © New Paradigm Learning Corporation, 1996.

president and CEO of Viacom, "TV is at bottom, a passive experience, which is its beauty." In other words, the great thing about television is that you can come home after a long day of work and veg-out in front of the TV.

Indeed, opportunities for vegging in the digital economy will be even greater than today, but passive viewing is only one component of the emerging interactive multimedia experience. For example, video is already used interactively on 30 million American television sets. Nintendo makes more money than ABC, CBS, and NBC combined. This audience can't be dismissed as "just kids" because kids grow up. The consumer of the future is downstairs in the rec room right now. Imagine how the intensity and involvement of video games will change transactional services in the future when applied to the tacky business of today's home shopping networks.

Most people don't know or care what firm publishes the CD, so radio stations are best positioned to serve their listener/user by selling the music they play and offering promotional services as well. Those who say that the internet is all about a bigger crop of couch potatoes not only have a too cynical view of humanity, they also ignore the nascent experience with interactive technologies. In fact, the shift is more like from couch potato to Nintendo jockey. And as technology proliferates and becomes pervasive—interpreting kinesthetic feedback—even physical passivity will (if the user wants it) disappear. For example, customers of Caterpillar won't just watch a video about new machines, they may test drive it in cyberspace.

Function: From Consumer to Information Producer or Programmer. As users interact in this multimedia world, they create information. When a business sends video mail to a customer or an individual sends a video happy birthday greeting to her sister in Los Angeles, everyone is creating "programming" through the network. Similarly, should Black & Decker disintermediate and attempt to move away from their current retail distribution channels, such as Kmart and Walmart, to sell directly to the consumer through the home information appliance, Black & Decker will become a producer of content, not just a vendor. In that case, B&D becomes an entertainment company and information provider, for both information and programming become part of what the company is taking to the marketplace.

Location: From Home to Everywhere. The nomadic information appliance will be with us everywhere. Overall, this is good news for everyone. For providers, the market (share of mind and time) expands dramatically. Informational and motivational programming for the office environment will have huge potential. There will be desktop training videos as well as computer-based learning as companies look to new technologies to transform their skill sets and knowledge and become learning organizations.

The Changing Business

All of which leads to a third set of profound shifts that will affect the very nature of the business of broadcasting itself. As Marshall McLuhan said, "In TV, the sender is sent." In the new economy, the recipient will also be the sender. See Figure 9.4.

Control: From Broadcaster to Customer. Because of the power of the customer to interact with multiple databases and to have far-reaching choices in programming content, control shifts from the broadcaster to the customer.

Schedule: From Prime Time to Any Time. In the past, broadcasters did research, assessed customer interest, developed content for the market, and devised a schedule. In so doing, they acted as the audience's agent or scheduling representative, attempting to foresee the interest of customers and maximize the audience. In the next wave, this is turned on its head. In the on-demand interactive environment, the customer has choice. Yes, the customer may still tune in for a scheduled event, such as a football game, newscast, or the first showing of a weekly sitcom—but the "tune-in" may not occur when the "tune" is played. For the most part, rather than tuning in to a broadcast, the customer will access a multimedia database of programming. As a result, the role of the broadcaster shifts from being scheduler to content provider. As an article in *The Economist* says in a thoughtful discussion of broadcasting: "[T]he broadcast networks are creatures of a time when television was a medium of scarcity, oligopoly, and mass consumption. As it grows to be more like publishing, TV will become

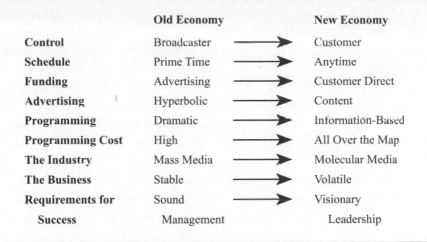

	Old Economy		New Economy
Control	Broadcaster	⟶	Customer
Schedule	Prime Time	⟶	Anytime
Funding	Advertising	⟶	Customer Direct
Advertising	Hyperbolic	⟶	Content
Programming	Dramatic	⟶	Information-Based
Programming Cost	High	⟶	All Over the Map
The Industry	Mass Media	⟶	Molecular Media
The Business	Stable	⟶	Volatile
Requirements for	Sound	⟶	Visionary
Success	Management		Leadership

FIGURE 9.4 *Shifts in Broadcasting: The Business*. SOURCE: © New Paradigm Learning Corporation, 1996.

a medium of abundance, competition, and personalization. A few viewers will be producers, more will be participants, the rest will simply do what they have always done when handed greater choice: use it."[4]

Funding: From Advertising to Customer Direct. Broadcast today is funded primarily through advertising. Although it's a relatively new concept, *pay-per-view* is an old paradigm term not dissimilar to *horseless carriage*. In the latter, a new modifier (horseless) was used to define an old paradigm concept (carriage); so, too, a new modifier (pay) changes an old concept term (view). In the interactive multimedia environment of the digital economy, vast numbers of commercial transactions affecting every aspect of human work, learning, entertainment, and social life will be conducted on a new type of network very different from CBS. For such transactions, customers will pay, commensurate with the value they attribute to the service or information. Companies will pay for video training delivered to the office or the home. Customers will pay "tuition" for computer-based learning programs. Customers will pay to access a movie or sports event. Health-care providers will pay for patients to be diagnosed remotely over the network rather than be airlifted for a consultation at the nearest medical center. Shoppers will pay a transaction fee for purchases, or such fees may be built into the cost of a product or service.

Advertising: From Hyperbole to Content. A role will remain for advertising in the new environment but advertising in this on-demand world will be very different from that in the current broadcast world. Remote control devices already allow TV viewers to graze across the channels or mute advertisements, but in the new broadcast world customers can choose what advertisements they'll experience.

There is good news in this scenario for both the sender and the sent. The best market for auto advertising is consumers who are looking for a vehicle. Such consumers will seek out advertisements about cars, and they want information amid the clutter. Consumers, for example, may want to compare standardized crash test results across different auto manufacturers. As a result, ads in the new environment will tend to become more factual and richer in content, downplaying the hyperbole. As advertisers become more like information providers, ad agencies that are solely in the business of creating hyperbole will need to readjust their strategies. In a disintermediating world, they live a tenuous existence. The man (or woman) in the gray flannel suit is no more.

Programming: From Dramatic to Information Based. People want drama in their lives, so dramatic programming will continue to be important. A four-part miniseries on *Scarlett* is but this generation's version of the weekly installments by Charles Dickens of *Great Expectations*. "We tell ourselves stories," said Joan Didion, "in order to live." Research has shown, however, that hours spent interacting with information on a personal computer tend to come at the expense of hours watching television. This suggests that more active participation will tend to displace passive viewing. It also raises questions regarding the perceived value of dramatic programming in the new on-demand environment.

The dynamics of someone selecting a program in the interactive environment will be quite different from that in broadcasting, because many of these programs have been sanitized to the point at which people's perceived value of them, compared for example to a feature film running in theaters or later played on television, is low. As diversity, choice, and the transactional nature of the medium increase, the result will be a shift in perceived value away from what we currently know as dramatic programming.

Programming Cost: From High to All Over the Map. Network programming has been expensive. The usual rule of thumb applied is that it takes $5,000 to produce a minute of television. Although developing interactive multimedia content can be equally costly, or in some cases even more expensive, many new content areas are far less expensive. Studios are being replaced by the computer with its capability for special effects. An early version of this was *Death Becomes Her*, with Meryl Streep and Goldie Hawn, a wacky film in which heads were on backward and holes appeared where stomachs had been. When John Candy died on the set of *Wagons East* in Durango, Mexico, the final scenes were shot with a double and rendered usable by using computer generation.

With the ready availability of cheap digital production and editing tools, the gritty effect of *NYPD Blue's* camcorder has inspired many young producers to create lower-budget clones. Coming soon to a motion picture screen near you will be *My Dinner with Marie*, the home-produced version of a date in Des Moines. Or maybe you've learned how to refinish antique boats and can assemble a program showing how to do it and make it available on the Internet. Unlike the Walkman, a technological revolution that created isolation, the next wave will be all about community, communications, and sharing what we know.

Industry: From Mass Media to Molecular Media. Broadcasters were at the heart of the creation of the mass media. They aimed for the largest possible markets, driven by what Eli Noam of Columbia University calls "body count economics." Cable TV has done little to address the "one size fits as many as we possibly can" mentality. The answer is not simply to increase the number of channels from 50 to 100 or even 500. Instead, channels as they now exist will disappear as surely as a flock of geese from the pond when migration time arrives. Because of the Net, there will instead be thousands (or millions) of channels—or sources of information—that will be accessible through an information appliance.

As everyone potentially becomes a producer, the shift will be from the mass media to the molecular media, enabling customers to access information services and people in an infinite multiplicity of sources. This is not to say that all databases or programs will be focused on a narrow targeted audience. Molecules can combine to create significant mass. But one thing is clear: The mass media, as the concept has existed for most of the modern era, are in their final days.

Business: From Stable to Volatile. All of this is taking the broadcasting industry into a period of far-reaching change. John Malone, CEO of TCI, has said that he has no idea where 60% of his company's revenue will come from in three years. There are many unknowns as the stable and relatively predictable environment ends. At one time, good market research combined with accurate ratings information provided a solid basis for planning a schedule. In the digital economy, where the consumer is programmer, researching is a mug's game.

Requirement for Success: From Sound Management to Visionary Leadership. All this is changing the fundamental requirement for success for any broadcasting business. There's really no growth left in broadcasting as it's currently conceived. Advertising revenues and viewing hours are static. Although new channels are being created, each tends to nibble away at the existing viewership. Although the core business of many broadcasters still generates significant cash flow, the challenge for change is about as harrowing as replacing a light fixture without turning off the power. The only other choice is to follow the maxim of a former Sears CEO who said, "All Sears has to do in the future is do what it did in the past, only better." That's a prescription for rot, as Sears, IBM, and GM discovered, a strategy characterized by hanging tough until the centrifugal pressures of technology and the emerging marketplace allow more nimble competitors to sashay by. The Walmart approach, or the Hewlett-Packard approach, or the Toyota approach is to reinvent a company proactively in order to ride the next wave.

Will We Become Couch Potatoes?

To think that the information highway is going to usurp all our activities is crazy. Sometimes I think some people dream for the day when we're going to take our brain out of our body and put it in a jar of formaldehyde, hook some wires to the thing, and maybe also one hand with some electrodes attached to it as well, which will be connected to a clicker, and there will be a camera hooked to our brain, and the camera will be focused on a TV, and we're going to spend our whole life, just kind of clicking and surfing through channels, ordering up cyber-sex, ordering cyber-pizzas, cyber-hats for our brain, or whatever, and we will forever be stuck in this jar of formaldehyde. It's just ridiculous. People are still going to get up and go out to see the movies, or to buy a loaf of bread, or meet other people because it's fun. But there will be a much wider choice and there will be opportunities for distance learning, video conferencing, and for information on demand, which I think is the real key.

Scott McNealy, CEO Sun Microsystems

ADVERTISING GOES DIGITAL

The advertising industry began earlier this century when regional newspapers seeking advertisements found an agent to link them up with suppliers wanting to reach the paper's audience. Nascent agencies solicited ads from, say, Schwinn bicycles and offered to create the advertisements for the papers in exchange for a commission of advertising revenues of 15%. In other words, the agencies performed the function of linking, or *mediating* between the producer and the newspaper. Their payment was a transaction fee for carrying out the transaction. This model works well when the cost of the media (publishing the ad in a paper or later on television) dwarfs the cost of production. The cost of producing a television ad may be $30,000 and the cost of running the ad $500,000. A commission of 15% is $75,000—leaving a healthy profit for the advertising agency.

The new media turn this model on its head, for the costs of the media (placing an ad on the Net) are trivial compared to the creation and production costs of traditional ads. As David Carlick of Poppe Tyson advertising agency explains, "As the cost of content exceeds the costs of media, the commission structure dies. It's like speech writing. If I got a commission on the cost of the paper I would be in trouble."

More important, what is the role for the agency in the newly disintermediated world? As the mass media become the molecular media, companies wanting to advertise can go directly to their markets—markets that are becoming electronic. Advertisers will no longer need someone to arrange the transaction. They may even acquire their own in-house talent to create the ads. (Today many companies already do their own Home Page development.) The shifts in advertising are indicated in Fig. 9.5.

In the physical world the trend today is pinpointing messages and markets. The message—"Volvo is the safety car"—is targeted to pinpointed demographic groups—yuppies with families. The messages are delivered through the mass media to the correct audiences (upscale publications, specific radio and television programs). Or else they are delivered through direct marketing and are aimed at selected city boroughs, streets, and even individuals. But when the media becomes molecular and pervasive and based on choice, messages can ironically become comprehensive. Volvo can become the "everything car." You access information about Volvos, and sure enough they have great safety features. You access information about acceleration, and sure enough they do well there. You look for information about mileage, and Volvos do well in that regard as well. Says Carlick, "Instead of having one feature that suits many people, you can have many features that suit one person. Interactivity allows that one person to explore products and services according to their own interests and find out what is important to them."

And what is the role of the agent in this world? Time to move up the chain from transactions to becoming a trusted advisor for clients. The agent's role in the future is as a marketing partner—helping clients to create and guide their messages into the electronic marketplace. The commission structure will shift initially to fees for service. Eventually revenue will come from performance—payment

Prinpointed Messages	Comprehensive Messages
Pinpointed Markets	Molecular Markets
Commission Revenue	Fee for Service Revenue
Free for Service Revenue	Contingent Performance Revenue
Execution of Transactions	Marketing Partner

FIGURE 9.5 *Shifts in Advertising.* SOURCE: © New Paradigm Learning Corporation, 1996.

based on actual success in the market—which in an electronic marketplace is easily measurable. Advertising effectiveness can be measured in "hits" on the Net and in actual orders generated. Carlick explains: "There is an infinitely greater level of accountability on the Net than there has been in any previous medium. You can tell to a greater and greater degree what kind of people came, why they came, what they looked at and why they bought."

Most of the advertising agencies have now set up new media divisions that try to become the supplier of new paradigm advertising to clients.

Quite often an on-line presence serves a number of purposes. It may have an area for presenting corporate brochures and reports, advertising, human resources recruitment, design references, product marketing, sales promotion and contests, customer support, and references. This is creating a convergence within internal functions and also external suppliers of these services.

"I've been involved in the sea changes in our industry over the last two decades," says Carlick. "This is the most interesting of all—more than desktop publishing. It's where the changes in technology (our Silicon Valley clients) impact the changes in media (our world). Desktop publishing only changed our work—the media. It gave us new tools to do the same old work. These are new tools and a whole new medium."

INTERNET ROADKILL—THE SHAKEOUT IN COMPUTING AND TELECOMMUNICATIONS

Digitization is blurring the lines between companies in the computing, communications, and content industries. It is also blurring the lines between companies that are in the businesses of numbers, text, voice, audio, image, and video/film. As both of these axes become continuous rather than discrete,

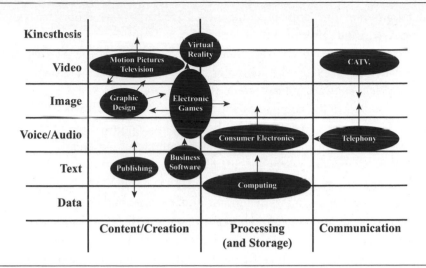

FIGURE 9.6 *Colliding Industries.* SOURCE: © New Paradigm Learning Corporation, 1996.

new opportunities and perils are arising for every business. There is no place to hide. This is depicted in Fig. 9.6.

The dark horse in all this change is the consumer electronics industry, which in many ways is an innovation leader, as evidenced by the spectacular growth of electronic games. These companies are now well positioned to provide networks for integration of various information appliances in the home and beyond. Production values of the industry approach those of Hollywood, and the industry, more than any other, has brought interactivity to the population. Consumer electronics touch each of us in a very personal way, and many businesses in the industry have not been constrained by old paradigms regarding, for example, what a computer is or what it should do. The industry shakeout can be seen in seven themes.

Theme 1: The Number of General-Purpose Hardware Suppliers Shrinks Dramatically

There were more than 1,000 automobile companies at the turn of the century in the United States. A few decades later there were three. Similarly, there are hundreds of companies manufacturing computers today. By the end of this decade, there will be only a handful.

The first wave of this trend has already hit the mainframe and minicomputer companies. In 1980 dozens of unique hardware architectures were supplied by mainframe and minicomputer companies. Each had its own proprietary operating system and software. But customers needed continual innovation—new applications to make businesses competitive. No company could create such applications by itself, so the computer companies fostered the growth of an independent software industry to do the job. Naturally, the software companies gravitated to the companies with the largest installed base, leaving the second-tier computer companies with no application growth (and therefore no reason why companies should purchase computers from them).

Three companies weathered this first wave of consolidation with their proprietary architectures still going strong: IBM because of a huge installed base and high margins for its mainframe and AS/400 minicomputers; Digital because of its domination of the minicomputer market; and Tandem, which had a unique product offering called fault tolerance (their computers never stop working). The other mainframe and minicomputer companies dropped their proprietary architectures and embraced the UNIX operating system (which has flavors running on all computers, and which provides a fairly uniform platform for independent software developers to create applications). The BUNCH—the previously impervious giants—have been forced through the grinder so much that Control Data, for example, has (wisely) decided to become a services company. Burroughs and Univac (renamed Sperry) combined to become Unisys Corp., embracing open systems. NCR, quick to abandon its proprietary architecture, successfully adopted UNIX and open systems. AT&T, which had laid the golden UNIX egg and never hatched it, wanted a computer company, so it acquired NCR. Honeywell retreated into the control industry, leaving the company in the hands of France's Bull Group. Ditto for the minicomputer companies with the exceptions of Digital and Tandem. (Hewlett-Packard was an early adopter of open systems. Because it dropped its proprietary architecture and adopted UNIX early, completely, and effectively, it was able to avoid the fate of the other minicomputer companies.)

The next wave of consolidation was caused by the microprocessor, thus spelling the end for the traditional approaches to computing. This also led to a proliferation of new computer companies creating PCs and workstations. Commodity microprocessors from Intel, Motorola, IBM RISC, Sun's SPARC, and others found their way into hundreds of computer brands.

However, an Intel PC is pretty much an Intel PC, as are various flavors of workstations based on IBM's Power-PC chip. Differentiation comes from software. As a result, a similar shakedown will occur in providers of PCs and workstations.

Even in the area of software a degree of commoditization is occurring. For example, although different operating systems have different features and functions, more and more they are looking very similar with similar capabilities and can run on the same hardware and enable the execution of the same or similar software applications. In fact, growing numbers of software applications, such as word processing packages, have a similar look and feel, perform similar functions, and run on similar gear.

Theme 2: Vertical Integration Gives Way to Alliances and a New Division of Labor in the Industry

The first period of the computer industry was based on the notion of vertical integration. Like their automotive predecessors, the big computer companies sought to perform all aspects of the product value chain. They designed and manufactured chips. They bent metal. They built disk drives, printers, and other peripherals. They created their own operating systems. They programmed their own software applications. They had a direct sales force and performed their own service. Now, because of standards, a division of labor is possible within the industry and no one, including IBM, seeks to be vertically integrated. Rather, alliances to complete the value chain are the only route to success.

As computers become pervasive and commoditized and as differentiation becomes more difficult, companies need to find their place in the new value network. This place can exist only through partnerships. "The reason you can rent a car and drive it away is that all cars are essentially the same," says HP's Birnbaum. "In 1915 some of those cars had steering wheels in the back and some of them ran on steam and they all had starting sequences and so forth. As computers built into appliances become the same, companies need to form partnerships to add value. And that means that the alliances that will make sense in the information age are the alliances that enable a company to concentrate on what it does best, looking to others to provide the more routine or commodity-like parts of the situation."

Theme 3: The Number of Providers of Specialized Hardware Products Increases

In the past the focus has been on processors: large computers, servers, general-purpose personal computers, and workstations. Multimedia will create new product categories, for example, the new digital "television." Like your home computer, the TV will be a computer with a high-resolution screen and communications hardware and software. But the appliance (formerly called the TV) in the family room may also have high-quality audio output, a smaller, more portable keyboard, a larger screen, and possibly other components—including a camera. Analog audio tape recorders and VCRs will disappear because they won't be necessary once your home appliance and its storage device are connected to a digital network.

One of the growth areas will be sensor-based systems that will monitor or measure physical processes. There will be markets for devices that monitor pollution in rivers, traffic on roads, asbestos in a ceiling, changes in the atmosphere, kinesthetic feedback in entertainment, and commercial virtual reality applications. In fact, the intersection between the digital and physical worlds will be rich with opportunity for new products. Markets for digital cameras, microphones, scanners, and biosensors will be huge.

Theme 4: The Number of Carriage Providers Shrinks Dramatically

Consolidation will occur as bandwidth becomes a commodity, as deregulation breaks down the walls between telephone companies on the one hand and telephone, cable, satellite, and terrestrial broadcasting on the other, and as networks integrate. As Dick Notebaert, CEO of Ameritech puts it, "My guess on the transport side is that a decade or so from now, we will be down to a handful of mega companies—organizations formed by alliances that integrate the core competencies of various industry leaders."

The cable companies will likely be the big losers because they have long enjoyed being monopolies and have been slow to respond. Many have been concerned with migrating into the telephone industry—a nonstarter at best. Unlike the telephone network, which carries its own power source, cable networks crash when there is a storm. Given this, the importance of the Internet, the silliness of HDTV, and the diversion of the set-top box, cable companies should be focusing more on how to interoperate with the Internet and how to deliver interactive services to the PC.

Theme 5: The Software and Services Industries Will See Unprecedented Growth

Another way of measuring the sea change is to look at how money is being spent by corporate customers. In 1989, the expenditure on hardware was double the amount spent on software and services. Now, spending on software and services is far greater and makes up the vast majority of profits in the industry. Hardware has declined dramatically as a vehicle for adding value; the action is shifting to software and services. The authors of a 1991 *Harvard Business Review* article titled "The Computerless Computer Company" will be proven at least partially right. They argue that by 2000 the most successful computer companies will be those that buy computers rather than build them. "The leaders will leverage fabulously cheap and powerful hardware to create and deliver new applications, pioneer and control new computing paradigms, and assemble distribution and integration expertise that creates enduring influence with customers... .The future belongs to the computerless computer company."[5]

"The specialized product suppliers for the information highway will not only be software companies and content companies, but all the companies that will provide services like assuring security, matching for interoperability across systems, and connecting legacy databases," says HP's Birnbaum. "And the size of that industry can be confidently predicted to be enormous compared to those people just supplying hardware platforms."

Where the "The Computerless Computer Company" authors erred is in assuming that it will not be possible to build successful hardware companies in the developed world (and their conclusion that fabrication by North American and European manufacturers should be abandoned). Compaq, HP, and Sun Microsystems have all shown that hardware manufacturing in a tough commodity world can be profitable. In fact, the authors cite the market value of Microsoft (the second most valuable computer company in the world) as evidence. But today Microsoft has been equaled by HP, which, although paying attention to software and services, is still primarily a manufacturing company. The authors also overlooked the rise of the specialized hardware industry.

Theme 6: The Entertainment Industry Will Grow Significantly, Driving Content and Software Development

As computing, telecommunications, and content converge, content will become king. Computing and telecommunications will become commoditized, leaving services and some software to create value. But significant value on the Net will be created by content providers. These are not the handful of electronic database providers of old who would sell you access to stock information, bibliographies, news wires, and credit information. Rather, there will be millions (literally) of companies and individuals with information, software programs, games, situation comedies, university notes, art, photographs, home improvement stories, music, vacation videos—you name it (and you likely will)—that will become the true value of the new media sector.

Multimedia is transforming the content business. And in an interesting twist of fate, entertainment is beginning to drive much of the content. This was already becoming clear as far back as 1987 when I participated in a multiclient investigation of the integration of data, text, voice, and image.[6] At that time the idea that entertainment was an important information technology application was met with some skepticism.

Entertainment software is now at the heart of leading-edge business applications. The type of software that created the terrifying, morphing robot in *Terminator II* is at the heart of many of today's visualization applications. Thank Hollywood when you helicopter through the stock market or go for a walk in an office building that you are designing.

Disney has a greater market value than Digital Equipment Corporation, Compaq, and Bell South combined. That is not to say the action is moving to Hollywood. The electronic games industry (1995 revenues of $17 billion) has greater revenue than the entire American motion picture industry.

Theme 7: Open Competition Is Transforming the Relationship Between Customers and Suppliers of Computing and Telecommunications

For decades the major computer and telecommunications vendors dominated markets. Competition was puny and customers had little or no real choice. In computing, the big hardware companies controlled customers through software lock-in. Because software was proprietary—working only on the computer of one vendor—customers stuck it out with that supplier. For most customers the alternative, a conversion, was unthinkable. A conversion required rewriting their company's software to work on the computers of another vendor. Vendors euphemistically called this process "account control." The presence of the Amdahl coffee mug on an MIS executive's desk was often somewhat effective but typically led to savings no greater than 10%.

The deregulation of the telephone industry killed account control. In computing the rise of the personal computer on the desktop and of open standards in larger systems meant that software became portable. Customers found freedom and companies were able to build multicomputer environments. The behemoths of the first era of computing—the mainframe and minicomputer companies, each with its own proprietary architectures—were left holding the proverbial bag. Overall, power in the industry shifted from suppliers to customers. But how will this change relationships between the two?

In the early 1990s many pundits predicted that commodity hardware would lead to commodity-style relationships between suppliers and customers. You go to the grain market and buy the most grain for the least amount of money. Others argued that account control would be replaced with a new era of promiscuity with vendors. But the world has evolved differently. Customers recognize the value of freedom of choice, but they do not wish to exercise this freedom unnecessarily. Changing suppliers frequently adds to costs; stable relationships can be in everyone's interest. The difference is that such relationships are based on free will and a more open market, but vendors must deliver. FTD CIO Dave Carlson puts it metaphorically: "If three truckloads of potatoes show up, there is an opportunity for us to look at the potatoes, judge the quality, the supplier, and their long-term viability. We may not necessarily choose the cheapest. We may rely on our long-term supplier because the long-term benefits of a relationship outweigh the short-term advantages of cost."

Some criteria for vendor selection have not changed. As *Paradigm Shift* described, customers still want good product features and functions, service and support, reliability and serviceability. Interestingly, and seemingly paradoxically (given the freedom of the new paradigm), customers are also looking for vendor stability. But new criteria are also emerging.

Customers want industry leadership in product architecture, as evidenced by the success of Microsoft. Microsoft products are designed to work together. Such standards compliance is important to customers who want standards followers (as well as leaders). Compatibility with existing products in the vendor's family used to be important; now compliance with industry standards is important, too. Products must comply with the right set of standards and enough of them, so that customers can avoid using vendor value-added functions that surreptitiously produce lock-in.

As for hardware, customers focus on price performance and conduct benchmark tests for speed, capacity, and other features such as graphics quality. Benchmarks once were difficult to compare because applications often worked on only one computer family. Don't select this week's price performance leader. Instead, look for suppliers of general-purpose hardware who have a good chance of weathering the coming industry shakeout.

Customers are also looking beyond hardware and software for expertise. The transformation of their technology, their business, and their cultures is proving to be a formidable challenge, and customers are looking for help. As a result, both hardware and software companies will find that they must get into the services business seriously—and not just because there are revenue opportunities from services. Increasingly, companies with services linked to their product offerings will be the companies that customers will seek, for customers will trade the trust of account control for the trust of the new partnerships.

This trend is causing many suppliers to shift from a product orientation to a relationship orientation. As Eric Benhamou, CEO of 3Com Corporation, says, "Customers are becoming less interested in technology and more interested in solutions." Suppliers' marketing forces need to shift focus from the product to the overall business solution; from the deal to the customer; from selling to the IT manager to selling to the businessperson; from emphasizing product features to business impact; from reacting to customer requests to building long-term relationships in which the supplier can provide advice and critical expertise for the big changes underway. "We are shifting from being box sellers to becoming trusted advisors," says Wim Roelandts, HP senior vice president. And that requires leadership for transforming the enterprise, the topic of the next chapter.

Notes

1. Neil Gros and Peter Coy, "The Technology Paradox: How Companies Thrive as Prices Dive," *Business Week*, March 6, 1995.
2. *Interactive Multimedia in High Performance Organizations: Wealth Creation in the Digital Economy*, case study by the Alliance for Converging Technologies, November 1994.
3. Clifford Stoll, *Silicon Snake Oil: Second Thoughts on the Information Highway*, Doubleday, 1995.
4. "A Survey of Television," *The Economist*, February 12, 1994.
5. Andrew S. Rappaport and Shmuel Halevi, "The Computerless Computer Company," *Harvard Business Review*, July-August 1991. The article set off a torrent of controversy in subsequent issues, in which many argued what is true for corporate strategy is not necessarily true for national policy and the United States would be ill-advised to withdraw from the manufacturing of hardware.
6. Art Caston and Don Tapscott, "Stage IV Report: The Integration of Data, Text, Voice and Image." This program was conducted by a team at Montreal-based DMR Group Inc. The $2.5 million dollar investigation was funded by 100 vendors and customers of information technology. © DMR Group, Montreal, 1987.

20th Anniversary Edition Commentary on Chapter 10: Leadership for the Internetworked Business

'M STRUCK BY how the leadership challenges described in this chapter persist today. For sure, the old command-and-control model of the leader has proved to be ineffective. It's true that as the chapter says: Leadership Can Come from Anywhere in an Organization; Leadership in the New Economy Is Leadership for Learning; Collective Leadership Is Becoming Possible; Internetworked Leadership Can Be (enhanced) Digital; Internetworked Leadership Is Incomplete Without the CEO.

Reflecting on the last 20 years the department that has adapted best is not the information technology (IT) department (you might think they'd lead as people who understand the technology) or human resources (HR) (isn't the digital revolution all about people?). It's the marketing department. Clearly the tonic of market forces is causing those focused on customers to wake up and change their practices.

The human resources function has for decades been in the business of executing HR functions. So it was understandable that they would miss the fundamental idea that in a networked world, "talent" and "human resources" can be *outside* the boundaries of the firm. Regardless, the intersection of the Net and the Net Generation entering the workforce requires a rethinking of talent management, and, for that matter, HR.

The current model of talent management is recruit, train, manage, retain. I believe the new credo for managing employees of all ages should go like this: initiate, engage, collaborate, and evolve. Instead of recruiting, companies should think about initiating relationships, and using social networks wherever possible. Instead of holding training sessions that are separate from work, companies should make learning happen *on the* job. Instead of holding annual performance reviews, companies should let employees ask for comments and advice and make performance improvement and feedback a daily thing.

And instead of trying to retain talented people, companies should realize that lifelong relationships, in a variety of forms, work much better. Let me explain:

1. *Don't Recruit; Initiate Relationships.* In the old model of human resources, potential new hires were solicited using one-way broadcast advertising methods, such as newspaper classified ads. Today advertising to attract young people is a waste of time and money. Companies can use social media to influence young people about their company and get to know them.

Old-style job interviews were much like FBI interrogations in which potential employees were grilled on their strengths and weaknesses, knowledge and skills. This approach should be completely revised. Employers who seek to identify, attract, and hire the best talent should see the process as a dialogue. And starting early, even in high school, companies can use challenges, projects, part-time jobs, internships, summer employment, and the like to get to know the best and brightest. When it's time to hire them there is no "recruiting" to be done, as you already know whom you want. It's simply a boundary change, where you bring your collaborator inside the boundaries of your firm.

2. *Don't Train: Create Work-Learning Environments.* Working and learning in the knowledge economy are basically the same thing. What are you doing right now reading this book? Working or learning? So rather than sending off employees to separate training and educational activities, why not use the new media to increase the learning component of their work? Rather than training them, engage them in rich working-learning environments for lifelong learning.

Net Generation employees, in particular, will respond well if mentored and coached to contribute to corporate policies, strategy, and business performance. Thus, employers must use creativity and flexibility when organizing the first few months of work to expose the new recruit to various leaders, work situations, and work content. Greater transparency, and exposure to, and interactivity with, the broader organization during this initiation phase will lead to a win-win outcome. Companies that make the effort will benefit from less turnover, shorter ramp-up speeds, higher levels of engagement, and earlier and greater returns on their investments in employees.

3. *Don't Manage: Collaborate.* Increasingly, traditional approaches to supervision and management are not effective. Good managers build teams and engage employees through distributing authority, power, and accountability. A growing number of firms are decentralizing their decision-making function, communicating in a peer-to-peer fashion, and embracing new technologies that empower employees to communicate easily and openly with people inside and outside the firm. In doing so, they are creating a new corporate meritocracy that is sweeping away the hierarchical silos in its path and connecting internal teams to a wealth of external networks.

Collaboration is a two-way street. It is an open flow of communication relaying the specific needs of the employee and the organization. "What's in it for me?" and "What's in it for you?" are questions that must be clearly addressed, with both employee and employer held accountable for delivery of their commitments. Work styles, workflow models, workday and workplace parameters, career paths, and professional development offerings should be examined and potentially retooled by organizations to maximize fit with the generational mix of employees.

As they enter the workforce, young employees bring their experience as digital authorities with them. This challenges fundamental concepts of corporate hierarchy—where, for example, a boss in any business unit is viewed as an authority on everything that takes place in that unit. He or she is the superior supervisor. Instead, the boss needs to understand that he or she is a student in some areas, for example, with regard to new use of wikis, blogs, and social networks for collaboration.

The tools of what Anthony D. Williams and I call in *Wikinomics*, "the Wiki Workplace" are the foundation of the new workplace collaboration. The nature of work itself is changing. Work has become more cognitively complex, more team-based and collaborative, more dependent on social skills, more time-pressured, more reliant on technological competence, more mobile, and less dependent on geography.

4. *Don't Retain: Evolve Lasting Relationships.* Talent doesn't need to be inside the boundaries of your enterprise. As I have explained, the Web drops transaction and collaboration costs and companies can find uniquely qualified minds to create value anywhere. This opens a new world of relationships between talent and firms. Using the analogy of the university's alumni network, companies should think of employees as a web of contacts. They should be perceived as networks, with a wealth of knowledge about the company's inner workings, which possess the opportunity to add great value, even after leaving the company. Social networking, communities of practice, and other Web platforms allow employees and ex-employees alike to exchange resources and disseminate information. Net Generation employees will embrace this kind of thinking as it comes naturally to them, having grown up in online communities such as Facebook.

My own company works with a network of individuals, many of them former employees. I don't try to "retain" then in a traditional way (like the way a person might try to retain water). I evolve my relationships with them, where sometimes they work on a part-time basis and sometimes they move back inside my boundaries. The old expression, "our most precious asset goes out the elevator every night," may be bypassed today. Today, your most precious talent may never see your elevator or drop in occasionally as mutually required. So think networks and relationships not just retention.

5. *Don't Do Annual Reviews: Improve Performance in Real Time.* If you're a manager, you may have noticed that your 20-something employees need feedback—plenty of it and seemingly all the time. It's part of their mindset. They are entering the workforce with attitudes honed by a lifetime of immersion in digital technology—the Internet and mobile phones and social networks, often running all at the same time.

This digital technology is, at its very core, interactive. It has had a profound effect on the Net Generation's mental habits and their way of doing things. They've grown up to expect a two-way conversation, not a lecture from a parent, a teacher, or an employer. They've also grown up connected, so they're used to constant and quick feedback from friends about everything—their homework, the new gadgets they want to buy, and now, their jobs.

The annual performance appraisal, in which the boss tells the underling how he or she rates against corporate objectives, makes even less sense for young employees. It's a one-way "appraisal"—boss to employee—that usually downplays the employee's wishes and desires. It happens once a year—long after the performance took place. It rewards or punishes individual performance—not the collaboration that the new workforce treasures. It's more about compensation and promotions than about improving performance. So how do you give feedback to a generation that has an insatiable desire for it? How do you do it in a way that makes sense to people under 30?

There are new software packages, such as Work.com, which offer software that generates real-time feedback. Instead of waiting an entire year to find out what managers think of them, employees can send out a quick (50 words or less) question to people they trust—a manager, a coworker sitting in the meeting, even a client, or a supplier. Baby Boomers like me still wonder whether software like this will make our e-mail inboxes overflow with requests for "advice." But I think managers will stop complaining once they see that employees are using this information to quickly improve their performance.

The IT Function and the Chief Information Officer

Twenty years ago, the IT Function headed by the chief information officer (CIO) was in the business of developing applications for the business. User departments made requests and then got in the queue, which was sometimes years long. IT managers also worked on developing infrastructure.

The IT function has been under duress for many years. Prior to the introduction of the personal computer, the IT department controlled all technology use. With the PC and, then later, the early days of the Web, many business departments—such as marketing, R&D, and supply chain management—increasingly went outside of IT to procure and meet their technology needs. This trend has accelerated with the rise of mobile apps and the availability of services on the Cloud. This has caused some analysts, including the industry behemoth Gartner, to conclude that the days of the CIO are over.

The business units have a point. Every business is becoming a digital business and it's positive that managers everywhere in the enterprise are interested in IT and are taking responsibility for it. They are tired of a multiyear backlog of application development, especially when they can fund publicly available services that meet many of their needs, often for a few dollars a month on the Cloud. Further, the new paradigm in technology threatens many companies' legacy infrastructure and IT know-how.

But there is a problem with all this enthusiasm and self-organizing activity throughout the organization. IT challenges are enterprise challenges. Companies need to have an integrated, enterprise architecture to have a single version of the truth and to harness the power of Big Data. They need to have security standards and systems to protect them from bad actors. They need back-up capabilities to ensure business continuity. They need an enterprise strategy for collaboration tools and systems to cut across business silos. They need to have elite IT talent to deal with the many complexities of becoming a digital business.

There is a solution to this dilemma. A new model of the IT function is emerging, and one that makes the CIO more important than ever. I call it "the IT Services Supermarket." Here's how it works: The CIO anticipates business needs and provides a rich supply of services, from standards for mobile devices to architecture compliant applications and Cloud services—all on the "shelves" of a supermarket. The business customer goes to the supermarket—a self-service portal or catalogue and pulls up the available IT. The business customer chooses the services and the level of services required, and combines them to meet its technology needs.

Because these services are running in the Cloud, they are delivered in a location-agnostic manner. Where the application is running—in the private, public, or hybrid Cloud on a virtualized machine, in virtualized storage, or over a virtualized network—no longer matters. Decisions like that are determined by cost and regulatory decisions. The Supermarket has costs associated with various technologies and service-level agreements for response time and other variables. Given the large economy of scale achieved by centralized purchasing, the costs are lower, affected by the needs for response time, governance, security, redundancy isolation, and other operational drivers. The fixed costs will end up being shared across a broader base, lowering them and making them variable. Given the advances in technology, services orientation, and the Cloud, there can be more focus on how to assemble capability like Lego blocks rather than custom building them from scratch.

With this vision, the CIO becomes a true business partner who is working on anticipating the future as opposed to satisfying the dated requirements of the past. But the CIO needs to change. The CIO's role must evolve for the progressive enlightened enterprise to something else —perhaps a Chief Innovation Officer, a Chief Integration Officer, or a Chief Inventory Officer (like a supermarket manager). Says Hunter Muller, who as the founder of HMG Strategies has built a community of CIOs in 30 cities, "The new CIO must be connected to the C-suite as a peer to drive market-facing, revenue-generating initiatives." Muller emphasizes the new corporate culture for the digital enterprise whereby the CIO must be aligned with corporate culture and market needs. "If there is culture or role incongruence, CIOs need to work with the C-suite to redefine the position and role potential." And in this new model, the CIO needs to lead through influence and persuasion rather than authority. This is only achievable through being a business Janus—looking forward and back, with a telescope and microscope, and being both a visionary and a detailed-oriented executor of platforms and solutions for the IT Supermarket.

The CIO also needs to be a practitioner of Maslow's "hierarchy of needs," a psychological theory proposed by Abraham Maslow in 1943. In this hierarchy, the most fundamental human needs, *physiological*, are at the bottom—like breathing, food, water, and sleep. At the next level is *safety* followed by *love* and *belonging*, followed by *esteem*, followed finally by *self-actualization* at the top. The idea is that if a tiger is chasing you, the fact that nobody loves you is not big on your mind.

So it goes with IT in an enterprise. The CIO needs to pay attention to the basics first; systems, no matter how elegant, need to work and not fail.

Systems need to be secure and protect the privacy of customers and other stakeholders. Countless CIOs have lost their jobs because they didn't see that a tiger was chasing them.

In fact, CEOs should pay attention too. In 2014, Target CIO Beth Jacob had to resign because of an IT breach that led to the theft of some 40 million credit and debit card records, along with another 70 million customer records. Months later, Target's CEO had to leave the company In the wake of the massive data breach.

Abraham Maslow would have taken note!

LEADERSHIP FOR THE INTERNETWORKED BUSINESS

I guess I see the Internet as sort of like the wilderness of the Wild West. Eventually civilization will move in and make rules about what is or is not acceptable. And as systems and services grow, the place will become more civilized in its own interest. But like the West, there will always remain some interesting wilderness areas to visit.

Vint Cerf, MCI, 1995

Traditional management may be appropriate for stable times, but in transformational times, leadership is required. If finding the right leadership for reengineering was a challenge, creating the leadership for business transformation in the digital economy can seem overwhelming. The old saw, "Companies that are failing tend to be overmanaged and underled," rings truer than ever as we enter the digital economy. As described in *Paradigm Shift*, the old model of technology in business:

> ... created structures that inhibit individual and team involvement in systems. It created a view of the technology and its application in business which is fundamentally outmoded. It created approaches to systems planning, software development, implementation and managing change which are becoming obstacles to making the shift. Through massive investments, it created legacy systems that have caused inertia that boggles even the most progressive executive mind.[1]

Old paradigms do die hard. Vested interests fight change. The Italian writer and political theorist Niccolo Machiavelli wrote that there is nothing so perilous as bringing about a new order of things. Those few people who might benefit from change are lukewarm supporters; the many who prospered under the old regime are enemies. In many companies today there is bound to be someone who first uttered the words, "We need to have a Home Page on the Net." That person knows full well what it is like to be received with puzzlement or coolness. "A *Home Page* you say? What on earth is that?"

This is compounded by the problem described in *Paradigm Shift* that "the leaders of the old are often the last to embrace the new." Whether Newtonian physicists, Swiss watchmakers, mainframe computer companies, or old retail giants, success in the old paradigm becomes inertia in the new. Some business leaders are savvy enough to understand this effect. Lew Platt, CEO of Hewlett-Packard Company, is concerned about how the company's success could prevent them from changing for the future. "Yesterday's recipe for success clearly will not be tomorrow's recipe for success. I am concerned about complacency at HP. We're having some pretty good times right now, and I'm worried that people are going to start believing that we can just extend what we're doing on into the future. We all know what's happened to companies that have done that."

Another leader, Dick Notebaert, CEO of Ameritech, puts the challenge of changing a highly successful regional bell operating company this way: "Decades of an entitlement mindset die hard. ...It is too easy to fall back into the familiar, comfortable ways of doing business, even though the new environment demands that you do otherwise. Turning a corporate culture around is no easy task. The progress that we have made began with the acknowledgment that our success in a monopoly background did not arm us with many of the skill sets that are absolutely vital to success in the competitive environment."

How will your organization find the leadership for transformation? Often senior management has an old-paradigm view of technology (e.g., the automation of business processes or existing ways of working). Or management may believe that thinking about technology is someone else's responsibility. Many businesspeople remain skeptical, even cynical, about the claims, arcane language, and perceived territorial motives of technologists. Information technology managers are often so busy fighting the fires of the technology legacy that it's difficult to find the time, let alone the will, resources, knowledge, or skills to make the transition to the new technology. Many technology suppliers are having difficulty providing leadership because they are in disarray as the industry goes through its first, serious restructuring. Human resource managers—the very people you would think should be at the fore of this transformation—are often locked into old models of their role in change. Even outside experts and consultants often seem wedded to the old economy and old-technology ways of thinking.

The Six Themes of Internetworked Leadership

The old model of technology was based on the mainframe; all intelligence was in the host computer. Similarly, the old model of leadership was focused in a single, powerful individual. Great leaders were often those with the biggest brain or brain/mouth combination. They created a vision and sold it down to others, just as mainframes communicated with peripherals down the hierarchical network. Command-and-control computing worked well with the command-and-control organization and the old style of leadership.

In the Age of Networked Intelligence leadership is internetworked. This approach to leadership is the antithesis of the old-style, brilliant visionary, take-charge, rally-the-troops type. In the past, Winston Churchill, Thomas Watson, and Lee Iacocca embodied the single dominant leader. Today, the leader is a collective, networked, virtual force with powers flowing from a jointly created and shared vision.

Just as the internetworked business is not under one roof or corporate structure, leadership is not necessarily embodied in a single individual. In the past, vision was transmitted only one way. In the future, vision will be achieved and transmitted collectively. Information technology is creating deep inside the organization whole networks of human intelligence and new knowledge power as people work to transform both the enterprise and themselves.

This book has introduced the concept of internetworked leadership as an effective approach for business transformation for the new enterprise. Internetworked leadership embodies a number of key concepts regarding the kind of leadership that companies need to achieve for the new economy.

Theme 1: Achieving Internetworked Leadership Is Your Personal Opportunity and Responsibility

I asked a group of 400 managers this question: "Excluding yourself, where is the leadership for transformation currently coming from in your organization? Please rank the top three." The managers were able to record their responses on a keypad in 13 categories representing different positions within or external to the organization. The data were then scaled to give a percentage of the total group who responded to each category. The results are shown in Fig. 10.1 and are striking. They show that leadership is currently coming from many different sources within companies. Leadership indeed can come from anywhere—senior manager, professional, nurse, travel agent, or secretary.

FIGURE 10.1 *Leadership Can Come from Anywhere.* SOURCE: © New Paradigm Learning Corporation, 1996.

Audrey Howe started out in a clerical role and became the critical person in the transformation of a division of Citibank. She had what it took to be a leader—she willed change. Leadership is percolating up through companies and coming from a multiplicity of sources.

"The best companies know without a doubt where the real productivity comes from," says General Electric Chairman and CEO Jack Welch. "It comes from challenged, empowered, excited, rewarded teams of people. It comes from engaging every single mind in the organization, making everyone part of the action, and allowing everyone to have a voice in the success of the enterprise. Doing so raises productivity not incrementally but by multiples."

One conclusion that can be drawn from this trend is that leadership for transformation is your opportunity, not just an opportunity for your boss, subordinate, or coworker, but *your* opportunity. Each of us has a choice to participate actively in transformation, to observe passively, or to resist. If you act, you can shape your future, even if you're not a member of the senior management group.

At root, it's a question of taking control of your destiny for a new age. No less a philosopher than rock singer Meatloaf has advice on why we need to take charge of our lives: "There is only one thing that will take away everything you've ever wanted—fear." Mahatma Gandhi was even more specific when he said, "We must be the change we wish to see in the world."

Theme 2: Leadership in the New Economy Is Leadership for Learning

Okay, so you've mustered the courage to allow change and to lead it. Is your firm open to the kind of transformation you know is necessary? Does it have the entrepreneurial interior in which people feel they have a chance to shine? "The new philosophy of organization and management is built on different assumptions about motivation and behavior. The entrepreneurial process creates the context that individuals *can* take the initiative, and it creates the context and mechanics necessary for them to do so," say Sumantra Ghoshal and Christopher A. Barlett, authors of *Managing Across Borders: The Transnational Solution.*[2]

Leadership can come from anywhere and be networked, because the best leadership is leadership for learning. The notion of the learning organization is catching on in transformational businesses because it works. Increasingly, the only sustainable competitive advantage is an organization's ability to overcome what Peter Senge calls its "learning disabilities," and to learn.[3] The days when a great leader at the top could learn *for* the entire organization are gone. As Senge points out, "In an increasingly dynamic, interdependent and unpredictable world, it is simply no longer possible for anyone to 'figure it all out at the top.'"[4] For Senge "'leaders are designers, stewards, and teachers. They are responsible for building organizations where people continually expand their capacities to understand complexity, clarify vision, and improve shared mental models—that is, they are responsible for learning."[5]

Still, too many CEOs see communication as a two-way street where, as one military leader put it, "We have a responsibility to communicate vision to our subordinates and they have a responsibility to be open and receive our communication."[6] Today, that kind of approach is nonsense on stilts. You can't have a "sell down" vision. You need a shared vision.

Theme 3: Internetworked Leadership Is Collective Leadership

Internetworked leadership is born in teams through collective action of individuals working to forge a new vision or solve problems. The whole is greater than the sum of the parts. Leadership is not simply achieved through one individual but through the collective action of many. At Xerox, as a case study described later in the chapter shows, one base team for achieving transformative leadership is "the dyad"—a pairing of individuals who work together. This extends to "communities of practice," where the synergy of diverse individuals combines for cultural change and breakthrough thinking.

The intellectual power generated through networking minds for collective vision will far surpass the intellectual prowess of the smartest boss. Equally important, strategies developed collectively have an infinitely higher probability of actually being implemented. Collective thinking leads to collective action.

Theme 4: Internetworked Leadership Can Be Digital

Leadership can and will increasingly be achieved virtually on computer networks. Human intelligence can be networked just like computer power. In the old days the supercomputer was a uniprocessor—a single, very large, and fast computer. Today it's hard to sell such a device. Supercomputers have been replaced by massively parallel or client/server systems that link many uniprocessors (microprocessors) together. The computer is no longer the powerful host—it is the infinitely more powerful network. Similarly, the leader is no longer simply the brilliant CEO. The leader becomes a network of human intelligence that has infinitely greater capacity for pervasive vision and collective action.

The old technology limited the evolution of such internetworked leadership. But as we achieve telepresence on the network—as people share not just their verbal ideas but facial expressions, body language, designs, notes, drawings, historical information, and tools—the potential for collective thinking and action explodes across the enterprise and beyond. Because of this, the technology infrastructure of the corporation is a learning infostructure. It enables the new media of human communication to be brought to the challenge of organizational learning, and in so doing provides the foundation of transformational leadership.

Theme 5: Internetworked Leadership Is Incomplete Without the Ceo

Mainframes have not disappeared; their roles have changed. In many companies they have become the most important server on a client/server network. So, too, with the CEO's role in achieving leadership. A CEO who fights business transformation acts as a straitjacket on a company's efforts to break free for the new economy. Conversely, a CEO who stewards internetworked leadership can springboard an enterprise into transformation.

A good example is Rich Barton, the former CEO of Xerox Canada. "My biggest problem in reinventing Xerox Canada was that it was profitable," says Barton. He wondered, "Where is the motivation to change? We're successful and have been so for years. There was no driver, no incentive for managers to break from the old paradigm."

Barton worked with a core team to put together a change agenda with many components, including a new technology infrastructure. It also included a massive program of systems literacy for all top managers. Groups of managers were brought together to kickstart the program through an intensive five-day workshop. The goal was to shift from being a copier and duplicator company based on light-lens analog technology to a document management company based on digital and management solutions. After the first session, the management team had forged a new vision, which is described in part in Figure 10.2.

Barton personally participated in the sessions where the program was rolled out to 300 managers. His message was unmistakable: "The world is changing. The marketplace is changing. The technology is changing. The needs of our customers are changing. Xerox is changing and each of us needs to change as well. If we join together in creating a change agenda we will have an exhilarating time transforming this company and we will all benefit. If you choose not to join in this program, that's okay, too ... but I really think you should consider working somewhere else."

As voice and text messages diffused rapidly throughout the company, the impact was immediate. The change agenda worked. And the results were spectacular. In the middle of the recession, 1992 sales at Xerox Canada were up year over year by only 3%, but profit was up 55% to $61 million on revenues of $1 billion. In 1993, Barton was named head of customer operations in the United States and in that capacity is carrying out the change agenda there.

Copier/Duplicator		Document Management
Focus on paper	➤	Focus on electronic documents
Mature market	➤	Growth market
Established competition	➤	New competitors
Standalone	➤	Integrated
Partial solution	➤	Total solution
Hardware focus	➤	Hardware/software/services focus
Administrative purchaser	➤	Multiple purchases (including IS)
Commodity orientation	➤	Value-added orientation
Short-term sales cycle	➤	Longer sales cycle
Vertical sector independent	➤	Industry knowledge/marketing required
Knowledge of features required	➤	Continuous learning required
Product sell	➤	Consultative sell
Installation	➤	Implementation
Xerox well known	➤	Xerox not initially seen as a major player

FIGURE 10.2 *Shifting Market for Xerox*. SOURCE: Xerox Corporation, used with permission.

Theme 6: Personal Use of the Technology Creates Leaders

The "ah-*ha*" phenomenon is a psychological term developed through experiments with rhesus monkeys in the 1960s. Experimenters hung a banana high in the monkey's cage. If the monkey could figure out how to screw together two poles that had been left in the cage, it could reach the banana and knock it down. The monkey would first try to reach the banana by jumping, then grab one pole and then the other in a failed effort to knock down the fruit. Finally, the monkey would look at the poles, look at the banana, and suddenly a look would come over its face that could only be described as the expression a human gets when a breakthrough in thinking occurs and the person says "ah-*ha*."

Many people are getting to "ah-*ha*" these days as they go onto the Net for the first time. The big driver for change is the growing personal use of technology by everyone. To be a with-it (not to mention an effective) manager you need to use an internetworked computer.

It wasn't long ago when jokes in business circles about the personal use of technology would get a laugh. "My VCR at home is still blinking 12:00." "Sure I use a computer. It's on my secretary's desk." "I'm a real Luddite myself." "You'll never catch me typing." Today, such comments are more likely to be received by whispers to the effect: "Who's the loser?" or "Do we really need this person in our group?"

As technology matures, personal use is more likely to be liberating, rather than infuriating. Personal use of technology opens horizons and creates curiosity. It also raises issues, problems, and challenges for individuals and their organizations.

As a starting point in your quest for leadership, if you haven't done so already, get on the Net! Just do it. Ask your information systems (IS) manager, IT supplier, or your teenager to get you a Web browser like Netscape or to get you onto a service like Microsoft Network, Prodigy, America Online, CompuServe, or GEnie. Just do it! If you haven't done it, the single most important thing you can learn from this book is that you should!

And if you have done it, reach out to colleagues and get them onto the Net as well.

BUSTING LOOSE FROM THE TECHNOLOGY LEGACY

Most companies are locked in a struggle with a little detail called "the technology legacy." The irresistible force of the new technology is meeting the immovable object of a $3 trillion installed base of legacy systems. Unfortunately, taking a bulldozer to the data center is not a viable strategy (sometimes referred to as the scorched earth, blue sky, or greenfield strategy). The legacy is composed of operational systems; unplug them and the business usually stops.

How does a company get from here to there? How to link old and new? How can you create the conditions by which new investments contribute to a desired future rather than building up the legacy—perpetuating the past. Yes, God is alleged to have created the world in six days, but he didn't have an installed base to work with.

One important technology migration theme is the idea of three-tiered computing. The way to handle the legacy is to leave it alone—to treat it as data. A middle "functionality" tier of servers uses the new technology and links to the legacy as appropriate. A desktop presentation tier handles all the work of the user interface and "client" aspect of applications.

More broadly, an enterprise strategy is required. The key to breaking free from the legacy is to create an enterprise architecture, a model of the future. By mapping that to the legacy, you can do a gap analysis and build a set of migration scenarios and plans so that investments can be made on target rather than on legacy platforms.

In the past an architecture was really the *design* of a system that had been created to meet specific application needs. In the new business environment, organizations have little idea what their application needs will be in 2, let alone 5 or 10 years. Consequently, we need architectures that can enable the exploitation of unforeseen opportunities and meet unpredictable needs.

As well, past architectures were often product architectures—dubbed "productectures" in the book *Paradigm Shift*—and were owned by an IT vendor. The new architecture is not restricted to one system or department but is an enterprise architecture that may reach out to external organizations. Dave Cox, CIO of Northern Telecom says:

> We need a rich, deep infrastructure to support change in the business. This requires a multilevel architecture that's defined not by you but by the way the business operates. If you don't do it, the company will find a way to do it because it is mandatory to business operations and success.

For Cox, the old idea of the infrastructure as being the boring, rusting iron in the basement is gone.

Infrastructure has become the essential structure for the high-performance organization as it transitions into the twenty-first century.

Those that plan architecture will be further ahead than those who just let it happen. We've built this in terms of network and computing capability. Now we're starting to work on applications and data, so that we can put "lite" functionality on top very quickly.

For example, because we have an architecture, we're implementing a complete new forecasting system for the corporation which is taking four months from start to finish, rather than four years. In 1991, when we restructured our business, it took 18 months to rework our organizational systems—reporting, financial, systems, HR. In 1994, we did it in four months. Soon, we will be able to do it in weeks, and then days. The goal is to be able to build our systems instantly.

Or as Paul Hoedeman, CIO of AlliedSignal, says, "We're trying to get away from thinking about and implementing systems where you've got a payroll system and its got its own interface built into it, its own communications—all monolithic, fully integrated applications. Rather, we want to create an infrastructure that has these capabilities and rapidly build application functions on this as the changing business demands."

Says Hewlett-Packard's Joel Birnbaum, "The information infrastructure is key. Like any other infrastructure it needs to be inconspicuous. That means you don't think about it until it fails. We don't worry about the water infrastructure until the water turns brown or goes away. It has to be dependable like the telephone infrastructure. It will be ubiquitous. It must be consistent. By definition it will be catalytic. It will catalyze not only new ways of doing business that we're in, it will catalyze new business. Nuclear power at one end and laser disc players at the other. Surely not in the mind of the people who built the plug 100 years ago."

"Infrastructure is a mindset issue," says Cox. "From the customer's standpoint it means service on demand and paying for what you use. From the provider view it means deploying and investing in anticipation of demand." Many things that Northern Telecom used to think of as "standalone"—such as e-mail, groupware, and collaborative applications—are now managed as infrastructure.

Architectures that lead to such infrastructures are based on models of the business, organization, information, application functions, and technology. This is a challenge for businesspeople and not just technologists. The architectural principle adopted by some banks, as is discussed in Chapter 3, stated,

"All customers will be treated as a customer of the bank." Businesspeople, not only technologists, must adopt such a principle. It will result in a transformation of a company's business if it is implemented by groups composed primarily of businesspeople, not techies.

Moreover, experience has shown that the process of architecture is first and foremost a process of organizational change. More daunting than the technology legacy is a cultural legacy left over from the first era. Through a process of architecture, however, business managers can come together and understand their common self-interest. The challenge of organizational change far outweighs the technological difficulties of migration from legacy systems to the new technology. Such change is also facilitated by quick implementations of systems and standards along the way. Quick-hit successes bring credibility and momentum to the process.

When it comes to actual implementation, San Francisco-based consultant and colleague Brad Bruce says the new technology is like barbecues that say, "Some assembly is required." Bruce could have added the words," Not all parts included or available." The immaturity of the new technologies is a problem. For example, John Hancock's Diane Smigel describes how that firm had to revolutionize the operational support processes for systems for client/server. "Problem resolution, capacity planning, security, disaster recovery, and other operational support services that have been around for decades in the mainframe world had to be reinvented. The problem here is that there aren't yet the tools to do these things in the new environment."

Increasingly the functionality required by systems won't have to be constructed internally by your company. It will be available on the Net. At the turn of the twentieth century, many companies had an internal power plant to provide electricity. The internal IS department with its mainframes is not completely dissimilar. As the publicly available information utility grows in capabilities, it will be possible to move some IS functions out onto the Net.

"We intend to move much of our internal IS onto the utility," says Cox. "It will depend on how rich the public utility is to provide the services we need. The boundary layers are already blurred. We have no vested interest in operating anything that we don't have to, unless it adds a competitive capability. As more of the market moves to the utility, companies need to be there."

Ron Ponder, CIO of AT&T, has similar views:

At some point we will have a virtual network with intelligence on the core of the network, at the edges of the network, and along the network. Infrastructures today are contained within organizations but as capabilities move out on the public network we'll need the robustness and dependability we like today. We're at the early days of understanding how this will be done. We aren't going to learn from the past. Eventually there will be a telecommunications environment where we will be telecomputing—where all of the computing is in the network.

THE TRANSFORMATION OF THE INFORMATION SYSTEMS (IS) FUNCTION

The pressures of the digital economy are placing huge demands on the IS function and the CIO. Typically, this function arose to address the needs of the old technology and the old economy, and it is becoming inappropriate to address the demands of the new economy. This is causing a problem no different from what happens when your car wheels get out of alignment. Information systems and the businesses they serve are often not properly aligned. Companies need to achieve strategic alignment (so that business strategies and IT plans are harmonized); architectural alignment (so that IT infrastructures correspond to business infrastructures); and organizational alignment (so that IT human resources are located and structured within the business to maximize IS contribution to the business).

One of the toughest jobs these days is that of the chief information officer (CIO). When David Cox became vice president of information systems and CIO at Northern Telecom in 1990, the firm consisted of what he called "warring tribes." Since then, Northern Telecom's 50 separate IS organizations have been centralized into a global network that connects more than 250 hosts to 50,000 workstations. Today NT is the world's fourth largest telecommunications company with $8 billion in revenues, 60,000 employees, manufacturing facilities in 20 countries, and sales in 90 nations. All infrastructure resources now come under worldwide management. Despite geographic growth, the number of host computing sites dropped from 60 in 1991 to 21 in 1994. The number of proprietary and legacy hosts is falling while the number of UNIX hosts is rising. The 43 computing support groups have become two. At the same time, use has skyrocketed. Videoconference hours went from 2,000 in 1990 to 68,000 in 1994. Audio conference hours rose from 5,400 to 96,000. Cox states:

We live in a world of very competitive, large players with new partners, competitors, and hybrid niche players emerging every day. The business vision of global processes drove us toward understanding the need for an information utility—a core network and computing infrastructure that provided seamlessness, consistency, and service. We're moving into—if we aren't already in—a world where the business environment demands a no compromises and no tradeoffs approach to the role of the CIO. Our users want their cake and they want to eat it, too.

CIOs are expected to give visionary leadership, yet at the same time are being asked to get back to basics and deliver the goods. We're told we have to be close to the business front line, yet build an invisible, enabling infrastructure. Both statements are true and our job is to make it so. The old style of thinking global and acting local has to be turned on its head; the opportunity is a new work style enabled by the confluence of information technology and new business thinking.

Being a catalyst and leader is not just the privilege of the CIO, it is the right and duty of every IS person, says Cox. For him, partnership and true fusion mean that individual affinity isn't to IS or the organization, but to the team. "Leadership is a lot more than just arm-waving. Leadership means having your own resources involved, sharing responsibility and risk in the outcome," he says.

Says Ponder, "The CIO has to be a guardian as well as a missionary. Those people who lead us will understand networking, computing, and systems with equal depth."

The Transformation of the Human Resources (HR) Function

The human resources function in general and human resources professionals in particular should be uniquely positioned to provide leadership for the transformation of the enterprise. After all, if the key obstacles blocking this shift toward the reinvention of the corporation are attitudes, ways of working, and people and legacy cultures, shouldn't the very department that's specifically responsible for "people issues," the human resource function, be the natural leader?

Although some human resources professionals are rising to the challenge, too many are not. The basic problem is that in the first era, human resources professionals were mere suppliers of human resource functions such as staffing needs and compensation planning. This may have made a lot of sense during a period of stability and steady growth. But as we move into the digital economy, the human resources profession needs to reinvent itself and forge partnerships with others in the organization for the transformation of the corporation.

Two human resources managers at AT&T in Morristown, New Jersey, Jeana Wirtenberg and Jill Conner, provide a good example of the new thinking. While working to bring about fundamental changes within AT&T as it repositions itself for interactive multimedia and the new marketplace, Wirtenberg and Conner have identified a number of important shifts required in the "mind-set" or mental model of human resources professionals.

Human resources professionals must make the shift from being administrators to being leaders for the transformation of the company. Rather than being rule makers, HR professionals need to become consultants and business partners so that the objectives of HR and the business are aligned. When that occurs, the powerful outcome will be that the walls between the two begin to break down. Rather than continue to be a functional orientation dealing with traditional issues such as staffing and compensation, HR must acquire a business orientation. When that occurs, the perspective will shift from a narrow bias to a broad understanding of both human resources and the burning issues that face the business. At the same time, the focus of the function will shift from an internal view to an external customer-oriented target. Rather than "one size fits all," for example, where there is a single, restraining company policy addressing career planning, HR needs to help the business to implement customized or tailored programs for individuals.[7]

As HR shifts from its traditional approach to leadership readiness for the digital economy, the department must transform itself from a group with little business expertise to one with significant business skills. It needs to shift from activities and processes where professionals can lose sight of the outcome and focus instead on business effectiveness and the impact on transforming the business as a whole.

Rather than being reactive, for example, and waiting for a manager to come to HR with a problem, the HR professional needs to become a proactive leader, looking for opportunities to help the organization learn and adapt for the new environment. The structure of HR itself needs to alter from a centralized corporate role to become instead a distributed, empowered function that provides a framework for others to make their own decisions in the context of an overall plan. Such a positive step would bring about a shift toward positive partnering and away from the mutual distrust of the past where line managers viewed HR as the naysayers who tried to stop them from doing certain things while HR saw line managers as schemers who were always trying to "get away with something."

Changing a Culture to Catch the Future

Xerox Corp. began corporate life 50 years ago as The Haloid Co. Its Palo Alto Research Center (PARC), founded in 1970, has long been the home of the most exciting research into computers. It was 25 years ago at PARC when Alan Kay dreamed up Dynabook, then a notebook-sized computer that could not only recognize handwriting but also communicate with larger systems through radio frequencies. Kay didn't develop his vision fully at the time, but when he later joined Apple it was that PARC thinking that was instrumental in shaping the Macintosh. PARC also developed the first prototype of a laser printer as well as Smalltalk, the first object-oriented computer language. The phrase that described PARC best is this one: "The easiest way to predict the future is to invent it."

As Douglas K. Smith and Robert C. Alexander wrote in *Fumbling the Future*, Xerox lost ground in the 1970s and 1980s when Japanese competitors, such as Sharp and Canon, grabbed market share in such areas as small copiers.[8] "Xerox has not created any substantial new businesses outside its copier core," say Gary Hamel and C. K. Prahalad, authors of *Competing for the Future*.[9] "In fact, Xerox has probably left more money on the table, in the form of underexploited innovation, than any other company in history. Why? Because to create new businesses, Xerox would have had to regenerate its core strategy: the way it defined its market, its distribution channels, its customers, its competitors, the criteria for promoting managers, the metrics used to measure success, and so on. A company surrenders today's business when it gets smaller faster than it gets better. A company surrenders tomorrow's business when it gets better without changing."[10]

Of course, Xerox isn't the only company to miss the mark at various points in its corporate history. When Bell Labs invented the laser, they almost didn't apply for a patent because they couldn't see how lasers might be applied to the telephone. Although the laser has gone on to be used in many fields, communications is the sector in which it has had the most profound impact. As recently as the mid-1960s, transatlantic cables could carry only a few score conversations. Today's fiber optic cables carry millions of conversations simultaneously.

After an ill-fated foray into financial services, Xerox is getting back on track, moving from a copier/duplicator company to a document company. To stress this fact, the name has been changed to The Document Company Xerox Corp.

At the same time, some of the firm's earlier inventions such as the photocopier have been upgraded. The best machines now contain nearly three dozen microprocessors linked by LANs that keep tabs on how the copier is operating and tell the user what's going on at that precise moment. "The big challenge is of creating a research organization that can invent new paradigms and on the other hand transfer that to the rest of the company for exploitation," says John Seely Brown, Xerox vice president and director at Xerox PARC. "Complementing the formal processes, we're paying attention to the informal processes or social fabric within which these processes exist, the relationship between people in the business and people in research in which each is bringing something to the business."

For Brown, PARC's most important invention will be the reinvention of the corporation itself. So what Xerox is doing now is going beyond micro-circuits and software to change what happens among people. The company continues to invent new aspects of IT but is trying to push computers out of sight so that they become just so much wallpaper in an organization. Brown calls the process "active listening" and wants it to extend to the customer as well.

"We're focused on the whole document environment on the basis that the document contains knowledge, whether it is an electronic document or paper document," says Xerox Corp. CIO Patricia Wallington. Although the company name may officially be "The Document Company," the working words to customers are more likely to be "Are you satisfied?" The new focus on customer service began when managers realized customers didn't want just better products from Xerox, they wanted better and broader service. Wallington was recruited in 1989 to head IS and works out of the Stamford, Connecticut, head office, overseeing CIOs in all the other divisions. She sees herself as a coach who has helped to put in place a workgroup orientation for field service staff everywhere. "There's a real dearth of leaders," admits Wallington. "Our real challenge is to find, nurture, and help champion people throughout the organization who are early adapters and are willing to take risks. You should be trying to seek them out, make them role models and help them in any way you can."

 For Wallington, changing the human environment means connecting the new economy directly with individual effectiveness. Just as I urge you to get on the Net, Wallington is urging the formation of dyads within Xerox that use Net skills. She calls the result the microenterprise unit, and it works whether the dyad is within the organization or consists of an employee relating to a customer through the Net.

> It's the technology and the individual and not much in between. The world consists of a global enterprise made up of individuals. One person representing Xerox has the ability to satisfy the customer whatever the problem might be. Technology is the enabler so we're focusing on the ability to support that globally with as much reusability and leverage as possible. The key was the engagement of the leadership of the company. Seamless global management is the real opportunity and technology can help overcome the barriers.

Crucial to the engagement of leadership is the understanding of the internal social fabric at Xerox based on "communities of practice" that define where the work will get done. "There is the authorized organization and the emergent organization," says Brown. "The authorized organization is where the business processes live, which help to structure what the work is. The emergent organization is those communities of practice where the actual work gets done. Most companies are putting in technologies that support the formal process, but not the actual work practices. We've created social computing infrastructure that supports these new work processes." In such a scenario, IT allows the emergence of competing agents and enhances the interrelationships.

This different way of thinking is heavily design-dependent and requires some different skills and abilities than those that currently exist. While planning for the future, Xerox must also continue doing what it is doing now. "It's very hard to make change while standing in the middle of a present that needs to be delivered," Wallington says. "Change is scary, people tend to try and stay safe." One of the solutions is outsourcing. Xerox outsourced all of its $700 million annual budget for information management functions (telecommunications, datacenter, etc.) to Electronic Data Systems (EDS). Some 1,700 Xerox employees transferred to EDS in this IT alliance that allows Xerox to get on with future IT planning—such as object-oriented design—and not worry about the day-to-day running of installed legacy systems. "It's enabling our transformation; it removes a lot of barriers. I'll buy the best of breed and let someone else manage the obsolescence curve," says Wallington. "It gives us the opportunity to do what the company needs. We were so focused on keeping the business running we couldn't create the future. There will be bridges that have to be built to the legacy, but after time that becomes less critical."

Meanwhile, Xerox is creating dyads that consist of an employee and a customer. "We restructured to bring ideas to customers so we have a greater line of sight into customers," says Wallington. "The microenterprise unit is one person representing Xerox with the ability at his or her disposal to satisfy the customer's needs, no matter what that might be. The true essence of empowerment is using the tools and information to satisfy the customer."

What Xerox is trying to do is to create the capacity to assemble solutions around the world rather than to build organizations around the world. "If I'm sitting at a PC and have digital technology available that allows me to fully understand my customer, the marketplace, the artificial intelligence to best meet that customer's needs, then it allows me to take that order at the customer's site, tell them everything they need to know about the order, then customize that order so that I can enable the customer's processes to be more simplified," says Wallington.

Teams of engineers are assigned to specific customers and each workgroup is backed up by two information systems. "This view of who we are builds on our strength from the past and the digital transformation. The ability of working together without getting together can't happen if you don't have an enterprise infrastructure perspective," says Wallington. "What is particularly challenging for us is that we don't have totally independent businesses so our customers overlap. But you want deeper market focus and you want to keep your business small. This is the best of being small, and the best of being big."

Key to the emergent leadership work being done at Xerox is The Center for Organizational Transformation, run by Shirley Edwards at PARC and Rose Fass in Stamford. Edwards is a 30-year Xerox veteran who started as a clerk and worked in every function except manufacturing. Before forming the Center, she was director of real estate, heading a department of 250 employees. After a time there, Edwards found herself looking into the mirror in the morning, asking, "What do I do?" In December 1993, Edwards went to Brown and told him her questions. "How does work happen? How are we supporting the work through management? Do our structures support where we need to go?" For a company like Xerox with Management Resource Planning (MRP) that guides employee careers, these were fundamental and transformational questions. With MRP, the individual usually thinks of herself in terms of the organization, as in, "Where will I fit?" But the real question became "What excites me?" says Edwards. "It is also the heart of what can get lost in an organization."

Organizations have lost their way, too. "People keep talking about nonjobs," she says. "Much of what is now written suggests you go from project to project.

People are uncomfortable with that. It's like the midlife question—people ask, 'Could I do something that excites me?'" The questions Edwards was framing were also laced with a certain irony. Why ask about the meaning of work at a firm like Xerox that was downsizing? But with John Seely Brown's support, Edwards is now on a voyage of personal and professional discovery that could change the very culture of Xerox itself.

Central to her thesis is the dyad, which simply means two people functioning together. Edwards created the first dyad by teaming with Rose Fass whose 20 years with Xerox were in sales. The two created the Center in May 1994, with a simple philosophy. "The dyad is the genesis of teams and the beginning of a community," says Edwards. "We need to create and enable conditions for empowerment. Empowerment is the outcome."

Like a lot of large organizations, Xerox has gone through a variety of revamps. In 1988, the company created partnerships in each of its 65 districts by bringing together the functions of sales, service, and finance in a series of regional partnerships. Edwards was part of the creation that saw each partner share bonuses and leadership. Although there were common goals (profit, customer satisfaction, and employee satisfaction), no one person had the business experience to lead the group as a general manager.

That arrangement lasted until 1995 when the number of districts was reduced to 37 and a vice president and general manager appointed for each. Some of the vice presidents were the result of internal promotion, others were recruited from outside Xerox. For Edwards, the progress since 1988 occurred at about the right rate. "Six years is not a long time for people to collaborate and really share contacts and past work experiences," says Edwards. For her, the next step is to create dyads and extend that concept into other aspects of the organization.

Already, the benefits of her dyad with Rose Fass are obvious. "When we're together, our diversity is clear. When we do things together, it more than doubles what's in the room. Sometimes you keep your mouth shut and sometimes you lead. You disagree and find ways to work it out." Specifically, the Center is trying to facilitate the EDS/Xerox deal. Although Edwards and Fass operate on the periphery of that arrangement (the two heads of that organization have their own dyad), "We're trying to help them with the water that the fish swim in."

Information technology is critical. Because Edwards and Fass spend much of their time on different coasts, they use PictureTel, a PC videoconferencing function. "There's so much that happens through facial expressions that it enhances what we do," says Edwards. "Seeing somebody's facial expression helps dialogue. This enables the virtual office." The dyad work is also supported by a live board, a white board with electronic picturing capacity. "Technology will support collaborative work, teams of 2 or 10, the High-Performance Organization and the Integrated Organization," she says.

The dyad concept has grown to something that Xerox calls $2 \times 2 \times 2$. Here's how it works. CIO Wallington and her CFO Bob Hope meet with two people from 12 divisions quarterly for two hours. So, $2 \times 2 \times 2$ is two people with two people for two hours. "It's a community gathering to pull work practices together where value can be created," says Edwards. "There's power in bringing these four people together." If another meeting is required, two days are allowed to pass for appropriate reflection and that session is dubbed $2 \times 2 \times 2 \times 2$.

Once their own dyad was functional, Edwards and Fass established learning groups that met every six weeks for $1 1/2$ days over an 18-month period. The two dozen participants came from a range of Xerox departments; the meetings alternated between PARC and Stamford. "Everyone must come with a learning partner. Learning is social, we learn better with others. It's emergent, but dyads take the fear out of risk, the shame out of failure, and the arrogance out of success," says Edwards. Edwards and Fass also network with other transformational peers at different organizations. "The reason to go digital is because we'll want to talk to more people," says Edwards. "Internet communication means the capacity to talk to them daily."

As Shirley Edwards and Rose Fass demonstrate, leadership can now come from anywhere. With the availability of the Net, communication is possible on all levels. The person at the top of the organization no longer controls all aspects of that organization's outreach. And just as the old organizational structure has become obsolete, so have the requirements for leadership. In the old model, where General George S. Patton was everyone's hero, the troops would blindly follow wherever he went. Well, that obedience simply doesn't work anymore. There's no longer any need to be the forgotten person at the bottom of the organization.

"There is a merge between being informed and participating in the world," says John Seely Brown. "You can't really be informed unless you participate; and you can't really meaningfully participate unless you're informed." Brown calls it "engagement through being." And information technology is a critical vehicle. If you will it, you can be a leader in the transformation.

NOTES

1. Don Tapscott and Art Caston, *Paradigm Shift: The New Promise of Information Technology*, McGraw-Hill, New York, 1993, p. 281.
2. *Harvard Business Review*, January-February 1995, p. 96.
3. Peter M. Senge, *The Fifth Discipline: The Art and Practice of the Learning Organization*. Senge has been instrumental in the change of thinking on leadership. His book *The Fifth Discipline* is the best single source on the topic. See also Peter Senge, Art Kleiner, Charlotte Roberts, Richard Ross, and Bryan Smith, *The Fifth Discipline Fieldbook: Strategies and Tools for Building a Learning Organization*, Doubleday, New York, 1994.
4. Peter M. Senge, "The Leader's New Work: Building Learning Organizations," *Sloan Management Review*, Fall 1990.
5. Ibid., p. 340.
6. Direct quotation from the intervention of the Admiral of a NATO country in a management planning session. Identity not disclosed to protect the guilty.
7. This view is based, in part, on discussions with AT&T professional development practitioners Jeana Wirtenberg and Jill Conner. Both are examples of the new HR leaders. For further material on their work see "Managing the Transformation of Human Resources Work," *Human Resource Planning*, Vol. 16, Issue 2.
8. Douglas K. Smith and Robert C. Alexander, *Fumbling the Future*, William Morrow & Company, New York, 1990.
9. Gary Hamel and C. K. Prahalad, *Competing for the Future*, Harvard Business School Press, Boston, 1994.
10. *Harvard Business Review*, July-August 1994, p. 126.

PART FOUR

LEADERSHIP FOR THE DIGITAL FRONTIER

20th Anniversary Edition Commentary on
Chapter 11: Privacy in the Digital Economy

THIS CHAPTER'S MAJOR discussion of privacy in 1995 was ill-timed. Back then, the Web was a platform for the presentation of content; the browser cookie had barely been invented; there was no "Big Data," Facebook, Google, and government eavesdropping was restricted to primitive wiretapping. When I said that privacy would be a defining issue of the digital age, the main reaction was a shrug.

Today, privacy has become that issue. New risks and threats such as identity fraud and identity theft are growing in a networked world, along with new forms of discrimination, social engineering, and even oppression made possible by the explosion of data capture and analysis. This is important because personal information—be it biographical, biological, genealogical, historical, transactional, locational, relational, computational, vocational, or reputational—is the stuff that makes up our modern identity. It must be managed responsibly and carefully protected.

However, much water has gone under the bridge in the last 20 years, and our strategies for safeguarding our right to privacy have changed. Let me explain.

"Big Brother?"

The recent National Security Agency (NSA) revelations reveal the extent of (government) assembly of massive dossiers about citizens and foreigners alike. In *The Digital Economy,* I discussed "Big Brother" in reference to George Orwell's iconic text *Nineteen Eighty-Four* about a dystopian society where a totalitarian state rules in its own interests and everyone is under constant surveillance by authorities. This was often correctly alleged about the totalitarian Eastern Bloc countries during the Cold War. It is unfortunately increasingly true of Western democracies today. In the name of national security, governments are collecting real-time information from us; sampling phone calls, e-mails, and social networks; and taking our biometrics at airports and a growing list of other places.

We have little idea of what governments are doing with this flood of personal information.

However, in hindsight, the allusions to Orwell or even Jeremy Bentham's panopticon prison, or an Eastern Bloc police state during the Cold War are not fully apt. Those are metaphors from another era that depended upon a single, all-knowing and malevolent power seeking control. The more appropriate metaphor for the growing loss of privacy today is found in Franz Kafka's *The Trial* in which the central character awaits trial and judgment from an inscrutable bureaucracy for a crime that he is not told about, using evidence that is never revealed to him, in a process that is equally random and inscrutable. In likewise manner, we too will be judged and sentenced in absentia by unknown public and private bureaucracies having access to our personal data. We will be the targets of social engineering, decisions, and discrimination, and we will never really know what or why.

Yes, we still need to resist attempts of governments to collect unnecessary information. We still need to fight for the basic privacy principle of *data minimization*, of limiting the information collected to clearly definable and socially helpful purposes. There should be no tapping of phones or anything else without due process. If a government agency proposes to set up video cameras in your neighborhood, you need to decide if the benefits of possible crime reduction outweigh the possible dangers of unknown governments being able to watch you constantly.

However, increasingly we need to make demands on our governments to limit their data collection activities and also the use of that data. Setting aside the question of whether Edward Snowden's behavior in releasing confidential information about the NSA's surveillance activities was appropriate, his revelations were a stunning reminder about how we must be vigilant. We must all vigorously oppose the collection of unnecessary personal information by governments.

"Little Brother"

The next problem is so-called "Little Brother" or corporations. As the Internet becomes the basis for commerce, work, entertainment, health care, learning, and much human discourse, each of us is leaving a trail of digital crumbs as we spend a growing portion of our day touching networks. The books, music, and stocks you buy online; your pharmacy purchases and the prescription drugs you buy; groceries scanned at the supermarket or bought online; your child's research for a school project; the card reader at the parking lot; your car's conversations with a database via satellite; the online publications you read; the shirt you purchase in a department store with your store card; and the hundreds of other network transactions in a typical day point to the problem.

Using the tools of Big Data analytics, computers inexpensively link and cross-reference such databases to slice, dice, and recompile information about individuals in hundreds of different ways. That means that companies want to know more and more about what makes each of us tick—our motivations, behavior, attitudes, and buying habits. The good news is that companies can give us highly customized services based on this intimate knowledge, *and build trusting relationships*. Sometimes it is great to have highly customized ads. I don't want to hear or see car ads except when I am interested in buying a new car. When I am, I would like to advise the car companies to bring it on!

But there is an obvious dark side. Companies can use our personal information to our disadvantage. Some of these are rogue "bad actors." In the Rupert Murdoch tabloid scandal in the United Kingdom, cellular phone company technicians could sell the location of a specific phone. This way Murdoch's reporters could track down celebrities.

However, many companies have no problem trying to convince customers to do things that are not in their interests. Millions of homeowners got a taste of this in the subprime mortgage scandal. They were seduced into purchasing homes they couldn't afford.

Now, imagine a world where corporations have near-perfect information about each of us. As the aphorism goes "Knowledge is Power." Could firms go beyond fairly influencing us, to being able to manipulate us? Could they abuse their detailed knowledge and cause us to purchase goods or services, or take other actions that are not in our interests?

We already live in a consumer society where people go into debt to purchase things they really can't afford. If corporations had information about our every purchase, articles we read, movies we watch, things we say, places we go, food we eat, medications we take, and Big Data from myriad other sources, how could they use that asymmetrical power to advance their interests against ours?

"Baby Brother"

Hundreds of millions of individuals—call them "Baby Brother"—reveal detailed data about their identities, activities, and preferences online every day. Almost unwittingly, we each make our separate Faustian deals with providers of online services, allowing them to collect our trails of digital crumbs into giant treasuries of information for private commercial benefit.

This situation has turned traditional privacy laws and regulations upside down. Privacy and data protection laws emphasize the responsibility of organizations to collect, use, retain, and disclose personal information in a confidential manner. But collaborative networks encourage individuals to share—explicitly and implicitly—their most intimate personal details, quite opposite from the principle of data minimization.

Before Facebook arrived, who would have predicted that hundreds of millions of people would voluntarily log on to the Internet and record detailed minute-by-minute data about themselves, their activities, their likes and dislikes, and so on? To make things worse, some social networking leaders confuse the right to privacy with transparency, arguing that transparency is good for individual relationships. This is misguided. Transparency applies to organizations, not people. Organizations are increasingly obliged to communicate pertinent information to their customers, shareholders, business partners, and so on. This is not the case for individuals. Indeed, individuals have an *obligation* to themselves to safeguard their personal information. And institutions should be transparent about what they do with our personal information.

This situation poses an unprecedented challenge for government and regulators because it has turned traditional privacy laws and regulations upside down. Privacy and data protection laws ensure that organizations collect, use, retain and disclose our personal information in a confidential manner. But today all of us are participating willfully in the destruction of our own private life. There are probably thousands of recent university graduates who didn't get that dream job because the employer did a "reference check" online and found them doing something inappropriate.

The bottom line is that the new ubiquitous computing environment forces us to rethink the issue of privacy and how to protect it. In *The Digital Economy*, I argued that one critical way to protect privacy is for each of us to show great care with what information we give away. This was consistent with the emerging field of privacy advocates who promoted policies of data minimization.

However, with the rise of social media, ubiquitous computing, cameras everywhere, geospatial systems, Big Data, and myriad other technologies, this is no longer feasible. Prudent, cautious approaches to giving up our personal information are woefully inadequate. Rather, the emphasis needs to shift to the collectors and owners of data. We need new norms and clear rules governing how these data will be used and for what purposes.

Endnote: Openness Is for Institutions, Not Individuals

The issue of personal information has been muddled with the opportunity for corporations to become more transparent. To be sure, as David Ticoll and I wrote over a decade ago in *The Naked Corporation* (2003), firms can gain huge benefits from sharing pertinent information with customers, employees, and other stakeholders. But corporations are fundamentally different from people. Corporations are institutions of society that we create or permit to achieve collective goals. As such, corporations have obligations to us, including being appropriately transparent. Individuals have no such obligations. We abhor institutions that are secretive. But we have and should continue to respect individuals who are "very private persons."

Yes, when companies become transparent they also may find themselves releasing personal information, like the compensation levels of corporate management. But senior executives control the institution and, as such, are not simply private individuals. In their corporate capacity, they have a social obligation to reveal some personal information. It should go with the job. Conversely, they have an obligation to fiercely protect the privacy of their employees, customers, and other stakeholders.

But today I find myself in a completely unexpected debate. There are a growing number of people who argue that the notion of having a private life in which we carefully restrict what we share with others is, in fact, a bad idea.

This view goes beyond the famous aphorism of Scott McNealy, the former CEO of Sun Microsystems, who in 1999 stated, "You have zero privacy anyway. Get over it."[1] The new view holds that we should all be more open—share intimate, personal information with others—and this is good for each of us and for everyone.

This is not a fringe movement. The proponents of this view are some of the smartest and most influential thinkers and practitioners of the digital revolution.

Jeff Jarvis, in his thoughtful book *Public Parts: How Sharing in the Digital Age Improves the Way We Work and Live*, makes the case for sharing and he practices what he preaches. We learn about everything from details of his personal income to his prostate surgery and malfunctioning penis. "I'm a public man," he says. "My life is an open book."[2] And he provides elaborate evidence on why this has been an enormously positive effect on his life, arguing that if everyone were more like him the world would be a better place. He concludes that while sharing should be a personal choice, privacy regulation should be avoided.

But unfortunately the debate about personal "openness" has obscured and muddled these important differences.

As the new movement for "personal openness" grows, there is a bizarre new danger that private people become stigmatized. "We know nothing about her vacation location." "He refuses to publish his DNA sequencing." "What are they hiding?"

Personally, I think we all need a balance between the public and the private. Just as the complete loner and hermit lifestyle is not optimal (we all need and benefit from human interaction and relationships) so being a completely public person undermines one essence of what it is to be human—to be private, reserved, and discreet.

By all means, be as open as you want but realize that with openness can come vulnerabilities, especially for your children. And as the expression goes, "Discretion is the better part of valor," which means that it makes sense to be careful in the face of risks. And most important, demand that all use your personal information in a responsible manner.

Yes, we need new understandings in society. As Tim Berners-Lee, creator of the World Wide Web says: "Just as there are laws that prevent discrimination based on gender, race, and age we need a law banning discrimination on the basis of something you said on Facebook before the age of nineteen."[3] But lacking such, a parent's mantra should be "sharer beware." Just as my parents talked to me about the dangers of playing in the street, one of the new responsibilities of parenting is to educate and collaborate with your children about their personal privacy strategy.

Notes

1. Polly Sprenger, "Sun on Privacy: 'Get Over It,'" *Wired*, January 26, 1999, http://archive.wired.com/politics/law/news/1999/01/17538.
2. Jeff Jarvis, *Public Parts: How Sharing in the Digital Age Improves the Way We Work and Live*. Simon & Schuster, 2011.
3. Don Tapscott, "Real Dangers of Thoughtless Sharing," *Toronto Star*, June 23, 2012.

PRIVACY IN THE DIGITAL ECONOMY

If, or is it when?—computers are permitted to talk to one another, when they are interlinked, they can spew out a roomful of data on each of us that will leave us naked before whomever gains access to the information. ... But we must be vigilant against their misuses, either accidentally or intentionally.

Walter Cronkite, 1980

THE EMERGING FIRESTORM

Privacy has been an important issue since the first person peeked around the corner of a cave to see what his fellow cave-dweller had caught for dinner. Since then, various philosophers, writers, politicians, unionists, businesspeople, and concerned citizens have written about and debated the many dimensions of the issue.

In precomputer times, if you wanted to surreptitiously learn a lot about someone, you would have to go to a lot of trouble. Let's say you wanted to trace the activities of a fictitious Jeremy Smith, described in my new book on privacy, coauthored by Ann Cavoukian, titled *Who Knows? Safeguarding Your Privacy in a Networked World.*[1] In an entirely paper-based world, you would have to physically travel to each location where paper files and records of Smith's paper-based transactions were located, and review each piece of paper. This would be a laborious exercise requiring considerable resources. If Smith lived in or traveled to various countries, the problem would be compounded. Surveillance of Smith's activities would likewise require considerable resources. It might have been feasible to track the activities of one or two people in this manner, but it would not be feasible to track the activity of thousands on a routine basis.

The computer began to change this. It became easier to follow an electronic trail and do it without physically leaving a central location. However, before information highway times, computer-based threats to privacy were finite as a result of lack of database integration, the low penetration of access devices, the relative unsophistication of users, poorly connected networks, and an overall limited use of information technology in business and social affairs. Such limitations are now fewer in number and should cause us to pause for concern.

Privacy, confidentiality, and security are related but different concepts. Let's use an example to explain.

The hotel industry is struggling with how to bring travel and tourism planning and bookings onto the Net. Weak security of the Net and the challenge of putting proper procedures and safeguards in place are a problem. For example, what happens if someone from Hilton books all the rooms of Hyatt worldwide—or vice versa? Systems can be put into place to help avoid such mischievous or fraudulent activity. But that is just the beginning.

Hotel industry executive John Davis describes the challenge:

> If I can break the network security, think about the information you provide when you book a hotel room on the Net. I've got your name, address, city, state, ZIP, phone number, and credit card number. I know where you're going; where you're staying; when you'll be there; how much you're going to pay, and a rough idea of your income because of your choice of hotel. I've got enough information to apply for a credit card. I know whether you're going to be staying alone or not. I even know what day to back my van up your driveway and start unloading your possessions. I'm in business big time!

The example helps to clarify the key concepts. Bad systems security leads to potential breaches of confidentiality, which cause an invasion of privacy, which results in violations of the security of the person or property.

There are many definitions of privacy, none of which is perfect. Like freedom, privacy is best understood when it is being undermined—you know what privacy is when someone is trying to take it away. Privacy involves the right to be left alone and to determine with whom we share the details of our personal lives or personal information.

Confidentiality is a narrower concept. Violation of the confidentiality of your personal information undermines privacy. But privacy can be achieved without confidentiality. You may choose not to share your information in the first place—that is, not entrust others to keep it confidential. Security is required to maintain confidentiality and therefore privacy.

Privacy is the overriding concept. It must be balanced with other values. As with all rights, there are trade-offs and competing rights and interests that must be respected. Economic interests may cause consumers to trade privacy for convenience such as occurs in credit card shopping. Efficient government requires personal information for taxes, drivers' licenses, or health care. Privacy may also conflict with publicly accepted principles of law enforcement and public safety.

Two other related concepts are censorship and free speech. These issues have been raised because of the overstated but very real problem of smut on the Net. Members of Congress who seek to pass and enforce laws prohibiting communications of certain material on the Net become censors. The problem is not simply that censorship is infeasible on the Net; it is a dangerous approach to solving the problem of obscenity because it prohibits free speech between consenting adults. This is not to say that criminal activities on the Net should be tolerated. Threatening another person with death, conspiring to commit a felony, or conducting an illegal drug transaction are crimes that should be enforced whether they occur in cyberspace or the street.

But many advocates of policing cyberspace go beyond this, arguing that it should be a crime to communicate obscene material—even between consenting adults. So if Bob, Carol, Ted, and Alice share a kinky fantasy in cyberspace they are breaking the law! The implications for both freedom of speech and privacy are clear.

If censorship is unworkable and undesirable, then how do we protect our children? The solution lies in two areas.

1. We need a multitude of rating services reflecting the different values we hold.
2. We need technological screens so that parents can control what information comes on to their children's workstations.

There should be a Southern Baptist rating service and one from the civil liberties association and hundreds more to provide you with a choice that corresponds to your sense of ethics and approach to childrearing.

You subscribe to the service and implement the corresponding filter for your family. Already there is software such as Vancouver-based "Net Nanny," which catches certain words or phrases you select (such as "where do you live") and shuts down your child's computer. There are solutions that don't take the draconian step of killing freedom of expression and leading us down the slippery slope of the erosion of privacy.

Back to privacy. The relentless expansion of the digital economy is causing growing concerns about privacy, as evidenced by numerous studies. For example, a 1994 Gallup Poll conducted for Andersen Consulting showed that 85% of the sample expressed concern about the personal information that might be collected about them on the information highway.[2]

Such results show that there is an emerging firestorm on this issue. The internet will intensify concerns about privacy, as interpersonal communications, human work, social development, and entertainment transactions become based on the network. Companies that do not manage this issue are at risk of severe damage in the marketplace as consumer and public sensitivity grows.

Ethical issues apart, every business needs to develop appropriate policies and practices to address these issues, regarding both employees and customers. Effective privacy strategies will become a requirement for effective business strategies as business shifts to the new information infrastructure. Proactive strategies to address privacy problems can contribute to good information and resource integrity and can help to manage the transition to the new environment. Companies need to be proactive in order to avoid being saddled with possible inappropriate regulations made by governments, unions, or other parties.

As the electronic web grows, the day-to-day activities of consumers, employees, game players—people communicating with one another—will leave an ever-larger digital trail. Computers will be able to record what movies we watch, what databases we access, what goods we buy, with whom we interact, and the content of our communications.

"Every time you make a telephone call, purchase goods using a credit card, subscribe to a magazine, or pay your taxes, that information goes into a database somewhere," writes leading cryptography expert David Chaum. "Furthermore, all of these records can be linked so that they constitute, in effect, a single dossier of your life—not only your medical and financial history but also what you buy, where you travel, and whom you communicate with."[3] But the danger is more complex than this.[4]

♦ *Transactional Data and Personal Profiling.* Information that had previously been stored in a vast number of separate databases can now be merged, sorted, and analyzed, resulting in the creation of a personal profile or data image of a subject based on his or her electronic data composite. As described in *Who Knows?*, "Not only is it possible to track someone's activities, but also to sketch a fairly accurate picture of that person, enabling you to visualize them without ever knowing them and without them ever knowing. These technological developments have led to the creation of a massive information-gathering industry."[5] Credit card companies sell their lists and their transactional data to other companies. This may be acceptable when the firms involved are reputable financial institutions; the costs to privacy may be offset by the benefits of being able to use a credit card. But in the new digital economy, every business large or small—reputable or not—will have the capacity to generate information files on its customers or to purchase data from other sources.

- *Individual Authentication.* As more and more consumer transactions and communications are conducted on the Net, it becomes critical to have effective identification of the sender and receiver. For example, the extension of banking terminals or credit card purchasing into the home raises many new issues of authentication. Conversely, how will a person rejected for a job discover that the reason was an incorrect entry on the personal database that's equivalent to today's credit bureau?

- *The Extension of Smart Products.* As chips become embedded in everything, privacy problems are exploding. For example, as smart cards proliferate, the pressure for reliable authentication grows, including biometric indicators such as thumbprints or bioretinal scans. But do such techniques lead us toward a society in which it is necessary to carry identification documents on one's person at all times? Or when you wear a shirt with a chip in it, your shirt may carry a vast range of personal information including who you are, where you bought it, the cost, and even personal financial information. Without getting too paranoid, let your mind consider some truly bizarre possibilities. Millions of people have pacemakers. There are now chips that can be inserted into breast implants. Perhaps chips would be inserted into other parts of peoples' bodies for nonmedical reasons. We could track repeat offender pedophiles, or repeat offenders in general, or offenders in general, or maybe just offensive people. Microprocessor-based products can be attached to children to discourage abduction or locate missing kids. What about chips in children for extra and permanent safety?

- *Confidential Information.* As society moves toward managed health care, it is clear that comprehensive cradle-to-grave patient records could facilitate better health care and reduce costs. But what procedures will be used to ensure that information cannot be inappropriately accessed both inside and outside the health care system?

- *Surveillance.* In Orwell's dystopian *1984*, citizens were watched by Big Brother using video cameras. Although such surveillance is growing, the larger danger comes from "little brother"—the capacity to monitor activity through the use of detailed personal information. "Dataveillance," as Roger Clarke calls it, "is supplanting conventional surveillance techniques."[6] The new technology brings a chilling capacity for surveillance on every individual, whether as a student, customer, employee, taxpayer, or recipient of government services. For example, to whom and how should we give the right to access employees' electronic mail (text, voice, and soon multimedia)? What levels of monitoring of workstation activity (for example, in a telework situation) will be acceptable? The very whereabouts of a given individual will be readily known by locating that person's portable telephone or other information appliance.
- *Physical Security.* As people conduct more banking, work, utility and appliance management, and other monitoring activities in the home, security concerns will grow about the networks involved and the individuals operating them. It's one thing to have a secure system in an office environment. How will security be similarly controlled on so many offsite locations? The home may become a target for intruders who could force the transfer of funds or engage in other illegal activities.

"Big Brother Doesn't Need to Watch!"

You might be wondering where all the information contained in these databases is coming from. You don't recall giving away any information that could be used to pry into your life. Really? Have you done any of the following lately: bought a car, bought a house, bought a dress, bought a book, bought something for indigestion at the supermarket, bought an airline ticket, reserved a room at a hotel, ordered underwear from a mailorder catalogue, joined a book club, used a telephone, used a bank machine, opened a bank account, ordered a pizza, rented a video, filled out a product warranty card, subscribed to a magazine, applied for a government program, applied for a job, applied for a loan, applied for insurance, sent an e-mail message, gone to the hospital, had a baby, had a blood test, had a prescription filled ... get the picture?"[7]

Government Guidelines

Over the years, governments have taken steps to protect privacy. Significantly, in September 1980, the OECD (Organization for Economic Cooperation and Development) developed a set of guidelines to assist in the protection of personal information. The principles contained in these guidelines are commonly referred to as the Code of Fair Information Practices (FIPs) and form the basis of all privacy legislation worldwide. The essence of these principles is quite simple:

- Limit the collection of information (collect only information you need).
- Where possible, collect information directly from the individual to whom it pertains; inform the subject of the purpose of the collection (tell them why you need it).
- Use the information only for the purpose intended and for which the subject was informed.
- Give subjects the opportunity to access their personal information and the right to seek its correction if incorrect.

The guidelines have been widely accepted among privacy advocates and more broadly by many governments and businesses. The guidelines are more than 15 years old, however; they urgently need to be updated to incorporate the implications of the information highway.

In contrast to Europe, the United States has tended to support voluntary codes of practice. The information highway is causing government and business to take a new look at the issue. The Privacy Working Group, one of several working groups of the National Information Infrastructure task force, is looking at the issues of privacy and integrity of information. The group has developed a set of principles and guidelines for fair information practices on the information highway.[8] This is intended to update the OECD code to make it more applicable to electronic environments as well as to update the codes developed in the early 1970s in the United States.

The basic assumption is that individuals are entitled to a reasonable expectation of information privacy. Furthermore, the responsibility of all participants is to ensure that information on the National Information Infrastructure (NII) has integrity— that it is secure through the use of whatever means are appropriate—as well as accurate, timely, complete, and relevant for the purpose for which it is given.

To achieve this, the NII has developed principles for information collectors (i.e., entities that collect personal information directly from the individual), information users (i.e., information collectors and entities that obtain, process, send, or store personal information), and individuals who provide personal information. Some critics argue that the new code departs from the OECD's approach that confers rights upon data subjects and responsibilities for data users (the organizations responsible for collecting personal information). The effect, critics say, would be to shift emphasis for protecting privacy away from data users and onto individuals. The language of the newly proposed code is directed not just at governments but to private enterprises as well as individuals. For the first time, individuals will be expected to take some responsibility for the protection of their personal information, especially in highly networked environments where the occurrence of multiple disclosures will probably be the norm, not the exception.

There are many privacy initiatives underway in Canada, both at the federal and provincial level. For example, the federal government's Industry Canada has published a paper "Privacy and the Information Highway," which outlines the main questions and solicits responses from interested parties.[9] In January 1994, Quebec introduced privacy legislation that extended coverage to the private sector. This is the first jurisdiction in Canada or the United States in which commercial enterprises will now be subject to privacy protection laws.

PRIVATE SECTOR INITIATIVES

More and more it will make good business sense to pay attention to privacy issues. Corporations that act ethically and with a sense of social responsibility in keeping with public and market expectations will be more likely to weather the firestorm, protect intellectual property, and preserve societal norms.

Many of the major telephone and cable companies in North America have privacy initiatives underway. The Direct Marketing Association (DMA)—the organization of companies that use direct marketing techniques, telephone solicitations, and growing networked-based marketing—has made considerable effort to tackle this problem. The Canadian Direct Marketing Association has developed a privacy code respecting the personal information obtained regarding its members' customers. Both organizations offer a "do not call" and "do not mail" service, allowing people to opt-out so that their names and addresses are not given to other companies for marketing purposes.

With the implementation of its Privacy Action Plan, DMA and its Privacy Task Force continue to lead in ushering in a new era of effective self-regulation for direct marketers. The Privacy Action Plan initiatives include intensive analysis of self-regulatory programs, increased industry education programs, expanded consumer education, and redoubled legislative outreach efforts.[10]

ALTERNATIVE APPROACHES TO THE ISSUE

There are five main approaches to the issue of privacy:

Laissez Faire

This view, expressed by those who say "why should you worry if you have nothing to hide," is held by fewer and fewer people these days, especially as the world is introduced to the chilling potential for a cyberspace invasion of our personal and business lives. Some believe in laissez faire.

Voluntary Codes and Standards

Voluntary privacy standards, the norm in North America, provide the flexibility for organizations in different sectors to customize their approaches in keeping with the needs of their customers, employees, and regulatory environments. Further voluntary codes can be as strong or stronger than those enforced by law. However, the matter of enforceability raises several questions: Who is ultimately accountable? Where does an aggrieved consumer go for redress? As the value of personal information increases with the growth of the information economy, how can voluntary codes ensure protection? Past experience has not been encouraging.[11]

Regulation

The trend in new technology is away from regulation to enable market forces to be more competitive and to accelerate the evolution toward a new infrastructure. There is widespread evidence that consumers favor legislation for privacy protection, however. Arguably, harmonization of basic rules that apply to information protection could be good for business and could also reduce the excessive bureaucracy created by the various patchwork approaches practiced in North America. Clear rules could also add to consumer confidence and help to avert privacy concerns by establishing a level playing field for all corporations—providers and/or users of technology as well as individuals.

Consumer Education

An active and informed public is the surest and most rational way to achieve privacy protection. It is only when society collectively comes to understand its common interests in these matters that privacy issues can be managed without excessive government involvement.

Technology Solutions

Ironically, technology may become one of the best ways to protect personal privacy and safeguard information. For example, the technology already exists that allows for unconditionally untraceable exchanges to take place. Encryption technology can be incorporated into software, embedded as chips in equipment such as telephone sets or palm-sized computers, or used in smart cards to provide fraud-proof authorization while at the same time allowing the holder to remain anonymous. The same technology can be used to provide reliable yet untraceable electronic cash. Such cash, stored in bits, can be loaded onto your disk or a smart card in your wallet and used as freely and anonymously as cash. David Chaum suggests a form of encryption based on public key cryptography and blind digital signatures. "In one direction lies unprecedented scrutiny and control over peoples' lives. In the other, secure parity between individuals and organizations. The shape of society in the next century may depend on which approach predominates."[12] *Business Week's* Amy Cortese and Kelly Holland describe it as follows:

> With [digital cash] the encryption not only protects the money from snoops and thieves, but also obscures the identity of the owner. Here's how: When you want cash, you make an electronic withdrawal from your bank account. The bank issues electronic currency—a series of encrypted serial numbers representing dollar bills and coins. Once encrypted money leaves your account, it can no longer be traced back to you—not even by the issuing bank. When you spend it, your digital coins get deposited directly into the merchant's cash account."[13]

Europe already has telephone systems that can be designed to "forget" the last few digits of a telephone number after placing the call, in order to protect privacy in billing statements. Electronic mail systems can be developed that provide ephemeral messages for personal use, a form of electronic disappearing ink.[14]

THE ROAD AHEAD

Clearly, government guidelines, consumer education, and technology solutions will be important in avoiding the privacy firestorm. But responsible protection of privacy by business, acting out of self-interest, is also important to the future.

To begin, businesses need to build secure systems. An example of the dangers is a Home Page called "The Blacklist of Internet Advertisers." This is a list "intended to curb inappropriate advertising" on the Net. "It works by describing offenders and their offensive behaviors, expecting that people who read it will punish the offenders in one way or another." A list of 10 ways to punish offenders is provided in the database. One popular way is to break into and disable or destroy their corporate systems. Life in the digital frontier can be dangerous, especially if your cattle ranch fences are not secure.

Each element in the "network of networks" requires appropriate levels of password protection, tiered levels of security, partitioned access according to the sensitivity of files, and rigorously enforced operating procedures and physical controls.[15] But that will not be enough. Peter G. Neumann, an expert on computer security, argues that collective action will be needed at a variety of levels if security is to be taken seriously and our existing "head in the sand" mentality has to change. He feels that an information campaign is necessary to make both computer users and systems administrators alike aware of the severity of the problem—"aware of how vulnerable their systems are to attack so that they will be motivated to employ defensive techniques. This must be a shared responsibility among vendors, customers, universities and government organizations."[16]

A key to the solution may be a change in thinking on the property rights and dollar value of information. Ann Cavoukian and I argue that your personal information (everything from your weight to your social security number) belongs to you. You own it. It is your property. Others who obtain your personal information act as its custodians and are entrusted with its care. If such information has value, the owner should receive compensation for its use. "If people stop giving away their information and start thinking about it as they do other forms of property, expecting to have some control over it, and get paid for its use, then things would begin to change. For example, why not a royalty payment system for the commercial uses of your personal information?"[17] We argue that there are dangers in extending this concept to treating privacy as a commodity, to be sold and traded in the marketplace. "Any consideration of economic gain in exchange for one's personal information should only be made in the private sector, in the context of commercial transactions. Legislated protections must continue to safeguard our fundamental rights, and the restrictions on the uses of our information must continue to apply to government organizations." But, we argue, what would stop someone from establishing a property right to personal information, which in turn would ensconce the right to control over your property?[18]

Businesses can implement the "privacy makes good business sense" view in other ways. For example, you can offer your customers a range of options, including some that are privacy-friendly. Industry associations can adopt codes for their members that can have considerable weight. Businesses should cooperate with government in developing formal legislation in everyone's shared interest. Companies can cooperate to ensure the growth of proper security measures on the Net. And every company needs to conduct a privacy audit of its own practices, evaluating the requirements of customers, employees, and the public and implementing policies to ensure that this basic right is not obliterated.

Admittedly, this is not easy. Many Catch-22 situations arise. Customers expect you to make life convenient by using information you have about them. When you take on a new service at the bank, you don't want to fill out a form providing information the bank already has. But making things easy for the customer can cause grief, as one bank executive told us. Their management had a two-hour discussion about issues such as whether to acknowledge that they already had personal information on file. One debate was whether to use the first or last name when a customer opened another account. Or should the thank-you letter read "Thank you for opening another account with us?" or "Thank you for opening an account with us?" In many situations they decided the latter enabled better customer relations.

Privacy is only one of a much broader set of concerns that are leading to new responsibilities for business.

NOTES

1. Ann Cavoukian and Don Tapscott, *Who Knows: Safeguarding Your Privacy in a Networked World*, Random House, Toronto, 1995.
2. Geoffrey Rowan, "Snoopophobia Haunts Information Highway: 85% Fear New Network Will Mean Loss of Privacy," *Globe & Mail*, May 3, 1994.
3. Chaum, David, "Achieving Electronic Privacy," *Scientific American*, 1992, p. 96.
4. The following categories are based on a thoughtful paper titled: "Privacy and the Canadian Information Highway," published by Industry Canada, 1994.
5. Cavoukian and Tapscott.
6. Roger Clarke, "Information Technology and Dataveillance," in *Communications of the ACM*, May 1988, Vol. 31, No. 5, pp. 498–512.
7. Cavoukian and Tapscott.
8. Draft Principles for Providing and Using Personal Information, April 21, 1994, produced by the Information Infrastructure Task Force's Privacy Working Group, chaired by Robert Veeder.
9. *Privacy and the Canadian Information Highway*, Industry Canada, 1994.
10. 1993 Annual Report, Direct Marketing Association.
11. *Privacy and the Canadian Information Highway*, Industry Canada, 1994.
12. Chaum, p. 101
13. Amy Cortese and Kelly Holland, "E-Cash," *Business Week*, May 29, 1995.
14. Amy Cortese and Kelly Holland, "What's the Color of Cybermoney?" *Business Week*, February 27, 1995.
15. *Privacy and the Canadian Information Highway*, Industry Canada, 1994.
16. Cavoukian and Tapscott.
17. Peter G. Neumann, "Computer Insecurity Issues," *Science and Technology*, Fall 1994, pp. 50–54. Cited in Cavoukian and Tapscott.
18. Cavoukian and Tapscott.

20th Anniversary Edition Commentary on Chapter 12:
The New Responsibilities of Business

A s WE ENTER the new age, every institution in society is being challenged. I can't remember why I named the closing chapter of *The Digital Economy* "The New Responsibilities of Business," but in hindsight it was a good choice to call on business leaders to think differently about their roles in the new age. Let me pick up two of the big issues where a lot of water has gone under the bridge: the nature of the corporation and the future of democracy. Then I will provide some closing thoughts.

Corporations in Society and in Change

It was many years ago that I first heard the optimistic adage, "Companies do well by doing good." Back then advocates of so-called Corporate Social Responsibility (CSR) were trying to make a business case for good corporate behavior. They didn't get very far in convincing anyone.

The main reason for lack of success in winning support for the "doing good adage," is that it was not true. Many companies did well by doing bad. Creative accounting, unfair labor practices, corporate secrecy, monopolistic behaviors, externalizing costs, and shady environmental behaviors could help beef up the bottom line. Not to mention that corporate executives could "do well" by paying astronomical bonuses to themselves, even while their companies were struggling.

But today, all this is changing. The paralysis of the financial systems and the global economic crisis of 2008 were a wakeup call to the world. It's become clear that business can't succeed in a world that is failing. We need to rethink and rebuild many of the organizations and institutions of the past around a new set of principles and behaviors.

In fact, the crisis and its continuing aftereffects represents more than a recession. It is a punctuation point in history. Arguably many of the pillars of economic and social life have come to the end of their life cycles. The financial services industry, for example, needs more than a fresh infusion of capital or some new regulations; it needs a whole new operating model. Our transportation system, based on the internal combustion engine, is changing the climate of Earth and there is no more important challenge than creating a green energy grid and a reindustrialization of the planet for sustainability. The American auto industry, the epitome of the industrial economy, collapsed during the crisis. As companies in other sectors cut their costs to stay alive, many began to see that hunkering down, while necessary, was insufficient for success. From manufacturing to retail, businesses have begun to initiate long overdue changes to their structures and strategies. There is a growing appreciation that conventional wisdom isn't going to cut it for success in this century. We need to reinvent our institutions.

At the same time, an old force with new power is rising in business, one that has far-reaching implications for most everyone. Nascent for half a century, this force has quietly gained momentum through the last decade; it is now triggering profound changes across the corporate world. Evidence suggests firms that embrace this force and harness its power will thrive. Those who ignore or oppose it will suffer. The force is *transparency*.

Globalization, instant communications, organized civil society, and a crisis in trust have changed the rules of the game. Firms are being held to complex and changing sets of standards—from unrelenting webs of "stakeholders" who pass judgment on corporate behavior to regulations, new and old, that govern and often complicate everyday activities. In an ultra-transparent world of instant communications, every step and misstep is subject to scrutiny. And every company with a brand or reputation to protect is vulnerable.

Customers can evaluate the worth of products and services at levels not possible before. Employees share formerly secret information about corporate strategy, management, and challenges. To collaborate effectively, companies and their business partners have no choice but to share intimate knowledge with one another. Powerful institutional investors today own or manage most wealth, and they are developing x-ray vision. Finally, in a world of instant communications, whistleblowers, inquisitive media, and Googling, citizens and communities routinely put firms under the microscope.

I've produced a few "studies in bad timing" in my life. One stellar example was a book I coauthored with the brilliant business strategist David Ticoll, *The Naked Corporation: How the Age of Transparency Will Revolutionize Business*. As people researching how technology changes things, we became interested in how the Internet would change the use and communication of information. We defined *transparency* as "access to pertinent information by stakeholders." By *pertinent*, we meant information that can help if you have it and hurt if you don't.

It has been over a decade since the book was published. We argued that the corporation is becoming naked, and as a result will have no choice but to rethink values and behaviors—for the better. Our tagline was "you're going to be naked, so you'd better be buff!" Reviewers either loved the book or hated it, and sales were modest. My deepest regret, in hindsight, was that clearly the book was not read and heeded by the leaders of our financial services industries. Lacking "fitness," they brought down the industry and with it the global economy.

To paraphrase Victor Hugo, there is nothing so powerful as an idea whose time has come—again. To build trusting relationships and succeed in a transparent economy, growing numbers of firms in all parts of the globe are being forced to behave more responsibly than ever. Disgraced banks represent the old model, a dying breed. Business integrity is on the rise, not just for legal or purely ethical reasons but because it makes economic sense. Companies need to do good—act with integrity—not just to secure a healthy business environment, but for their own sustainability and competitive advantage. Firms that exhibit ethical values, openness, and candor have discovered that they can better compete and profit.

Of course many companies are still shrouded in secrecy. And there is an epic battle shaping up between the forces of transparency and the forces of opacity. Furthermore, it makes sense to have some corporate secrets. However, today's winners increasingly "undress for success." Our research suggests that open corporations tend to perform better. Transparency is a new form of power, which pays off when harnessed. Rather than to be feared, transparency is becoming central to business success. Rather than be unwillingly stripped, smart firms are choosing to be open. Over time, what we call "open enterprises"—firms that operate with candor, integrity, and engagement—are most likely to survive and thrive. And any bank executive who thinks he or she can return to the old ways long term is mistaken.

Get ready for a growing debate on the role of the corporation in the new economy. Societies grant firms a license to operate and increasingly people everywhere are demanding appropriate behavior. The main axis of this battle will be with the "Masters of the Universe" that run Wall Street. In other industries—like manufacturing, retail, and technology—companies have improved their behavior, largely out of market pressures that transparency brings. But the financial services industry is home to executives who are shielded from such pressures and who innovate complex financial instruments, maneuver, and do deals shrouded in secrecy. They will be the last to change; and evidence suggests they will not go willingly.

The Case of Apple

You are being reasonable to criticize the perspective outlined above, arguing that it is obviated by the success of one company —Apple. Apple has been called "the world's most secretive company." It seems to hoard its intellectual property (IP). It's sitting on $160 billion of cash reserves, and it is a philanthropic miser. Foxconn, the high-profile electronics company that builds Apple's iPhone and other products in China, has been in and out of the headlines for poor working conditions, worker riots at its Taiyuan factory, and a series of employee suicides.

Fang Zhongyang, one of the factory workers, told *Bloomberg BusinessWeek*:

> The guards here use gangster style to manage. We are not against following rules, but you have to tell us why. They won't explain things, and we feel like we cannot communicate with them.

A labor rights group reported that Foxconn workers had gone on strike over production demands for the iPhone 5. The company denied there was a strike.

Although employees at Apple and Foxconn are treated very differently, the two companies are known for keeping their workers and others in the dark. Yet both are enormously successful, causing many people to question whether the popular management advice in favor of "openness" actually makes business sense.

I was reminded of this when speaking at last year's TEDGlobal Conference. The conference's theme was "radical openness," an idea I helped develop a number of years ago in *The Naked Corporation*.

My talk argued that "openness" has several meanings, and for each there is a corresponding principle. One meaning of openness refers to "transparency," with a company making available pertinent information to stakeholders such as customers, employees, business partners, and shareholders. I believe companies can often benefit from being more transparent with these groups. Another meaning of openness applies to the "sharing of intellectual assets." I believe a company can benefit by sharing some of its (IP), given the right conditions.

But when you look closely at Apple, a different picture emerges. Apple has become more open in a number of areas, and the pressures of the market forces I describe are forcing it to open up even further.

To begin, Apple is more transparent than one might think. Like all companies, it has four major stakeholders: customers, employees, business partners, and shareholders.

Apple is obviously super-secretive with its customers about product announcements. And at the moment it can get away with this behavior because it is so powerful in the niche markets in which it operates, and it has a small array of products. But as it tries to expand its share of the corporate market, business customers will demand to be well-briefed regarding Apple's intentions and its product road maps.

Research in Motion (RIM) is a good example of this. The struggling company was forced to share details about its BlackBerry 10 platform before its release, trying feverishly to pump up the buzz around the software to encourage its customers to stay loyal and developers to make apps. And as Apple's iOS continues to lag well behind Android in market share, eventually it will also be forced to be more open with consumers.

Apple's customers aren't alone in being kept in the dark; the company treats its employees the same way. The vast majority of them have few details about what is in the company's product pipeline. But such opacity does not derive from some inherent benefits of closed work systems. Rather, it is purely to ensure the secrecy of its product strategy from its customers.

Apple doesn't want its workers leaking information to the media or the blogosphere. But increasingly Apple pays a price for this employee secrecy. It doesn't get the serendipitous collaboration across company silos that many other businesses enjoy. That, among other things, could have prevented the premature release of defective mapping software on the iPhone 5. Think of Google and how its workers are encouraged to dream up new products.

In terms of its supply chain, Apple itself has huge transparency and visibility. It can see down through Foxconn all the way down to suppliers, two levels below. True, this visibility has not been extended to the rest of the world, but in this age of transparency Apple can no longer keep its supply chain practices secret.

As a result, everyone knows about Foxconn's labor relations: how its factories are run under tight security; how its employees are treated and compensated poorly. This is an enormous problem for Apple, not just for its reputation, but also the disruptions such working conditions can cause in the supply chain. So as Apple becomes naked, it is being forced to get buff—to clean up its supply chain practices.

In 2012, a report on working conditions at Foxconn by auditors from the Fair Labor Association, a watchdog group hired by Apple, found serious violations of worker rights and salaries too low to cover living expenses. Foxconn promised to improve conditions, and Apple said, "We think empowering workers and helping them understand their rights is essential."[1]

As for transparency with its shareholders, Apple is actually very open. It is respected as being one of the best companies on the planet for providing shareholders with pertinent information. The only area in which it had been faulted is whether it had been sufficiently candid about Steve Jobs's declining health.

Paradoxically, Apple's success is largely due to another kind of openness. The iPhone or iPad are nice pieces of hardware, but that's not what created their market success. By opening up what are called "application programming interfaces," Apple has enabled its customers and the world of software developers to build apps on its platform. In this sense, Apple's corporate borders are quite open and porous. It is a design-and-marketing company at the heart of an enormous business web of suppliers and software developers, based on openness.

To be sure, Apple is obsessed with guarding its intellectual property and it has sought refuge in outmoded intellectual property laws and in courts that today stifle innovation in our economy. But increasingly this comes at a cost, too. Android, the open-source software platform developed by Google, quickly became the dominant operating system in the mobile marketplace. Open-source software stimulates creativity and attracts attention, and over time openness tends to win out in the market.

Google was smart to release the Android software's inner workings so that manufacturers could tweak the operating system to their specific devices. Other companies have made equally smart moves. IBM gave away $400 million worth of software to the open-source Linux movement and in exchange received billions of dollars in savings and new business.

Apple also has failed miserably in terms of sharing within society and the global community. It is not only sitting on mountains of cash, but during the Jobs era Apple made little effort to be a good corporate citizen and reach out to the larger community. It has long provided lower-cost computers to schools and universities, but purely as a marketing strategy, and otherwise has done little to help America's education system. It has been a philanthropic miser and has declined to take part in important social partnerships.

With Tim Cook's appointment as CEO in 2011, Apple seems to be increasingly aware that in the long term, business cannot succeed in a world that's failing. It has started to make more donations and is joining social causes, which will prove popular with its customers, especially with young people who increasingly want to do business with companies that behave well.

In fact, it would be in the interests of shareholders and customers for Apple to take a portion of its $160 billion in cash and apply it to transforming some important institutions like education. Such a bold move would benefit everyone, including shareholders, and Apple could be positioned to dominate some important emerging markets.

The conclusion is that Apple became the world's most valuable company for a number of complex reasons, including the design genius of its brilliant founder. But when you look under the surface, it is more open than you might think, and there is no real evidence that Its secrecy has helped it succeed. Increasingly, as it comes under more intense competitive pressures, Apple will need to become an even more open company.

The Internet and Western Democracy

Most Americans think that the U.S. Congress is dysfunctional and deeply corrupt. And for good reason. U.S. politicians are beholden to wealthy contributors and interest groups, and many members of Congress go on to become lobbyists. The insurance industry prevented the country from joining the rest of the developed world with a single payer health-care system. Fully 92% of Americans want background checks of people buying guns, but the rich and powerful National Rifle Association (NRA) thwarts any legislation. The notion that Congress is "government of the people, by the people, for the people" is risible.

The same problems loom across the Atlantic. The British were outraged by their MPs' secretive and outlandish expense claims. Italians were appalled by the immoral and illegal actions of former Prime Minister Silvio Berlusconi. Everywhere, it seems government leaders are behaving badly. Mayor Rob Ford of Toronto and his crack-smoking binge-drinking habits generated headlines around the world. New Jersey Governor Chris Christie's office closed bridges in order to create traffic jams to punish those who didn't vote for him. And there is now open discussion among leading thinkers that global institutions like the United Nations or the World Bank are no longer "fit for function." Many wonder if global problems are just too hard to solve, or if our model is outdated and inadequate.

This points to a much bigger problem—an emerging crisis of legitimacy of our democratic institutions. A growing number of citizens aren't voting, reasoning that their ballots won't change anything. Not since the dawn of universal suffrage In the established democracies have voters been angrier with their governors. Nor have so many citizens in so many countries acted on the bumper sticker exhortation: "Don't Vote! It Only Encourages Them!"

During the past 20 years, voter turnout has dropped in most Western democracies, in some cases quite dramatically. In the 1992 U.S. presidential election, 89.9% of voters went to the polls. In the 2012 contest, the turnout plunged to 66.6%. Voter turnout has also fallen in countries such as the United Kingdom, France, Germany, Italy, Sweden, and Canada. In particular, young people are looking for ways other than voting to bring about social change and a new youth radicalization is fully underway. The American political sociologist Seymour Martin Lipset wrote that legitimacy is "the capacity of a political system to engender and maintain the belief that existing political institutions are the most appropriate and proper ones for the society."[2]

The ongoing abuse of trust by office holders is not simply a series of isolated incidents, but manifestations of a deep and widespread rot. The result is a full-blown crisis in legitimacy. We need more than changes to politics. It's time to reinvent democracy itself.

The first era of democracy created "representative institutions." But with weak mandates, passive citizens, and politicians beholden to powerful funders and special interests, we now have "broadcast democracy." It was only a matter of time before such a model would run its course.

We need to replace this old model with a new era of "participatory democracy" built around five principles: integrity, accountability, interdependence, engagement with citizens, and transparency.

Integrity. Integrity is basically about doing the right thing. To rebuild the public's trust in political institutions, elected officials need to embrace integrity, which is honesty and consideration. Honest politicians establish trusting relationships with voters. Politicians need to be open and fairly disclose information. They must be truthful, accurate, and complete in communications. They must not mislead or be perceived to mislead.

Considerate officials don't cause traffic jams for those who disagree with them. They have regard for the interests, desires, or feelings of others, especially the electorate. They don't spy on their citizens and undermine their basic right to privacy. They don't kill good political discussion with negative attack ads. Politicians everywhere know that negative advertising is toxic to democracy, poisons reasoned political debate, and dumbs down the discussion. Nevertheless, they trash their opponents with attack ads alienating voters and adding to the legitimacy crisis.

Accountability to the Electorate. We need to divorce politicians from relying on big money. In the United States, citizens thought they had a system that limited big donations, but the right-wing Supreme Court clearly became alarmed at the possibility of wealthy donors not being able to influence elections. In the notorious Citizens United case, the court effectively lifted the limits on political donations, and a casino magnate promptly pledged $100 million to fight Obama's reelection. Stanford Law Professor Larry Lessig is right that the United States needs to adopt the policies of other countries that place strict controls on campaign financing.

Interdependence. Elected officials need to recognize that the public, private sector, and civil society all have a role to play in sustaining a healthy society. As Jeffrey Sachs has argued, there is a price to civilization and we need strong, good government. When politicians say the best role of government is "to get out of the way," they are shirking their responsibilities. Strong regulations saved Canadian banks from being sucked into the U.S. subprime mortgage crisis. The Canadian banks and Canada are healthier because of this. Similarly corporations and nongovernmental organizations (NGOs) are becoming pillars of society, and we all need new ways of collaborating on shared interests.

Engagement with Citizens. We need on-going mechanisms for government to benefit from the wisdom and insight that a nation can collectively offer. Using the Internet, citizens can become involved, learn from each other, take responsibility for their communities and country, and learn from and influence elected officials, and vice versa. It is now possible to have a three-day "digital brainstorm" with the electorate of a country. Challenges, participatory budgeting, and electronic town halls have all proven effective in turning voters into participants in democracy.

Transparency. Almost everything should be done in the full light of day. Sunshine is the best disinfectant, and the Internet is the perfect vehicle to achieve this. Transparency is critical to trust. The question "What are they hiding?" encapsulates the relationship between transparency and trust. It implies that if government leaders hold secrets, they do so for a nefarious reason and therefore are not deserving of trust. Citizens know that the fewer secrets leaders keep, the more likely they will be trusted.

Transparency, even radical transparency, is becoming central to building trust between stakeholders and their institutions. To restore legitimacy and trust, we need a second era of democracy based on integrity and accountability, with stronger, more open institutions, active citizen citizenship, and a culture of public discourse and participation.

Promise or Peril?

The final chapter of *The Digital Economy* is worth a read. It raises deep concerns about the impact of the digital revolution on issues like employment, equity in society, democracy, quality of life, and global problems. Reflecting on this list, the last 20 years and projecting forward to the next 20 years, I must confess to being deeply concerned about the future.

The Internet has bestowed many wonders on us, accelerating innovation, connecting us more than ever before, helping us learn, and making life more fun. But these wonders have not fully translated into the benefits that really matter in society: full employment, social development, societal cohesion, security, true empowerment, protection of our planet, governments that act in our interests, and peace. Astonishingly the world is becoming more unequal, more unsustainable, and more conflicted.

Is it possible that the digital revolution is unfolding at a pace that outstrips our ability as humans, corporations, governments, and societies to comprehend, let alone manage or embrace it? After decades of doubling and redoubling, we are now achieving gargantuan leaps in all facets of information technologies, in keeping with the second half of the chessboard metaphor I described in Chapter 4. We see mind-boggling acceleration in computing power, storage capacity, and bandwidth. Examples are everywhere, from Intel's computer chips to low-cost consumer electronics. When the MP3 player debuted in 1998, it stored less than a dozen songs. Now 160-gigabyte iPods store 40,000 songs. Network bandwidth is now limited by our demand not their capacity. The recent Consumer Electronics Show had 22,000 new products released. Google CEO Eric Schmidt first made the now-famous aphorism that between the dawn of civilization and 2003 there were 5 exabytes of data collected (an exabyte equals 1 quintillion bytes). Today 5 exabytes of data get collected every 2 days. Soon there will be 5 exabytes every few minutes.

Most of us are wondering what this environment is doing to the way we process information, learn, and even think. Young people—digital natives—seem to be more adept at dealing with this new environment. I'm hopeful that the changes to their brains of growing up digital will be positive ones. But many people worry, and justifiably so, as there is much that we don't know about the human brain and human behavior. Will we all end up in "the shallows" as Nicholas Carr describes in his book *The Shallows: What the Internet Is Doing to Our Brains*,[3] where we lose our capacity for deep thought? Will we abandon reading deeper and longer works to end up flittering around from one data source to another, like a bee in a garden of flowers? Will this affect our relationships with others as we are consumed by thousands of weak ties on social media and have less time for our real friends and those we love? Will this new world change not only how we think and relate but also how we are—what kinds of values we have and stand for?

I've written that we need to adopt a much more take-charge attitude about how we manage these tools and all this information, and for that matter how we live. More than ever before, we need to step back and consciously design our lives. We need to decide explicitly what we stand for and whether we are the slave or the master of the new technologies.

When I was a kid, life for my parents was blissfully simpler. There was one daily newspaper in our house and three TV channels. Dad went to work. Mum didn't. Workers put in their hours in factories or planned their day at the office, with the only source of interruption being the telephone. We had clear values—taught by our mother in the home and reinforced weekly at church. There was no pornography in the house or for that matter even on the newsstands in our town. This was the late 1950s, and the cause célèbre was whether Ed Sullivan would show Elvis Presley grinding his pelvis on Sullivan's hugely popular Sunday night TV variety show. The decision: No. All images of Elvis were from the waist up.

Smart companies are taking initiatives to help their employees cope with the new technology-rich world. They give their employees training on time management and becoming values-based enterprises. They ensure that integrity is part of their corporate DNA. They design business models, structures, and business processes to ensure that work systems best serve the organization and maximize the effectiveness of its people.

Smart people and families should do the same. On the personal front, most of us in our daily lives, at work, and in our families muddle through this new data-rich, networked world hopping from device to device, app to app, decision to decision, or crisis to crisis without an overarching strategy. All of us should be applying principles of design to our lives. Make conscious choices about how to upgrade your capacity to filter data and about when to use new technologies and what to believe in.

Adopt a values statement for yourself and your family—and constantly revise it as the world and conditions change. Don't complain about technological overload. Know how to adjust and even turn off the shower. Harness the power of new technologies and transparency for the good, design them, rather than having them control you.

Hundreds of years ago, Martin Luther called the printing press "God's highest act of grace." With today's communications revolution we have been bestowed with a second great act of grace. We have an historic occasion to rebuild business and the world. Hopefully we will have the wisdom and the will to seize the time. Personally I have come to the conclusion that there are countless battles and conflicts shaping up and that the period ahead will be very difficult, which is the theme of my next book. Stay tuned.

Notes

1. John Paczkowski, *Fair Labor Association Wins Some OT Relief for Apple's Foxconn Workers*, allthingd.com, March 29, 2012, http://allthingsd.com/20120329/fairlabor-association -wins-some-ot-relief-for-apples-foxconn-workers/.
2. Seymour Martin Lipset, *Political Man: The Social Bases of Politics*, 2nd ed., Heinemann, 1983, p. 64.
3. Nicolas Carr, *The Shallows: What the Internet Is Doing to Our Brains*, New York: W.W. Norton, 2010.

THE NEW RESPONSIBILITIES OF BUSINESS

Like the printing press, the new computer media will bring forth its own very special ways to think about the complexities we have not been able to deal with up to now—especially for complex chaotic systems such as the AIDS epidemic and the ecological balance of our planet. But much care has to be taken ... in order for the change to be positive. We don't have natural defenses against fat, sugar, salt, alcohol, alkaloids—or media.... Television should be the last mass communications medium to be naively designed and put into the world without a surgeon-general's warning!

Alan Kay, Apple Computer[1]

This is a time of promise and of peril. There are storm warnings that go far beyond concerns about privacy. Rising inequalities and dislocations are leading to a breakdown in the social fabric. The growing discordance has huge social ramifications. The dark side of the new economy is posing profound questions regarding leadership for the transformation underway, and it is placing, I believe, new responsibilities on business. The business community needs to rethink many assumptions about its role in the economy and society.

For example, there is a growing concentration of wealth and income in the United States that exceeds all other developed countries. According to the Federal Reserve, 1% of American households own nearly 40% of the nation's wealth. The top 20% of American households—worth $180,000 or more—own 80% of the country's wealth. Wealth and income skewing is accelerating faster in the United States than in any other developed nation. The rich are getting richer, and it's not just the poor who are getting poorer—so is everyone else. Moreover, this is happening faster on a scale greater than ever before or anywhere else.[2] Because the development of the new economy is most advanced in the United States, this should give us and the rest of the world cause for concern regarding what the future holds.

To what extent are these conjunctional problems caused by the recession of the early 1990s, tax cuts to the rich in the 1980s, windfall profits from the markets, or other short-term factors? Can these problems be eliminated as the new infrastructure grows in capacity, function, and penetration? Or are these problems endemic to the new economy, only to be exacerbated as the internet and new economic relations are extended throughout society?

Will the internet be used not only to further stratify society (as a result of some people having access and others not) but to accelerate cocooning of the wealthy from everyone else, particularly from the growing underclass? Will we create new electronic communities on the Net where we identify more closely with our new neighbors in cyberspace than with the people in our physical communities—possibly changing our concept of local responsibilities? For all the talk about a global village, we still live in physical villages and cities and nation-states where, at least in the past, we have felt some responsibility to those around us. In the past we have held that public services and a social safety net were important, and we were willing to pay taxes to support public services. As we shift into cybercommunities, will that sense of local and national responsibility fade? Concern about these questions is reflected in a controversial *Harper's Magazine* article by Christopher Lasch:

> To an alarming extent, the privileged classes—by an expansive definition, the top 20 percent have made themselves independent.... They send their children to [private] schools, insure themselves against medical emergencies by enrolling in company-supported plans, and hire private security guards to protect themselves against mounting violence. It is not just that they see no point in paying for public services they no longer use; many of them have ceased to think of themselves as Americans in any important sense, implicated in America's destiny for better or for worse. Their ties to an international culture of work and leisure—of business, entertainment, information and "information retrieval"—make many members of the elite deeply indifferent to the prospect of national decline.[3]

The Age of Networked Intelligence is creating a borderless world where nation-states become less important. Money, communications, business transactions, and information are becoming bits that lack awareness and respect for national boundaries.

Other data about life in the new economy should give us cause for concern. If the new economy is creating new wealth, why do an estimated 25% of U.S. children live in poverty (a rate four times that of Europe and up from 15% in the past 20 years)?[4] Why do 35 million people in the United States have no health care? This generation of American children will be the first generation to experience a lower standard of living than their parents. Infant mortality ranks with some of the poorest Third World countries despite much higher per-capita health-care costs compared with other Western economies. Many people are becoming socially and economically marginalized through the growth of drug use. A murder takes place every 21 minutes; a rape every 5 minutes; a robbery every 48 seconds.[5] Correctional institutions are a growth business, with an American incarceration rate of five times that of other developed countries. Homelessness is a national disgrace. In 1995 the term "Third World country inside our country" became popular to describe the situation. At the same time, tens of millions of people learn daily how to hate a scapegoat by listening to talk radio and carrying out the new vanguard practices at a local militia camp.

Internationally, the situation is little better. The former Soviet bloc is a mess—with over 25% of the population voting for a fascist leader in Russia. Polarization is the product of discordance. In the 1995 French election more than one-third of the population voted for the extreme fascist right or Marxist left. In Latin America, Africa, and some parts of Asia, rural displacement has created urban nightmares of poverty, disease, crime, and despair.

The internet and the new economy offer promise and the hope for solutions. Former communist and undeveloped countries can leapfrog others in creating new infrastructures and generating new competitive economies. In doing so, they can begin the process of job creation and improving quality of life, but unplanned economic development can have devastating effects. For example, consider that 20% of the world's population inhabiting the developed countries consume 80% of the world's resources. (The average U.S. citizen consumes 50 times more steel; 56 times more energy; 170 times more newsprint; 250 times more fuel; and 300 times more plastic than the average Indian citizen.) Raising the level of consumption in the underdeveloped world to U.S. levels could, in the twenty-first century, result in a total ecological catastrophe. If, by 2050, world population reaches the expected (conservative estimate) of 11.5 billion inhabitants living on the level of U.S. 1988 standards, world petroleum reserves will be used up in 7 years; aluminum in 18; copper in 4; zinc in 3; carbon in 34; to mention only a few key minerals.[6] And more gravely, the rate of world pollution will have quadrupled. What kind of world will the new economy bring for our children? These are issues that thoughtful businesspeople cannot ignore.

Employment and Jobs

The Issue: What will be the impact of the new technology on employment? Firms need to understand this issue to plan their workforce and develop strategies for interenterprise partnering. More broadly, shifts in employment will strongly affect labor markets, consumer market growth, demands on the social safety net, government deficits, and social stability.

The relationship between technological growth and employment has always been complex, but no previous technological innovation matches the power and potential significance of the internet. This is leading to broad concern and debate about the potential impact of the information highway on jobs. Many commentators are cynical. For example, a recent article states, "[Promoters] say the [information] highway will be paved with jobs. Yet how is it that every week a phone company or computer company announces massive layoffs?"[7] Notwithstanding the difficulties some companies experience in weathering the first restructuring of the new information technology sector, the data show that this industry is the engine of economic growth and high-paying, high-value jobs.

In the United States the new media sector is close to 10% of the GDP. According to the U.S. Department of Commerce, business and consumer spending on information technology has accounted for 36% of economic growth since 1990. Individuals in the field fare better, too. Income of computer programmers since 1990 has risen 12% for males and 21% for females, compared to 6% and 13% for all male and female workers respectively. The United States is also running a huge ($3 billion) trade surplus in computer-related services.[8] World trade is growing five times more quickly in knowledge-related goods and services than in resources. Information technology (excluding content) in Canada in 1995 was almost a $50 billion dollar industry and accounted for more than 6% of the GDP. Most new employment is being created in software and services; the balance of payments for IT services is seeing unprecedented growth. The software industry alone is responsible for 21% of all R&D in Canada.[9] European and Japanese hardware manufacturers, software companies, information systems, and network services providers have been growing strongly for years.[10] Revenues of software firms selling to large international companies have grown by more than 150% between 1988 and 1992, and information services have grown by more than 70%. Texas Instruments is Japan's most competitive producer of chips.[11] Sales of the Japanese information services industry grew by more than 300% between 1985 and 1991.[12]

There is, however, a larger point. Information technology is not just a sector but the basis of all sectors as we enter an economy based on computer networks. As the "service economy" grew in the 1980s, there was much hand-wringing that most of the population would end up in low-paying jobs flipping burgers, changing beds, or working retail. The concern is no longer justified. As Michael Mandel says: "The worry was that if the United States lost its manufacturing industries, it would have a difficult time selling enough services abroad to pay for its imports of cars, consumer electronics, and other goods. [But] fear not: Like adolescence, the service economy has turned out to be a temporary stage."[13]

Furthermore, there is strong evidence that the wage gaps and productivity gaps between manufacturing and services are narrowing. For example, in 1992 the median goods-producing job paid only $19 per week more than the median service job, according to an unpublished study by the Federal Reserve Bank of Cleveland.[14] Most companies are trying to reinvent themselves for the new competitive, global marketplace; people and information are the critical resources for transformation. In most cases, new employment growth is not occurring in large companies but in start-ups and smaller companies. The internet is the engine of new employment, and unlike previous predictions, most jobs are not low-skilled service jobs but high-value and high-paying jobs.

However, success of individual companies does not translate into full employment in the society as a whole. Many larger companies have sought "strategic efficiencies," such as downsizing, rather than effectiveness. The recession of the early 1990s, coupled with the awkward gestation of the new economy and the downward pressures on the cost structure of Western companies caused by the end of the Cold War, forced many companies to restructure their cost base. Reengineering was a response to this situation. As explained in Chapter 1, the primary objective of nearly all reengineering programs has been to cut costs through the streamlining of business processes.

The main types of employees targeted were middle managers, operators, and clerical workers; this trend will continue. According to the Bureau of Labor Statistics, between 1992 and 2005 a number of job types will decline by a significant percentage: computer operators (39%); billing, posting, and calculating machine operators (29%); telephone operators (28%); typists and word processing operators (16%); and bank tellers (4%).

The new technologies will also contribute to downsizing. Unlike reengineering, however, the likely targets will shift to front-line customer service employees, professionals, and middle-to-senior managers as they become disintermediated and as customers become "prosumers." We can expect reductions in many types of jobs, including agents (sales, real estate, life insurance, travel), wholesalers (food, dry goods, clothing), teachers (primary and high school), distributors (postal workers, retail trade), to name a few. Moreover, the extension of the new technologies into the manufacturing sector is likely to accelerate the decline of that sector as a contributor to employment in the developed countries. Manufacturing automation technologies are judged to have reduced employment in that sector from 34% of all American employment in 1950 to 17% in 1990.[15]

In the past, job loss has always been more than compensated for by a parallel process of job creation in new industries, firms, and occupations. Technological change has led to higher real incomes and greater employment.[16] But just as companies that don't embrace the technology will become uncompetitive, any nation that dallies will also face competitive decline—facing the specter of massive structural unemployment. Capital and jobs will be attracted to economies with state-of-the-art infrastructures and innovative, affordable services. Countries that lag in developing the new information highways will tend to become backwaters of economic activity.

Japan and Europe have already fallen far behind in this race. Japan has only a third as many PCs as the United States per capita. Only 10% of Japanese businesspeople use PCs, and only 13% of those are connected to networks, compared to over 50% in the United States, where there are 50 million computers. Only 20 years ago, there were 50,000 computers in the world; now that many are being installed daily. In the United States more than two-thirds of homes are connected to cable, but only 10% in Japan.[17] The main impediments are likely the difficulties of accessing devices with a Japanese character-set keyboard, overregulation, and a strong hierarchical model of the organization that discourages individuals from creating, presenting, and realizing innovative ideas and breakthrough concepts.

The same problems of overregulation and stubborn hierarchical structures have inhibited the evolution of networks and new technology in Europe as well. Notwithstanding some bold investments such as France's Minitel (most homes have a telephone-based VDT that provides them access to directory information and other information services), the lack of a competitive telephone market has left much of Europe with antiquated telephone systems, not to mention a slow start on the information highway. However, the prospect of deregulation has heated up the investment environment. The European Union plans to invest $76 billion in the next five years for broadband networks and services.[18] Ironically, many countries may gain advantage over the United States because deregulation will eliminate local and long-distance monopolies at once.

Singapore illustrates that it is not only highly developed countries that are able to build an infrastructure. But are civil rights the price to pay for national leadership? Many developed countries are saddled with a massive installed base of the old networks and old technologies.[19] Most economists expect that technology-stimulated growth (economies, jobs) will be greatest in the developing world over the next decade. Overall, the evidence is strong that employment growth from new types of businesses, new sectors, and smaller entities will far outstrip the decline of the old megacorporation. Although there will be growth in many high-paying types of jobs by 2005 (including professional, growing 12% in terms of the share of total employment, and technical growing by 8.3%), there will also be a painful process of structural adjustment for the workforce involving skills, knowledge, tools, and location.

We can also expect that networking will dramatically affect the physical location of the workforce. This is already occurring. Citibank moved its back-office banking operations from Huntington, New York, to Sioux Falls, South Dakota. Regulations covering interest rates and out-of-state banks were changed to allow the new corporate citizen to take up residence, but without the new technology nothing would have been possible. As a result of the move, the local South Dakota economy boomed. Some 40% of the new Citibank employees had no jobs before Citibank hired them. Omaha, Nebraska, has followed a similar course and now calls itself the telemarketing capital of the world. The local economy enjoys full employment by using technology to gain leverage from its situation. In this case, Omaha had long been a site for the Strategic Air Command. So, when toll-free calling began, there was a natural fit between new ways of doing business and the telecommunications already in place.

In summary, some directions are emerging, as follows:

+ *Likely outcome:* Many larger companies and governments will seek and achieve downsizing, not only of clerical but also of professional and managerial staff, through the new technologies. In most sectors, small- and medium-sized companies that embrace internetworking effectively will tend to be more successful and will achieve growth in revenue and jobs.

- *Likely outcome:* The cumulative effect of growth in the new sector (convergence of computing, telecommunications, and content) combined with the stimulative effect of the new technology in the growth of small- and medium-sized companies will lead to significant employment growth for those developed countries that succeed in building a world-class infrastructure.
- *Likely outcome:* Japan and Europe are both in a catch-up mode, with the edge going to Europe. Growth in developing countries will be stronger than in the developed world.
- *Likely outcome:* There will be significant growth in high-paying jobs—in particular professional and technical—as well as some lower-paying jobs in the service industry. There will also be a significant decline in old economy jobs, including operators, administrative support, laborers, sales, and farm and forestry.
- *Likely outcome:* Networking will dramatically affect the physical location of the workforce as the proximity of knowledge workers to markets, plant, and other traditional factors become less important.

ACCESS AND EQUITY

The Issue: Is universal access of all persons regardless of income, disability, or location a desirable goal? If yes, how can it be feasibly and most readily achieved? Will differences in access to the internet create a two-tiered society, increasing gaps, for example, between haves and have-nots, knowers and know-nots, men and women, north and south, whites and minorities, skilled professionals and unskilled hourly workers? Concerns regarding these issues could slow consumer acceptance. Inappropriate mechanisms to achieve these goals could slow capital investment and the open evolution of the marketplace. Business leaders need to formulate views on these issues—not just the principle but implementation approaches.

Universal service has been an accepted principle since the early days of the post office, and it has been extended to telecommunications. Some 94% of U.S. households have telephones. Almost 100% have radios and televisions, two-thirds have a VCR, and 60% have cable TV. About one-quarter of households have a personal computer, a level that's growing quickly because personal computers now outsell televisions. But even with the relatively primitive technology of today, problems are arising because we are creating a new have and have-not society. Some smaller communities have antiquated telephone systems. Some Native-American communities have one phone in the whole community—often in a town hall that gets locked at night.

As technology becomes more important for economic success and social well-being, this problem will become more significant.

According to a 1995 survey of telephone and computer ownership conducted by the National Telecommunications and Information Administration, Washington, D.C., inner-city households in the Northeast have the smallest percentage of telephone subscribers, and rural poor are least likely to own a computer. Black households own the smallest percentage of computers among all inner-city racial groups, followed by inner-city Hispanics. Native-American households have the lowest level of telephone service 75.5% in rural areas. Rural blacks have the lowest rate of computer ownership, 6.4%. Among rural whites, 95.4% have telephone service and 24.6% own computers. Among racial categories, Asians have the highest computer ownership rate (36%), blacks the lowest (9.5%). About 28% of white households and 12% of Hispanic households have computers. According to the NTIA study, people over the age of 55 are least likely to own a computer, followed by households headed by people younger than 25.[20]

The federal government has recognized this problem in one of its five principles for the National Information Infrastructure: "Preserving and enhancing universal service to avoid creating a society of information 'haves' and 'have nots.'"[21] One goal is that by 2000, all classrooms, libraries, hospitals, and clinics in the United States will be connected to the NII (National Information Infrastructure). "This is not a matter of guaranteeing the right to play video games. It is a matter of guaranteeing access to essential services," says Vice President Gore. "We cannot tolerate—nor in the long run can this nation afford—a society in which some children become fully educated and others do not; in which some adults have access to training and lifetime education, and others do not. Nor can we permit geographic location to determine whether the information highway passes by your door."[22]

This perspective is not held by everyone. One industry leader recently stated, "People should have reasonable access to all and any services that they can reasonably afford."[23] However, there is a strong consensus emerging that this is one area that can't be left to the market.[24] The mechanisms for achieving access are less than clear, however. Notwithstanding difficulties in getting telecommunications legislation through Congress, the administration is seeking to achieve access and equity through the following steps:

♦ Making the preservation and enhancement of universal service an explicit objective of the Communications Act, in order to establish the goal that advanced services be available to rural and urban lower-income users, to users in areas where the costs of service are high, and to social institutions, especially schools and health-care facilities

- Charging the FCC and the states with continuing responsibility to review the definition of universal service to meet changing technological, economic, and societal circumstances
- Establishing a federal/state joint board to make recommendations concerning the FCC and state action on the fundamental elements of universal service. In its deliberations, the joint board must gather input from nongovernmental organizations
- Obliging those who provide telecommunications services to contribute to the preservation and advancement of universal service.[25]

As the information infrastructure expands, so will understanding and definition of the services deemed to be essential. And as the environment becomes less regulated, we need to take steps to ensure that technology is serving people.

Without access there can be no equity. A second key determinant of equity is, of course, education level. In the new economy those without knowledge (which is by definition specialized) will be marginalized. Already American men with postgraduate education have incomes 130% higher than those who did not complete high school. This gap is nearly double what it was in 1980, but technology can be a great leveler.

What about differences between men and women? The vast majority of Internet users are men—pointing to a potential problem. Yet many new-economy companies have a large proportion of women workers. Microsoft employs 17,000 people—over one-third are women. Peter Drucker and others have pointed out that knowledge work has no *gender bias*. Optimists conclude that we are moving into a new era of egalitarianism. Men and women should have equal opportunity in the new economy. There are no physiological requirements necessary for being a physician, systems analyst, engineer, or organizational consultant in a new-economy factory.

However, it wasn't physical demands of work that kept women out of the industrial economy or relegated them to lower-paying jobs in the first place. True, being a construction laborer may require considerable physical strength. But for most job types in the old economy women were not hampered primarily by their strength but by other factors. Women were seen as a reserve pool of labor and a source of cheap labor. In the steel plant or construction company, they worked as low-paid secretaries. But when it was deemed socially necessary, such as during World War II, they were moved onto the plant floor or the construction site. And "Rosie the Riveter" did just fine. When the war was over, the pictures of Rosie in *Life* magazine were replaced with photos of cheery women with baby prams or women working in their shiny kitchens waiting for their husbands to come home. The needs of business and the fabric of society determined women's fate, not some alleged physical, mental, or emotional inferiority.

However, the new media will forever destroy the "biology is destiny" justification for streaming women into lower-income vocations. In an economy where brains, not brawn, counts, and where networks enable people to participate fully in the economy, the reasons for income gaps and professional imbalances can only be viewed as societal, not chromosomal.

The new media actually provide many new vehicles for women to redress imbalances. In cyberspace no one needs to know what gender you are. Furthermore, research has shown that the new media provide opportunities to overcome gender differences. Computer conferencing (a written meeting taking place over a defined period of time) and Net discussion groups have been found to change criteria for leadership—moving the most succinct (often women), rather than the forceful and verbose, to the fore. Japan Telescene reports that many Japanese women are opting to visit Nissan's Internet site to get information on cars rather than brave the male-dominated showrooms. You can bet that if dealers want to stay in business they will make showrooms less gender-biased in the future.

And as for women who choose to be homemakers, the internet can reduce rather than increase isolation and stratification. The internet provides an infrastructure to network them and their families with others—friends, extended family, schools, community groups, churches. It provides a foundation for lifelong learning, so that should they return to the workforce, they will not have fallen behind. (All recent studies show that women who leave the workforce can expect to return at lower levels than they left.) It provides a basis for income generation as economic activity moves onto the internet.

As for differences between old and young, there is little doubt that the generation of 10- to 25-year-olds are effortlessly embracing the new media. Rather than a generation gap, there is a danger of a *generation lap* where cyberspace is part of life for one generation and an uncomfortable place for preceding ones. But senior citizens need not fall behind. The Department of Veterans Affairs worried that veterans would reject electronic banking of payments; its concerns were misplaced. The woodworking class in an East Coast veterans' center has low enrollment; there is a long lineup for the PC class. If there is access and if there is societal will for equity, technology can help to reduce gaps, not increase them. But those are two big "ifs."

Quality of Life

The Issue: What will happen to quality of work life (QWL) and quality of life overall in the digital economy? Both perception and reality need to be managed on the organizational and societal levels. Concerns about extreme deterioration of quality of life are retarding consumer acceptance. Actual deterioration in quality of life for most people is unnecessary and undesirable. But managers need new knowledge and skills to design the new work systems—sociotechnical systems that jointly optimize social and technological components of the new work, with the joint objective of dramatically improving performance on the one hand and worker motivation, satisfaction, and QWL on the other. More broadly, far-reaching issues are raised about life in the Age of Networked Intelligence.

Discussion of the possibility of mothers working from home often conjures up fears of pieceworkers teleworking in isolation in their basements. That's a debate that has raged for years. Now, as business is poised to move onto the Net, the debate is moving to new levels of intensity. Some skeptics have raised the specter of a disembodied, contingent workforce toiling from home over a keyboard. Others point to the impact of the first era of IT in creating some pretty deadening jobs. Although it is just beginning, new directions are emerging regarding what work can and may be like in the digital economy. Some of these themes are positive and some are not.

Theme 1: The Shift to Knowledge Work Increases the Potential for Satisfying Work

The new economy is a knowledge-based economy, raising new potential for quality of work life (QWL). In popular vernacular, this means a shift to the white-collar job—up from 20% of the workforce in 1900 to almost 60% today. Blue-collar work has declined from almost 40% of the workforce to just over 20% today—a level that does not fully reflect the fact that many production, agricultural, construction, and other jobs are becoming knowledge work. Knowledge-based jobs tend to require greater skills and have greater variety and potential for good QWL.

It is true that many jobs involving computer systems have entailed deadly and boring routines. In early days, systems were single function, and job design alternatives were restricted. For example, when word processing came along, many companies took away all the interesting things that secretaries did and made them single-task, power keyboarders. This latter day Taylorism—which assigns a single task to a worker—created results for companies and employees that were not happy.[26]

Most authorities in organizational design have come to the conclusion that Taylorism is now inappropriate, especially compared to the new approaches of building high performance work systems enabled by new media technologies. In the new era we have multifunction work/learn stations that integrate data, text, voice, image, and (soon) video. This has far-reaching implications for the design of jobs and work systems, making it possible to design "whole jobs" and high-performance work systems that actually significantly improve quality of work life.

There is no joy in unproductive activities—playing telephone tag, waiting for things to happen, looking for information, duplicating work. People receive job fulfillment from productive work, which more and more is enabled by the new technology. Furthermore, the new enterprise and work systems cannot succeed without high employee motivation and identification. In the new economy, high-performance work systems and quality of work life tend to go hand in hand.

Theme 2: The Concept of a "Job for Life" Is Declining

Given the opportunity of networks to enable new ways of structuring work, many companies are attempting to create a flexible "contingent workforce." Blue Cross/Blue Shield of Rhode Island reduced its workforce in a time of retrenching without laying off any full-time employees. Similarly, companies can "staff up" rapidly to meet the demands of new opportunities. The internet-worked enterprise reaches out through technology to individuals and other entities to respond to its human resource and business demands. On a more cynical note, use of knowledge workers on a part-time basis can reduce costs, because such workers are often paid fees equivalent to their old salaries without the benefits and overhead (often calculated to equal 40% of salary costs).

As for the knowledge workers themselves, many actually prefer such arrangements, which provide improved work variety and opportunity for skill enhancement. Contract employment and self-employment are growing, the number of new businesses is skyrocketing, and part-time employment is growing as people look for more flexible arrangements to enable them to manage the challenges of working and family life.

As for the QWL implications of this trend, the jury is out. Many "sole practitioners" say there is no other way. They report enjoying the autonomy and independence they require; they take responsibility for the development of their own custom knowledge; they can increase their incomes through competition for their services; and they have a variety of work experiences. Many commentators, however, worry about undermining one of the primary sources of self-esteem and personal security—the job. As one put it: "The danger I see is that the intangible but indispensable values I discovered at work will be lost: the sense of community, the shared goals, the spirited exchange of ideas, the pride of achievement."[27]

There is, however, no reason (other than the intransigence of old paradigms) that should prevent management and, for that matter, societies, from creating a new kind of contract between employers and themselves. Whether part-time, mobile, teleworking, contingent, contract, or all of the above, the experience to date shows that relationships can be forged that are based on clear expectations, mutual support and trust, commitment, and community.

Theme 3: The Concept of a "Career" Is Declining

The theme of organizational learning has been driving many efforts for corporate reinvention for half a decade. The idea—popularized by Peter Senge—is that companies will be able to compete only if they can learn, as organizations, faster than their competitors. Companies need to overcome their organizational learning disabilities to be able to learn and constantly change to meet changing demands. Just as companies need to be able to learn continuously for their ongoing transformation, so individuals need to undertake lifelong learning. In the old economy, individuals learned a skill, trade, or profession, and they simply kept up with changes in that field. In the new economy, individuals can expect to fundamentally change their knowledge base and skill set several times throughout their working lives.

The majority of office workers in the United States have learned to use a very new and different tool over the past decade and a half—the computer. More important, they are now learning how to make decisions, handle information, and communicate differently. They are learning new ways to design buildings, save patients, and plan urban communities. In the future they will learn whole new areas of human professional activity.

This raises challenges for management and workers alike. Management must take significant responsibilities for knowledge development, knowing full well that they are equipping their employees or contractors with skills applicable to other organizations. And employees or contractors must also invest continuously in their own development. But despite the large amount of company-sponsored training, U.S. employers are still spending relatively little—1.4% of payroll. And according to research by *Training* magazine, spending by U.S. companies with more than 100 employees was up only 11% in the period from 1990 to 1994—less than the inflation rate.[28]

Theme 4: There Are Far-Reaching Issues of Compensation, Income, and the Social Distribution of the Benefits of the New Economy, That We Are Only Now Beginning to Tackle

Over the past decade real incomes of the vast majority of the workforce have declined. This trend is worst for high school dropouts (–23%); bad for high school graduates (–14%); and still bad for college graduates (–7%). At the same time that incomes are dropping, management is requiring workers to be highly motivated, customer-focused, capable, constantly upgrading their knowledge and skills, and accepting of ever-increasing responsibilities—empowered. The storm warnings were there years ago when I wrote in a 1981 book on office automation:

> When it comes to employment and quality of work life, computers are a double-edged sword. To date they have resulted in a net growth in jobs and a net improvement in the interesting, creative, and skill-demanding positions available in the work force. Yet they have also destroyed many specific jobs and even occupations in the process, while at the same time created very tedious and alienating positions. Unfortunately, people, when discussing the problem, often look only at one edge or the other.

We are soon entering a period where the nature of work and social organization will change and a question is posed: How will the benefits of the new technologies be distributed? Without such distribution it is likely in the short term and even in the long term that large numbers of people will see only the negative side of the sword. These people [will be] confronted with a glaring contradiction: the magnificent potential of the technology versus a reality in which they are the victims of technological progress."[29]

In the new economy the means of production increasingly become the minds of the producers. More and more it is knowledge that creates wealth. The key assets of a company shift from money and physical plant to the intellectual—skill, knowledge, and information. Business awareness of this issue is now at the point where cover stories in major business magazines discuss the challenges of measuring intellectual capital.[30] However, although means of production may have shifted from the plow to the assembly line and increasingly to the brains of knowledge workers, their share of the wealth they create is declining. As Art Caston and I point out: "However, the owners of these crackling brains still have no or little ownership in the wealth they create, other than a salary and maybe a bonus plan. As the shift evolves, and as their power grows, the issue of ownership of wealth will, we believe, be posed."[31]

Theme 5: Nothing Inherent in the Technology Will Necessarily Result in Improvements in Quality of Work Life

Amid the promise, there are new forms of job stress. Psychologists warn that multitasking—talking on the phone, reading and answering e-mail, flipping through a fax—makes stressful lives more so and makes vacations and leisure less restful. "The technologies don't come with a notice: 'WARNING! This is going to break into your downtime and lead to stress-related disorders.' But that may be true," says the chief medical officer at the University of Pennsylvania Medical Center. At executive seminars run by Harvard Medical School, technology-induced exhaustion is now the most popular session.[32] The combination of new tools and the new fast-paced, global business environment has, for many, created a new tempo and rhythm for work. For many, we've gone from Mozart to M. C. Hammer.

So, too, for the way work is organized. In one nightmare scenario, MIT's Thomas Malone explores what would happen if the trend to use technology and markets to organize relationships were taken to the extreme. All work relationships between people could be mediated by the market, and every individual could function as a company working in constantly changing alliances and ventures. A leading business think tank—the Aspen Institute—concluded that such extreme atomization would not only be an undesirable way to construct human work but would also be ineffective as a way of conducting business.[33]

It is not technology that creates work systems. People do. Managers need to be not only humane but smart—building simultaneously for performance and quality of work life. The same is true for telework. Many who have a home office find their time very productive and enjoyable.[34] The technology enables people to work more effectively and improves quality of work life. Clearly, the way to ensure that things go the right way is not to inhibit the capabilities of networks and stop the march of new media and the highway, but to take steps to ensure that things go the right way. People, not technology, design work systems and organizations.

When it comes to quality of life *beyond work*, the promise is striking. Smart cards and health networks will reduce drug interactions and thereby save lives and reduce health costs. Home information appliances will offer a vast array of services that will improve everything from managing our finances to shopping to our enjoyment of the arts.

The new technology can transform learning through virtual colleges and lifelong learning programs. But when it comes to telecommunications, schools are the most impoverished institutions in our society. We need to learn for the new technology and economy and we need the new technology for learning.

The Net is also helping to protect the environment. The Los Angeles earthquake propelled that city into telework projects as twisted highways forced people to work from home or new locations. Among other things, this will result in a reduction of emissions from the internal combustion engine that propels automobiles. The targets for reduction the city has set cannot be achieved by carpools. New technology-enabled work systems will be required.

The Net enables new forms of communications, making the world a smaller place and holding considerable promise. It will provide new simulated travel experiences for people from their homes, schools, or churches. It holds the potential of transforming the democratic process in ways we can only imagine.

But will we all drown in data, as Neil Postman and others have argued? As management lecturer Tom Peters recently said, "I'm concerned that this global economy will in fact be garbage at the speed of light."

Raw data are indeed disaggregated, empirical facts. When organized and defined in some intelligible fashion, data become information. Information that has been interpreted and synthesized, reflecting certain implicit values, becomes knowledge. And knowledge that carries profound, transhistorical insights might become wisdom.[35] Ironically the new capability of technology enables us to move up the wisdom chain if we want to. The information database industry, for example, is not only the purveyor of databases but is entering the business of helping to organize data into information and more. If the industrial economy created mass production, the new economy is creating mass customization—the mass production of customized goods and services—including data.

For example, as discussed earlier, companies will sell you a custom newspaper delivered each day. Today you can define network profiles of the data, news, and entertainment that you want. Such profiles will contain information in multiple media including video. The fear of creating illiterate couch potatoes is also ironic given that the current technology is called broadcast—a one-way dump that excludes text and reading. The new technology is interactive. It is based on the active involvement—not just viewing and listening but also the reading, thinking, and decision making of the customer in addition to the computer-enabled communications between human beings. Look to the Internet for the model, not to television. Research so far suggests that consumers will actually "watch" (as currently defined) less television.[36] A recent survey supports this view, placing interest in interactive education and training programs way ahead of movies on demand, television shows, and games.[37] As Dick Notebaert, CEO of Ameritech, says, "The redefinition of television will occur as people demand to be stimulated instead of vegetated—when they stop 'watching' and start 'using' their televisions."

Of course there are dangers. Will, for example, some people select information about sports and violent crime for their profiles? But these dangers are human, not technological.

ELECTRONIC DEMOCRACY AND THE NEW BODY POLITIC

The Issue: What are the implications of the emerging networks for the electoral process itself and more broadly for democracy? What are the broader changes in economic and political power that are being precipitated by the new economy? Tectonic technological and economic shifts bring far-reaching changes in the political infrastructure. Changes in political institutions, processes, and power in turn deeply affect the business environment, not to mention the rate of penetration of the new technologies and growth of new markets.

The implications of the information highway for the "reinvention of government"—a euphemism for fundamental changes to the business of government and the delivery of government programs enabled by the new technology—were discussed in Chapter 6. However, there has been recent considerable discussion about the information highway and its implications for the democratic process itself.[38]

This influence was highlighted by the past two national elections in the United States. In the 1994 midterm elections, some candidates used the Internet to answer questions and deliver campaign pitches. Fed up with vacuous and vitriolic television sound bites, hundreds of thousands of voters used their computers for comparison shopping—finding out where candidates stood on issues and reviewing their voting records. The League of Women Voters established Project Vote Smart, which provided voting records, campaign financial data, and performance evaluations of candidates by special-interest groups. The California Online Voter Guide, a nonpartisan service funded by groups of organizations ranging from the California Teachers' Association to Pacific Bell, provided similar information.

Many candidates used electronic mail to answer voter questions, and some even established "Web servers," where people browsing the Net could find information about their campaign. For example, Kathleen Brown, Democratic challenger to California governor Pete Wilson (who also used the Net extensively), set up multimedia kiosks in shopping malls for people who did not have computers. Claiming to break new ground in a political campaign, Brown said that the technology "combines two elements that have contributed to California's economy and creativity—Hollywood and Silicon Valley."[39] On election day, the Internet was also used for instant news on election returns.

In the 1992 election, many people cringed when Ross Perot proposed the electronic town hall, conjuring up the image of an electronic mob. To many observers, voting "yes" or "no" from your home or place of work could be dangerous. In addition to possible manipulation, such daily referenda could actually undermine a true democratic process, which is based on participation. Motions put to a vote are usually well-refined distillations of large and complex issues. They result from a long process involving conflicts, contradictions, and compromises. To understand a motion and to vote responsibly, citizens need to participate in some form of refining process. The notion of an instant referendum conducted electronically has been widely viewed with skepticism by most analysts.[40] The Perot campaign did, however, serve to raise the issue of electronic democracy in a high-profile manner.

There are numerous ways networks could dramatically improve democratic participation. A thoughtful paper prepared for the Aspen Institute discusses several:

- *Representation.* As an alternative to the electronic town hall, they propose "The Town Hall Revisited." In this scenario, technology is used to tap into the diverse insights and expertise in a community. An interactive system could allow people to ask questions, make suggestions, and give opinions to a central forum, such as a city council. This input influences the council, who as elected representatives are the final decision makers.
- *Reorganizing.* Here the network could enable new groups of like interests and views to come together in ways that previously would have been infeasible or impractical. Instead of relying on geographical boundaries, which are subject to gerrymandering, voting districts could be allocated to affinity groups that reach certain thresholds of size.

- *Intermediaries.* Intermediation involves the collaboration between citizens and new intermediaries (replacements for the disintermediated individuals of the old paradigm). For example, through an electronic newspaper or forum of journalists and editors, specialists are able to share information as well as to debate issues or elaborate on information not otherwise available through normal distribution channels such as a newspaper. Instead of seeing online databases as simple substitutes for edited hard-copy news, the local newspaper "uses electronic technology as a way to complement the special community significance of publishing a newspaper."
- In a section called "New Strategies for Interpretation," the authors explore ways the new technology can help one group come to understand the very different perspectives of another. Networks don't simply enable people of like views and interests to organize but can help to overcome boundaries between groups—for example, different groups of voters or lawmakers.[41]

The technology can also be used to simulate various outcomes and to understand the impact of various decisions. For example, rhetoric about cuts to social programs for deficit reduction is easy. Through simulating the impact of cuts on other aspects of the economy, various demographic and racial groups, lawmakers, and other stakeholders can come to a deeper understanding of the impact of legislation on complex systems.

While the debates regarding networks and the democratic process rage on, more far-reaching issues are posed. Democracy in many Western countries is stagnating, some would say atrophying. Voter cynicism is at an all time high. Political corruption in high places is unabated. Governments everywhere seem ineffective and out of touch.

Yet at the same time "marketplace" democratic processes are surging. Instant polling is already an everyday phenomenon, and by many accounts it is creating a hyperdemocracy in which elected leaders are buffeted daily by the capricious winds of pollsters and the public mood. Superficial electronic democracy is used daily to make consumers and voters sovereign. We vote with our dollars or our opinions, guiding the decisions of CEOs and politicians. Yet, all of this responsiveness to the "will of the people" has failed. It has failed to overcome political alienation and cynicism. Notwithstanding the laudable efforts of some government leaders, it has failed to create flexible, responsive, or efficient government. It has failed to renew our political parties or the ideologies that guide them. Today's publicity- and feedback-driven democratic institutions are in a deep crisis of credibility and functionality.

Technology helped to create this depressing and dangerous situation. Industrial society created the mass media and its crowning media achievement—the television. Apple CEO Michael Spindler says that television has become the paradigm for today's conception of public information. "The television news is built on principles such as: 'bite size is best,' 'nuances are dispensable,' and 'visual stimulation is a good substitute for thought.'" He argues that the TV commercial is a serious attack on audiences, bringing together in 15 or 30 seconds all the arts of showbiz for maximum emotional appeal, often at the expense of the truth. In addition to shifting resources in the economy from product research to marketing, TV advertising has a second debilitating effect on the body politic: "The TV commercial has become the main instrument for presenting political ideas," Spindler says.

The new media are interactive, however. The user has control. Even so, can the new media really change things? "Layering faster, more transparent and highly accessible information technology on top of a dysfunctional body politic will achieve very little," says Riel Miller, Alliance contributor. "Interactive multimedia in a digital world of ubiquitous networks cannot work magic. No alchemy of the body politic can turn today's parliamentary arterial sclerosis into the healthy flow of democratic dialogue and mutually respectful exercise of power."[42]

Miller is right. Don't look to the new media as technological quick fixes of the chronic problem of Industrial Age democracy. Rather, the new technology is at the heart of a more fundamental change in economic relationships that, if we will it, can lead to a truer democracy. The technological whirlwind that encompasses us today can significantly affect the political process. Political rejuvenation, if it emerges at all, will be fundamentally linked to technological change because the relentless technological and competitive forces overturning the way we earn a living are opening up new frontiers. On the horizon, in innovative firms and community organizations, the digital economy is coming into sight. Historical, technological, economic, and political change are inextricably linked.

Harold Innis and his student, Marshall McLuhan, pointed out that new media have precipitated political changes throughout history. As Innis wrote in the early 1950s: "Monopolies or oligopolies of knowledge have been built up ... [to support] forces chiefly on the defensive, but improved technology has strengthened the position of forces on the offensive and compelled realignments favoring the vernacular." Or as put by Alliance President David Ticoll: "Libraries based on clay documents enabled the priest-based monopoly of knowledge in ancient Babylon. The invention of papyrus scrolls and the alphabet was a key to the limited democracy of Greek city states and the rule of law in ancient Rome. The improved portability, ease of use and durability of parchment-based, bound books created by the papacy and monastic orders were critical to the speed of conversion to Christianity. Paper and the printing press reproduced religious text in the vernacular and led to the Reformation, the end of feudalism and the emergence of parliamentary democracy in tandem with the industrial revolution."

In ancient civilizations, slaves had no access to knowledge and consequently no economic or political power. In the agricultural age, knowledge began to disperse, first to the feudal nobility and to some extent to the serfs—who acquired access to land and its fruits for their efforts. In the nineteenth century, access to machinery created the industrial revolution. In the industrial age, the silk-hatted tycoons dominated, but the worker was more than a cog in the machine. Work became social, rather than done in isolation; literacy and knowledge rose in the population. Workers could organize to acquire formal strength through trade unions to defend their interests. The tycoons acquired wealth, but the standard of living of others rose as well as did their economic power. Unions took political action in the nineteenth century through the creation of political parties—which continue today as the social democratic parties of most developed countries.

In the twenty-first century, wealth will flow from knowledge—an asset more widely and freely available than ever before. The distribution of real power, if not formal power, is changing. The Age of Networked Intelligence could bring new power and freedom, particularly for the two-thirds of the workforce who are knowledge workers.

As Miller describes the current situation: "Once again, with vast political consequences, the economic genie has been unleashed from its bottle. Summoned, perhaps unwillingly or unknowingly by the blind drive for profit, the genie is applied to achieve greater competitiveness. And in the process we are redrawing the political power grid established by the old order of economic life."

Figure 12.1 summarizes the historical changes. Starting with very tight control over the physical production by slaves of the Roman Empire or Egyptian Pharaohs, the dispersion of political power has marched hand in hand with the dispersion of control over knowledge. None of the transitions between one economic or political system and another has been easy. Nor, up until now, have any of the transitions been peaceful. Shifts in power have largely been marked as the outcome of bloody battles with very high costs for people and economic institutions.

FIGURE 12.1 *Knowledge and Political Power Over Time: Distinguishing Different Economies.* SOURCE: Riel Miller, David Ticoll, Don Tapscott. © Alliance for Converging Technologies, 1996.

So far, the revolution underway in developed countries is mostly quiet. As networks proliferate and new companies and individuals innovate to create wealth (using the new infrastructure) knowledge is dispersing and along with it—economic and political power.

More than ever knowledge is power. In the emerging digital economy, what people know matters. What they know about new production processes. What they know about where to find information on organic bread or energy efficient heating. What they know about the occupational health or learning needs and services of their community. Today, as most innovative organizations already understand, the capacity for knowledge in action is the predominant source of economic advantage. People are the source of knowledge in action. People are the prime engine of economic power. In innovative start-ups, such power can correspond to income and wealth. In larger companies there is still dissonance between contribution and rewards—between ownership of the new means of production and ownership of wealth. But as Miller says, the genie is out of the bottle.

The Net, like the revolutionary media of the past, is central to this quiet and radical reallocation of political and economic power—the creation of a new political economy. The internet is the technological enabling mechanism. The internet offers the technological possibility for firms to become direct personal suppliers and for consumers to personalize their consumption. By cutting the cost and improving the quality of knowledge exchange, the Net opens the door to making learning the basic transaction of society.

Reaching this Age of Networked Intelligence, where learning is the primary relationship between producers and consumer, will not be the outcome of quick technological fixes. Realizing this degree of decentralization and innovative initiative depends conversely on significant political reform. The task is to encourage another leap up the timeline toward greater democracy. Democracy is about choice, being able to make choices that determine the future.

"The Net can have a great impact on 'the culture of choice.' Not the choice among a dozen different types of toothpaste, nor the choice among a dozen grinning politicians," says Miller. "Choice in the new economy goes beyond selecting from predetermined options to changing the content of the options—what and how you produce something, what and how you consume. Interactivity is only a slogan if the interaction does not actually add content or value to one or both sides of the transaction."

However, the fact that the Net makes it possible to gain the knowledge required to change what you produce or consume, or your participation in new democratic processes, does not mean society will accomplish anything. Cynicism and ignorance do not disappear overnight. Reinventing the corporation or government is not a simple task. Overcoming the reflexes of the mass-production and mass-consumption age will not be easy. Most people are accustomed to a world in which most choices are predetermined—such as what you do at work, what you can buy in the supermarket, and which political parties you vote for.

The internet offers the technological possibility for firms to become direct personal suppliers and for consumers to personalize their consumption. Achieving this more pervasive and substantive democracy can occur only if we change the way we work and live and organize. The move away from the alienating characteristic of "mass society" will occur only if there is really a greater degree of control—and the capacity to exercise that formal control—in the workplace, in your backyard, and in the world around us. We can expect that there will be considerable conflict as real power of knowledge workers conflicts with formal structures of power, both political and economic.

THE INTERNET, THE MACROECONOMY, AND THE NATION-STATE

There is evidence that the internet will result in geopolitical disintermediation, undermining the role of everything in the middle, including the nation-state. That is, broadband networks may accelerate *polarization* of activity toward both the global and the local, enabling a higher diversity and density of economic connections. Rising from the ashes of the Great Depression and World War II came a modern map of nations and the leaders that managed them. Over time the many open questions and uncertainties posed by the dark track record of the first half of this century have been replaced by expectations and habits forged from the stability of the second half. Governments and bank economists, along with many others, helped to establish the molds. Macroeconomic policies were introduced to calm the fluctuations of commerce that had plagued the past.

Nation-states introduced pensions, unemployment insurance, and social and health-care systems to stabilize income and well-being. A virtuous circle of reinforcing expansion where the bountiful supply (productivity) of mass production helped to both fuel (with wages) and feed (with product) the demand of mass consumption. This complementarity corresponded well with the ambitions and capabilities of the nation-state. Countries, secure within their borders, could address the need for basic productive infrastructure, such as roads and schools, of the mass production age.

Slowly, over a span of 40 years, competition and development undermined this congruence of supply and demand by both increasing and spreading the knowledge (technological and managerial) required to survive in the marketplace. Knowledge diffusion encouraged the development of strong new competitors both globally and locally. Increases in knowledge, particularly in the form of technologies that embody new knowledge (or new uses for the knowledge), also disrupted the stable patterns of investment, employment, and enterprise organization.

Gradually, the comfortable reach of the nation-state as revenue raiser and infrastructure provider has collapsed into jobless growth, fiscal crisis, and investor relocation. Borders crisscrossed by road, rail, and fiber optic cable became more permeable to goods, services, finance, and knowledge. Control over space, the geographic buffers of the nation, started to melt away with the decline of the so-called Golden Age of mass production. Compounding these changes in what, how, and where we produce are the profound changes in East-West and North-South relationships as the binary balance of terror decentralizes into a multiplicity of local conflicts. The combined impact of lifting many Cold War constraints and the proliferation of regional conflicts is giving rise to new trading patterns, investment flows, and global migration.

Redirecting global flows of money, information, products, and people creates significant demographic shock waves. Patterns of regional economic integration are recast in cases, for example, where a surge in immigration from the Pacific Rim to North America alters a range of institutions and practices, from financial sources to production methods. New networks and ways of working are springing up. New clients, products, and ways of doing business are disrupting traditional habits, laws, and customs. As regional giants and nimble local entrepreneurial communities take the stage, nation-states and the macroeconomic policies that were their calling card are fading into the background of history.

Within this seemingly chaotic and sometimes terrifying whirlwind, global disintermediation is occurring. On one level, supranational state systems (EC, NAFTA, APEC) are reducing the risks and costs of market transactions on a wider geographic field. At another level, local and community-based markets are blossoming as common interests and capabilities are forced together by the collapse of the old economy. Overall, an erosion is taking place in the effectiveness of the traditional tools of the nation-state.

This situation is posing more questions than answers. How can we protect and extend the public services and social safety net that has been the task of the nation-state, when that state is being undermined? What new forms of international collaborations and possible government structures are required to correspond to the new global situation? Alvin and Heidi Toffler argue effectively that we need a new form of "decision division" in which some decision making is "moved up" from the nation-state to transnational structures and some "moved downward from the center."[43] But in practice, such transnational structures are weak, and it is far from clear whether state and local governments are prepared, able, or willing to take on new responsibilities delegated from the national level. Does such talk about decision division provide ideological justification for members of Congress who would simply eliminate federally funded social programs and other functions of government? People like Newt Gingrich (who wrote the foreword to the Tofflers' book) have used decision division as the rationale to hand off government functions to local and transnational halfbacks who aren't even on the field. Will we use new economy cyberspeak as a way of shirking our responsibility to others, especially the less fortunate? As the internet grows in reach and capabilities, as the institutions of the old economy crumble, such issues will become more sharply posed.

FIVE VIEWS ON SOCIETAL TRANSFORMATION

The printing press enabled a new paradigm in human communication and learning. Over the years the press has been used to print the Bible, Nazi propaganda, *Hamlet*, manuals for nuclear weapons, Barbie brochures, first-grade readers, *Scientific American*, and magazines glorifying the exploitation of children. The new technology is proving to be even more malleable. The new technology can be just about anything we want it to be: textbook, telephone switch, meeting place, adventure game, word processor, flight simulator, calculator, or driving aid. The application of new technology and ultimately the character of new institutions, governance, rules, social structures, and cultures will be socially created—that is, they will be created by people and societies.

But through what process will this occur?

There are various competing views on how the economic and social transformation can best be achieved, although arguably such views are not completely mutually exclusive.[44]

View 1: It'll All Come Out in the Wash

This view, alternately named the "leave it to the market" view, or the "optimist" view, holds that the transformation of business and society will happen naturally through market forces.[45] The view has credence, given the widespread consensus that an open competitive marketplace is critical to the rapid deployment and acceptance of the new technologies. This consensus is now being extrapolated beyond a policy for infrastructure growth, technology diffusion, and sectoral strategy to a broad social policy. Business leaders who make such extensions of open market principles to societal views often discharge themselves from any responsibility beyond the interests of their customers and shareholders.

View 2: Societal Transformation Is the Responsibility of the Social Sector

The main advocate of this view is Peter Drucker, most recently in the cover story of the November 1994 issue of the *Atlantic Monthly* magazine. Posing the question, "Who takes care of the social challenges of the knowledge society?" he replies a separate and new sector—the social sector—different from public or private sectors. This new social sector consists of nongovernmental organizations (for profit or not) with the task "to create human health and well-being" and to create "citizenship," that is, responsible and informed participation in society (beyond voting every few years and paying taxes all the time).

Volunteers and the concept of charity are key to social sector organizations. The sector will be central to the cohesion of the knowledge society and thereby the performance of the new economy. Government, Drucker says, cannot fulfill this role because it has proven itself to be moribund and ineffective. "We do not have even the beginnings of political theory of the political institutions needed for effective government in the knowledge-based society of organizations."[46]

View 3: Societal Transformation Is the Responsibility of Government

The issues raised are too large to be resolved at the individual corporation or organization level; considerable planning, legislation, and enforcement are required. Governments in a democratic society are charged with repre-senting the common interest, and many challenges transcend the interests of individual companies, sectors, and stakeholder groups. That govern-ments are ineffective is not relevant. We need to reinvent government to make it an appropriate instrument for the new economy. Variants of this view range from extreme government involvement (Japan, Singapore)—in not only policy but also in the actual construction of the highway—to gov-ernment regulation and initiatives (United States, Canada) to encourage private investment, protect competition, provide open access to the net-work, and help to manage the social impact of the new infrastructure and the fundamental changes in society.

View 4: Consumers, Users, and Others Must/Will Demand That Technology Serve Social and Human Needs

This view holds that those to be affected by these changes can rely on no one but themselves. Workers, interest groups, unions, users in organizations, and consumer associations have all launched initiatives—some considerable in size and scope—to ensure that technology is not used only for narrow profit-oriented purposes. The activity on the Internet, the initiatives in pubic sector unions, and increased talk of white-collar unionization are reflective of this trend. In the extreme cases, it is said that the contradiction between growing wealth and prosperity contrasted with the growing income disparity between the few and the many will lead to massive social conflict and revolutionary changes. If Marxism in its Stalinist form has been forever discredited, there is an apparent growth of neoleft radical thinking, which argues that true democ-racy, distributed power, social planning, and the application of market forces can work together well.

As economic development consultant Phil Courneyeur put it in a discussion on the Net:

> Our system today paradoxically generates stupendous wealth alongside even more stupendous want, poverty, and waste. The technological revolution, in its current context, only quickens the pace of planet Earth's rush to disaster, or rather to the fork in the road on the world history line where we must and will make a decision of life and death consequences for civilization as we know it. Time is running out for a world order based on ever-concentrating corporate ownership of wealth and driven primarily by the needs of profit. Technology can be used effectively to take us into an age of barbarism that will make fascism look like an exercise in charity and human progress.

> But that same revolution equips us with a means to tackle this problem rationally, that is socially; to move beyond the blind corporate drive for profit into a world of awareness, information, knowledge, empowerment, imagination, cooperation, commitment, and freedom.

View 5: Business Has a New Responsibility for Leadership for Transformation

The new economy and society raise new imperatives for business leaders. The shift is, at its core, economic. Appropriate leaders for societal transformation are the new business leaders of the new economy—those shaping innovation and the creation of wealth and jobs. Increasingly it can be argued that it will be difficult and inappropriate for businesspeople to say "these issues are someone else's problem." Or "my only responsibility is to my shareholders." We're all developing new responsibilities to ourselves, our families, our fellow human beings, and our planet.

LEADERSHIP FOR SOCIETAL TRANSFORMATION

Which approach(es) is (are) right? Shifts like these cause dislocation, confusion, uncertainty. They raise far-reaching issues for societies to tackle. As discussed earlier, a new political economy is emerging, and every institution in the society—businesses, the organizations of business, government, unions, educational institutions, the media, the regulators, and in many ways, every individual—will have to change.

It is clear in North America and to a lesser extent in South America, Europe, and a number of Pacific Rim countries that an open, competitive marketplace is the best environment for rapid growth of the new technologies. And "coming out of the wash" will be innovative technologies, high-speed interoperable networks, applications growth, and extensive use. We need to move to an open, competitive market for information technology—absolutely. Investments will come from the private sector—absolutely. However, an open marketplace does not a social strategy make. It is hard to imagine how a broader social transformation will occur without conscious effort and leadership at every level of society. Market determinism is not the answer to the challenges being discussed here.

Drucker's views on the social sector are important and interesting. They fit well with the views outlined herein regarding the polarization between local and global sectors. Local, grassroots organizations, in touch with the changing needs of their constituencies or clients, can contribute. But who will achieve any standards in terms of quality of life? Will the fate of the have-nots be left to the uneven determination of volunteer workers, the capricious whims of donors and charities, the luck of the geographic draw, or the unpredictable resources of the local social organization. Who will attempt to strike a balance, establishing basic principles of conduct and quality of life?

The most disturbing aspect of the application of market determinism beyond the economy to society is a sinister new social Darwinism. We hear that not only companies, but people and social groups who are able, motivated, and effective should rightly rise to the top and those who aren't should rightly fall behind. Societies, it is said, are not responsible for the care and advancement of the less fortunate—individuals are. This notion appeared in the last century when some extended Darwin's theory of natural selection to the social systems of the industrial economy. The idea was rejected by previous democracies who created a social safety net, public education, and access to health care. But it has now raised its head as we enter the new economy.

Because of this, governments do have a role to play. The approach developed by the government of Ontario is noteworthy. It was the first North American jurisdiction to develop a comprehensive approach to the information highway. The approach is balanced, and it was developed by a consensus process involving business, labor, government, community groups, and others. Moreover, it is actually being implemented by various partnerships throughout the province. The strategy rested on the view that the information highway must be developed and funded by the private sector but that government could play a useful role in several areas:[47]

- Create the regulatory conditions for an open competitive marketplace for the evolution of the information infrastructure.
- Use the new technologies to reinvent itself to cut costs and improve the delivery of government programs. In doing so governments would not only deliver better and cheaper services but as a significant purchaser place considerable demand on the market.
- Take steps to ensure that technology serves people by implementing policies and programs to ensure universal access, equity, privacy, and security.
- Act as a catalyst for new kinds of partnerships that would encourage demands for networks, the growth of applications, and the use of the new technologies. Variations on this view have now been adopted by numerous other provinces, states, and the NII council.

Beyond this, what roles are emerging for government in managing the transition to the new economy and ensuring that promise, not peril, wins? Miller says:

> Arguing supply-side versus demand-side policies is getting to be a stale pastime. Even the passionate exchanges on incentives versus disincentives or social solidarity versus atomistic fear-induced competition are rooted in the institutional and cultural traditions of the fading industrial economy. We are witnessing a change in the way governments—as the promoters of the general social interest and the agents of collective action—undertake the task of economic "intervention." In an age when how, what, and when we produce and consume are erasing the once neat division between supply and demand, governments cannot use blunt macro tools.

True, the digital economy brings up a finer mesh, a more detailed level of analysis and action. Transactions are information-rich at the micro level whereas generalized macroeconomic aggregations lack detail. The new economy depends on a much greater transaction density. Connecting so many economic agents and dealing with so many personalized products provides new challenges for business, governments, and other organizations. At the local level or through the network, the challenge is to ensure sufficient access, transparency, and veracity to the infrastructure that will help the economy to function.

This is a radical departure from the mass production and mass consumption of the past. It involves a shift away from traditional macroeconomic policy using the fiscal (tax and spend) tools of national government. It means a transformation in the security provided by the welfare state away from the passive and paternalistic, after-the-fact redistribution of income to a new "equality of opportunity," and "plugging" everyone in. Community becomes more important, whether it is a geographically specific area or a set of intense common interests, as the basis for joint wealth creation and market exchange.

Unfortunately, most public institutions are carried along by the inertia of policies and legal systems crafted to meet the needs of the past. As a result, they are often incapable of addressing the serious challenges of, say, stimulating the reskilling of a workforce or providing leadership for the social distribution of the benefits of the new economy.

Blunt, standardized administrative methods are often associated with ideas of universal services by which every citizen has the same rights. Nondiscrimination, an important principle, is embedded in this type of mass access. Specialized, personalized products, including those from the public sector, bring the risk of privileging one part of the population against another.

The internet does not reduce this type of risk. Instead, knowledge, with its tendency to escape ownership and invade privacy, tends to provoke discriminatory access and insight. Reforms spurred by these tensions attempt to address the symptoms.

Mostly, however, efforts to reform public sector infrastructure are caught up in the pressures and parameters of existing practices. As Miller says: "There is still little recognition that the learning culture of the new economy entails a reexamination of the basic power relationships of the workplace, marketplace, household, and society. Knowledge work, the new consumer sovereignty, localized infrastructure for the Net, all of these demand a reconfiguration of public participation and administration."

Overcoming the cynicism born of outdated policies attempting unsuccessfully to address pressing problems is a serious political obstacle. Equally, the administrative logic of public sector institutions, entrenched in the laudable notions of professionalism and objectivity (avoidance of corruption), now seem unable to adjust to the way power can be distributed in the new economy. For these reasons, governments are not fully able to play the kind of leadership role that is required. New kinds of partnerships, often led by business, will be required.

BUSINESS AND LEADERSHIP
FOR TRANSFORMATION

The business community needs to rethink its role in the new economy. Business should provide leadership for the broader changes to come, not only through altruism but also through self-interest. The success of businesses will depend on the rapidity and smoothness of the societal changes that are being unleashed by the internet. Business in any nation-state can succeed only if it has a new-economy workforce—one that is educated, motivated, stable, and healthy. And domestic markets will be viable only if they are supportive of innovations, see the social benefit to themselves, and have confidence about their personal privacy.

Corporations have never lived in a social vacuum. They have always had an interest in the sociopolitical environment. Companies give to charities, support political parties, invest in social projects. Conversely, companies have been able to operate in unstable volatile environments, but that's not where they put their head offices and key assets. However, as the shift to the new economy gains momentum, the links between economic and social transformation become intense. The federal deficit is a tame problem compared to the potential social deficit lurking in the wings of a poorly managed transition to the new economy. Furthermore, as the world becomes a smaller place both for companies and customers, such links grow on a global scale.

The old institutions and value systems are collapsing: the hierarchy; the unwritten contract between companies and employees of a lifetime job in exchange for loyalty and hard work; public respect for governments.

In the rising search for values, to whom can people look? Not, it appears, to the old establishment. Stockbrokers are in jail for fraud, and priests are imprisoned for the sexual assault of children. Some business leaders profess no responsibility other than to their shareholders. Executive compensation for some—unrelated to useful measures of performance—skyrockets through seven to eight figures while employees tighten their belts and try to deal with serious erosion of their real income. White, wealthy lawmakers fight for cuts in taxes on the one hand and reductions in social services that, on the other hand, will further degrade the lives of the poor and people of color.

More than any other time in history, humanity is at a crossroads. Is it unthinkable that business could lead in the forging of new values for a new economy? Can a new generation of business leaders understand their common self-interest in achieving social justice and a smooth societal transformation? Clearly the technological and market forces driving us forward must be tempered by deeper nonmarket human values. Can business leaders meet this challenge, avoiding the alternative of massive social conflict and turmoil? What are the implications of management remaining locked into the old models regarding the social responsibilities of business?

The digital economy requires a new kind of businessperson: one who has the curiosity and confidence to let go of old mental models and old paradigms; who tempers the needs for business growth and profit with the requirements of employees, customers, and society for privacy, fairness, and a share in the wealth they create; one who has the vision to think socially, the courage to act, and the strength to lead in the face of coolness or even ridicule. The digital economy requires yesterday's managers to become tomorrow's leaders. As we enter the new age, the future won't just happen. It will be created. And if we all get involved, our values, aspirations, and growing expectations will shape and drive the transformation of our businesses and our world.

Past technological paradigms—the broadcast media and the old model of the computer—were hierarchical, immutable, and centralized. As such, they carried the values of their powerful owners. The new media are interactive, malleable, and distributed in control. As such, they cherish an awesome neutrality. Ultimately, they will be what we want them to be. They will do what we command of them.

This fact should give us not only great hope but determination to shape the future for the common good—to create a new social consciousness and conscience. If we act, rather than passively observe, we can seize the time. And the Age of Networked Intelligence will be an age of promise fulfilled.

NOTES

1. Alan Kay. From a speech given to the Superhighway Summit at the University of California at Los Angeles, 1994. As cited in *WIRED*, May 1994, p. 76.
2. Keith Bradsher, "Gap in Wealth in U.S. called Widest in West," *New York Times*, April 12, 1995.
3. Christopher Lasch, "Revolt of the Elites: Have they Cancelled Their Allegiance to America?" *Harpers Magazine*, November 1994.
4. David Wessel and Bob Davis, "In the Middle of the Middle: Two Families Stories," *Wall Street Journal*, March 29, 1995, Bl.
5. David Olive, "Bankrupt America," *Globe and Mail Report on Business*, April 1995.
6. Dr. Juan Antonio Blanco, "Tercer Milenio: Apuntes para una reflexion [Third Millenium—Notes for Reflection]," NGP Centro Felix Varela, Havana, October 1994.
7. Antonia Serbisias, "Who Will Control the Wired World?" *Toronto Star*, January 29, 1994.

8. Michael Mandel, "The Digital Juggernaught," *BusinessWeek*, 1994, p. 22.

9. From Industry Canada data.

10. Christopher Freeman and Luc Soete, Information Technology and Employment, OECD, November 1993.

11. *Datamation*, June 15, 1993.

12. Freeman and Soete.

13. Mandel, p. 22

14. Ronald Henkoff, cited in "Service Is Everybody's Business," *Fortune*, June 27, 1994, p. 49.

15. Paul R. Krugman and Robert Z. Lawrence, "Trade Jobs and Wages," *Scientific American*, April 1994, pp. 44–49.

16. Freeman and Soete.

17. Neil Gros, "A Game of Catch-Up," *Business Week, The Information Revolution*, Special Issue, 1994, p. 38

18. Gail Edmondson, "Brave Old World," *Business Week, The Information Revolution*, Special Issue, 1994, p. 42.

19. Pete Engardio, "Third World Leapfrog," *Business Week, The Information Revolution*, Special Issue, 1994, pp. 47–49.

20. Paige Darden, NTIA, http:\www.ntia.doc.gov.

21. Background paper on the "Administration's Telecommunications Policy Reform Initiative," available through the NII, January 11, 1994, p. 1.

22. Vice President Al Gore, from a presentation to the Television Academy, UCLA, January 11, 1994.

23. Cited by FCC Chairman Reed Hundt in his address to the Networked Economy conference, Washington, D.C., September, 1994.

24. "Administration's Telecommunications Policy Reform Initiative."

25. Ibid., p. 7.

26. Frederick Taylor's 1887 theory of scientific management assigned a single task to a worker. Recently there have been a number of attempts to rehabilitate Taylor, arguing that his theories and approaches were actually quite progressive for the social context and time. See Marvin R. Weisbord, *Productive Workplaces: Organizations for Dignity, Meaning and Community*, Jossey-Bass Publishers, San Francisco, 1991.

27. Jack Patterson, "Welcome to the Company That Isn't There," *BusinessWeek*, October 17, 1994, p. 87.

28. Cited in "The New World of Work," *Fortune*, October 17, 1994, p. 87.

29. Don Tapscott, *Office Automation: A User-Driven Method*, Plenum Press, New York, 1981, p. 222.

30. Thomas A. Stewart, "Your Company's Most Valuable Intellectual Asset: Intellectual Capital," *Fortune*, October 3, 1994, p. 68–74.

31. Don Tapscott and Art Caston, *Paradigm Shift: The New Promise of Information Technology*, McGraw-Hill, New York, 1993, p. 313.

32. *Wall Street Journal*, B1, April 4, 1995.

33. "The Promise and Perils of Emerging Information Technologies," A Report on the Second Annual Information Roundtable, The Aspen Institute, 1993.

34. Data cited in the keynote presentation given by Don Tapscott to the National Telework Symposium, New Paradigm Learning Corporation, Toronto, October 1994.

35. "The Promise and Perils of Emerging Information Technologies," A Report on the Second Annual Information Roundtable, The Aspen Institute, 1993.

36. Don Tapscott, Keynote address to the Canadian Association of Broadcasters Annual Conference, October 1994. New Paradigm Learning Corporation, Toronto, 1994.

37. Andersen Consulting Report on Canadian consumers interest in the information highway, Andersen Consulting, Toronto, 1994.

38. Sandra Braman, "The Autopoetic State: Communication and Democratic Potential in the Net," *Journal of the American Society for Information Science*, July 1994; Brenda Dervin, "Information—Democracy: An Examination of Underlying Assumptions," *Journal of the American Society for Information Science*, July 1994; Gary H. Anthes, "Digital Democracy," *Computerworld*, April 12, 1993; Richard J. Varn, "Electronic Democracy: Jeffersonian Boom or Teraflop?" *Spectrum: The Journal of State Government*, Spring 1993; Steven E. Miller, "From System Design to Democracy," *Communications of the ACM*, June 1993; Shirley Bloomfield, "Bringing Democracy Home," *Rural Telecommunications*, July/August 1993; Giuseppe Mantovani, "Is Computer-Mediated Communication Intrinsically Apt to Enhance Democracy in Organizations?," *Human Relations*, January 1994; Nancy Millichap, "The People's Right to Know: Media, Democracy, and the Information Highway," *Online*, July 1994; Michael E. Martinez, "Access to Information Technologies Among School-Age Children: Implications for a Democratic Society," *Journal of the American Society for Information Science*, July 1994; Su-Lien Sun, George A. Barnett, "The International Telephone Network and Democratization," *Journal of the American Society for Information Science*, July 1994.

39. Louise Kehoe, "American Politicians Seek Votes on Global Network," *Financial Times*, November 3, 1994.

40. Bruno S. Frey, Direct Democracy: Politico-Economic Lesson from the Swiss Experience, *AEA Papers and Proceedings*, Vol. 82, No. 2, May 1994, p. 439.

41. The Promise and Perils of Emerging Information Technologies, A Report on the Second Annual Information Roundtable, The Aspen Institute, 1993. The four points in this list come from a paper by John Seely Brown, Paul Duguid, and Susan Haviland, entitled "Towards Informed Participation: Six Scenarios in Search of Democracy in the Electronic Age."

42. These comments are based on a discussion with economist and visionary Riel Miller, who is currently consulting to the OECD, the Alliance for Converging Technologies and other organizations and governments.

43. Alvin and Heidi Toffler, *Creating a New Civilization*, Andrews and McNeel, 1995.

44. For a good discussion of these views, see Don Tapscott, *Office Automation: A User-Driven Method*, Plenum Press, New York, 1981.

45. Ibid.

46. Peter F. Drucker," The Age of Social Transformation," *Atlantic Monthly*, November 1994.

47. Telecommunications: Ensuring Ontario's Future. Report of the Advisory Committee on a Telecommunications Strategy for Ontario, Toronto, 1992.

APPENDIXES

COMPARISON OF MULTIMEDIA OUTPUT: 1996 AND 2005

New Media Industry 1996: $953 billion

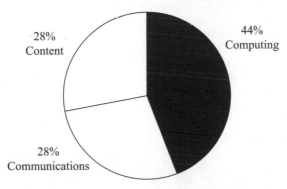

28%
Content

44%
Computing

28%
Communications

New Media Industry 2005: $1.47 trillion

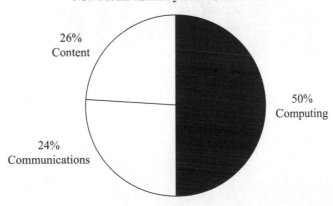

26%
Content

50%
Computing

24%
Communications

THE NEW MEDIA INDUSTRY: JOB GROWTH, 1992–2005

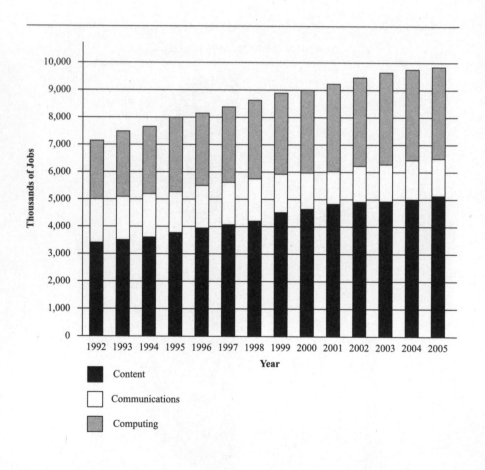

THE NEW MEDIA INDUSTRY: OUTPUT GROWTH, 1992–2005

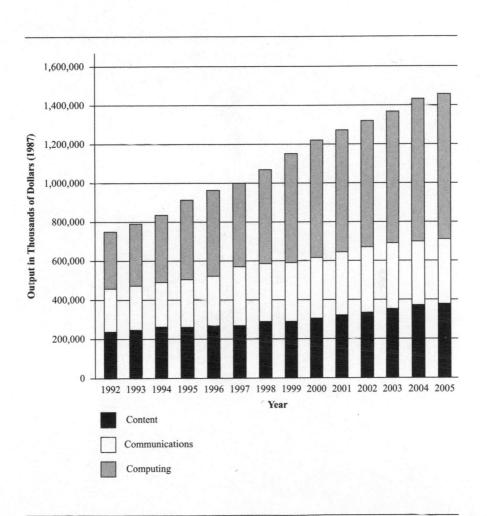

COMPARISON OF JOB GROWTH TO OUTPUT GROWTH

Job Growth, 1992–2005

7% Multimedia Total

93%
Nonmultimedia Total

Output Growth, 1992–2005

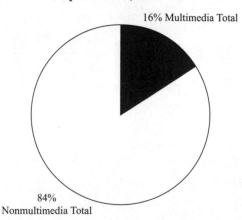

16% Multimedia Total

84%
Nonmultimedia Total

CLASSIFICATIONS FOR NEW MEDIA INDUSTRY ANALYSIS

New Media Triangle Components

Communications
    Communications facilities
    Household A/V equipment
    Telephone & telegraph equipment
    Broadcasting and communications equipment
    Communications, except broadcasting
    Radio & TV broadcasting

Computing
    Computer equipment
    Semiconductors & related devices
    Miscellaneous electronic components
    Electrical equipment & supplies
    Search & navigation equipment
    Computer & data processing services, software
    Electrical repair shops

Content
    Newspapers
    Periodicals
    Books
    Miscellaneous publishing
    Greeting card publishing

Advertising
Photocopying, commercial art, photo finishing
Business services
Motion pictures
Video tape rental
Producers, orchestras, and entertainers
Libraries, vocational and other schools

Source: List of Industry Classifications, U.S. Bureau of Labor Statistics.

SELECTED READINGS

Ackoff, Russell L., *The Democratic Corporation*, Oxford University Press, New York, 1994.

Argyris, Chris and Schön, Donald A., *Organizational Learning: A Theory of Action Perspective*, Addison-Wesley Publishing Company, Reading, MA, 1978.

Aston, Robert and Schwarz, Joyce, ed., *Multimedia: Gateway to the Next Millennium*, AP Professional, Cambridge, 1992.

Badaracco, Joseph L. Jr. and Ellsworth, Richard R., *Leadership and the Quest for Integrity*, Harvard Business School Press, Boston, 1989.

Beck, Nuala, *Shifting Gears: Thriving in the New Economy*, HarperCollins Publishers, New York, 1992.

Bennis, Warren and Nanus, Burt, *Leaders: The Strategies for Taking Charge*, Harper & Row, New York, 1985.

Block, Peter, *Stewardship: Choosing Service Over Self-Interest*, Berrett-Koehler Publishers, San Francisco, 1993.

Boone, Mary E., *Leadership and the Computer*, Prima Publishing, Rocklin, CA, 1991.

Bradley, Stephen P., Hausman, Jerry A., and Nolan, Richard L., *Globalization, Technology and Competition*, Harvard Business School Press, Boston, 1993.

Carroll, Jim and Broadhead, Rick, *The Canadian Internet Advantage*, Prentice Hall Canada, Inc., Scarborough, Ontario, 1995.

Cavoukian, Ann and Tapscott, Don, *Who Knows: Safeguarding Your Privacy in a Networked World*, Random House, Toronto, 1995.

Champy, James, *Reengineering Management*, Harper Collins Publishers, Inc., New York, 1995.

Chomsky, Noam, *The Chomsky Reader*, Pantheon Books, New York, 1987.

Cronin, Mary J., *Doing Business on the Internet: How the Electronic Highway Is Transforming American Companies*, Van Nostrand Reinhold, New York, 1994.

Davenport, Thomas H., *Process Innovation*, Harvard Business School Press, Boston, 1993.

Davidow, William H. and Malone, Michael S., *The Virtual Corporation: Structuring and Revitalizing the Corporation for the 21st Century*, HarperBusiness, New York, 1992.

Davis, Stan and Botkin, Jim, *The Monster Under the Bed*, Simon & Schuster, New York, 1994.

Davis, Stan and Davidson, Bill, *2020 Vision: Transform Your Business Today to Succeed in Tomorrow's Economy*, Simon & Schuster, New York, 1991.

Drucker, Peter F., *Managing for the Future*, Truman Talley Books/Dutton, 1992.

Drucker, Peter F., *Post-Capitalist Society*, Harper Business, New York, 1993.

Drucker, Peter F., *The New Realities*, Harper & Row, New York, 1989.

Ferguson, Marilyn, *The Aquarian Conspiracy: Personal and Social Transformation in the 1980s*, J.P. Tarcher, Inc., Los Angeles, 1980.

Friedhoff, Richard Mark and Benzon, William, *The Second Computer Revolution: Visualization*, Harry N. Abrams, Inc., New York, 1989.

Gilder, George, *Microcosm: The Quantum Revolution in Economics and Technology*, Simon & Schuster, New York, 1989.

Gore, Al (Vice President), *Creating a Government That Works Better and Costs Less: Reengineering Through Information Technology, Accompanying Report of the National Performance Review*, Plume Books, Washington, 1993.

Hamel, Gary and Pralahad, C.K., *Competing for the Future: Breakthrough Strategies for Seizing Control of Your Industry and Creating the Markets of Tomorrow*, Harvard Business School Press, Boston, 1994.

Hammer, Michael and Champy, James, *Reengineering the Corporation*, HarperCollins, New York, 1993.

Handy, Charles, *The Age of Paradox*, Harvard Business School Press, Boston, 1994.

Handy, Charles, *The Age of Unreason*, Harvard Business School Press, Boston, 1989.

Harrington, H. James, *Business Process Improvement*, McGraw-Hill, Inc., New York, 1991.

Johansen, Robert, *Groupware*, The Free Press, New York, 1988.

Keen, Peter, *Competing in Time*, G.W. Ballinger Publishing Company, New York, 1988.

Keen, Peter, *Shaping the Future*, Harvard Business School Press, Boston, 1991.

Kelly, Kevin, *Out of Control*, Addison-Wesley Publishing Company, Reading, MA, 1994.

Kropl, Ed, *The Whole Internet*, O'Reilly and Associates, Sebastopol, CA, 1992.

Meyer, Dean N. and Boone, Mary E., *The Information Edge*, Holt, Rinehart & Winston of Canada, Limited, 1987.

Naisbitt, John, *Global Paradox*, William Morrow & Company, Inc., New York, 1994.

Negroponte, Nicholas, *being digital*, Alfred A. Knopf, New York, 1995.

Nohria, Nitin and Eccles, Robert G., *Networks and Organizations: Structure, Form, and Action*, Harvard Business School Press, Boston, 1992.

Ohmae, Kenichi, *The Borderless World*, McKinsey & Company, Inc., 1990.

Ohmae, Kenichi, *The Mind of the Strategist: The Art of Japanese Business*, McGraw-Hill, New York, 1982.

Osborne, David and Gaebler, Ted, *Reinventing Government*, Addison-Wesley Publishing Company, Inc., Reading, MA, 1992.

Parker, Marilyn, M. and Benson, Robert J., *Information Economics*, Prentice Hall, Inc., New Jersey, 1988.

Parker, Marilyn M., Trainor, H. Edgar, and Benson, Robert J., *Information Strategy and Economics*, Prentice-Hall, Inc., NJ, 1989.

Perelman, Lewis J., *School's Out*, Avon Books, New York, 1992.

Petrozzo, Daniel P. and Stepper, John C., *Successful Reengineering: Now You Know What It Is—Here's How to Do It!*, Van Nostrand Reinhold, New York, 1994.

Pinchot, Gifford and Pinchot, Elizabeth, *The End of Bureaucracy and Rise of the Intelligent Organization*, Berrett-Koehler Publishers, San Francisco, 1994.

Pine, B. Joseph II, *Mass Customization: The New Frontier in Business Competition*, Harvard Business School Press, Boston, 1993.

Porter, Michael E., *The Competitive Advantage of Nations*, The Free Press, New York, 1990.

Quinn, James Brian, *Intelligent Enterprise: A Knowledge and Service Based Paradigm for Industry*, The Free Press, New York, 1992.

Reich, Robert B., *The Work of Nations*, Vintage Books, New York, 1992.

Rifkin, Jeremy, *The End of Work*, G. P. Putnam's Sons, New York, 1995.

Rockart, John F. and Bullen; Christine V., ed., "The Rise of Managerial Computing: The Best of the Center for Information Systems Research," *Sloan School of Management*, Massachusetts Institute of Technology, Irwin, IL, 1986.

Rushkoff, Douglas, *Media Virus: Hidden Agendas in Popular Culture*, Ballantine Books, New York, 1994.

Senge, Peter M., *The Fifth Discipline*, Doubleday, New York, 1990.

Senge, Peter M., *The Fifth Discipline Fieldbook: Strategies and Tools for Building a Learning Organization*, Doubleday, New York, 1994.

Strassmann, Paul A., *The Business Value of Computers*, The Information Economics Press, New Canaan, CT, 1990.

Tapscott, Don, *Office Automation*, Plenum Press, New York, 1982.

Tapscott, Don, *On Ramp: Your Guide to the Information Highway*, Globe & Mail, Toronto, 1994.

Tapscott, Don and Caston, Art, *Paradigm Shift: The New Promise of Information Technology*, McGraw-Hill, New York, 1993.

Tapscott, Henderson, and Greenberg, *Planning for Integrated Office Systems*, Holt, Rinehart & Winston of Canada, Limited, 1985.

Tichey, Noel M. and Devanna, Mary Anne, *The Transformational Leader*, John Wiley & Sons, Inc., 1986.

Toffler, Alvin, *Powershift*, Bantam Books, New York, 1990.

Toffler, Alvin, *The Third Wave*, William Morrow & Co., Inc., 1980.

Toffler, Alvin and Toffler, Heidi, *Creating a New Civilization*, Turner Publishing, Inc., Atlanta, 1994.

Treacy, Michael and Wiersema, Fred, *The Discipline of Market Leader*, Addison-Wesley Publishing Company, Reading, MA, 1995.

Tufte, Edward R., *Envisioning Information*, Graphics Press, Cheshire, CT, 1990.

Utterback, James M., *Mastering the Dynamics of Innovation*, Harvard Business School Press, Boston, 1994.

Wheatley, Margaret J., *Leadership and the New Science*, Berrett-Koehler Publisher, San Francisco, 1992.

Wired (every issue).

Zuboff, Shoshana, *In the Age of the Smart Machine*, Basic Books, Inc., New York, 1988.

INDEX

ABOUT THE AUTHOR

Don Tapscott is one of the world's leading authorities on innovation, media, and the economic and social impact of technology. Named one of the world's most important living management thinkers by Thinkers50, he advises business and government leaders around the globe. Tapscott is the author or coauthor of some of the most widely read and cited books on technology in society, including *Paradigm Shift, Growing Up Digital, Grown Up Digital, The Naked Corporation, Digital Capital Wikinomics,* and *Macrowikinomics*